Ford Fiesta Owners Workshop Manual

by J H Haynes
Member of the Guild of Motoring Writers

Models covered:

UK
Fiesta   Base, L and Ghia, 957 cc
Fiesta   Base, L, Sport (S) and Ghia, 1117 cc
Fiesta   Base, L, Sport (S) and Ghia, 1298 cc
USA
Fiesta Decor, Sport (S) and Ghia, 97 cu in (1588 cc)

ISBN 0 85696 334 8

HAYNES PUBLISHING GROUP
SPARKFORD YEOVIL SOMERSET ENGLAND
distributed in the USA by
HAYNES PUBLICATIONS INC
861 LAWRENCE DRIVE
NEWBURY PARK
CALIFORNIA 91320
USA

Acknowledgements

Special thanks are due to the Ford Motor Company in the UK and USA for the supply of technical information and certain illustrations. Castrol Limited provided lubrication data, and the Champion Sparking Plug Company supplied the illustrations showing the various spark plug conditions. The bodywork repair photographs used in this manual were provided by Lloyds Industries Limited who supply 'Turtle Wax', 'Dupli-color Holts', and other Holts range products.

The Section of Chapter 8 dealing with the suppression of radio interference, was originated by Mr. I.P. Davey, and was first published in *Motor* magazine.

Lastly, thanks are due to all those people at Sparkford who helped in the production of this manual. Particularly, Brian Horsfall and Leon Martindale (Member of the Master Photographers Association), who carried out the mechanical work and took the photographs respectively, Stanley Randolph who planned the layout of each page, and John Rose who edited the text.

About this manual

Its aims

The aim of this book is to help you get the best value from your car. It can do so in two ways. First, it can help you decide what work must be done, even should you choose to get it done by a garage, the routine maintenance and the diagnosis and course of action when random faults occur. But, it is hoped that you will also use the second and fuller purpose by tackling the work yourself. This can give you the satisfaction of doing the job yourself. On the simpler jobs it may even be quicker than booking the car into a garage and going there twice, to leave and collect it. Perhaps more important, considerable expense can be saved by avoiding the costs a garage must charge to cover labour and overheads.

The book has drawings and descriptions to show the function of the various components so that their layout can be understood. Then the tasks are described and photographed in a step-by-step sequence so that a novice can cope with complicated work. Such a person is the very one to buy a car needing repair yet be unable to afford garage costs.

The jobs are described assuming only normal spanners are available, and not special tools unless absolutely necessary. But a reasonable outfit of tools will be a worthwhile investment. Many special workshop tools produced by the makers merely speed the work, and in these cases guidance is given as to how to do the job without them. On a very few occasions a special tool is essential to prevent damage to components, then its use is described. Though it might be possible to borrow the tool, such work may have to be entrusted to the official agent.

To avoid labour costs a garage will often give a cheaper repair by fitting a reconditioned assembly. The home mechanic can be helped by this book to diagnose the fault and make a repair using only a minor spare part.

The manufacturer's official workshop manuals are written for their trained staff, and so assume special knowledge; therefore detail is left out. This book is written for the owner, and so goes into detail.

Using the manual

The manual is divided into ten chapters. Each Chapter is divided into numbered Sections which are headed in **bold** type between horizontal lines. Each Section consists of serially numbered paragraphs.

There are two types of illustration: (1) Figures which are numbered according to Chapter and sequence of occurrence in the Chapter. (2) Photographs which have a reference number in their caption. All photographs apply to the Chapter in which they occur so that the reference figures pinpoint the pertinent Section and paragraph number.

Procedures, once described in the text, are not normally repeated. If it is necessary to refer to another Chapter the reference will be given in Chapter number and Section number thus: Chapter 1, Section 16. Cross-references given without the use of the word 'Chapter' apply to Section and/or paragraphs in the same Chapter, eg, 'see Section 8' means also in this Chapter.

When the left or right side of the car is mentioned it is as if one is seated in the driver's seat looking forward.

Whilst every care is taken to ensure that the information in this manual is correct, no liability can be accepted by the authors or publishers for loss, damage or injury caused by any errors in, or omissions from, the information given.

Contents

In addition each Chapter contains, where applicable: Specifications, General description and Fault diagnosis.

Use of English

As this book has been written in England, it uses the appropriate English component names, phrases, and spelling. Some of these differ from those used in America. Normally, these cause no difficulty, but to make sure, a glossary is printed below. In ordering spare parts remember the parts list will probably use these words:

Glossary

English	American	English	American
Aerial	Antenna	Interior light	Dome lamp
Accelerator	Gas pedal	Layshaft (of gearbox)	Countershaft
Alternator	Generator (AC)	Leading shoe (of brake)	Primary shoe
Anti-roll bar	Stabilizer or sway bar	Locks	Latches
Battery	Energizer	Motorway	Freeway, turnpike etc.
Bodywork	Sheet metal	Number plate	Licence plate
Bonnet (engine cover)	Hood	Paraffin	Kerosene
Boot lid	Trunk lid	Petrol	Gasoline
Boot (luggage compartment)	Trunk	Petrol tank	Gas tank
Bottom gear	1st gear	'Pinking'	'Pinging'
Bulkhead	Firewall	Propeller shaft	Driveshaft
Camfollower or tappet	Valve lifter or tappet	Quarter light	Quarter window
Carburettor	Carburetor	Retread	Recap
Catch	Latch	Reverse	Back-up
Choke/venturi	Barrel	Rocker cover	Valve cover
Circlip	Snap ring	Roof rack	Car-top carrier
Clearance	Lash	Saloon	Sedan
Crownwheel	Ring gear (of differential)	Seized	Frozen
Disc (brake)	Rotor/disk	Side indicator lights	Side marker lights
Drop arm	Pitman arm	Side light	Parking light
Drop head coupe	Convertible	Silencer	Muffler
Dynamo	Generator (DC)	Spanner	Wrench
Earth (electrical)	Ground	Sill panel (beneath doors)	Rocker panel
Engineer's blue	Prussian blue	Split cotter (for valve spring cap)	Lock (for valve spring retainer)
Estate car	Station wagon	Split pin	Cotter pin
Exhaust manifold	Header	Steering arm	Spindle arm
Fast back (Coupe)	Hard top	Sump	Oil pan
Fault finding/diagnosis	Trouble shooting	Tab washer	Tang; lock
Float chamber	Float bowl	Tailgate	Liftgate
Free-play	Lash	Tappet	Valve lifter
Freewheel	Coast	Thrust bearing	Throw-out bearing
Gudgeon pin	Piston pin or wrist pin	Top gear	High
Gearchange	Shift	Trackrod (of steering)	Tie-rod (or connecting rod)
Gearbox	Transmission	Trailing shoe (of brake)	Secondary shoe
Halfshaft	Axle-shaft	Transmission	Whole drive line
Handbrake	Parking brake	Tyre	Tire
Hood	Soft top	Van	Panel wagon/van
Hot spot	Heater riser	Vice	Vise
Indicator	Turn signal	Wheel nut	Lug nut
Interior light	Dome lamp	Windscreen	Windshield
		Wing/mudguard	Fender

Miscellaneous points

An Oil seal is fitted to components lubricated by grease!

A Damper is a Shock absorber, it damps out bouncing, and absorbs shocks of bump impact. Both names are correct, and both are used haphazardly.

Note that British drum brakes are different from the Bendix type that is common in America, so different descriptive names result. The shoe end furthest from the hydraulic wheel cylinder is on a pivot; interconnection between the shoes as on Bendix brakes is most uncommon. Therefore the phrase 'Primary' or 'Secondary' shoe does not apply. A shoe is said to be Leading or Trailing. A 'Leading' shoe is one on which a point on the drum, at it rotates forward, reaches the shoe at the end worked by the hydraulic cylinder before the anchor end. The opposite is a trailing shoe, and this one has no self servo from the wrapping effect of the rotating drum.

Introduction to the Fiesta

The Fiesta models were first introduced in the United Kingdom in February 1977. This two door small car with the upward lifting tail-gate is unique to the Ford UK range in having front wheel drive, with a transverse engine and a separate transmission assembly. This transmission incorporates four forward and one reverse gear, and also the differential gear.

Economy in both running and maintenance costs are the keynote of this car. For this reason, the original Fiesta was available with three engine options - 957 cc low compression, 957 cc high compression and 1117 cc high compression. These engines are based on the well proven Ford UK in-line engine, but with a three main bearing crankshaft.

Because of the growing demand from people who wanted even more power in their Fiesta, Ford UK began fitting the 1300 cc, five main bearing engine - as used in the Escort and Cortina - in September 1977. With this increase in power, came the need for a two piece driveshaft on the longer length.

Finally, towards the end of 1977 the Fiesta was introduced in the United States, this time with the 1600 cc five main bearing engine.

The Fiesta is available in several trim levels and also has a wide range of options from sports road wheels to a sunshine roof.

Fiesta (Base) 957 cc - UK specification

Fiesta L 1117 cc - UK specification
This is the actual car used as our workshop project vehicle. Vinyl roof optional

Fiesta Ghia 1117 cc - UK specification

Fiesta Sport - North American specification

Buying spare parts and vehicle identification numbers

Buying spare parts

Spare parts are available from many sources, for example: Ford garages, other garages and accessory shops, and motor factors. Our advice regarding spare part sources is as follows:

Officially appointed Ford garages - This is the best source of parts which are peculiar to your car and are otherwise not generally available (eg, complete cylinder heads, internal gearbox components, badges, interior trim etc). It is also the only place at which you should buy parts if your car is still under warranty - non-Ford components may invalidate the warranty. To be sure of obtaining the correct parts it will always be necessary to give the storeman your car's vehicle identification number, and if possible, to take the 'old' part along for positive identification. Remember that many parts are available on a factory exchange scheme - any parts returned should always be clean! It obviously makes good sense to go straight to the specialists on your car for this type of part for they are best equipped to supply you.

Other garages and accessory shops - These are often very good places to buy materials and components needed for the maintenance of your car (eg, oil filters, spark plugs, bulbs, fan belts, oils and greases, touch-up paint, filler paste, etc). They also sell general accessories, usually have convenient opening hours, charge lower prices and can often be found not far from home.

Motor factors - Good factors will stock all of the more important components which wear out relatively quickly (eg, clutch components, pistons, valves, exhaust systems, brake cylinders/pipes/hoses/seals/shoes and pads etc). Motor factors will often provide new or reconditioned components on a part exchange basis - this can save a considerable amount of money.

Vehicle identification numbers

Although many individual parts, and in some cases sub-assemblies, fit a number of different models it is dangerous to assume that just because they look the same, they are the same. Differences are not always easy to detect except by serial numbers. Make sure therefore, that the appropriate identity number for the model or sub-assembly is known and quoted when a spare part is ordered.

The vehicle identification plate is mounted on the right-hand front wing (fender) apron, and may be seen once the bonnet is open. Record the numbers from your car on the blank spaces of the accompanying illustration. You can then take the manual with you when buying parts; also the exploded drawings throughout the manual can be used to point out and identify the components required.

Emission control decal. All Federal models have an emission control decal in the engine compartment. This gives information such as spark plug type and gap setting, ignition initial advance setting, idle speeds, maintenance schedule code letter and basic details of engine tune-up procedures.

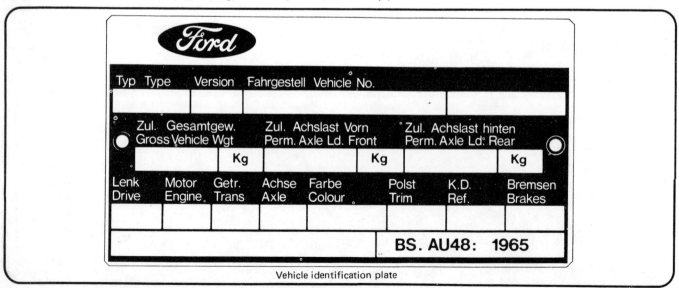

Vehicle identification plate

Routine maintenance

Maintenance is essential for ensuring safety, and desirable for the purpose of getting the best in terms of performance and economy from your car. Over the years the need for periodic lubrication - oiling, greasing and so on - has been drastically reduced, if not totally eliminated. This has unfortunately tended to lead some owners to think that because no such action is required, components either no longer exist, or will last forever. This is a serious delusion. It follows therefore that the largest initial element of maintenance is visual examination and a general sense of awareness. This may lead to repairs or renewals, but should help to avoid roadside breakdowns.

In the summary given here the 'essential for safety' items are shown in **bold type.** They must be attended to at the regular frequencies shown in order to avoid the possibility of accidents and loss of life. Other neglect results in unreliability, increased running costs, more rapid wear and depreciation of the vehicle in general.
Note: For vehicles operating within the United States, any local or Federal legislation pertaining to vehicle servicing or maintenance must overrule anything stated below.

Every 250 miles (400 km), weekly or before a long journey

Steering
    Check tyre pressures (when cold)
    Examine tyres for wear and damage
    Check steering for smooth and accurate operation

Brakes
    Check reservoir fluid level. If this has fallen noticeably, check for fluid leakage (Fig. 1).
    Check for satisfactory brake operation

Lights, wipers, horns, instruments
    Check operation of all lights
    Check operation of screen wipers and washers and washer leads (Fig. 2).
    Check that the horn operates
    Check that all instruments and gauges are operating

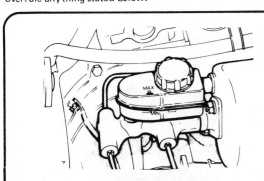

Fig. 1. Brake fluid reservoir

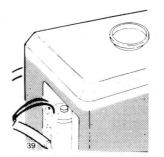
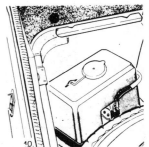

Fig. 2. Screen washer reservoirs

Engine compartment
Check engine oil level; top-up if necessary (photo 1)
Check radiator coolant level (Fig. 3)
Check battery electrolyte level (Fig. 4)

Every 6,000 miles (10,000 km) or 6 months, whichever occurs first

*Renew engine oil and oil filter (photo 2)
Clean all HT leads, top of coil, distributor cap and rotor arm (Fig. 5)
Check rotor arm and points for wear and adjust gaps (photo 3)
*Clean spark plugs and reset gaps (Fig. 6)
Lubricate distributor
*Check ignition timing
*Check valve clearances (photo 4)
*Check tightness of inlet and exhaust manifold bolts
Check condition of exhaust system
*Check condition and tension of all drivebelts (Fig. 7)
*Adjust slow idle speed
Clean/tighten battery terminals, check electrolyte level
Check transmission oil level, top-up if required (photo 5)
Lubricate handbrake linkage and clutch cable at release arm
Check front brake for wear (photo 6)
Check rear brake linings for wear (Fig. 8)
Examine brake hoses for leaks and chafing
Check steering linkage for wear and damage
Check front suspension linkage for wear and damage
Check steering, suspension and driveshaft gaiters for security and condition
Check operation of all doors, catches and hinges. Lubricate as necessary
Check condition of seatbelts and operation of buckles and inertia reels
Adjust air cleaner spout for seasonal condition (Fig. 9)
Check engine compartment and underbody for leakage of oils and fluids

Every 18,000 miles (30,000 km) or 18 months, whichever occurs first

* Change air cleaner element (photo 7)
* Clean or replace crankcase emission orifice in oil filler cap
* Renew crankcase emission filter (located inside air cleaner casing) — later 1300 models only
* Check fast idle speed

Every 24,000 miles (40,000 km) or 2 years, whichever occurs first

Renew all rubber seals and hoses in braking systems. Renew brake fluid.
* Drain engine coolant. Renew antifreeze or inhibitor coolant mixture

For USA vehicles, refer to the next Section for these items.

Emission control system scheduled maintenance
The following items must be checked at the intervals shown, or more frequently where this is more convenient when following the Routine Maintenance schedule above.

	Mileage in thousands or time in months whichever occurs first						
	1.5	7.5	15	22.5	30	37.5	45
Change engine oil (See notes 1, 2)		GH	GH	GHJ	GH	GHJ	GH
Change engine oil filter (See notes 1, 2)		GH	GH	GHJ	GH	GHJ	GH
Check/adjust valve clearances	GH		GH		GH		GH
Check coolant condition and strength (See note 3)					GH		
Change coolant (See note 4)							GH
Check cooling system hoses and clamps (See note 4)							GH
Check/adjust drive belt tension	GH		GH		GH		GH
Check air cleaner temperature control							GH
Inspect fuel vapour system							GH
Check/adjust static ignition timing	GH						
Replace spark plugs (see note 2)			G		GH		G
Clean PCV valve			G		GH		G
Check/adjust fast idle speed	GH						

Top up engine oil level

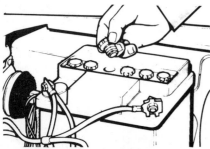
Fig. 4. Battery electrolyte level

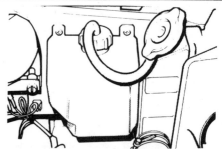
Fig. 3. Engine coolant level

Renew engine oil filter

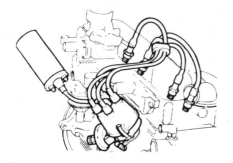

Fig. 5. Clean HT components

Adjust distributor points gap

Fig. 6. Adjust spark plug gap

Adjust valve clearances

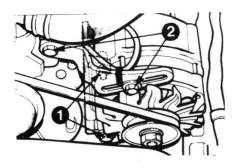

Fig. 7. Adjust alternator belt tension

Top up transmission oil level

Check front brake pads

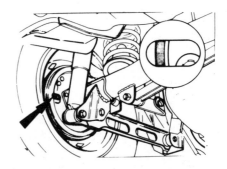

Fig. 8. Check brake lining wear

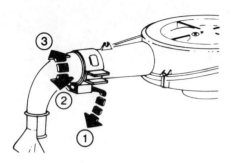

Fig. 9. Adjust air cleaner spout position

Change air cleaner element

	Mileage in thousands or time in months which-ever occurs first						
	1.5	7.5	15	22.5	30	37.5	45
Check/adjust slow idle speed	GH		G		GH		G
Check carburettor bowl vent	GH		G		GH		GH
Check function of choke system			GH		GH		GH
Replace air cleaner and crankcase emission filter (see note 5)					GH		
Check cylinder head inlet and exhaust manifold bolt/nut torques	GH						

Notes:
1 Change engine oil and filter every 7,500 miles or 6 months.
2 If operating under
   a) Stop/start or low speed operation
   b) temperatures below 10⁰F and short journeys (10 miles or less) or
   c) Severe dusty conditions,
change engine oil every 3,000 miles or 3 months and filter every 6,000 miles or 6 months.
3 If coolant is dirty or rusty in appearance it should be renewed.
4 Every 36 months or 45,000 miles.
5 More often if operating in severe dusty conditions.

The code letters G, H and J refer to a schedule which will be listed on the emission control decal attached to the bonnet lock apron.

Jacking and towing

Jacking points

To change a wheel in an emergency, use the jack supplied with the vehicle. Ensure that the roadwheel bolts are released before jacking up the car and make sure that the arm of the jack is fully engaged with the body bracket and that the base of the jack is standing on a firm surface.

The jack supplied with the vehicle is not suitable for use when raising the vehicle for maintenance or repair operations. For this work, use a trolley, hydraulic or screw type jack located under the front crossmember, bodyframe side-members or rear axle casing, as illustrated. Always supplement the jack with axle stands or blocks before crawling beneath the car.

Towing points

If your vehicle is being towed, or is towing another vehicle, the tow rope must be attached to the towing eyes where these are fitted. Otherwise, the rope can be attached to the right- or left-hand tie rod at the front, as shown. At the rear, the rope should only be attached to the left-hand end of the axle tube to avoid damage to the suspension or brake components.

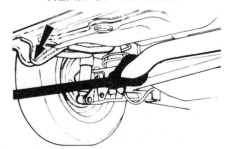

Car jacking point (for use only with car jack)

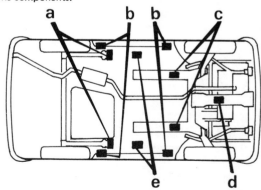

Car jacking points (for maintenance and repair operations)

REAR OF VEHICLE

FRONT OF VEHICLE

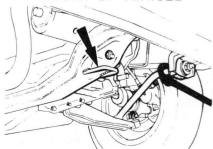

Tow rope attachments to car (arrows indicate towing eyes when fitted)

Terry Davey
© HAYNES

Recommended lubricants and fluids

Component					Capacity		Castrol product
1 Engine - including filter	...	...			5.75 Imp pint (3.25 litre) (6.9 US pint)	...	**Castrol GTX**
- excluding filter	...	...			4.85 Imp pint (2.75 litre) (5.8 US pint)	...	**Castrol GTX**
2 Transmission	...	...	...	...	5 Imp pint (2.8 litre) (6.0 US pint)	...	**Castrol Hypoy Light (80EP)**
3 Wheel bearings	..	...	...	...	—		**Castrol LM Grease**
4 Steering gear	...	...	...	...	0.17 Imp pint (95 cc) (0.2 US pint)	...	**Castrol Hypoy B (90EP)**
Brake master cylinder	...	...	...		—		**Castrol Girling Universal Brake and Clutch Fluid**
Cooling system - 960/1100 cc		...	...		9.27 Imp pint (5.27 litre) (11.12 US pint)		
1300/1600 cc		...	...		11 Imp pint (6.25 litre) (13.2 US pint)		
Antifreeze	...	...	...	...	Refer to Chapter 2 ...	...	**Castrol Antifreeze**
Fuel tank	...	...	...	...	7.5 Imp gall (34 litre) (10 US gall)		

Tools and working facilities

Introduction

A selection of good tools is a fundamental requirement for anyone contemplating the maintenance and repair of a motor vehicle. For the owner who does not possess any, their purchase will prove a considerable expense, offsetting some of the savings made by doing-it-yourself. However, provided that the tools purchased are of good quality, they will last for many years and prove an extremely worthwhile investment.

To help the average owner to decide which tools are needed to carry out the various tasks detailed in this manual, we have compiled three lists of tools under the following headings: Maintenance and minor repair, Repair and overhaul, and Special. The newcomer to practical mechanics should start off with the 'Maintenance and minor repair' tool kit and confine himself to the simpler jobs around the vehicle. Then, as his confidence and experience grows, he can undertake more difficult tasks, buying extra tools as, and when, they are needed. In this way, a 'Maintenance and minor repair' tool kit can be built-up into a 'Repair and overhaul' tool kit over a considerable period of time without any major cash outlays. The experienced do-it-yourselfer will have a tool kit good enough for most repairs and overhaul procedures and will add tools from the 'Special' category when he feels the expense is justified by the amount of use these tools will be put to.

It is obviously not possible to cover the subject of tools fully here. For those who wish to learn more about tools and their use there is a book entitled 'How to Choose and Use Car Tools' available from the publishers of this manual.

Maintenance and minor repair tool kit

The tools given in this list should be considered as a minimum requirement if routine maintenance, servicing and minor repair operations are to be undertaken. We recommend the purchase of combination spanners (ring one end, open-ended the other); although more expensive than open-ended ones, they do give the advantages of both types of spanner.

Combination spanners - 10 to 22 mm AF
Adjustable spanner - 9 inch
Engine sump/gearbox/rear axle drain plug key (where applicable)
Spark plug spanner (with rubber insert)
Spark plug gap adjustment tool
Set of feeler gauges
Brake adjuster spanner (where applicable)
Brake bleed nipple spanner
Screwdriver - 4 in. long x 1/4 in. dia. (plain)
Screwdriver - 4 in. long x 1/4 in. dia. (crosshead)
Combination pliers - 6 inch
Hacksaw, junior
Tyre pump
Tyre pressure gauge
Grease gun (where applicable)
Oil can
Wire brush (small)
Funnel (medium size)

Note: *For some applications TORX internal drive head screws are being progressively introduced. Suitable tools should be available through Ford dealers.*

Repair and overhaul tool kit

These tools are virtually essential for anyone undertaking any major repairs to a motor vehicle, and are additional to those given in the Basic list. Included in this list is a comprehensive set of sockets. Although these are expensive they will be found invaluable as they are so versatile - particularly if various drives are included in the set. We recommend the 1/2 square-drive type, as this can be used with most proprietary torque wrenches. If you cannot afford a socket set, even bought piecemeal, then inexpensive tubular box spanners are a useful alternative.

The tools in this list will occasionally need to be supplemented by tools from the Special list.

Sockets (or box spanners) to cover range in previous list
Reversible ratchet drive (for use with sockets)
Extension piece, 10 inch (for use with sockets)
Universal joint (for use with sockets)
Torque wrench (for use with sockets)
'Mole' wrench - 8 inch
Ball pein hammer
Soft-faced hammer, plastic or rubber
Screwdriver - 6 in. long x 5/16 in. dia. (plain)
Screwdriver - 2 in. long x 5/16 in. square (plain)
Screwdriver - 1 1/2 in. long x 1/4 in. dia. (crosshead)
Screwdriver - 3 in. long x 1/8 in. dia. (electricians)
Pliers - electricians side cutters
Pliers - needle noses
Pliers - circlip (internal and external)
Cold chisel - 1/2 inch
Scriber (this can be made by grinding the end of a broken hacksaw blade)
Scraper (this can be made by flattening and sharpening one end of a piece of copper pipe)
Centre punch
Pin punch
Hacksaw
Valve grinding tool
Steel rule/straight-edge
Allen keys
Selection of files
Wire brush (large)
Axle stands
Jack (strong scissor or hydraulic type)

Special tools

The tools in this list are those which are not used regularly, are expensive to buy, or which need to be used in accordance with their manufacturers instructions. Unless relatively difficult mechanical jobs are undertaken frequently, it will not be economic to buy many of these tools. Where this is the case, you could consider clubbing together with friends (or a motorists club) to make a joint purchase, or borrowing the tools against a deposit from a local garage or tool hire specialist.

The following list contains only those tools and instruments freely available to the public, and not those special tools produced by the vehicle manufacturer specifically for its dealer network. You will find occasional references to these manufacturers special tools in the text of this manual. Generally, an alternative method of doing the job without the vehicle manufacturers special tool is given. However, sometimes, there is no alternative to using them. Where this is the case and the relevant tool cannot be bought or borrowed you will have to entrust the work to a franchised garage.

> Valve spring compressor
> Piston ring compressor
> Ball joint separator
> Universal hub/bearing puller
> Impact screwdriver
> Micrometer and/or vernier gauge
> Carburettor flow balancing device (where applicable)
> Dial gauge
> Stroboscopic timing light
> Dwell angle meter/tachometer
> Universal electrical multi-meter
> Cylinder compression gauge
> Lifting tackle
> Trolley jack
> Light with extension lead

Buying tools

For practically all tools, a tool factor is the best source since he will have a very comprehensive range compared with the average garage or accessory shop. Having said that, accessory shops often offer excellent quality tools at discount prices, so it pays to shop around.

Remember, you don't have to buy the most expensive items on the shelf, but it is always advisable to steer clear of the very cheap tools. There are plenty of good tools around, at reasonable prices, so ask the proprietor or manager of the shop for advice before making a purchase.

Care and maintenance of tools

Having purchased a reasonable tool kit, it is necessary to keep the tools in a clean and serviceable condition. After use, always wipe off any dirt, grease and metal particles using a clean, dry cloth, before putting the tools away. Never leave them lying around after they have been used. A simple tool rack on the garage or workshop wall, for items such as screwdrivers and pliers is a good idea. Store all normal spanners and sockets in a metal box. Any measuring instruments, gauges, meters, etc., must be carefully stored where they cannot be damaged or become rusty.

Take a little care when the tools are used. Hammer heads inevitably become marked and screwdrivers lose the keen edge on their blades from time-to-time. A little timely attention with emery cloth or a file will soon restore items like this to a good serviceable finish.

Working facilities

Not to be forgotten when discussing tools, is the workshop itself. If anything more than routine maintenance is to be carried out, some form of suitable working area becomes essential.

It is appreciated that many an owner mechanic is forced by circumstance to remove an engine or similar item, without the benefit of a garage or workshop. Having done this, any repairs should always be done under the cover of a roof.

Wherever possible, any dismantling should be done on a clean flat workbench or table at a suitable working height.

Any workbench needs a vice: one with a jaw opening of 4 in (100 mm) is suitable for most jobs. As mentioned previously, some clean dry storage space is also required for tools, as well as the lubricants, cleaning fluids, touch-up paints and so on which soon become necessary.

Another item which may be required, and which has a much more general usage, is an electric drill with a chuck capacity of at least 5/16 in (8 mm). This, together with a good range of twist drills, is

virtually essential for fitting accessories such as wing mirrors and reversing lights.

Last, but not least, always keep a supply of old newspapers and clean, lint-free rags available, and try to keep any working area as clean as possible.

Spanner jaw gap comparison table

Jaw gap (in.)	Spanner size
0.250	1/4 in. AF
0.275	7 mm AF
0.312	5/16 in. AF
0.315	8 mm AF
0.340	11/32 in. AF/1/8 in. Whitworth
0.354	9 mm AF
0.375	3/8 in. AF
0.393	10 mm AF
0.433	11 mm AF
0.437	7/16 in. AF
0.445	3/16 in. Whitworth/1/4 in. BSF
0.472	12 mm AF
0.500	1/2 in. AF
0.512	13 mm AF
0.525	1/4 in. Whitworth/5/16 in. BSF
0.551	14 mm AF
0.562	9/16 in. AF
0.590	15 mm AF
0.600	5/16 in. Whitworth/3/8 in. BSF
0.625	5/8 in. AF
0.629	16 mm AF
0.669	17 mm AF
0.687	11/16 in. AF
0.708	18 mm AF
0.710	3/8 in. Whitworth/7/16 in. BSF
0.748	19 mm AF
0.750	3/4 in. AF
0.812	13/16 in. AF
0.820	7/16 in. Whitworth/1/2 in. BSF
0.866	22 mm AF
0.875	7/8 in. AF
0.920	1/2 in. Whitworth/9/16 in. BSF
0.937	15/16 in. AF
0.944	24 mm AF
1.000	1 in. AF
1.010	9/16 in. Whitworth/5/8 in. BSF
1.023	26 mm AF
1.062	1 1/16 in. AF/27 mm AF
1.100	5/8 in. Whitworth/11/16 in. BSF
1.125	1 1/8 in. AF
1.181	30 mm AF
1.200	11/16 in. Whitworth/3/4 in. BSF
1.250	1 1/4 in. AF
1.259	32 mm AF
1.300	3/4 in. Whitworth/7/8 in. BSF
1.312	1 5/16 in. AF
1.390	13/16 in. Whitworth/15/16 in. BSF
1.417	36 mm AF
1.437	1 7/16 in. AF
1.480	7/8 in. Whitworth/1 in. BSF
1.500	1 1/2 in. AF
1.574	40 mm AF/15/16 in. Whitworth
1.614	41 mm AF
1.625	1 5/8 in. AF
1.670	1 in. Whitworth/1 1/8 in. BSF
1.687	1 11/16 in. AF
1.811	46 mm AF
1.812	1 13/16 in. AF
1.860	1 1/8 in. Whitworth/1 1/4 in. BSF
1.875	1 7/8 in. AF
1.968	50 mm AF
2.000	2 in. AF
2.050	1 1/4 in. Whitworth/1 3/8 in. BSF
2.165	55 mm AF
2.362	60 mm AF

Chapter 1 Engine

Specifications

Engine (general)

	950 cc	1100 cc	1300 cc	1600 cc
Engine type	Four cylinder in-line, overhead, push rod valves		Four cylinder in-line, overhead, push rod valves	
Firing order	1 - 2 - 4 - 3	1 - 2 - 4 - 3	1 - 2 - 4 - 3	1 - 2 - 4 - 3
Bore	2.91 in (73.96 mm)	2.91 in (73.96 mm)	3.188 in (80.98 mm)	3.188 in (80.98 mm)
Stroke	2.19 in (55.70 mm)	2.56 in (64.98 mm)	2.48 in (62.99 mm)	3.06 in (77.62 mm)
Cubic capacity	957 cc (58.4 cu in)	1117 cc (68.16 cu in)	1298 cc (79.21 cu in)	1588 cc (96.87 cu in)
Compression ratio (low) ...	8.3 : 1	—	—	8.5 : 1
(high)	9.1 : 1	9.1 : 1	9.0 : 1	
Compression pressure at starter speed (low) ...	137 - 166 lb/in^2 (9.5 - 11.5 kg/cm^2)	—	—	
(high) ...	159 - 188 lb/in^2 (11 - 13 kg/cm^2)	159 - 188 lb/in^2 (11 - 13 kg/cm^2)	142 - 170 lb/in^2 (10 - 12 kg/cm^2)	—
Idling speed	775 - 825 rpm	750 - 850 rpm	775 - 825 rpm	775 - 825 rpm
Maximum engine speed (LC) ...	5800 rpm	—	—	5800 rpm
(HC)	6300 rpm	6300 rpm	6300 rpm	
Engine bhp (DIN) (LC)	40 @ 5500 rpm	—	—	63 @ 5300 rpm
(HC)	45 @ 6000 rpm	53 @ 5700 rpm	66 @ 5600 rpm	
Maximum torque (DIN) (LC) ...	47 lb ft @ 2700 rpm	—	—	79 lb ft @ 3000 rpm
(HC)	48 lb ft @ 3000 rpm	59 lb ft @ 3000 rpm	67 lb ft @ 3000 rpm	—

Specifications

	950 cc	1100 cc	1300 cc	1600 cc
Cylinder block				
Cast number	77 BM - 6015 - CC	77 BM - 6015 - CC	711 M - 6015 - AA	711 M - 6015 - BA
Number of main bearings ...	3	3	5	5
Cylinder liner bore in (mm) ...	3.0349 - 3.0359 (77.086 - 77.112)	3.0349 - 3.0359 (77.086 - 77.112)	3.311 - 3.314 (84.112 - 84.175)	3.311 - 3.314 (84.112 - 84.175)
Cylinder bore diameter in (mm)				
Standard	2.9122 - 2.9136 (73.97 - 73.98)	2.9122 - 2.9136 (73.97 - 73.98)	3.1873 - 3.1889 (80.957 - 80.998)	3.1873 - 3.1889 (80.957 - 80.998)
Oversize 0.015 in	—	—	3.2022 - 3.2038 (81.336 - 81.377)	3.2022 - 3.2038 (81.336 - 81.377)
0.02 in	2.9331 - 2.9335 (74.50 - 74.51)	2.9331 - 2.9335 (74.50 - 74.51)	—	—
0.03 in	—	—	3.2169 - 3.2185 (81.709 - 81.750)	3.2169 - 3.2185 (81.709 - 81.750)
0.04 in	2.9528 - 2.9531 (75.00 - 75.01)	2.9528 - 2.9531 (75.00 - 75.01)	—	
Main bearing shell inner diameter in (mm)				
Standard	2.2444 - 2.2455 (57.009 - 57.036)	2.2444 - 2.2455 (57.009 - 57.036)	2.126 - 2.128 (54.013 - 54.044)	2.126 - 2.128 (54.013 - 54.044)
Undersize 0.01 in	2.2344 - 2.2391 (56.755 - 56.872)	2.2344 - 2.2391 (56.755 - 56.872)	2.116 - 2.118 (53.759 - 53.790)	2.116 - 2.118 (53.759 - 53.790)
0.02 in	2.2244 - 2.2255 (56.501 - 56.528)	2.2244 - 2.2255 (56.501 - 56.528)	2.106 - 2.108 (53.505 - 53.536)	2.106 - 2.108 (53.505 - 53.536)
0.03 in	2.2144 - 2.2155 (56.247 - 56.274)	2.2144 - 2.2155 (56.247 - 56.274)	2.096 - 2.098 (53.251 - 53.282)	2.096 - 2.098 (53.251 - 53.282)
Main bearing bore in (mm)				
Standard	2.3867 - 2.3872 (60.623 - 60.636)	2.3867 - 2.3872 (60.623 - 60.636)	2.271 - 2.2715 (57.683 - 57.696)	2.271 - 2.2715 (57.683 - 57.696)
Oversize	2.4017 - 2.4022 (61.003 - 61.016)	2.4017 - 2.4022 (61.003 - 61.016)	2.286 - 2.2865 (58.064 - 58.077)	2.286 - 2.2865 (58.064 - 58.077)
Camshaft bearing in (mm)				
Standard	1.6885 - 1.6897 (42.888 - 42.918)	1.6885 - 1.6897 (42.888 - 42.918)	1.6885 - 1.6897 (42.888 - 42.918)	1.6885 - 1.6897 (42.888 - 42.918)
Oversize	1.7085 - 1.7094 (43.396 - 43.420)	1.7085 - 1.7094 (43.396 - 43.420)	1.7085 - 1.7094 (43.396 - 43.420)	1.7085 - 1.7094 (43.396 - 43.420)
Crankshaft				
Endfloat in (mm)	0.003 - 0.011 (0.075 - 0.280)	0.003 - 0.011 (0.075 - 0.280)	0.003 - 0.011 (0.075 - 0.280)	0.003 - 0.011 (0.075 - 0.280)
Main journal dia in (mm)				
Standard	2.2433 - 2.2441 (56.980 - 57.000)	2.2433 - 2.2441 (56.980 - 57.000)	2.125 - 2.126 (53.983 - 54.003)	2.125 - 2.126 (53.983 - 54.003)
Undersize 0.01 in	2.2333 - 2.2341 (56.726 - 56.746)	2.2333 - 2.2341 (56.726 - 56.746)	2.115 - 2.116 (53.729 - 53.749)	2.115 - 2.116 (53.729 - 53.749)
0.02 in	2.2233 - 2.2241 (56.472 - 56.492)	2.2233 - 2.2241 (56.472 - 56.492)	2.105 - 2.106 (53.475 - 53.495)	2.105 - 2.106 (53.475 - 53.495)
0.03 in	2.2133 - 2.2141 (56.218 - 56.238)	2.2133 - 2.2141 (56.218 - 56.238)	2.095 - 2.096 (53.221 - 53.241)	2.095 - 2.096 (53.221 - 53.241)
Main journal to bearing Clearance in (mm)	0.0003 - 0.002 (0.009 - 0.056)	0.0003 - 0.002 (0.009 - 0.056)	0.0004 - 0.0024 (0.010 - 0.061)	0.0004 - 0.0024 (0.010 - 0.061)
Crankpin diameter in (mm)				
Standard	1.6925 - 1.6933 (42.99 - 43.01)	1.6925 - 1.6933 (42.99 - 43.01)	1.937 - 1.938 (49.195 - 49.215)	1.937 - 1.938 (49.195 - 49.215)
Undersize 0.01 in	1.6827 - 1.6835 (42.74 - 42.76)	1.6827 - 1.6835 (42.74 - 42.76)	1.927 - 1.928 (48.941 - 48.961)	1.927 - 1.928 (48.941 - 48.961)
0.02 in	1.6728 - 1.6736 (42.49 - 42.51)	1.6728 - 1.6736 (42.49 - 42.51)	1.917 - 1.918 (48.687 - 48.707)	1.917 - 1.918 (48.687 - 48.707)
0.03 in	1.6630 - 1.6638 (42.24 - 42.26)	1.6630 - 1.6638 (42.24 - 42.26)	1.907 - 1.908 (48.433 - 48.453)	1.907 - 1.908 (48.433 - 48.453)
0.04 in	—	—	1.897 - 1.898 (48.179 - 48.199)	1.897 - 1.898 (48.179 - 48.199)
Camshaft				
Number of bearings	3	3	3	3
Drive	Chain and sprocket	Chain and sprocket	Chain and sprocket	Chain and sprocket
Camshaft bearing dia in (mm) ...	1.5596 - 1.5604 (39.615 - 39.635)	1.5596 - 1.5604 (39.615 - 39.635)	1.5596 - 1.5604 (39.615 - 39.635)	1.5596 - 1.5604 (39.615 - 39.635)
Bearing shell inner dia in (mm)...	1.5615 - 1.5620 (39.662 - 39.675)	1.5615 - 1.5620 (39.662 - 39.675)	1.5615 - 1.5620 (39.662 - 39.675)	1.5615 - 1.5620 (39.662 - 39.675)

	950 cc	1100 cc	1300 cc	1600 cc
Endfloat in (mm)	0.0024 - 0.0076 (0.062 - 0.193)	0.0024 - 0.0076 (0.062 - 0.193)	0.0024 - 0.0076 (0.062 - 0.193)	0.0024 - 0.0076 (0.062 - 0.193)
Cam lift in (mm) inlet	0.236 (5.985)	0.236 (5.985)	0.236 (5.985)	0.231 (5.865)
exhaust	0.232 (5.894)	0.232 (5.894)	0.232 (5.894)	0.232 (5.894)
Cam length (heel to toe) in (mm)				
inlet	1.3011 - 1.3041 (33.049 - 33.125)	1.3011 - 1.3041 (33.049 - 33.125)	1.3011 - 1.3041 (33.049 - 33.125)	1.313 (33.357)
exhaust	1.3106 - 1.3135 (33.288 - 33.364)	1.3106 - 1.3135 (33.288 - 33.364)	1.3106 - 1.3135 (33.288 - 33.364)	1.3106 - 1.3135 (33.288 - 33.364)

Pistons

	950 cc	1100 cc	1300 cc	1600 cc
Diameter in (mm)				
Standard	2.9106 - 2.9116 (73.930 - 73.955)	2.9106 - 2.9116 (73.930 - 73.955)	3.187 - 3.188 (80.954 - 80.974)	3.187 - 3.188 (80.954 - 80.954)
Oversize 0.015 in	—	—	3.201 - 3.203 (81.294 - 81.354)	3.201 - 3.203 81.294 - 81.354)
0.02 in	2.9315 - 2.9325 (74.460 - 74.485)	2.9315 - 2.9325 (74.460 - 74.485)	—	—
0.03 in	—	—	3.216 - 3.218 (81.674 - 81.734)	3.216 - 3.218 (81.674 - 81.734)
0.04 in	2.9512 - 2.9522 (74.960 - 74.985)	2.9512 - 2.9522 (74.960 - 74.985)	—	—
Ring gap (fitted in block) in (mm)				
top and centre	0.0098 - 0.0177 (0.25 - 0.45)	0.0098 - 0.0177 (0.25 - 0.45)	0.009 - 0.014 (0.23 - 0.36)	0.009 - 0.014 (0.23 - 0.36)
bottom	0.0079 - 0.0157 (0.20 - 0.40)	0.0079 - 0.0157 (0.20 - 0.40)	0.009 - 0.014 (0.23 - 0.36)	0.009 - 0.014 (0.23 - 0.36)
Ring gap position - top	180° to bottom ring gap	180° to bottom ring gap	180° to bottom ring gap	180° to bottom ring gap
centre	90° to bottom ring gap	90° to bottom ring gap	90° to bottom ring gap	90° to bottom ring gap
bottom	in-line with gudgeon pin	in-line with gudgeon pin	in-line with gudgeon pin	in-line with gudgeon pin

Gudgeon pin

	950 cc	1100 cc	1300 cc	1600 cc
Diameter in (mm)				
1 - white	0.8119 - 0.8120 (20.622 - 20.625)	0.8119 - 0.8120 (20.622 - 20.625)	0.8119 - 0.8120 (20.622 - 20.625)	0.8119 - 0.8120 (20.622 - 20.625)
2 - red	0.8120 - 0.8121 (20.625 - 20.628)	0.8120 - 0.8121 (20.625 - 20.628)	0.8120 - 0.8121 (20.625 - 20.628)	0.8120 - 0.8121 (20.625 - 20.628)
3 - blue	0.8121 - 0.8122 (20.628 - 20.631)	0.8121 - 0.8122 (20.628 - 20.631)	0.8121 - 0.8122 (20.628 - 20.631)	0.8121 - 0.8122 (20.628 - 20.631)
4 - yellow	0.8122 - 0.8124 (20.631 - 20.634)	0.8122 - 0.8124 (20.631 - 20.634)	0.8122 - 0.8124 (20.631 - 20.634)	0.8122 - 0.8124 (20.631 - 20.634)
Interference fit in piston in (mm)	0.0005 - 0.0017 (0.013 - 0.045)	0.0005 - 0.0017 (0.013 - 0.045)	0.0001 - 0.0003 (0.003 - 0.008)	0.0001 - 0.0003 (0.003 - 0.008)
Clearance in con-rod in (mm) ...	0.00015 - 0.0004 (0.004 - 0.010)	0.00015 - 0.0004 (0.004 - 0.010)	0.00015 - 0.0004 (0.004 - 0.010)	0.00015 - 0.0004 (0.004 - 0.010)

Connecting rods

	950 cc	1100 cc	1300 cc	1600 cc
Big end bore in (mm)	1.8380 - 1.8388 (46.685 - 46.705)	1.8380 - 1.8388 (46.685 - 46.705)	2.0823 - 2.0831 (52.89 - 52.91)	2.0823 - 2.0831 (52.89 - 52.91)
Small end bore in (mm) ...	0.8106 - 0.8114 (20.589 - 20.609)	0.8106 - 0.8114 (20.589 - 20.609)	0.8122 - 0.8126 (20.629 - 20.640)	0.8122 - 0.8126 (20.629 - 20.640)
Big end bearing inner dia in (mm)				
Standard	1.6935 - 1.6949 (43.016 - 43.050)	1.6935 - 1.6949 (43.016 - 43.050)	1.938 - 1.939 (49.221 - 49.260)	1.938 - 1.939 (49.221 - 49.260)
Undersize 0.01 in	1.6835 - 1.6850 (42.766 - 42.800)	1.6835 - 1.6850 (42.766 - 42.800)	1.928 - 1.929 (48.967 - 49.005)	1.928 - 1.929 (48.967 - 49.005)
0.02 in	1.6738 - 1.6752 (42.516 - 42.550)	1.6738 - 1.6752 (42.516 - 42.550)	1.918 - 1.919 (48.713 - 48.751)	1.918 - 1.919 (48.713 - 48.751)
0.03 in	1.6640 - 1.6656 (42.266 - 42.300)	1.6640 - 1.6656 (42.266 - 42.300)	1.909 - 1.913 (48.491 - 48.592)	1.909 - 1.913 (48.491 - 48.592)
0.04 in	1.6542 - 1.6555 (42.016 - 42.050)	1.6542 - 1.6555 (42.016 - 42.050)	1.898 - 1.899 (48.205 - 48.243)	1.898 - 1.899 (48.205 - 48.243)
Big end journal to bearing clearance in (mm)	0.0002 - 0.003 (0.006 - 0.064)	0.0002 - 0.003 (0.006 - 0.064)	0.0002 - 0.003 (0.006 - 0.064)	0.0002 - 0.003 (0.006 - 0.064)

Cylinder head

	950 cc	1100 cc	1300 cc	1600 cc
Cast marking	77 BM - 6090 - CD	77 BM - 6090	33	37
Valve seat angle	44° 30' - 45° 00'	44° 30' - 45° 00'	44° 30' - 45° 00'	44° 30' - 45° 00'
Valve stem bush bore in (mm) ...	0.3113 - 0.3125 (7.907 - 7.938)	0.3113 - 0.3125 (7.907 - 7.938)	0.3113 - 0.3125 (7.907 - 7.938)	0.3113 - 0.3125 (7.907 - 7.938)
Bush bore in head in (mm) ...	0.438 - 0.439 (11.133 - 11.153)	0.438 - 0.439 (11.133 - 11.153)	0.438 - 0.439 (11.133 - 11.153)	0.438 - 0.439 (11.133 - 11.153)

	950 cc	1100 cc	1300 cc	1600 cc
Inlet valve				
Opens	21° BTDC	21° BTDC	21° BTDC	21° BTDC
Closes	55° ABDC	55° ABDC	55° ABDC	71° ATDC
Clearance (cold) in (mm)	0.009 (0.22)	0.009 (0.22)	0.010 (0.25)	0.010 (0.25)
Length in (mm)	4.152 - 4.191 (105.45 - 106.45)	4.152 - 4.191 (105.45 - 106.45)	4.357 - 4.396 (110.67 - 111.67)	4.357 - 4.396 (110.67 - 111.67)
Head diameter in (mm)	1.3 (33.0)	1.5 (38.1)	1.5 (38.1)	1.55 (39.4)
Stem diameter in (mm)				
Standard	0.3098 - 0.3105 (7.868 - 7.886)	0.3098 - 0.3105 (7.868 - 7.886)	0.3098 - 0.3105 (7.868 - 7.886)	0.3098 - 0.3105 (7.868 - 7.886)
Oversize 0.003 in	0.3128 - 0.3135 (7.944 - 7.962)	0.3128 - 0.3135 (7.944 - 7.962)	0.3128 - 0.3135 (7.944 - 7.962)	0.3128 - 0.3135 (7.944 - 7.962)
0.015 in	0.3248 - 0.3255 (8.249 - 8.267)	0.3248 - 0.3255 (8.249 - 8.267)	0.3248 - 0.3255 (8.249 - 8.267)	0.3248 - 0.3255 (8.249 - 8.267)
Stem to guide clearance in (mm)	0.0008 - 0.0028 (0.021 - 0.070)	0.0008 - 0.0028 (0.021 - 0.070)	0.0008 - 0.0028 (0.021 - 0.070)	0.0008 - 0.0028 (0.021 - 0.070)
Valve lift (excluding clearance) in (mm)	0.372 (9.448)	0.372 (9.448)	0.347 (8.81)	0.347 (8.81)
Exhaust valve				
Opens	70° BBDC	70° BBDC	70° BBDC	63° BBDC
Closes	22° ATDC	22° ATDC	22° ATDC	29° ATDC
Clearance (cold) in (mm)	0.023 (0.60)	0.023 (0.60)	0.022 (0.55)	0.022 (0.55)
Length in (mm)	4.139 - 4.179 (105.15 - 106.15)	4.139 - 4.179 (105.15 - 106.15)	4.345 - 4.365 (110.36 - 110.87)	4.345 - 4.365 (110.36 - 110.87)
Head diameter in (mm)	1.142 - 1.152 (29.01 - 29.27)	1.142 - 1.152 (29.01 - 29.27)	1.234 - 1.244 (31.34 - 31.59)	1.331 - 1.339 (33.8 - 34.0)
Stem diameter in (mm)				
Standard	0.3089 - 0.3096 (7.846 - 7.864)	0.3089 - 0.3096 (7.846 - 7.864)	0.3089 - 0.3096 (7.846 - 7.864)	0.3089 - 0.3096 (7.846 - 7.864)
Oversize 0.003 in	0.3119 - 0.3126 (7.922 - 7.940)	0.3119 - 0.3126 (7.922 - 7.940)	0.3119 - 0.3126 (7.922 - 7.940)	0.3119 - 0.3126 (7.922 - 7.940)
0.015 in	0.3239 - 0.3246 (8.227 - 8.245)	0.3239 - 0.3246 (8.227 - 8.245)	0.3239 - 0.3246 (8.227 - 8.245)	0.3239 - 0.3246 (8.227 - 8.245)
Stem to guide clearance in (mm)	0.0017 - 0.0036 (0.043 - 0.092)	0.0017 - 0.0036 (0.043 - 0.092)	0.0017 - 0.0036 (0.043 - 0.092)	0.0017 - 0.0036 (0.043 - 0.092)
Valve lift (excluding clearance) in (mm)	0.3664 (9.306)	0.3664 (9.306)	0.341 (8.67)	0.341 (8.67)
Engine lubrication				
Oil grade	HD multi-grade	HD multi-grade	HD multi-grade	HD multi-grade
Viscosity −9 to +90°F (−23° to +32°C)	10W/30, 10W/40, 10W/50	10W/30, 10W/40, 10W/50	10W/30, 10W/40, 10W/50	10W/30, 10W/40, 10W/50
+10 to over 90°F (−12° to over 32°C)	20W/40, 20W/50	20W/40, 20W/50	20W/40, 20W/50	20W/40, 20W/50
Oil change without filter	4.85 Imp pints (5.82 US pints) (2.75 litres)	4.85 Imp pints (5.82 US pints) (2.75 litres)	4.85 Imp pints (5.82 US pints) (2.75 litres)	4.85 Imp pints (5.82 US pints) (2.75 litres)
Oil change including filter	5.75 Imp pints (6.9 US pints) (3.25 litres)	5.75 Imp pints (6.9 US pints) (3.25 litres)	5.75 Imp pints (6.9 US pints) (3.25 litres)	5.75 Imp pints (6.9 US pints) (3.25 litres)
Minimum oil pressure at 750 rpm	8.7 lb/in^2 (0.6 kg/cm^2)	8.7 lb/in^2 (0.6 kg/cm^2)	8.7 lb/in^2 (0.6 kg/cm^2)	8.7 lb/in^2 (0.6 kg/cm^2)
Minimum oil pressure at 2000 rpm	21.75 lb/in^2 (1.5 kg/cm^2)	21.75 lb/in^2 (1.5 kg/cm^2)	21.75 lb/in^2 (1.5 kg/cm^2)	21.75 lb/in^2 (1.5 kg/cm^2)
Warning light operates at	4.3 - 7.3 lb/in^2 (0.3 - 0.4 kg/cm^2)	4.3 - 7.3 lb/in^2 (0.3 - 0.4 kg/cm^2)	4.3 - 7.3 lb/in^2 (0.3 - 0.4 kg/cm^2)	4.3 - 7.3 lb/in^2 (0.3 - 0.4 kg/cm^2)
Relief valve opens at	35 - 40 lb/in^2 (2.4 - 2.75 kg/cm^2)	35 - 40 lb/in^2 (2.4 - 2.75 kg/cm^2)	35 - 40 lb/in^2 (2.4 - 2.75 kg/cm^2)	35 - 40 lb/in^2 (2.4 - 2.75 kg/cm^2)
Oil pump clearances in (mm)				
rotor to housing	0.0055 - 0.0102 (0.14 - 0.26)	0.0055 - 0.0102 (0.14 - 0.26)	0.0055 - 0.0102 (0.14 - 0.26)	0.0055 - 0.0102 (0.14 - 0.26)
inner to outer rotor	0.0020 - 0.0050 (0.051 - 0.127)	0.0020 - 0.0050 (0.051 - 0.127)	0.0020 - 0.0050 (0.051 - 0.127)	0.0020 - 0.0050 (0.051 - 0.127)
rotors to cover endfloat	0.0010 - 0.0024 (0.0256 - 0.06)	0.0010 - 0.0024 (0.0256 - 0.06)	0.0010 - 0.0024 (0.0256 - 0.06)	0.0010 - 0.0024 (0.0256 - 0.06)

Torque wrench settings	950 cc and 1100 cc		1300 cc and 1600 cc	
	lb f ft	kg f m	lb f ft	kg f m
Main bearing caps	70	9.0	57	7.7
Connecting rod bolts	22	3.0	33	4.6
Rear oil seal carrier	13	1.8	14	1.8
Flywheel	48	6.7	53	7.2
Clutch pressure plate	6.3	0.8	14	1.8
Chain tensioner	5.9	0.8	6	0.8

	950 cc and 1100 cc		1300 cc and 1600 cc	
Camshaft thrust plate	3.3	0.45	3.3	0.45
Camshaft gear	13	1.8	14	1.8
Timing cover	6.3	0.8	6	0.8
Water pump	6.3	0.8	6	0.8
Crankshaft pulley	41	5.6	26	3.5
Water pump pulley	6.3	0.8	6	0.8
Alternator to block	28	4.0	28	4.0
Fuel pump	13	1.8	13	1.8
Distributor clamp	2.6	0.35	2.6	0.35
Oil pump	13	1.8	14	1.8
Oil pump cover	7.4	1.0	6	0.8
Sump				
1st tightening	7	1.0	4	0.5
2nd tightening	7	1.0	7	1.0
3rd tightening	7	1.0	7	1.0
(warm)				
Sump drain plug	18	2.4	22	3.0
Oil pressure switch	10	1.4	10	1.3
Temperature sender	10	1.4	10	1.3
Rocker shaft supports	27	3.7	20	2.6
Cylinder head				
1st tightening	9	1.2	5	0.7
2nd tightening	33	4.5	25	3.5
3rd tightening	63	8.5	54	7.3
4th tightening	77	10.5	68	9.4
(after 10 min. wait)				
Rocker cover	3.3	0.45	3.5	0.45
Exhaust manifold	17	2.3	17	2.3
Inlet manifold	13	1.8	14	1.8
Carburettor	14	1.9	14	1.8
Thermostat housing	14	1.9	14	1.8
Fan temperature sender	21	2.8	21	2.8
Spark plugs	13	1.7	25	3.5
Engine mounts to block ...	66	9.0	66	9.0
Engine mounts to body ...	35	4.7	35	4.7
Inner wing engine mount ...	35	4.7	35	4.7
Engine mount to floor pan ...	35	4.7	35	4.7
Engine support to transmission	66	9.0	66	9.0
Transmission to engine	29	4.0	29	4.0

1 General description

The engine fitted to all models in the Fiesta range is the four cylinder overhead valve engine, available in 950 cc, 1100 cc, 1300 cc and 1600 cc versions.

The bore on the 950 cc and 1100 cc engine is the same as is the bore on the 1300 cc and 1600 cc engines. Variations in capacity are achieved by different crankshaft strokes and connecting rod lengths. All units are similar in design, differing only in the size of certain components, and the number of main bearings.

Two valves per cylinder are mounted vertically in the cast iron cylinder head and run in integral valve guides. They are operated by rocker arms, pushrods and tappets from the camshaft which is located at the base of the cylinder bores in the right-hand side of the engine. The correct valve stem to rocker arm pad clearance can be obtained by the adjusting screws in the ends of the rocker arms.

A crossflow cylinder head is used with four inlet ports on the right-hand side and four exhaust on the left. The 950 cc engine is available in both low and high compression versions, the difference being achieved by differing combustion chamber volumes in the cylinder head.

The cylinder block and upper half of the crankcase are cast together. The open half of the crankcase is closed by a pressed steel sump.

The pistons are made from an anodised aluminium alloy with solid skirts. Two compression rings and a slotted oil control ring are fitted. The gudgeon pin is an interference fit in the piston, and a clearance fit in the small end bush. The connecting rod bearings are steel backed, and may be of copper/lead, lead/bronze or aluminium/tin composition.

At the front of the engine a single chain drives the camshaft via the camshaft and crankshaft sprockets. This drive gear is enclosed in a pressed steel cover. The chain is tensioned automatically by a snail cam which bears against a pivoted tensioner arm. This presses against the non-driving side of the chain, so avoiding any backlash or rattle.

The camshaft is supported by three renewable bearings located directly in the cylinder block. Endfloat is controlled by a plate, bolted to the front bearing journal, and the sprocket flange. The balanced cast iron crankshaft is supported by threee (950 cc and 1100 cc) or five (1300 cc and 1600 cc) renewable main bearing shells which are in turn supported by webs which form part of the crankcase.

Crankshaft endfloat is controlled by semi-circular thrust washers located on each side of the centre main bearings.

The centrifugal water pump and the alternator are driven from the crankshaft pulley wheel by a flexible belt. The distributor is mounted toward the front of the right-hand side of the cylinder block and advances and retards the ignition timing by mechanical and vacuum means. The distributor shaft is driven at half crankshaft speed from a skew gear on the camshaft, while the fuel pump is driven by an eccentric on the camshaft.

The oil pump is mounted externally on the right-hand side of the engine under the distributor and is driven by a short shaft from the same skew gear on the camshaft as the distributor.

Bolted to the flange on the end of the crankshaft is the flywheel to which is bolted the clutch. Attached to the rear of the engine is the transmission housing.

2 Major operations possible with the engine in the vehicle

The following major operations can be carried out with the engine in place in the car. Certain of these operations require the engine to be

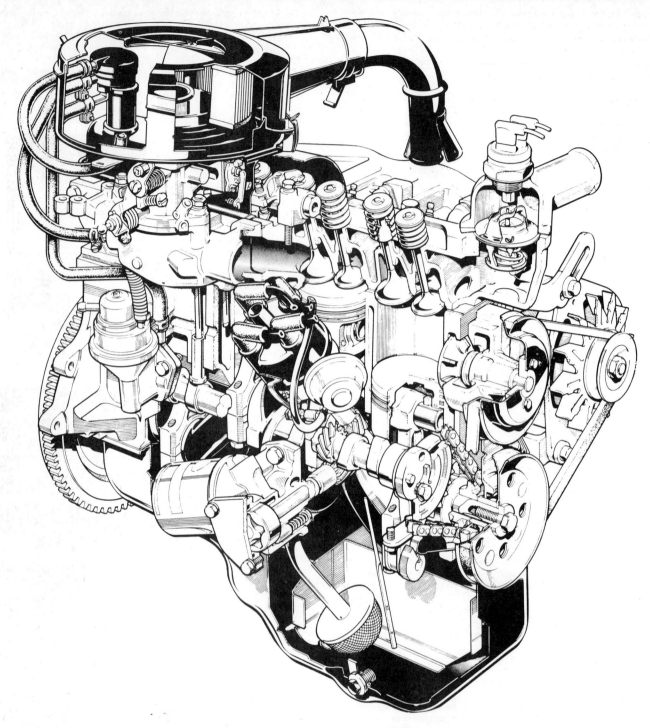

Fig. 1.1. Fiesta 950 cc and 1100 cc engine cut-away (Sec. 1)

supported from above. Removal and refitment of the:
1 Cylinder head assembly
2 Sump
3 Big-end bearings
4 Pistons and connecting rods
5 Oil pump
6 Engine mountings

engine removed from the vehicle. Removal and refitment of the:
1 Main bearings
2 Crankshaft
3 Flywheel
4 Rear bearing oil seal
5 Camshaft and bearings
6 Timing chain and gears

---

3   Major operations requiring engine removal

The following major operations can only be carried out with the

---

4   Method of engine removal

The engine complete with gearbox can be removed from the car as a unit. Because of the transverse mounting of the assembly, and the fact that both engine and gearbox are accessible from under the bonnet, this is normally the easiest and most practicable method of removal.

5 Engine and transmission - removal

1   This procedure entails lowering the engine and gearbox, and removing the unit from beneath the car. For this reason, certain items of equipment are necessary. A suitable engine hoist should be employed to lower the engine. A more difficult alternative would be to use a good trolley jack. Secondly, if an inspection pit is not available, four strong axle stands, capable of supporting the weight of the car, must be used. In addition, a willing friend will make the procedure easier.

2   Before commencing operations, select 4th gear to make gearshift adjustment easier on reassembly.

3   Open the bonnet and disconnect the battery cables.

4   Remove the radiator cap and place two trays under the engine to catch the coolant.

5   Remove the radiator bottom hose at the radiator (Fig. 1.2) and allow the coolant to drain into one of the trays. Unscrew and remove the cylinder block drain plug (front of block) and let the coolant drain into the second tray.

6   Disconnect the radiator top hose from the thermostat housing outlet and the radiator and remove the hose (Fig. 1.3).).

7   Disconnect the heater hoses from the pipe junction and inlet manifold.

8   Remove the three air cleaner securing bolts, slacken the breather hose clamp, pull off the hose and lift off the air cleaner (Fig. 1.4).

9   Pull off the spring clip from the accelerator cable end (photo) and pull the cable off the balljoint. Unscrew the two bracket retaining bolts and swing the cable and bracket to one side (Fig. 1.5).

10   Slacken the screw retaining the inner choke cable, and push out the spring clip retaining the outer choke cable (Fig. 1.6).

11   Unscrew and remove the two bolts which secure the exhaust pipe to the manifold. Unhook the exhaust system from its mounting rubbers and remove the system.

12   From the rear of the alternator, unclip the plug retaining clip and pull off the plastic loom plug.

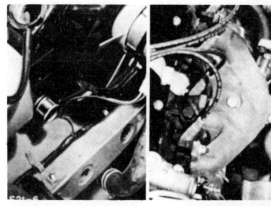

Fig. 1.2. Remove the radiator bottom hose (Sec. 5)   Fig. 1.3. Disconnect the top radiator hose (Sec. 5)

5.9 Pull off the accelerator cable clip

Fig. 1.4. Disconnect the breather hose and remove the air cleaner bracket bolts (Sec. 5, 8)

Fig. 1.5. Disconnect the accelerator cable and bracket (Sec. 5)

Fig. 1.6. Push out the choke cable (Sec. 5, 10)

5.14A Pull off the temperature sender unit wire ...

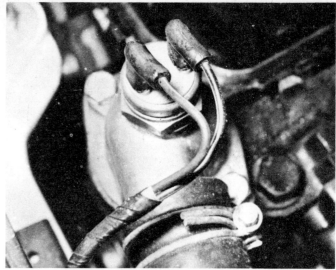

5.14B ... and the fan temperature probe wires

5.15 Pull off the centre ignition coil lead

5.17 Disconnect the engine earth strap

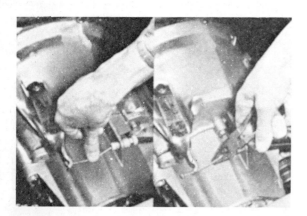

Fig. 1.7. Press down then unhook the clutch cable (Sec. 5)

Fig. 1.8. Disconnect the gear selector lever (Sec. 5)

13 Pull off the lead from the oil pressure switch, located below the distributor.

14 Pull off the lead from the temperature sender unit (photo) and, where applicable, the two leads from the fan temperature probe (photo).

15 Pull the centre lead from the ignition coil, and the smaller lead from the negative (—) terminal of the coil (photo).

16 Slacken the clamps and remove the vacuum servo hose and the breather hose from their inlet manifold locations.

17 Disconnect the engine earth strap from the front of the cylinder block (photo).

18 Disconnect the fuel inlet pipe (horizontal) from the pump. Plug the end of the pipe to prevent fuel loss.

19 Disconnect the three starter motor cables.

20 Unscrew the knurled nut and disconnect the speedometer cable from the rear of the transmission.

21 Press down on the clutch cable as shown (Fig. 1.7) and unhook the cable from the release arm. Pull the cable through its bracket.

22 If an inspection pit is not available, jack up the front and rear of the car and fit axle stands. There must be sufficient clearance to remove the engine and gearbox assembly from under the front of the car.

23 Unscrew the gear selector pinch bolt and disconnect the selector rod (Fig. 1.8).

24 Slacken both stabiliser insulator nuts, and remove the stud using an Allen key (Fig. 1.9).

25 Unscrew the two nuts securing the selector housing to the floor pan and lower the housing (Fig. 1.10). Turn the selector rod and stabilizer towards the rear of the car and suspend them from a convenient location with wire. Note that some variants have a spring between the selector rod and the body box member.

26 Remove the split pin and castellated nut from each of the two track rod outer ends, and separate the balljoint using a suitable tool (Fig. 1.11).

27 Remove the left-hand track control arm from the body mounting, and detach the balljoint from the pivot bearing at the outer end

(Fig. 1.12).

28 Disconnect the left-hand driveshaft joint from the transmission by inserting a large screwdriver between the gearbox and the joint. Knock the screwdriver down with the heel of the hand, while pulling the wheel and driveshaft outwards (Fig. 1.13). **Note:** As soon as this joint is disconnected, the transmission oil will leak out, so be ready with a drain tray!

29 Suspend the driveshaft with wire (Fig. 1.14) to avoid undue strain on the outer joint.

30 Place a suitable plug in position (Fig. 1.15) to avoid displacement of the drive pinions.

31 Remove the right-hand track control arm from the body mounting, and detach the balljoint from the pivot bearing at the outer end (Fig. 1.12).

32 Unscrew the three bolts and remove the right-hand suspension tie

Fig. 1.9. Remove the selector lever stabiliser stud (Sec. 5)

Fig. 1.11. Use a standard tool to disconnect the track rod ends (Sec. 5)

Fig. 1.10. Unscrew the two nuts and lower the gear lever housing (Sec. 5)

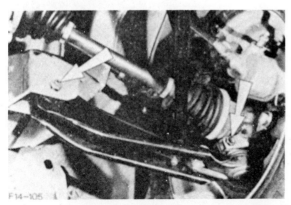

Fig. 1.12. Remove the left hand track control arm (right hand similar) (Sec. 5)

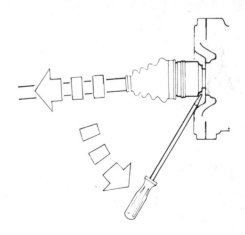

Fig. 1.13. Tap the left-hand drive shaft outwards (Sec. 5)

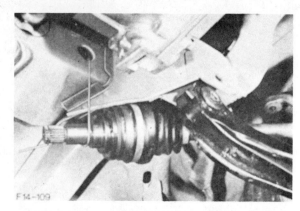

Fig. 1.14. Suspend the left-hand driveshaft (Sec. 5)

Fig. 1.15. Place a suitable plug in the transmission housing (Sec. 5)

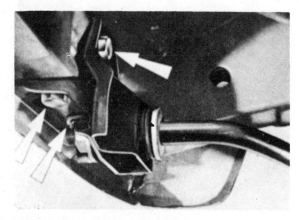

Fig. 1.16. Remove the right-hand tie bar bracket (Sec. 5)

Fig. 1.17. Tap out the right-hand driveshaft (Sec. 5)

Fig. 1.18. Support the engine and transmission assembly on a trolley jack (Sec. 5)

Fig. 1.19. Remove the engine mounting nut (Sec. 5)

bar bracket (Fig. 1.16).

33 *950 cc and 1100 cc models.* Using a large screwdriver between the transmission casing and the joint, tap out the right-hand driveshaft (Fig. 1.17). Suspend the driveshaft from the floor pan to prevent undue strain on the outer joint.

34 *1300 cc and 1600 cc models.* Unscrew and remove the Allen screws around the driveshaft joint at the centre of the right-hand driveshaft. Suspend the driveshaft from the floor pan to prevent undue strain on the outer joint.

35 *All models.* Support the weight of the engine and transmission.

This can be done by either:

a) *Arranging a wire sling around the engine sump, and a second sling around the transmission, and taking the strain on an overhead hoist or*

b) *Supporting the assembly from below, using a trolley jack and blocks of wood (Fig. 1.18).*

36 Remove the 'front' engine mounting from the right-hand wing by unscrewing the nut (Fig. 1.19).

37 Remove the engine crossmember bolts, two at the front and two at the rear (Fig. 1.20).
38 Either:

  a) *Lower the engine from above onto a suitable trolley (photo)* or
  b) *Lower the engine carefully on the trolley jack.*

39 Pull the engine and transmission assembly forward from under the front of the car (photo).
40 Thoroughly wash the exterior with paraffin or a water soluble cleaner such as Jizer. Wash off with a strong water jet and dry thoroughly.
41 The transmission may now be separated from the engine. Undo and remove the bolts that secure the starter motor to the bellhousing flange. Lift away the starter motor.
42 Unscrew and remove the bolt holding the rear engine stabiliser to the bellhousing (photo). Swing the stabiliser to one side.
43 Unscrew and remove the bolt holding the front engine stabiliser bar to the engine.
44 Unscrew and remove the two bolts passing through the engine crossmember and into the bellhousing. Slide the crossmember out from under the engine.
45 *1300 cc and 1600 cc models.* Unscrew the three nuts and remove the driveshaft bearing retaining bracket from the side of the engine.

46 *All models.* Undo and remove the remaining bolts that secure the clutch housing to the engine. The transmission may now be parted from the engine (photo). **Do not** allow the weight of the transmission to hang on the input shaft.

Fig. 1.20. Remove the engine crossmember bolts (Sec. 5, 13)

5.38 Lower the engine onto a suitable trolley ...

5.39 ... and pull it from under the front of the car

5.42 Remove the rear engine stabiliser

5.46 Support the engine while pulling off the transmission

6 Engine - dismantling - general

1   It is best to mount the engine on a dismantling stand, but if this is not available, stand the engine on a strong bench at a comfortable working height. Failing this, it will have to be stripped down on the floor.

2   During the dismantling process, the greatest care should be taken to keep the exposed parts free from dirt. As an aid to achieving this thoroughly clean down the outside of the engine, first removing all traces of oil and congealed dirt.

3   A good grease solvent will make the job much easier, for, after the solvent has been applied and allowed to stand for a time, a vigorous jet of water will wash off the solvent and grease with it. If the dirt is thick and deeply embedded, work the solvent into it with a strong stiff brush.

4   Finally, wipe down the exterior of the engine with a rag and only then, when it is quite clean, should the dismantling process begin. As the engine is stripped, clean each part in a bath of paraffin or petrol.

5   Never immerse parts with oilways in paraffin (eg, crankshaft and camshaft). To clean these parts, wipe down carefully with a petrol dampened rag. Oilways can be cleaned out with wire. If an air-line is available, all parts can be blown dry and the oilways blown through as an added precaution.

6   Re-use of old gaskets is false economy. To avoid the possibility of trouble after the engine has been reassembled **always** use new gaskets throughout.

7   Do not throw away the old gaskets, for sometimes it happens that an immediate replacement cannot be found and the old gasket is then very useful as a template. Hang up the gaskets as they are removed.

8   To strip the engine, it is best to work from the top down. When the stage is reached where the crankshaft must be removed, the engine can be turned on its side and all other work carried out with it in this position.

9   Wherever possible, refit nuts, bolts and washers finger tight from wherever they were removed. This helps to avoid loss and muddle. If they cannot be refitted then arrange them in a fashion that it is clear from whence they came.

10 No special tools are required to dismantle and reassemble the Fiesta engine, but access to certain proprietary equipment such as valve spring compressor, piston ring compressor and two-legged pullers will facilitate these operations.

7 Engine - removing ancillary components

Before basic engine dismantling begins, it is necessary to strip it of ancillary components:

a) **Fuel components**
Carburettor
Exhaust manifold
Fuel pump
Fuel line

b) **Ignition system components**
Spark plugs
Distributor

c) **Electrical system components**
Alternator
Starter motor

d) **Cooling system components**
Water pump pulley
Water pump
Thermostat housing and thermostat
Water temperature indicator sender unit

e) **Engine**
Oil filter
Oil pressure sender unit
Oil level dipstick
Oil filler cap and top cover
Engine mountings
Crankcase ventilation valve and oil separator

f) **Clutch**
Clutch pressure plate assembly
Clutch friction plate assembly

g) *Where emission control systems are installed (see Chapter 3), remove any additional items bolted to the cylinder block as its attachment.*

All nuts and bolts associated with the foregoing; some of these items have to be removed for individual servicing or renewal periodically and details can be found in the appropriate Chapter.

8 Rocker shaft and pushrods - removal (engine in car)

1   Open the bonnet and disconnect the battery.

2   Slacken the clamp and remove the breather hose from under the air cleaner (Fig. 1.4). Remove the three bolts and lift off the air cleaner complete.

3   Disconnect the breather hoses from the inlet manifold and the cylinder block and remove the oil filler cap with the breather hoses (Fig. 1.21).

4   Disconnect the HT leads from the spark plugs, disengage them from the clips on the rocker cover and swing them clear. Mark the HT leads in order to refit them in the correct order.

5   Remove the four rocker cover screws and spring washers and remove the cover.

6   Unscrew the four rocker shaft bolts evenly. When fully unscrewed, lift away the rocker shaft (Fig. 1.22).

7   The pushrods must be marked for correct reassembly, and removed by lifting from their locations (photo). A convenient method of ensuring that these and similar items are kept in the correct order is to punch eight holes in a shoe box or similar.

8   Refer to Section 54 for refitting.

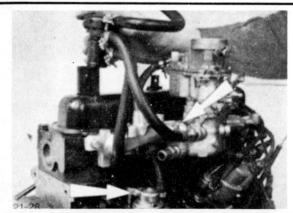

Fig. 1.21. Unclamp the breather hoses and remove the oil filler cap (Sec. 8)

Fig. 1.22. Remove the rocker shaft (Sec. 8)

8.7 Remove the pushrods

10.12 Lift away the inlet manifold and carburettor

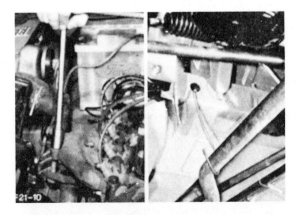

Fig. 1.23. Unscrew the exhaust pipe from the manifold and suspend the pipe (Sec. 10, 13)

9 Rocker shaft and pushrods - removal (engine on bench)

The procedure for removing the rocker shaft with the engine on the bench is similar to the procedure with the engine in the car. Refer to Section 8 and follow the sequence given in paragraphs 3 to 8 inclusive.

10 Cylinder head - removal (engine in car)

1 Open the bonnet and using a soft pencil mark the outline of the bonnet stay retaining bracket on the bonnet. Remove the bracket.
2 Refer to Chapter 10, Section 9 and remove the radiator grille.
3 Using a soft pencil mark the outline of the bonnet hinges.
4 With the help of a second person to take the weight of the bonnet, undo and remove the hinge securing bolts. There are two bolts to each hinge.
5 Lift away the bonnet and stand in a safe place. Place a pad of rag or thick newspaper on the edges which rest on the floor or against a wall.
6 Refer to Chapter 8, Section 2 and remove the battery.
7 Pull off the spring clip from the accelerator cable end (photo 5.9) and pull the cable off the balljoint. Unscrew the two bracket retaining bolts and swing the cable and bracket to one side (Fig. 1.6).
8 Slacken the screw retaining the inner choke cable, and push out the spring clip retaining the outer choke cable (photo).
9 Disconnect and remove the fuel line from the carburettor, and pull off the small vacuum line from the base of the carburettor.
10 Place a large drain tray under the radiator and disconnect the lower hose from the radiator, and the upper hose from the thermostat housing neck.
11 Disconnect the heater hoses from the pipe junction and from the inlet manifold. Disconnect the servo vacuum hose from the inlet manifold.
12 Unscrew and remove the five bolts retaining the inlet manifold and lift away the manifold with the carburettor (photo). Recover the inlet manifold gasket.
13 Unscrew the two bolts holding the exhaust pipe to the exhaust manifold, and suspend the exhaust manifold with a length of wire (Fig. 1.23).
14 Pull off the lead from the temperature sender unit and, where applicable, the two leads from the fan temperature probe (photo 5.14).
15 Refer to Section 8, paragraphs 2 to 7 inclusive, and remove the rocker shaft and pushrods.
16 Undo the cylinder head bolts half a turn at a time in a diagonal sequence. When all the bolts are no longer under tension they may be unscrewed from the cylinder head one at a time. Keep the bolts in their correct order, in the same way as the pushrods.
17 The cylinder head may now be removed by lifting upwards. If the head is stuck, try to knock it to break the seal. Under no circumstances try to prise it apart from the cylinder block with a screwdriver or cold chisel, as damage may be done to the faces of the cylinder head and block. If the head will not readily free, temporarily refit the battery and turn the engine over using the starter motor, as the compression in the cylinders will often break the cylinder head joint. If this fails to work, strike the head sharply with a plastic headed or wooden hammer, or with a metal hammer with an interposed piece of wood to cushion the blow. Under no circumstances hit the head directly with a metal hammer as this may cause the casting to fracture. Several sharp taps with the hammer, at the same time pulling upwards, should free the head.
18 Lift away the cylinder head and place to one side. Do not lay the cylinder head face downwards unless the plugs have been removed as they protrude and can easily be damaged.
19 Refer to Section 53 for refitting.

11 Cylinder head - removal (engine on bench)

The procedure for removing the cylinder head with the engine on the bench is similar to that for removal when the engine is in the car, with the exception of disconnecting the controls and services. Refer to Section 10, and follow the sequence given in paragraphs 15 to 19 inclusive.

'12 Flywheel and backplate - removal

1 With the clutch removed, as described in Chapter 5, lock the flywheel using a screwdriver in mesh with the starter ring gear and undo the five bolts that secure the flywheel to the crankshaft in a diagonal and progressive manner (photo).
2 Remove the bolts and lift away the flywheel.

13 Sump - removal (engine in the car or on the bench)

1 It is possible to remove the sump with the engine in the car provided a suitable hoist is available to take the weight of the engine in order to remove the crossmember.
2 With the car supported on axle stands, open the bonnet and disconnect the battery leads,
3 Unscrew the two bolts securing the exhaust pipe to the manifold, move the exhaust pipe to one side and support it with a length of wire (Fig. 1.23).
4 Using wire or rope slings around the inlet and exhaust manifolds, support the weight of the engine on a suitable hoist.
5 Position a large drain tray under the engine and remove the sump drain plug. Allow the engine oil to drain.
6 Remove the three clutch cover plate bolts (Fig. 1.24) and unscrew the two engine to crossmember stabiliser bars from their crossmember locations.
7 Remove the engine crossmember bolts, two at the front and two at

the rear (Fig. 1.20), and lift away the engine mounting crossmember.
8 Remove the sump by unscrewing and removing the securing bolts (Fig. 1.25). It may be necessary to free the sump by prising it off with a screwdriver.
9 To remove the sump with the engine on the bench is a simple matter of removing the securing bolts and prising off the sump (photo).
10 Refer to Section 49 to refit the sump.

14 Oil filter and pump - removal (engine in car or on bench)

1 The oil filter and pump are located on the 'rear' of the engine, and can be removed together or separately with the engine in the car or on the bench.
2 When removing the filter, position a small drain tray to catch any spilt oil.
3 The filter unscrews anti-clockwise, and the use of a chain wrench or similar proprietary tool may be found advantageous.
4 To remove the oil pump, unscrew and remove the three retaining bolts, and ease the pump from its location (photo).
5 To overhaul the pump, refer to Section 26.
6 To refit the pump, refer to Section 50.

15 Crankshaft pulley and front cover - removal

1 Because of the transverse mounting of the engine, it is not practicable to remove the front cover with the engine in the car.

12.1 Remove the flywheel securing bolts

Fig. 1.24. Remove the clutch cover plate bolts (Sec. 13)

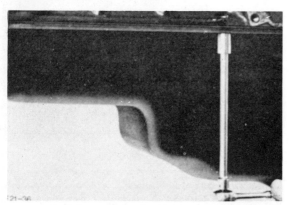

Fig. 1.25. Unscrew the sump bolts (Sec. 13)

13.9 Lift away the sump

14.4 Remove the oil pump, taking care of the gear teeth

15.2 Unscrew the crankshaft pulley retaining bolt

15.5 Lift away the front cover

16.2 Lift away the timing chain tensioner

2   Lock the crankshaft using a block of wood placed between a crankshaft web and the crankcase then using a socket, undo the bolt that secures the crankshaft pulley (photo). Recover the large diameter plain washer.

3   Using a large screwdriver, progressively ease off then remove the pulley.

4   Unscrew and remove the five bolts securing the timing chain cover, noting that one of these bolts also secures the water pump. If the sump has not already been removed, the front sump bolts must also be removed.

5   Lift away the timing chain cover (photo) and remove the gasket.

6   Lift off the crankshaft oil slinger.

16 Timing chain and gears - removal

1   Because of the transverse mounting of the engine, it is not practicable to remove the timing chain or gears with the engine in the car.

2   Unscrew and remove the two bolts holding the timing chain tensioner, lift off the tensioner (photo) then pull the tensioner arm off its dowel.

3   Check the chain for wear by measuring how much it can be depressed. More than ½ in (13 mm) means a new chain must be fitted on reassembly.

Fig. 1.26. Tap back the camshaft gear lock tabs (Sec. 16)

4   With a drift or screwdriver tap back the tabs on the lockwasher and undo the camshaft gear bolts (Fig. 1.26).

5   The camshaft gear and timing chain can now be lifted away from the cylinder block (photo).

6   The crankshaft gear can now be removed with a standard two legged puller (Fig. 1.27). If this is not available, then two suitable

16.5 Lift away the camshaft gear and timing chain

levers should be used alternately on opposite sides of the gear.

7   Once the gear has been removed, the Woodruff key can be pulled from the crankshaft using a pair of pliers.

17 Camshaft and tappets - removal

1   The camshaft can only be removed from the engine with the engine on the bench.

2   With the engine inverted, rotate the camshaft through one revolution, to ensure that all the tappets are clear of the cams.

3   Using a suitable drift or screwdriver, knock down the tabs on the camshaft retainer plate lockwasher.

4   Remove the two retainer plate bolts (Fig. 1.28) and slide the retainer upwards to remove it (photo).

5   Carefully pull the camshaft forward out of the engine (photo). Ensure that the cam lobes do not damage the camshaft bearings.

6   The tappets can now be lifted from their locations (photo). The tappets should be kept in the correct order, and this can be done by punching holes in a thin cardboard box.

18 Pistons, connecting rods and big-end bearings - removal

1   Note that the pistons have an arrow marked on the crown showing

Fig. 1.27. Use a standard puller to remove the crankshaft sprocket (Sec. 16)

Fig. 1.28. Remove the camshaft retainer plate bolts (Sec. 17)

17.4 Slide off the camshaft retainer plate

17.5 Withdraw the camshaft, taking care not to damage the bearings

17.6 Lift out the tappets, using a valve grinding tool

18.1 Connecting rod and big-end cap markings

18.3 Removing the big-end cap

Fig. 1.29. Check main bearing cap markings (950 cc/1100 cc shown) (Sec. 19)

19.2 Lift away the crankshaft rear oil seal carrier

the forward facing side. Inspect the big-end bearing caps and connecting rods to make sure identification marks are visible. This is to ensure that the correct end caps are fitted to the correct connecting rods and the connecting rods placed in their respective bores (photo).

2 Undo the big-end bolts and place to one side in the order in which they were removed.

3 Remove the big-end caps (photo) taking care to keep them in the right order and the correct way round. Also ensure that the shell bearings are kept with their correct connecting rods unless the rods are to be renewed.

4 If the big-end caps are difficult to remove, they may be gently tapped with a soft hammer.

5 To remove the shell bearings, press the bearing opposite the groove in both the connecting rod and its cap, and the bearing will slide out easily.

6 Withdraw the pistons and connecting rods upwards and ensure they are kept in the correct order for refitting in the same bores as they were originally fitted.

19 Crankshaft and main bearings - removal

1 Make sure that identification marks are visible on the main bearing end caps, so that they may be refitted in their original positions, and the correct way round (Fig. 1.29).

2 Unscrew and remove the four bolts which hold the crankshaft rear oil seal carrier, and lift away the carrier (photo). Remove the gasket.

3 Undo by one turn at a time the bolts which hold the main bearing caps.

4 Lift away each main bearing cap with its bearing shell, keeping the two together.
5 When removing the centre cap, note the semi-circular halves of the thrust washers, one half lying on either side of the main bearing. Lay them with the centre bearing cap, on the correct side.
6 Remove the crankshaft by lifting it away from the crankcase (photo).
7 Remove the remaining bearing shells, and place them with the corresponding caps, including the two semi-circular thrust washers at the centre main bearing.

20 Valves - removal

1 Once the cylinder head has been removed from the engine, the valves, valve springs and oil seals can be removed with the use of a standard valve spring compressor.
2 Using the valve spring compressor, press the valve spring retainer down far enough to free the collets (photo), then remove the collets.
3 Release the spring compressor and lift off the valve spring and retainer (photo). When using the valve spring compressor, ensure that the valve spring retainers do not damage the valve stem.
4 Lift off the rubber valve stem seals and remove the valves from the underside of the cylinder head.
5 Keep the valves, springs, retainers and collets in the correct order by using a piece of card with holes numbered from 1 (front of engine) to 8 (rear).
6 Refer to Section 52 for refitting.

21 Rocker shaft - overhaul

1 Once the rocker shaft has been removed from the engine, it may be dismantled as follows.
2 Remove the split pin from one end of the rocker shaft and lift off

the spring washer and flat washer.
3 The rocker arms, rocker pedestals and distance springs can now be slid off the end of the shaft, and should be kept in the correct order.
4 Refer to Section 37 and examine the components.
5 Refit the components in the order shown in Fig. 1.30. Note that the vertical grooves must be on the adjusting screw side. Use *new* split pins.

22 Gudgeon pin - removal

A press type gudgeon pin is used and it is important that no damage is caused during removal and refitting. Because of this, should it be necessary to fit new pistons, take the parts along to the local Ford garage who will have the special equipment to do this job.

23 Piston rings - removal

1 To remove the piston rings, slide them carefully over the top of the piston, taking care not to scratch the aluminium alloy, never slide them off the bottom of the piston skirt. It is very easy to break the cast iron piston rings if they are pulled off roughly, so this operation should be done with extreme care. It is helpful to make use of an old feeler gauge.
2 Lift one end of the piston ring to be removed out of its groove and insert under it the end of the feeler gauge.
3 Turn the feeler gauge slowly round the piston, and, as the ring comes out of its groove, apply slight upward pressure so that it rests on the land above. It can then be eased off the piston with the feeler gauge stopping it from slipping into an empty groove if it is any but the top ring that is being removed.

19.6 Lift out the crankshaft (950 cc/1100 cc shown)

20.2 Compress the valve spring to remove the collets.

20.3 Remove the valve spring retainer and spring

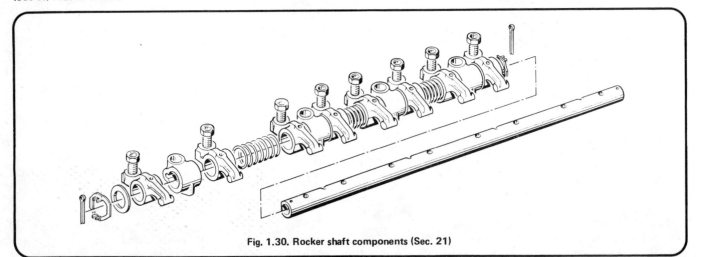
Fig. 1.30. Rocker shaft components (Sec. 21)

24 Lubrication system - description

1   The pressed steel oil sump, attached to the underside of the crank-case, acts as a reservoir for the engine oil. The eccentric twin rotor pump draws oil through a strainer located under the oil surface, passes it along a short passage and into the full-flow oil filter. The oil pressure is regulated by means of a pressure relief valve located within the oil pump.

2   From the filter, the oil flows to the pressure sender unit, and from there across the engine to the main oil gallery. From the main oil gallery, oil flows to each of the three main bearings, and from there through drillings to the three camshaft bearings.

3   Diagonal drillings in the crankshaft enable oil from the main bearings to be fed to the big-end bearings. From there, oil is splashed onto the gudgeon pins and the trailing side of the cylinders.

4   A cross drilling in the oilway from the front main bearing to the front camshaft bearing gives splash lubrication of the timing gears. A final drilling from the front camshaft bearing feeds oil to the hollow rocker shaft. From this shaft, oil is fed to the rocker arms and valve operating gear.

25 Crankcase ventilation system

1   The oil filler cap has three hose connections, and two one-way valves. During idling, some of the air entering the air cleaner is drawn through a hose to the filler cap. From here, the fresh air is drawn through a one-way valve, down a second hose into the crankcase. Crankcase fumes collect in the rocker cover, and are drawn through a second one-way valve, along the third hose and into the inlet manifold, when they are burnt in the combustion chamber.

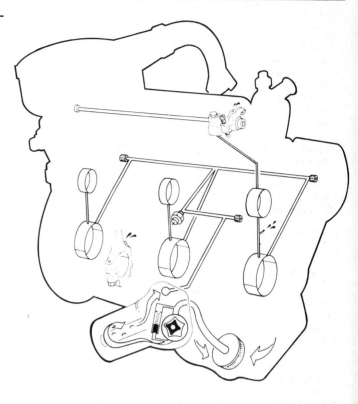

Fig. 1.31. 950 cc/1100 cc engine lubrication circuit (Sec. 24)

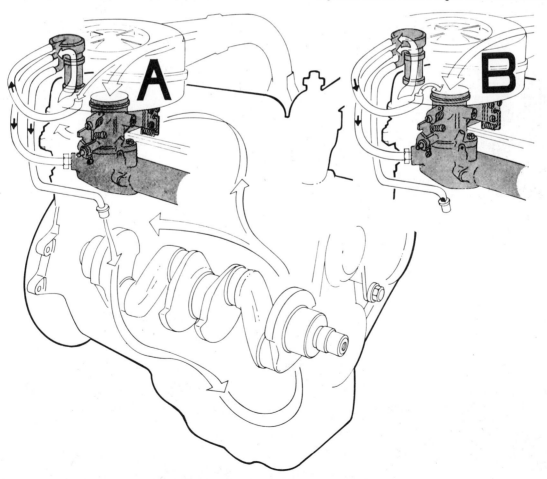

Fig. 1.32. Crankcase ventilation at idle (A), and with fully open throttle (B) (Sec. 25)

2 At full throttle, the greater proportion of crankcase fumes are dealt with by the need for air during combustion. In addition to the fumes being drawn into the inlet manifold, crankcase fumes are also drawn through the unrestricted hose and into the carburettor, together with the fresh air drawn through the air cleaner spout.

3 At the specified service intervals, the oil filler cap should be removed and all components washed in petrol to remove sludge and deposits. Any hoses suspected of deterioration should be renewed.

26 Oil pump - overhaul

1 If the pump is worn it is best to purchase an exchange reconditioned unit as an efficient lubrication system is the secret of long engine life. Generally speaking, an exchange pump should be fitted at a major engine rebuild.

2 If it is wished to renew or overhaul the oil pump, refer to Section 14 to remove it.

3 Undo and remove the three screws securing the cover and remove the 'O' ring (photo).

4 Check the clearance between the inner and outer rotors (photo), using feeler blades. This should not exceed 0.002 to 0.005 in (0.050 to 0.125 mm). Check the clearance between the outer rotor and the pump body using feeler blades. This should not exceed 0.0055 to 0.0102 in (0.15 to 0.25 mm).

5 Check the endfloat by placing a straight edge across the open face of the pump casing and checking the clearance between this and the rotor face using feeler blades. This should not exceed 0.001 to 0.0024 in (0.025 to 0.060 mm).

6 Replacement rotors are only supplied as a matched pair so that if any of the clearances are excessive, a new rotor assembly must be fitted. When it is necessary to renew the rotors, drive out the pin securing the skew gear and pull the gear from the shaft. Remove the inner rotor and driveshaft and remove the outer rotor. Install the outer rotor with the chamfered end towards the pump body.

7 Fit the inner rotor and driveshaft assembly, position the skew gear and install the pin. Tap over each end of the pin to prevent it loosening. Position a new 'O' ring in the groove in the pump body, fit the end plate and secure it with the three bolts and lockwashers.

8 Refit the oil pump assembly, with a new gasket, and secure it with the three bolts and lockwashers.

27 Engine components - examination for wear

When the engine has been stripped down and all parts properly cleaned decisions have to be made as to what needs renewal and the following Sections tell the examiner what to look for. In any border-line case it is always best to decide in favour of a new part. Even if a part may still be serviceable, its life will have been reduced by wear and

the degree of trouble needed to renew it in the future must be taken into consideration. However, these things are relative and it depends on whether a quick 'survival' job is being done or whether the car as a whole is being regarded as having many thousands of miles of useful and economical life remaining.

28 Crankshaft - examination and renovation

1 Look at the main bearing journals and the crankpins, and if there are any scratches or score marks then the shaft will need regrinding. Such conditions will nearly always be accompanied by similar deterioration in the matching bearing shells.

2 Each bearing journal should also be round and can be checked with a micrometer or caliper gauge around the periphery at several points. If there is more than 0.001 of ovality regrinding is necessary.

3 A main Ford Agent or motor engineering specialist will be able to decide to what extent regrinding is necessary and also supply the special undersize shell bearing to match whatever may need grinding off.

4 Before taking the crankshaft for regrinding check also the cylinder bores and pistons as it may be advantageous to have the whole engine done at the same time.

29 Main and big-end bearings - examination and renovation

1 With careful servicing and regular oil and filter changes, bearings will last for a very long time but they can still fail for unforeseen reasons. With big-end bearings the indication is a regular rhythmic load knocking from the crankcase. The frequency depends on engine speed and is particularly noticeable when the engine is under load. This symptom is accompanied by a fall in oil pressure although this is not normally noticeable unless an oil pressure gauge is fitted. Main bearing failure is usually indicated by serious vibration, particularly at higher engine revolutions, accompanied by a more significant drop in oil pressure and a 'rumbling' noise.

2 Bearing shells in good condition have bearing surfaces with a smooth even matt silver/grey colour all over. Worn bearings will show patches of a different colour when the bearing metal has worn away and exposed the underlay. Damaged bearings will be pitted or scored. It is always well worthwhile fitting new shells as their cost is relatively low. If the crankshaft is in good condition it is merely a question of obtaining another set of standard size. A reground crankshaft will need new bearing shells as a matter of course.

30 Cylinder bores - examination and renovation

1 A new cylinder is perfectly round and the walls parallel throughout

26.3 Lift off the oil pump cover and remove the 'O' ring (arrowed)

26.4 Check the rotor to body clearance at A, and the inner to outer rotor clearance at B

its length. The action of the piston tends to wear the walls at right angles to the gudgeon pin due to side thrust. This wear takes place principally on that section of the cylinder swept by the piston rings.

2   It is possible to get an indication of bore wear by removing the cylinder head with the engine still in the car. With the piston down in the bore first signs of wear can be seen and felt just below the top of the bore where the top piston ring reaches and there will be a noticeable lip. If there is no lip it is fairly reasonable to expect that bore wear is not severe and any lack of compression or excessive oil consumption is due to worn or broken piston rings or pistons (see Section 31).

3   If it is possible to obtain a bore measuring micrometer measure the bore in the thrust plane below the lip and again at the bottom of the cylinder in the same plane. If the difference is more than 0.003 in (0.08 mm) then a rebore is necessary. Similarly, a difference of 0.003 in (0.08 mm) or more across the bore diameter is a sign of ovality calling for rebore.

4   Any bore which is significantly scratched or scored will need reboring. This symptom usually indicates that the piston or rings are damaged also. In the event of only one cylinder being in need of reboring, it will be necessary for all four to be bored and fitted with new oversize pistons and rings. Your Ford agent or local motor engineering specialist will be able to rebore and obtain the necessary matched pistons. If the crankshaft is undergoing regrinding also, it is a good idea to let the same firm renovate and reassemble the crankshaft and pistons to the block. A reputable firm normally gives a guarantee for such work. In cases where engines have been rebored already to their maximum, new cylinder liners are available which may be fitted. In such cases the same reboring processes have to be followed and the services of a specialist engineering firm are required.

31 Pistons and piston rings - inspection and testing

1   Worn pistons and rings can usually be diagnosed when the symptoms of excessive oil consumption and lower compression occur and are sometimes, though not always, associated with worn cylinder bores. Compression testers that fit into the spark plug hole are available and these can indicate where low compression is occurring. Wear usually accelerates the more it is left so when the symptoms occur early action can possibly save the expense of a rebore.

2   Another symptom of piston wear is piston slap - a knocking noise from the crankcase not to be confused with the big-end bearing failure. It can be heard clearly at low engine speed when there is no load (idling for example) and is much less audible when the engine speed increases. Piston wear usually occurs in the skirt or lower end of the piston and is indicated by vertical streaks in the worn area which is always on the thrust side. It can also be seen where the skirt thickness is different.

3   Piston ring wear can be checked by first removing the rings from the pistons as described in Section 23. Then place the rings in the cylinder bores from the top, pushing them down about 1½ in (38 mm) with the head of a piston (from which the rings have been removed), so that they rest square in the cylinder. Then measure the gap at the ends of the ring with a feeler gauge. If it exceeds that given in the Specifications, they need renewal.

4   The grooves in which the rings locate in the piston can also become enlarged in use. The clearance between ring and piston, in the groove, should not exceed that given in the Specifications.

5   However, it is rare that a piston is only worn in the ring grooves and the need to replace them for this fault alone is hardly ever encountered.

32 Connecting rods and gudgeon pins - examination and renovation

1   Gudgeon pins are a shrink fit into the connecting rods. Neither of these would normally need renewal unless the pistons were being changed, in which case the new pistons would automatically be supplied with new gudgeon pins.

2   Connecting rods are not subject to wear but in extreme circumstances such as engine seizure they could be distorted. Such conditions may be visually apparent but where doubt exists they should be changed. The bearing caps should also be examined for indications of filing down which may have been attempted in the mistaken idea that bearing slackness could be remedied in this way. If there are such signs then the connecting rods should be renewed.

33 Camshaft and camshaft bearings - examination and renovation

1   The camshaft bearing bushes should be examined for signs of scoring and pitting. If they need renewal they will have to be dealt with professionally as, although it may be relatively easy to remove the old bushes, the correct fitting of new ones requires special tools. If they are not fitted evenly and square from the very start they can be distorted thus causing localised wear in a very short time. See your Ford dealer or local engineering specialist for this work.

2   The camshaft itself may show signs of wear on the bearing journals or cam lobes. The main decision to take is what degree of wear justifies renewal, which is costly. Any signs of scoring or damage to the bearing journals cannot be removed by grinding. Renewal of the whole camshaft is the only solution. **Note:** Where excessive cam lobe wear is evident, refer to the note in the following Section.

3   The cam lobes themselves may show signs of ridging or pitting on the high points. If ridging is light then it may be possible to smooth it out with fine emery. The cam lobes however, are surface hardened and once this is penetrated, wear will be very rapid thereafter.

4   Ensure that the camshaft oilways are unobstructed.

5   Examine the skew gear for wear, and damaged teeth. If either is evident, a replacement shaft must be obtained.

6   Carefully examine the camshaft thrust plate. Excessive wear will be visually evident and will require the fitting of a new plate.

34 Cam tappets - examination

1   Examine the surface of the tappets which bear on the camshaft. Any identation in this surface or any cracks indicate serious wear and the tappets should be renewed. Thoroughly clean them out, removing all traces of sludge.

2   It is most unlikely that the sides of the tappets have worn, but if they are a very loose fit in their bores they should be renewed.

35 Valves and valve seats - examination and renovation

1   With the valves removed from the cylinder heads examine the heads for signs of cracking, burning away and pitting of the edge where it seats in the port. The seats of the valves in the cylinder head should also be examined for the same signs. Usually it is the valve that deteriorates first but if a bad valve is not rectified the seat will suffer and this is more difficult to repair.

2   Provided that there are no signs of serious pitting, the exhaust valve should be ground with its seat. *The inlet valves are aluminised and must not be ground in.* If the inlet valve seats are badly pitted, use a spare valve for grinding the seat. If the inlet valve itself is pitted or burnt then it must be renewed.

3   Valve grinding is carried out by placing a smear of carborundum paste on the edge of the valve and, using a suction type valve holder, grinding the valve in situ. This is done with a semi-rotary action, rotating the handle of the valve holder between the hands and lifting it occasionally to re-distribute the traces of paste. Use a coarse paste to start with. As soon as a matt grey unbroken line appears on both the valve and seat the valve is 'ground in'. All traces of carbon should also be cleaned from the head and neck of the valve stem. A wire brush mounted in a power drill is a quick and effective way of doing this.

4   Another form of valve wear can occur on the stem where it runs in the guide in the cylinder head. This can be detected by trying to rock the valve from side to side. If there is any movement at all it is an indication that the valve stem or guide is worn. Check the stem first with a micrometer at points along and around its length and if they are not within the specified size new valves will probably solve the problem. If the guides are worn, however, they will need reboring for oversize valves or for fitting guide inserts. The valve seats will also need recutting to ensure they are eccentric with the stems. This work should be entrusted to your Ford dealer or local auto-engineering works.

5   When the valve seats are badly burnt or pitted, requiring renewal, inserts may be fitted - or replaced if already fitted once before - and once again this is a specialist task to be carried out by a suitable engineering firm.

6   When all valve grinding is completed it is essential that every trace

of grinding paste is removed from the valves and ports in the cylinder head. This should be done by thorough washing in petrol or paraffin and blowing out with a jet of air. If particles of carborundum should work their way into the engine they would cause havoc with bearings or cylinder walls.

36 Timing chain and gears - examination and renovation

1   Examine the teeth on both crankshaft and camshaft gearwheels for wear. Each tooth forms an inverted V with the gearwheel periphery, and if worn the side of each tooth under tension will be slightly concave in shape when compared with the other side of the tooth. If any sign of wear is present, the gearwheels must be renewed.
2   In addition to the check carried out before removal, Section 16, examine the links of the chain for side slackness and renew the chain if any evidence of excess wear is evident. It is a sensible precaution to renew the chain at about 30,000 miles (48,000 km) and at a lower mileage if the engine is stripped down for a major overhaul. The rollers on a very badly worn chain may be slightly grooved.
3   The timing chain tensioner arm should be renewed, as should the tensioning cam if the milled edge is excessively worn.

37 Rockers and rocker shaft - examination and renovation

1   Thoroughly clean the rocker shaft and then check it for distortion by rolling it on a piece of plate glass. If it is out of true, renew it. The surface of the shaft should be free from wear ridges and score marks.
2   Check the rocker arms for wear of the rocker bushes, for wear of the adjusting ball ended screws. Wear in the rocker arm bush can be checked by gripping the rocker arm tip and holding the rocker arm in place on the shaft, noting if there is any lateral rocker arm shake. If shake is present, and the arm is very loose on the shaft, a new bush or rocker arm must be fitted.
3   Check the top of the rocker arm where it bears on the valve head for cracking or serious wear on the case hardening. If none is present re-use the rocker arm. Check the lower half of the ball on the end of the rocker arm adjusting screw. Check the pushrods for straightness by rolling them on a piece of plate glass. Renew any that are bent.

38 Flywheel - examination and renovation

1   If the ring gear is badly worn or has missing teeth it should be renewed. The old ring can be removed from the flywheel by cutting a notch between two teeth with a hacksaw and then splitting it with a cold chisel.
2   To fit a new ring gear requires heating the ring to 400°F (204°C). This can be done by polishing four equally spaced sections of the gear, laying it on a suitable heat resistant surface (such as fire bricks) and heating it evenly with a blow lamp or torch until the polished areas turn a light yellow tinge. Do not overheat or the hard wearing properties will be lost. The gear has a chamfered inner edge which should go against the shoulder when put on the flywheel. When hot enough place the gear in position quickly, tapping it home, if necessary, and let it cool naturally without quenching it in any way.

39 Cylinder head and piston crowns - decarbonisation

1   When the cylinder head is removed, either in the course of an overhaul or for inspection of bores or valve condition when the engine is in the car, it is normal to remove all carbon deposits from the piston crowns and heads.
2   This is best done with a cup shaped wire brush and an electric drill and is fairly straightforward when the engine is dismantled and the pistons removed. Sometimes hard spots of carbon are not easily removed except by a scraper. When cleaning the pistons with a scraper, take care not to damage the surface of the piston in any way.
3   When the engine is in the car, certain precautions must be taken when decarbonising the piston crowns in order to prevent dislodged pieces of carbon falling into the interior of the engine which could cause damage to cylinder bores, piston and rings - or if allowed into the water passages - damage to the water pump. Turn the engine so that the piston being worked on is at the top of its stroke and then mask off

the adjacent cylinder bores and all surrounding water jacket orifices with paper and adhesive tape. Press grease into the gap all round the piston to keep carbon particles out and then scrape all carbon away by hand carefully. Do not use a power drill and wire brush when the engine is in the car as it will virtually be impossible to keep all the carbon dust clear of the engine. When completed carefully clear out the grease around the rim of the piston with a matchstick or something similar - bringing any carbon particles with it. Repeat the process on the other piston crown. It is not recommended that a ring of carbon is left round the edge of the piston on the theory that it will aid oil consumption. This was valid in the earlier days of long stroke low revving engines but modern engines, fuels and lubricants cause less carbon deposits anyway and any left behind tends merely to cause hot spots.

40 Sump - inspection

Wash out the sump in petrol and wipe dry. Inspect the exterior for signs of damage or excessive rust. If evident, a new sump must be obtained. To ensure an oil tight joint scrape away all traces of the old gasket from the cylinder block mating face.

41 Engine reassembly - general

All components of the engine must be cleaned of oil, sludge and old gasket and the working area should also be cleared and clean. In addition to the normal range of good quality socket spanners and general tools which are essential the following must be available before reassembling begins:

1   *Complete set of new gaskets.*
2   *Supply of clean lint-free cloths.*
3   *Clean oil can full of new engine oil.*
4   *Torque wrench.*
5   *All new spare parts as necessary.*

42 Crankshaft - refitting

Ensure that the crankcase is thoroughly clean and that all oilways are clear. A thin twist drill or a piece of wire is useful for cleaning them out. If possible blow them out with compressed air.

Treat the crankshaft in the same fashion, and then inject engine oil into the crankshaft oilways.

Commence work of rebuilding the engine by refitting the crankshaft and main bearings:
1   Wipe the bearing shell locations in the crankcase with a lint-free cloth.
2   Wipe the crankshaft journals with a soft lint-free cloth.
3   If the old main bearing shells are to be renewed (not to do so is a false economy unless they are virtually new) fit the upper halves of the main bearing shells to their location in the crankcase (photo).
4   Identify each main bearing cap and place in order. The caps are marked F (front), C (centre), and R (rear), or alternatively 1 (front) through to 5 (rear), and the arrow (where applicable) should point to the front of the engine (Fig. 1.33).
5   Wipe the end cap bearing shell location with a soft non-fluffy rag.
6   Fit the bearing half shell onto each main bearing cap.
7   Apply a little grease to either side of the centre main bearing so as to retain the thrust washers.
8   Fit the upper halves of the thrust washers into their grooves either side of the main bearing. The slots must face outwards (Fig. 1.34).
9   Lubricate the crankshaft journals and the upper and lower main bearing shells with engine oil (photo).
10 Carefully lower the crankshaft into the crankcase.
11 Lubricate the crankshaft main bearing journals again and then fit all bearing caps except the centre one. Fit the securing bolts but do not tighten yet.
12 Apply a little grease to either side of the centre main bearing end cap. Fit the thrust washers with the slots facing outwards.
13 Fit the centre main bearing cap and the two securing bolts.
14 Lightly tighten all main cap securing bolts and then fully tighten in a progressive manner to a final torque wrench setting as specified (photo).
15 Using a screwdriver ease the crankshaft fully forwards and with feeler gauges check the clearance between the crankshaft journal side

42.3 Fit the upper main bearing shell and thrust washers (centre bearing)

Fig. 1.33. Main bearing cap letter and arrow markings (950 cc/1100 cc shown)(Sec. 42)

Fig. 1.34. Thrust washer grooves facing outwards (Sec. 42)

42.9 Lubricate the main bearing shells with engine oil

42.14 Tighten the main bearing caps progressively (950 cc/1100 cc shown)

42.15 Check the crankshaft endfloat at the centre bearing

and the thrust washers. The clearance must not exceed that given in the Specifications. Oversize thrust washers are available (photo).

16 Test the crankshaft for freedom of rotation. Should it be stiff to turn or possess high spots, a most careful inspection must be made with a micrometer, preferably by a qualified mechanic, to get to the root of the trouble. It is very seldom that any trouble of this nature

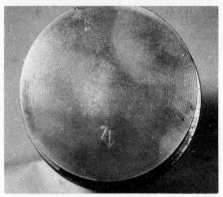
44.5 Arrow on piston crown must point to the front of the engine

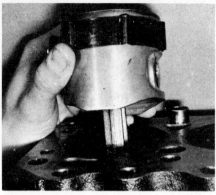
44.6 Fit the piston into the bore, using a piston ring compressor

45.3 Lubricate the crankpins with engine oil

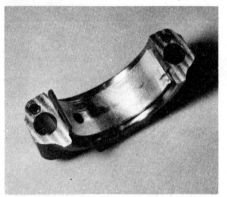
45.4 Fit the big-end bearing in the cap, with the bearing tongue in the locating groove

45.7 Tighten the big-end bearing cap bolts

46.1 Fit the tappets in their correct bores

46.4 Secure the camshaft retaining plate bolts with the tab washer

Fig. 1.35. Press on the crankshaft sprocket (Sec. 47)

47.2 Align the crankshaft and camshaft sprocket timing marks with the shaft centres

47.4 Secure the camshaft sprocket retaining bolts with the tab washer

47.5 Refit a new tensioner arm and secure the timing chain tensioner

will be experienced when fitting the crankshaft.

17 Using a screwdriver, prise out the circular rear crankshaft oil seal from its carrier.

18 Place a new oil seal squarely in the aperture, and tap into the carrier gently and evenly using a piece of wood to avoid damage to the seal.

19 Clean the mating faces, position a new gasket and secure the oil seal carrier in position with the four bolts.

43 Piston rings - refitting

1 Check that the piston ring grooves and oilways are thoroughly clean and unblocked. Piston rings must always be fitted over the head of the piston and never from the bottom.

2 The easiest method to use when fitting rings is to wrap a 0.020 in (0.5 mm) feeler gauge round the top of the piston and place the rings one at a time, starting with the bottom oil control ring, over the feeler gauge.

3 The feeler gauge, complete with ring can then be slid down the piston over the other piston ring grooves until the correct groove is reached. The piston ring is then slid gently off the feeler gauge into the groove.

4 An alternative method is to fit the rings by holding them slightly open with the thumbs and both of the index fingers. This method requires a steady hand and great care as it is easy to open the ring too much and break it.

44 Pistons - refitting

The piston, complete with connecting rods, can be fitted to the cylinder bores in the following sequence:

1 With a wad of clean rag wipe the cylinder bores clean.

2 The pistons, complete with connecting rods, are fitted to their bores from the top of the block.

3 Locate the piston ring gaps in the following manner:

Top: at 180° to bottom ring gap
Centre: at 90° to bottom ring gap
Bottom: in line with gudgeon pin

4 Well lubricate the piston and rings with engine oil.

5 Fit a universal piston ring compressor and prepare to insert the first piston into the bore. Make sure it is the correct piston-connecting rod assembly for that particular bore, that the connecting rod is the correct way round with the front of the piston (photo) facing the front of the engine.

6 Again lubricate the piston skirt and insert into the bore (photo).

7 Gently but firmly tap the piston through the piston ring compressor and into the cylinder bore with a wooden, or plastic faced hammer.

45 Connecting rods to crankshaft - refitting

1 Wipe clean the connecting rod half of the big-end bearing cap and the underside of the shell bearing, and fit the shell bearing in position with its locating tongue engaged with the corresponding cut out in the rod.

2 If the old bearings are nearly new and are being refitted then ensure they are refitted in their correct locations on the correct rods.

3 Generously lubricate the crankpin journals with engine oil and turn the crankshaft so that the crankpin is in the most advantageous position for the connecting rods to be drawn onto it (photo).

4 Wipe clean the connecting rod bearing cap and back of the shell bearing, and fit the shell bearing in position ensuring that the locating tongue at the back of the bearing engages with the locating groove in the connecting rod cap (photo).

5 Generously lubricate the shell bearing and offer up the connecting rod bearing cap to the connecting rod.

6 Refit the connecting rod nuts and pinch them tight.

7 Tighten the bolts with a torque wrench to the specified torque (photo).

8 When all the connecting rods have been fitted, rotate the crankshaft to check that everything is free, and that there are no high spots causing binding. The bottom half of the engine is now nearly built up.

46 Camshaft and tappets - refitting

1 With the engine still upside down, locate the camshaft tappets into their respective bores, as noted during removal (photo).

2 Generously oil the camshaft bearings with clean engine oil, and carefully insert the camshaft, ensuring that the cam lobes and skew gear do not damage the bearings.

3 Place the 'U' shaped retaining plate into the groove in the end of the camshaft.

4 Fit a **new** tab washer, secure the retaining plate with the two bolts, and bend up the ends of the tab washer using a suitable screwdriver or drift (photo).

47 Timing chain and gears - refitting

1 Fit the Woodruff key in its slot in the end of the crankshaft then press the crankshaft sprocket into position with the timing mark facing forward. The sprocket can be pressed on using the crankshaft pulley and bolt, Fig. 1.35.

2 The timing chain and camshaft sprocket should now be positioned so that the two sprocket marks align ie, on the imaginary line through each sprocket centre (photo).

3 The camshaft should now be rotated until the locating dowel aligns with the hole in the sprocket. Fit the sprocket and a **new** tab washer, and secure with the two bolts.

4 Using a screwdriver or suitable drift, bend up the locktabs (photo).

5 Slide a new tensioner arm onto its dowel, and fit the timing chain tensioner, and secure it with the two bolts and spring washers (photo).

48 Crankshaft pulley and front cover - refitting

1 Fit the oil slinger with the concave face outwards and the slot over the crankshaft key (photo).

2 Prise out the oil seal from the front cover. Position a new seal squarely in the aperture and tap in gently and progressively, using a wooden block to avoid damage to the seal.

3 Clean the mating faces and fit the float cover, with a new gasket. Secure the cover with the five bolts, noting that one bolt also assists in securing the water pump (photo).

4 The crankshaft pulley may be fitted at this stage, or after the sump has been fitted. Take care to align the slot in the pulley with the Woodruff key in the crankshaft. Secure the pulley with the bolt and large plain washer.

48.1 Fit the oil slinger to the crankshaft, facing outwards

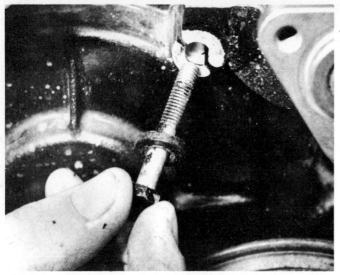

48.3 One of the bolts secures both the timing cover and the water pump

49.3 Align the tab on the sump gasket with the cut-out in the oil seal

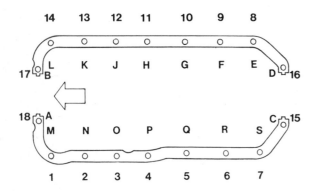

Fig. 1.36. Tighten the sump bolts in alphabetical, then numerical and finally alphabetical order (Sec. 36)

51.1 Locate the engine backplate over the two dowels

52.1 Insert the valves into their correct locations

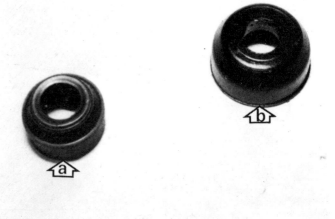

52.3 Exhaust (A) and inlet (B) valve stem seals

49 Sump - refitting

1   Wipe the mating faces of the underside of the crankcase and the sump.
2   Smear some non-setting gasket sealant on the underside of the crankcase.
3   Fit the sump gasket and end seals making sure that the bolt holes line up (photo).
4   Offer the sump up to the gaskets taking care not to dislodge, and secure in position with the bolts.
5   Tighten the sump bolts in a progressive manner, to a final torque wrench setting as specified, in the order shown in Fig. 1.36.
6   *Engine in the car.* Refit the engine crossmember, with the towing eye to the front, and secure it with the four bolts (two at the front, two at the rear) and spring washers.
7   Using two suitable drifts, align the engine mounting bolt holes with the holes in the crossmember, and fit two **new** bolts.
8   Refit the clutch cover plate, and secure with three **new** self-locking bolts.
9   Refit and secure the engine to crossmember stabilizer bars.
10 Release the weight of the engine from the hoist. Refit the exhaust manifold and secure it with the two bolts.
11 Reconnect the battery leads, lower the car to the ground and refill the engine with specified engine oil.

50 Oil filter and pump - refitting

1   Refit the oil pump after filling it with clean engine oil and turning the gear through 1 - 2 revolutions. Secure with the three bolts and spring washers.
2   Ensure that the oil filter sealing ring groove is clean, then fit the square section seal, taking care not to twist or distort the seal.
3   Screw in the oil filter cartridge until the seal contacts the housing, then tighten the cartridge a further ¾ turn. **Do not overtighten.**
4   Note that if this operation has been carried out with the engine in the car, the oil level should be topped up as required.

51 Flywheel and backplate - refitting

1   Wipe over the end of the cylinder block, and locate the engine backplate over the two dowels (photo).
2   Check that the flywheel bolts are in good condition and lightly oil them.
3   Refit the flywheel and secure with the five bolts.

52 Valves - refitting

1   With the valves ground in (Section 35) and kept in their correct order, start with No. 1 cylinder and insert the valve into its guide (photo).
2   Lubricate the valve stem with engine oil and slide on a new seal. To avoid damaging the seals it is useful to wrap a piece of foil around the stem grooves before fitting the seal.
3   Note that the exhaust valve stem seal has a helical spring (photo).
4   Fit the valve spring and cap.
5   Using a universal valve spring compressor, compress the valve spring until the split collets can be slid into position. Note these collets have serrations which engage in slots in the valve stem. Release the valve spring compressor.
6   Repeat this procedure until all eight valve springs are fitted.

53 Cylinder head - refitting

1   Wipe the mating faces of the cylinder head and cylinder block.
2   Carefully place a new gasket on the cylinder block and check to ensure that it is correct way up and the right way round.
3   Gently lower the cylinder head being as accurate as possible first time so that the gasket is not dislodged.
4   Refit the cylinder head bolts taking care not to damage the gasket if it has moved.
5   Tighten the cylinder head bolts in four stages, as specified in the Specifications, in the order shown in Fig. 1.37.

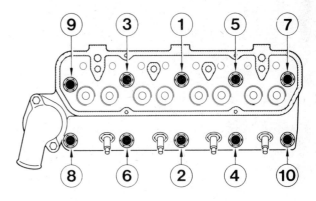

Fig. 1.37. Tighten cylinder head bolts in the order shown (Sec. 53)

6   *Engine in the car.* Refer to Section 54, paragraph 1 to 7 inclusive and refit the rocker shaft and pushrods.
7   Refit the leads to the temperature sender unit and, where applicable, the two leads to the fan temperature probe (photo 5.14).
8   Refit the exhaust manifold and secure with the two bolts.
9   Refit the inlet manifold gasket and manifold, complete with carburettor, and secure it with the five bolts.
10 Reconnect the heater hoses at the pipe junction and inlet manifold. Reconnect the servo vacuum hose to the inlet manifold.
11 Reconnect the upper and lower radiator hoses and refill the cooling system.
12 Reconnect the fuel and vacuum lines to the carburettor.
13 With the choke knob pushed fully home, and the choke plate fully open, remove all slack from the cable and secure the inner cable with the screw clamp and the outer cable with its spring clip (photo 5.10).
14 Refit the accelerator cable bracket and secure with the two bolts. Push the cable end onto the carburettor arm and secure with the spring clip. Refer to Chapter 3, Section 9 and adjust the accelerator cable.
15 Refer to Chapter 8, Section 2 and refit the battery.
16 With the help of a second person to take the weight of the bonnet, align the bonnet hinges with the pencil marks and refit the hinges. Check the bonnet alignment before fully tightening the bolts.
17 Refer to Chapter 10, Section 9 and refit the radiator grille.
18 Refit the bonnet stay bracket and secure.
19 Start the engine and check for leaks.

54 Rocker shaft and pushrods - refitting

1   Fit the pushrods into the same holes from which they were removed. Make sure the pushrods seat properly in the cam followers.
2   Lower the rocker shaft assembly into position (photo) and push the adjusting bolt ends into the pushrod sockets.
3   Tighten down the four rocker shaft retaining bolts.
4   Refer to Section 55, and adjust the valve clearances.
5   Fit a new cork gasket, refit the rocker cover and secure with the four screws and spring washers. Note that the distributor should be fitted before refitting the rocker cover, as the position of the valves will identify the firing stroke. Refer to Chapter 8 for details.
6   Refit the HT leads to the rocker cover clips and push them firmly onto the spark plugs (Fig. 1.38).
7   Reconnect the breather hoses to the inlet manifold and the cylinder block, and refit the oil filler cap (photo).

55 Valve clearances - checking and adjustment (engine in car)

1   Disconnect the breather hose from the underside of the air cleaner, remove the three air cleaner securing bolts and lift off the air cleaner.
2   Disconnect the breather hoses from the inlet manifold and cylinder block.
3   Disconnect the HT leads from the spark plugs, disengage them from the clips on the rocker cover and swing them clear. Mark the HT leads in order to refit them in the correct order.
4   Remove the four rocker cover screws and spring washers and remove the cover.

54.2 Lower the rocker shaft assembly into position

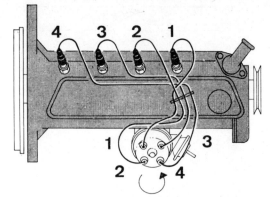

Fig. 1.38. Refit the spark plug leads in the order shown (Sec. 54, 55)

54.7 Reconnect the breather hoses to the engine and inlet manifold

55.7 Check and adjust the valve clearances, using a ring spanner

950 and 1100
Front: Exhaust, inlet, exhaust, inlet, exhaust, inlet, exhaust, inlet
1300 and 1600
Front: Exhaust, inlet, inlet, exhaust, exhaust, inlet, inlet, exhaust

7   To check the clearance, insert the appropriate feeler blade(s) between the valve stem and the rocker arm (photo). The clearance is correct when the gauge will just slide in and out without nipping.
8   To adjust the clearance, screw the adjusting screw up (to increase) or down (to decrease) using a ring spanner or socket.
9   Refit and secure the rocker cover (four screws and spring washers).
10 Refit the HT leads to the rocker cover clips and push them onto and spark plugs (Fig. 1.38).
11 Refit the air cleaner and three breather hoses.

5   The valve clearances should be checked and adjusted with the engine cold. The importance of the correct clearance cannot be over-stressed, since if the clearance is too great, the efficiency of the engine will be reduced, while if the clearance is too small, the valves may not close properly, causing burning of the valve head and seat.
6   Turn the engine in the normal direction of rotation until the crankshaft pulley mark aligns with the 'O' mark on the timing cover (see photo 15.6/8 on page 88). If the pulley is now turned to-and-fro a little, the valves of cylinder number 1 or cylinder number 4 will be seen to be rocking (rocker arms and pushrods moving in opposite directions). If the valves on cylinder number 1 are rocking, rotate the engine through 360° so that the valves on cylinder number 4 are rocking. Starting the adjusting sequence with cylinder number 4 valves rocking obviates the need to rotate the engine unnecessarily. Now adjust both valves on cylinder number 1 according to the Specifications. When adjustment is complete rotating the engine through 180° will bring the next pair of cylinders into the rocking and adjusting positions as shown in the following table.

Cylinder valves rocking	Cylinder valves to adjust
No 4	No 1
No 3	No 2
No 1	No 4
No 2	No 3

Number one cylinder is immediately behind the crankshaft pulley.

The valve arrangements are as shown in the next column, and commence from the crankshaft pulley end of the engine.

56 Valve clearances - checking and adjustment (engine on the bench)

The procedure for adjusting the valve clearances with the engine on the bench is similar to that for adjustment with the engine in the car, with the exception of disconnecting the controls and services. Refer to Section 55, paragraphs 5 to 7 inclusive.

57 Engine - refitting ancillary components

Refit all ancillary components referred to in Section 7. Where necessary, refer to the appropriate Chapter for full details. Particular care should be taken when refitting the distributor (Chapter 8), and the clutch (Chapter 5).

58 Engine and transmission - refitting

1   In the same way as for engine and transmission removal, the

availability of an engine hoist or trolley jack, and four axle stands or an inspection pit are essential. A second pair of hands will also make this job much easier.

2 Ensure that the engine backplate is correctly located on its dowels (photo 51.1), and that the clutch plate is centralised, Chapter 5.

3 With the engine on the floor and a wood block under the front of the sump, lift up the gearbox and insert the gearbox input shaft in the centre of the clutch and push so that the input shaft splines pass through the internal splines of the clutch disc.

4 If difficulty is experienced in engaging the splines try turning the gearbox slightly but **on no account** allow the weight of the gearbox to rest on the input shaft as it is easily bent.

5 With the gearbox correctly positioned on the engine backplate support its weight using a wooden block.

6 Secure the gearbox to the engine and backplate with the bolts and spring washers.

7 *1300 cc and 1600 cc models.* Refit the driveshaft bearing retaining bracket to the engine, and secure with the three nuts and spring washers.

8 *All models.* Slide the engine crossmember under the sump (photo), and secure with two **new** bolts through the crossmember and into the bellhousing.

9 Refit the front engine stabilizer bar to the crossmember (photo), and the rear engine stabilizer bar to the engine to bellhousing flange.

10 Position the Allen screw into its gearbox location, and lightly tighten the locknut against the crossmember bracket (photo).

11 Tuck all loose leads and hoses out of harms way, and position the engine and transmission assembly under the front of the raised car (photo).

12 Raise the assembly into the engine compartment by either:

   a) raising it on a trolley jack, with several pieces of wood to spread the load, or
   b) passing a wire sling under the engine and raising it from above with a hoist.

13 Refit and tighten the four crossmember bolts, two at the front and two at the rear (photos).

14 Refit the nut to the engine mounting at the right-hand inner wing, and tighten the nut, ensuring that the rubber insulator is not twisted.

15 Remove the engine lifting equipment, and refit the starter motor.

16 *1300 cc and 1600 cc models.* Refit the right-hand driveshaft joint, and secure it with the Allen screws.

17 *950 cc and 1100 cc models.* Fit a **new** circlip to the right-hand driveshaft end (Fig. 1.39), remove the plug from the transmission casing, and insert the driveshaft. Using a suitable screwdriver placed against the universal joint weld, tap the driveshaft fully home until the circlip engages (Fig. 1.39). If there is no weld, use a plastic or rubber mallet to drive the shaft home.

18 *All models:* Refit the right-hand suspension tie bar bracket, and secure it to the side rail with the three bolts.

19 Refit the ball joint in the pivot bearing of the right-hand track control arm, and reconnect to the body mounting (Fig. 1.40).

20 Fit a **new** circlip to the left-hand driveshaft end, remove the plug from the transmission case and refit the driveshaft as described in paragraph 17.

21 Refit the left-hand track control arm ball joint in the pivot bearing, then reconnect the arm at the body mounting (Fig. 1.40).

22 Reconnect the two track rod outer ends, and secure with the castellated nut and a **new** split pin (Fig. 1.41).

23 From under the car, locate the gear lever housing together with the linkage and stabilizer bar.

24 Loosen the Allen screw locknut from the bracket and pull the screw from its transmission location. Push the Allen screw through the stabilizer bar bush and into the transmission housing, and tighten the Allen screw.

25 Tighten the first nut against the stabilizer bar, and the second nut against the crossmember bracket (Fig. 1.42). Finally, tighten the outer locknut against the other side of the crossmember bracket.

26 Secure the gear lever housing to the floor pan with the two nuts (photo). Refit the gearchange linkage, adjust the linkage as described in Chapter 6, Section 14, and tighten the pinch bolt clamp.

27 Where applicable, refit the spring between the gearchange linkage and the body boxmember (photo).

28 If the car is raised on stands, it can now be lowered to the floor, since subsequent work is carried out more easily in this position.

58.8 Reposition the engine crossmember

58.9 Refit the front engine stabiliser

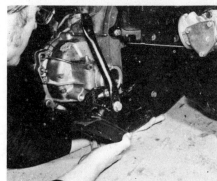
58.10 Loosely fit the Allen screw into its location in the transmission

58.11 Position the engine and transmission assembly under the car

58.13A Securely tighten the front ...

58.13B ... and rear crossmember retaining bolts

46

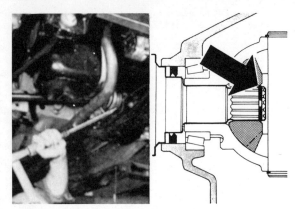

Fig. 1.39. Fit a new circlip (arrowed) and tap the shaft fully home (Sec. 58)

Fig. 1.40. Fit the right-hand track control arm (left-hand similar) (Sec. 58)

Fig. 1.41. Reconnect the track rod ends and secure (Sec. 58)

Fig. 1.42. Tighten the gear linkage stabiliser inner locknuts (Sec. 58)

58.26 Secure the gear lever housing to the floor pan

58.27 Refit the anti-vibration spring

29 Refill the transmission with the specified lubricant (Fig. 1.43).
30 Push the clutch cable through the bracket on the transmission,
ensuring that the outer cable is securely seated. Using a pair of pliers,
pull the inner cable through, and hook it into the release arm.
31 Push the speedometer cable into its location, and screw in the knurled nut (Fig. 1.44).
32 Reconnect the starter motor cables.
33 Remove the plug from the end of the fuel line, and reconnect it to
the fuel pump. Tighten the securing clamp.
34 Reconnect the earth straps to the front of the cylinder block, and
the floor pan (photo).
35 Reconnect the vacuum servo hose (where applicable), and the
breather hose from the oil filler cap, to the inlet manifold (Fig. 1.45).
36 Push in the centre lead on the ignition coil, and the low tension lead.
37 Push on the leads to the temperature sender unit, and the fan
temperature probe, where applicable.
38 Push the lead onto the oil pressure switch below the distributor
(photo).
39 Plug in the cable connector at the rear of the alternator, and secure
it in position with the spring clip.
40 Attach the exhaust system to its rear mounting (Fig. 1.46), refit the
pipe to the exhaust manifold and tighten the two securing bolts.
41 With the choke control knob pushed fully home, and the carburettor
choke plates fully open, remove all slack from the cable, and secure
the inner cable with the screw clamp, and the outer cable with its spring
clip (Fig. 1.47).

Fig. 1.43. Transmission oil filler plug (Sec. 58)

Fig. 1.44. Refit the speedometer cable (Sec. 58)

58.34 Refit the earth strap to the body

Fig. 1.45. Refit the breather hose and servo vacuum hose (Sec. 58)

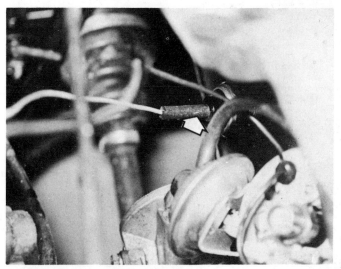

58.38 Refit the oil pressure sender lead

Fig. 1.46. Fit the exhaust system rear mounting (Sec. 58)

Fig. 1.47. Push in the choke cable clip (Sec. 58)

42 Refit the accelerator cable bracket and secure it with the two bolts.
Push the cable end onto the carburettor arm and slide on the sprung
sleeve. Refer to Chapter 3, Section 9 and adjust the accelerator cable.
43 Refit the air cleaner, reconnect the breather hose and tighten its
securing clamp. Refit the three air cleaner bracket securing bolts and
tighten them.
44 Reconnect the heater hoses at the pipe junction (Fig. 1.48) and at
the inlet manifold.
45 Reconnect the upper and lower radiator hoses, and tighten the retaining clamps securely.
46 Refill the engine with coolant, not forgetting the antifreeze if
necessary, and refit the radiator cap.
47 Refill with engine oil, allowing time for the oil to run into the
sump.
48 Reconnect the battery positive and negative leads.
49 With the help of an assistant, refit the bonnet, but do not fully
tighten the bolts until the bonnet alignment has been checked.
50 Finally, check that all leads have been connected, all hose clips
tightened and all tools, rags and other loose items removed from the
engine compartment. Also check to see there are no spare nuts, bolts
or washers.

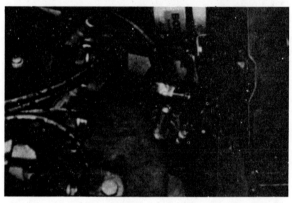

Fig. 1.48. Refit the heater hose at the pipe junction (Sec. 58)

59 Engine - initial start-up after overhaul or major repair

1   Make sure that the battery is fully charged and that all lubricants,
coolant and fuel are replenished.
2   If the fuel system has been dismantled it will require several
revolutions of the engine on the starter motor to pump the petrol up
to the carburettor.
3   As soon as the engine fires and runs, keep it going at a fast idle only
(no faster) and bring it up to normal working temperature. When the
thermostat opens the coolant level will fall and must therefore be
topped-up again as necessary.
4   As the engine warms up there will be odd smells and some smoke
from parts getting hot and burning off oil deposits. The signs

to look for are leaks of water or oil which will be obvious, if serious.
Check also the exhaust pipe and manifold connections as these do not
always find their exact gastight position until the warmth and vibration
have acted on them and it is almost certain that they will need tightening
further. This should be done, of course with the engine stopped.
5   When normal running temperature has been reached, adjust the
engine idle speed, as described in Chapter 3.
6   Stop the engine and wait a few minutes to see if any lubricant or
coolant is dripping out when the engine is stationary.
7   After the engine has run for 20 minutes remove the engine top
cover and recheck the tightness of the cylinder head bolts. Also check
the tightness of the sump bolts. In both cases use a torque wrench.
8   Road test the car to check that the timing is correct and that the
engine is giving the necessary smoothness and power. Do not race the
engine; if new bearings and/or pistons have been fitted it should be
treated as a new engine and run in at a reduced speed for the first 1000
miles (2000 km).

60 Fault diagnosis

Symptom	Reason/s	Remedy
Engine fails to turn over when starter operated	Discharged or defective battery	Charge or renew battery, push-start car.
	Dirty or loose battery leads	Clean and tighten both terminals and earth end of earth lead.
	Defective starter solenoid or switch	Run a heavy duty cable direct from the battery to the starter motor or bypass the solenoid.
	Engine earth strap disconnected	Check and retighten strap.
	Defective starter motor	Remove and repair.
Engine turns over but will not start	Ignition damp or wet	Wipe dry the distributor cap and ignition leads.
	Ignition leads to spark plugs loose	Check and tighten at both spark plug and distributor cap ends.
	Shorted or disconnected low tension leads	Check the wiring on the CB and SW terminals of the coil and to the distributor.
	Dirty, incorrectly set or pitted contact breaker points	Clean, and adjust.
	Faulty condenser	Check contact breaker points for arcing, remove and fit new condenser.
	Defective ignition switch	Bypass switch with wire.
	Ignition LT leads connected wrong way round	Remove and replace leads to coil in correct order.
	Faulty coil	Remove and fit new coil.
	Contact breaker point spring earthed or broken	Check spring is not touching metal part of distributor. Check insulator washers are correctly placed. Renew points if the spring is broken.
	No petrol in petrol tank	Refill tank.
	Vapour lock in fuel line (in hot conditions or at high altitude)	Blow into petrol tank, allow engine to cool, or apply a cold wet rag to the fuel line in engine compartment.
	Blocked float chamber needle valve	Remove, clean and replace.
	Fuel pump filter blocked	Remove, clean and replace.
	Choked or blocked carburettor jets	Dismantle and clean.
	Faulty fuel pump	Remove, overhaul and replace.
	Too much choke allowing too rich a mixture to wet plugs (manual choke)	Remove and dry spark plugs or with wide open throttle, push-start the car.
	Float damaged or leaking, or needle not seating	Remove, examine, clean and replace float and needle valve as necessary.
	Float lever incorrectly adjusted	Remove and adjust correctly.
Engine stalls and will not start	Ignition failure - sudden	Check over low and high tension circuits for breaks in wiring.
	Ignition failure - misfiring	Check contact breaker points, clean and adjust. Renew condenser if faulty.
	Ignition failure - in severe rain or after traversing water splash	Dry out ignition leads and distributor cap.
	No petrol in petrol tank	Refill tank.
	Petrol tank breather choked	Remove petrol cap and clean out breather hole or pipe.
	Sudden obstruction in carburettor	Check jets, and needle valve in float chamber for blockage.
	Water in fuel system	Drain tank and blow out fuel lines.
Engine misfires or idles unevenly	Ignition leads loose	Check and tighten as necessary at spark plug and distributor cap ends.
	Battery leads loose on terminals	Check and tighten terminal leads.
	Battery earth strap loose on body attachment point	Check and tighten earth lead to body attachment point.
	Engine earth lead loose	Tighten lead.
	Low tension leads to terminals on coil loose	Check and tighten leads if found loose.
	Low tension lead from distributor loose	Check and tighten if found loose.
	Dirty, or incorrectly gapped spark plugs	Remove, clean and regap.
	Dirty, incorrectly set or pitted contact breaker points	Clean, and adjust.
	Tracking across distributor cap	Remove and fit new cap.
	Ignition too retarded	Check and adjust ignition timing.
	Faulty coil	Remove and fit new coil.
	Mixture too weak	Check jets, float chamber needle valve and filters for obstruction. Clean as necessary. Carburettor incorrectly adjusted.

Symptom	Reason/s	Remedy
	Air leak in carburettor	Remove and overhaul carburettor.
	Air leak at inlet manifold to cylinder head, or inlet manifold to carburettor	Test by pouring oil along joints. Bubbles indicate leak. Renew manifold gasket as appropriate.
	Incorrect valve clearances	Adjust clearances.
	Burnt out exhaust valves	Remove cylinder head and renew defective valves.
	Sticking or leaking valves	Remove cylinder head, clean, check and renew valves as necessary.
	Weak or broken valve springs	Check and renew as necessary.
	Worn valve guides or stems	Renew valves.
	Worn pistons and piston rings	Dismantle engine, renew pistons and rings.
Lack of power and poor compression	Burnt out exhaust valves	Remove cylinder head, renew defective valves.
	Sticking or leaking valves	Remove cylinder head, clean, check and renew valves as necessary.
	Worn valve guides and stems	Remove cylinder head and renew valves.
	Weak or broken valve springs	Remove cylinder head, renew defective springs.
	Blown cylinder head gasket (accompanied by increase in noise)	Remove cylinder head and fit new gasket.
	Worn pistons and piston rings	Dismantle engine, renew pistons and rings.
	Worn or scored cylinder bores	Dismantle engine, rebore, renew pistons and rings.
	Ignition timing wrongly set. Too advanced or retarded	Check and reset ignition timing.
	Contact breaker points incorrectly gapped	Check and reset contact breaker points.
	Incorrect valve clearances	Adjust clearances.
	Incorrectly set spark plugs	Remove, clean and regap.
	Carburettor too rich or too weak	Tune carburettor for optimum performance
	Dirty contact breaker points	Remove, clean and replace.
	Fuel filters blocked causing top end fuel starvation	Dismantle, inspect, clean and replace all fuel filters.
	Distributor automatic advance weights or vacuum advance and retard mechanism not functioning correctly	Overhaul distributor.
	Faulty fuel pump giving top end fuel starvation	Remove, overhaul, or fit exchange reconditioned fuel pump.
Excessive oil consumption	Badly worn, perished or missing valve stem oil seals.	Remove, fit new oil seals to valve stems.
	Excessively worn valve stems and valve guides	Remove cylinder head and fit new valves.
	Worn piston rings	Fit oil control rings to existing pistons or purchase new pistons.
	Worn pistons and cylinder bores	Fit new pistons and rings, rebore cylinders.
	Excessive piston ring gap allowing blow-by	Fit new piston rings and set gap correctly.
	Piston oil return holes choked	Decarbonise engine and pistons.
Oil being lost due to leaks	Leaking oil filter gasket	Inspect and fit new gasket as necessary.
	Leaking rocker cover gasket	Inspect and fit new gasket as necessary.
	Leaking timing case gasket	Inspect and fit new gasket as necessary.
	Leaking sump gasket	Inspect and fit new gasket as necessary.
	Loose sump plug	Tighten, fit new gasket as necessary.
Unusual noises from engine	Worn valve gear (noisy tapping from top cover)	Inspect and renew defective parts.
	Worn big-end bearing (regular heavy knocking)	Fit new bearings.
	Worn main bearings (rumbling and vibration)	Fit new bearings.
	Worn crankshaft (knocking, rumbling and vibration)	Regrind crankshaft, fit new main and big-end bearings.

Chapter 2 Cooling and heating system

Contents

Specifications

Type	Pressurised, assisted by pump and fan

Heater type	Heat exchanger (radiator) within passenger compartment

Thermostat

Type	Wax
Location	Front of cylinder head
Starts to open	85 to 89°C (185 to 192°F)
Fully open	99 to 102°C (210 to 216°F)
Operating tolerance for used thermostat	$\pm$ 3°C ($\pm$ 5°F)

Radiator

Type	Corrugated fin
Pressure cap setting	13 lbf/in^2 (0.91 kgf/cm^2)

Water pump

Type	Centrifugal

Drive belt

Free-play	0.5 in (13 mm) at midpoint of longest span of belt

Fan

Type	Electrically operated, continuous or temperature switched

Cooling system capacity

Including heater:

960 cc and 1100 cc	9.27 Imp pints (5.27 litres/11.12 US pints)
1300 cc and 1600 cc	11.0 Imp pints (6.25 litres/13.2 US pints)

Torque wrench settings	lbf ft	kgf m
Water pump	5 to 7	0.69 to 0.97
Thermostat housing	12 to 15	1.66 to 2.07
Shroud to radiator	5 to 7	0.69 to 0.97
Motor to shroud	3 to 4	0.4 to 0.5
Pump pulley	5 to 7	0.69 to 0.97
Alternator mounting and adjusting bolts	15 to 18	2.07 to 3.5
Radiator to front panel	5 to 7	0.69 to 0.97

1 General description

1 The engine cooling water is circulated by the thermosyphon method, assisted by a water pump, and the system is pressurised. The radiator cap seals the cooling system with an internal spring, which pressurises the system to 13 lbf/in^2 (0.91 kgf/cm^2). This has the effect of considerably increasing the boiling point of the coolant.

2 If the water temperature rises above this increased boiling point, the extra pressure forces the internal spring off its seat and allows coolant to flow into the expansion tank. As the system temperature and pressure drop, the overflow is drawn from the expansion tank, through a vacuum relief valve in the filler cap and into the radiator. It is therefore important to check that the radiator cap is in good condition and that the spring has not weakened.

3 The impellor type water pump is mounted on the engine face, and is driven by the crankshaft pulley through a drive belt which also drives the alternator.

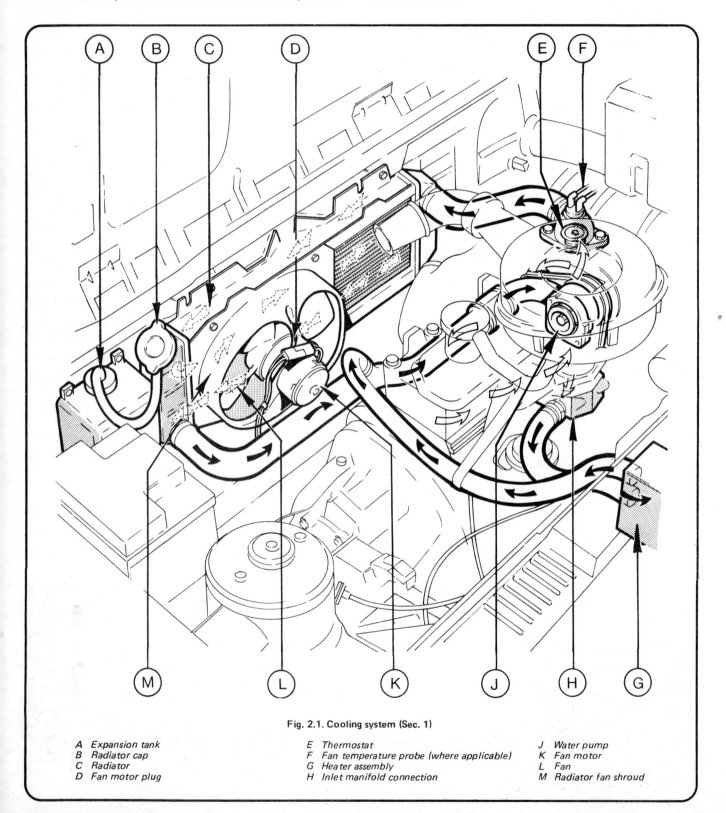

Fig. 2.1. Cooling system (Sec. 1)

A Expansion tank	E Thermostat	J Water pump
B Radiator cap	F Fan temperature probe (where applicable)	K Fan motor
C Radiator	G Heater assembly	L Fan
D Fan motor plug	H Inlet manifold connection	M Radiator fan shroud

4   The electrically operated water cooling fan is mounted on the
radiator, and operates all the time the ignition is switched on with
960 cc engines. The fan on all other engines is controlled by a thermal
switch mounted in the thermostat housing. As soon as the coolant
temperature rises above a certain point, the fan motor comes into
operation. It is therefore important, whenever working near the fan to
ensure that the ignition is **switched off.**
5   The system functions in the following fashion. Cold water in the
bottom of the radiator circulates up the lower radiator hose to the
water pump where it is pushed round the water passages in the cylinder
block, helping to keep the cylinder bores and pistons cool.
   The water then travels up into the cylinder head and circulates
round the combustion spaces and valve seats absorbing more heat, and
then, when the engine is at its correct operating temperature, travels
out of the cylinder head, past the open thermostat into the upper
radiator hose and so into the radiator header tank.
   The water travels down the radiator where it is rapidly cooled by
the in-rush of cold air through the radiator core, which is created by
both the fan and the motion of the car. The water, now much cooler,
reaches the bottom of the radiator when the cycle is repeated.
   When the engine is cold the thermostat (which is a valve that opens
and closes according to the temperature of the water) maintains the
circulation of the same water in the engine.
   Only when the correct minimum operating temperature has been
reached, as shown in the Specifications, does the thermostat begin to
open, allowing water to return to the radiator.
6   Engine coolant flows from an outlet on the inlet manifold, through
a hose to the heater radiator inside the car, and return water flows to a
pipe junction in the engine compartment. The heater radiator is
contained within the heater assembly, which also houses a heater
blower fan. External air enters the heater assembly through a hole in
the top, and two flap valves control the mixture of warm and cold air,
and the direction of air flow. The flap valves are moved by cables
linked to the instrument panel controls. The blower fan is used when
the vehicle is moving at slow speeds, and for enforced cold air
circulation.

2   Cooling system - draining

1   If the engine is cold, remove the filler cap from the radiator by
turning the cap anti-clockwise. If the engine is hot, then turn the
filler cap very slightly until pressure in the system has had time to be
released. Use a rag over the cap to protect your hand from escaping
steam. If with the engine very hot the cap is released suddenly, the
drop in pressure can result in the water boiling. With the pressure
released the cap can be removed.
2   If antifreeze is used in the cooling system, drain it into a bowl
having a capacity of at least that of the cooling system for re-use.
3   Unscrew the hose clamp and pull the bottom hose off the
radiator (photo). Allow the coolant to drain.
4   It is important to note that the heater on most models cannot be
drained completely during the cold weather so an antifreeze solution
must be used. Always use an antifreeze with an ethylene-glycol or
glycerine base.

3   Cooling system - flushing

1   In time the cooling system will gradually lose its efficiency as the
radiator becomes choked with rust, scale deposits from the water, and
other sediment. To clean the system out, remove the radiator filler cap
and bottom hose and leave a hose running in the filler cap neck for ten
to fifteen minutes.
2   In very bad cases the radiator should be reversed flushed. This can
be done with the radiator in position. Remove the top and bottom hoses
from the radiator, but leave a hose running in the bottom hose location.
3   To flush the engine, remove the top and bottom radiator hoses and
the thermostat, Section 7. Leave a hose running in the thermostat
location for ten to fifteen minutes.
4   It is recommended that some polythene sheeting is placed over the
engine to stop water finding its way into the electrical system.

4   Cooling system - filling

1   Reconnect the radiator upper and lower hoses and refit the
thermostat and housing, Section 7.
2   Fill the system slowly to ensure that no air lock develops. If the
heater has a water control valve check that it is open (control at hot),
otherwise an air lock may form in the heater. The best type of water to
use in the cooling system is rain water; use this whenever possible.
3   Do not fill the system higher than within ½ inch (13 mm) of the
filler neck. Overfilling will merely result in wastage, which is especially
to be avoided when antifreeze is in use.
4   It is usually found that air locks develop in the heater radiator so
the system should be vented during refilling by detaching the heater
supply hose from the elbow connection on the inlet manifold.
5   Pour coolant into the radiator filler neck whilst the end of the
heater supply hose is held at the connection height. When a constant
stream of water flows from the supply hose quickly refit the hose. If
venting is not carried out it is possible for the engine to overheat.
Should the engine overheat for no apparent reason then the system
should be vented before seeking other causes.
6   Only use antifreeze mixture with a glycerine or ethylene glycol
base, or a cooling system inhibitor.
7   Refit the filler cap and turn it firmly clockwise to lock it in
position.
8   Check the level of coolant in the overflow container, and fill to the
MAX line.

5   Radiator - removal, inspection and cleaning

1   Drain the cooling system as described in Section 2.
2   Unscrew the hose clamp and pull off the top radiator hose (photo).
Pull the expansion tank pipe off the filler neck.
3   Unscrew and remove the two lower radiator bolts from the front of
the car.
4   Disconnect the loom plug from the radiator fan, and unclip the lead
from the shroud.
5   Unscrew and remove the two upper radiator bolts from the engine

2.3 Remove the bottom radiator hose

5.2 Remove the top radiator hose

5.5 Unscrew the upper radiator retaining
bolts

compartment (photo) and lift the radiator upwards to remove it.
6   Remove the four bolts securing the fan and shroud assembly, and remove the assembly.
7   With the radiator away from the car any leaks can be soldered or repaired with a suitable proprietary substance. Clean out the inside of the radiator by flushing as described earlier in this Chapter. When the radiator is out of the car it is advantageous to turn it upside down and reverse flush. Clean the exterior of the radiator by carefully using a compressed air jet or a strong jet of water to clear away any road dirt, flies etc.
8   Inspect the radiator hoses for cracks, internal or external perishing and damage by overtightening of the securing clips. Also inspect the overflow pipe. Renew the hoses if suspect. Examine the radiator hose clips and renew them if they are rusted or distorted.

6   Radiator - refitting

1   Refitting the radiator and shroud is the reverse sequence to removal (see Section 5).
2   If new hoses are to be fitted they can be a little difficult to fit on to the radiator so lubricate them with a little soap.
3   Refill the cooling system as described in Section 4.

7   Thermostat - removal, testing and refitting

1   Partially drain the cooling system as described in Section 2.
2   Slacken the top radiator hose to the thermostat housing and remove the hose.
3   Undo and remove the two bolts and spring washers that secure the thermostat housing to the cylinder head.
4   Carefully lift the thermostat housing away from the cylinder head (photo). Recover the joint washer adhering to either the housing or cylinder head.
5   Lift the thermostat from its location in the cylinder head (photo).
6   Test the thermostat for correct functioning by suspending it on a string in a saucepan of cold water together with a thermometer. Heat

the water and note the temperature at which the thermostat begins to open. This should be as given in the Specifications. Continue heating the water until the thermostat is fully open. Then let it cool down naturally.
7   If the thermostat does not fully open in boiling water, or does not close down as the water cools, then it must be discarded and a new one fitted. Should the thermostat be stuck open when cold this will usually be apparent when removing it from the housing.
8   Refitting the thermostat is the reverse sequence to removal. Always ensure that the thermostat housing and cylinder head mating faces are clean and flat. If the thermostat housing is badly corroded fit a new housing. Always use a new gasket. Tighten the two securing bolts to the specified torque.

8   Water pump - removal and refitting

1   Refer to Section 2 and drain the cooling system.
2   Slacken the three water pump pulley bolts.
3   Slacken the two lower alternator mounting bolts, the alternator to adjusting arm bolt and the adjusting arm to body bolt.
4   Swing the alternator towards the engine and remove the drive belt.
5   Remove the three water pump pulley bolts and remove the pulley (photo).
6   Slacken the water pump hose clamp and pull off the hose.
7   Remove the three bolts securing the water pump, and lift out the pump (photo).
8   Refitting the water pump is the reverse sequence to removal. The following additional points should however be noted:

   a) Make sure the mating faces of the cylinder block and water pump are clean. Always use a new gasket.
   b) Tighten the water pump and fan bolts to the specified torque.
   c) Adjust the drive belt tension to give ½ in (13 mm) free play at the point shown (photo).

7.4 Unscrew and remove the thermostat housing

7.5 Lift out the thermostat

8.5 Remove the water pump pulley

8.7 Lift out the water pump

8.8 Adjust drivebelt free play at this point

9 Water pump - dismantling, overhaul and reassembly

1 Before undertaking the dismantling of the water pump to effect a repair, check that all parts are available. It may be quicker and more economical to replace the complete unit.

2 Refer to Fig. 2.2 and using a universal three legged puller and suitable thrust block draw the hub from the shaft.

3 Using a soft faced hammer drive the shaft assembly out towards the rear of the pump body.

4 The impeller vane is removed from the spindle by using a universal three legged puller and suitable thrust block.

5 Remove the seal.

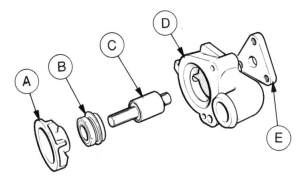

Fig. 2.2. Water pump (Sec. 9)

A Impeller D Pump body
B Seal E Pulley hub
C Bearing shaft

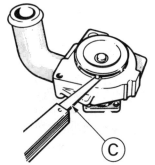

Fig. 2.3. Check impeller to body clearance (C) (Sec. 9)

10.2 Unplug the two wires and unclip from the shroud

6 Carefully inspect the condition of the shaft and bearing assembly and if it shows signs of wear or corrosion, new parts should be obtained. If it was found that the coolant was leaking from the pump a new seal should be obtained. If it was evident that the pulley hub or impeller were a loose fit they must be renewed.

7 To reassemble the water pump first fit the shaft to the housing.

8 Next press the pump pulley onto the front end of the shaft until the end of the shaft is flush with the end of the hub.

9 Place the new seal over the shaft and into the counterbore in the water pump housing and then press the impeller onto the shaft until a clearance of 0.03 in (0.76 mm) is obtained between the impeller and the housing face (Fig. 2.3).

10 Cooling fan motor - removal and refitting

1 Disconnect the battery leads.

2 Unplug the two wires from the fan motor, and unclip the wires from the shroud (photo).

3 Remove the four bolts holding the shroud to the radiator, and remove the shroud, fan and motor assembly.

4 Remove the spring clip retaining the fan, remove the washer and fan blades from the motor shaft (Fig. 2.4).

5 Unscrew and remove the three nuts and their washers, and remove the fan motor.

6 It is not normally practicable to overhaul this motor in the event of a failure, and a new unit should be fitted.

7 Refitting is the reverse procedure to removal.

11 Drive belt - removal and refitting

If the drive belt has worn or stretched unduly, it should be renewed. The most usual reason for renewal is that the belt has broken in service. It is recommended that a spare belt be always carried in the car.

1 Loosen the alternator mounting bolts and move the alternator towards the engine.

2 Slip the old belt over the crankshaft, alternator and water pump pulley wheels and lift it off.

3 Put a new belt onto the three pulleys and adjust it as described in Section 12. **Note:** After fitting a new belt it will require adjustment after 250 miles (400 km).

12 Drive belt - adjustment

1 It is important to keep the belt correctly adjusted and it is considered that this should be a regular maintenance task every 6,000 miles (10,000 km). If the belt is loose it will slip, wear rapidly and cause the alternator and water pump to malfunction. If the belt is too tight the alternator and water pump bearings will wear rapidly causing premature failure of these components.

2 The belt tension is correct when there is 0.5 in (13 mm) of lateral

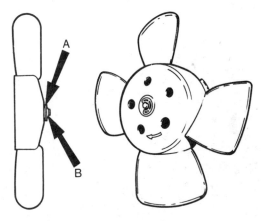

Fig. 2.4. Fan blade spring clip (B) and washer (A) (Sec. 10)

movement at the mid point position of the belt run between the alternator pulley and the water pump (photo 8.8).
3   To adjust the belt, slacken the alternator securing bolts and move the alternator in or out until the correct tension is obtained. It is easier if the alternator bolts are only slackened a little so it requires some effort to move the alternator. In this way the tension of the belt can be arrived at more quickly than by making frequent adjustments.
4   When the correct adjustment has been obtained fully tighten the alternator mounting bolts.

13 Temperature gauge - fault diagnosis

1   If the temperature gauge fails to work, either the gauge, the sender unit, the wiring or the connections are at fault.
2   It is not possible to repair the gauge or the sender unit and they must be replaced by new units if at fault.
3   First check that the wiring connections are sound. Check the wiring for breaks using an ohmmeter. The sender unit and gauge should be tested by substitution.

14 Temperature gauge and sender unit - removal and refitting

1   Information on the removal of the gauge will be found in Chapter 10.
2   To remove the sender unit, disconnect the wire leading into the unit and unscrew the unit with a spanner. The unit is located in the cylinder head just below the thermostat housing.
3   Refitting is the reverse sequence to removal.

15 Antifreeze and corrosion inhibitors

1   In circumstances where it is likely that the temperature will drop below freezing it is essential that some of the water is drained and an adequate amount of ethylene glycol antifreeze is added to the cooling system. If antifreeze is not used, it is essential to use a corrosion inhibitor in the cooling system in the proportion recommended by the inhibitor manufacturer.
2   Any antifreeze which conforms with specifications BS3151 or BS3152 can be used. Never use an antifreeze with an alcohol base as evaporation is too high.
3   Castrol antifreeze with an anti-corrosion additive can be left in the cooling system for up to two years, but after six months, it is advisable to have the specific gravity of the coolant checked at your local garage, and thereafter once every three months.
4   The table below gives the proportion of antifreeze and degree of protection:

Antifreeze	Commences to freeze		Frozen solid	
%	^oC	^oF	^oC	^oF
25	-13	9	-26	-15
33 1/3	-19	-2	-36	-33
50	-36	-33	-48	-53

Note: Never use antifreeze in the windscreen washer reservoir as it will cause damage to the paintwork.

16 Heater controls - adjustment

1   Remove the two retaining screws, and pull down the left-hand dash lower trim panel.
2   Slacken the bolt retaining each heater cable clamp on the heater body.
3   Move the temperature control on the instrument panel to a point 0.2 in (5 mm) from the right-hand (cold) stop position. Move the control on the heater to its upper (cold) position, and tighten the outer cable clamp bolt (Fig. 2.5).
4   Move the distribution control on the instrument panel to its left-hand (closed) stop, and check that the alignment notches on the heater valve gears are aligned (Fig. 2.6). If they are not aligned, pull off the cable arm and refit in the correct position.
5   Move the distribution control on the instrument panel to a point

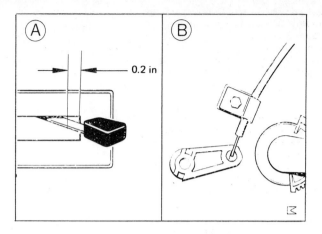

Fig. 2.5. Adjust the temperature control cable (Sec. 16)

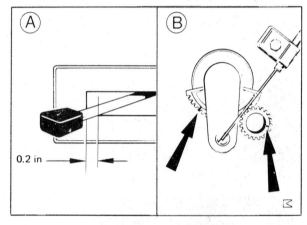

Fig. 2.6. Check the alignment marks (arrowed) and adjust the distribution control cable (Sec. 16)

0.2 in (5 mm) from the left-hand (closed) stop position. Move the control on the heater to its closed position, and tighten the outer clamp bolt (Fig. 2.6).
6   Make sure that the cable retaining clamps are not twisted while tightening the clamp bolts.
7   Finally check the controls for easy action along the **whole** length of their travel. Refit the dash lower trim panel.

17 Heater controls - removal and refitting

1   Remove the two retaining screws and pull down the left-hand dash lower trim panel.
2   Slacken the bolt retaining each heater cable clamp on the heater body, and unhook the cables (Fig. 2.7).
3   Pull the ashtray fully out, and remove the two screws and ashtray retaining bracket (Fig. 2.8).
4   Pull off the heater control knobs.
5   Where applicable, remove the four retaining screws, lift off the switch cover panel and pull off the cigarette lighter and heater controls illumination plug.
6   Remove the two heater control panel screws and withdraw the heater panel complete with cables (Fig. 2.9).
7   Refitting is the reverse procedure to removal, and the cables must be adjusted as described in Section 16.

18 Heater blower switch - removal and refitting

1   Disconnect the battery.
2   Pull out and remove the ashtray, and pull off the heater control knobs.
3   Where applicable, remove the four retaining screws, lift off the

switch cover panel and pull off the cigarette lighter and heater controls illumination plug.

4 Using a small screwdriver, carefully prise out the switch, protecting the control panel with a piece of cloth or wad of paper.

5 Pull off the connecting plug.

6 Refitting is a reversal of the above procedure.

19 Heater assembly - removal and refitting

1 Initially disconnect the battery.

2 Slacken the lower heater hose clamp, and pull off the hose, draining the coolant into a suitable container. Slacken and pull off the upper heater hose (Fig. 2.10). Secure both hoses in the engine compartment with the open ends pointing upwards above the level of the remaining coolant.

3 Remove the two screws, cover plate and gasket (Fig. 2.11). Plug the ends of the heater connections to avoid subsequent spillage.

4 From inside the vehicle, remove the four screws securing the right- and left-hand dash lower trim panel and remove each panel.

5 Pull the two vent hoses from the heater assembly.

6 Slacken the two control cable clamp bolts and disconnect the cables (Fig. 2.7).

7 Unscrew and remove the heater retaining bracket (Fig. 2.12).

8 Remove the two nuts retaining the heater to the bulkhead (Fig. 2.13).

9 Pull the heater assembly inwards until the connection necks are clear of the bulkhead.

10 Disconnect the heater motor plug and remove the heater assembly to the right. Drain remaining coolant from the heater radiator.

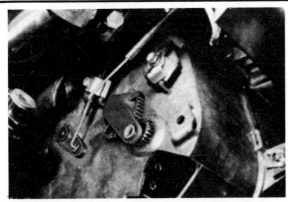

Fig. 2.7. Slacken the clamp bolts and unhook the cables (Sec. 17)

Fig. 2.10. Remove the hoses from the heater (Sec. 19)

Fig. 2.8. Remove the ashtray retaining bracket (Sec. 17)

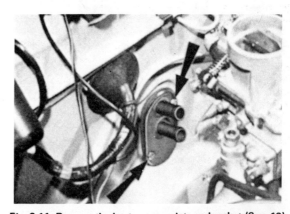

Fig. 2.11. Remove the heater cover plate and gasket (Sec. 19)

Fig. 2.9. Remove the heater control panel (Sec. 17)

Fig. 2.12. Remove the heater retaining bracket (Sec. 19)

11 Refitting is the reverse of the above procedure, noting the
following points:

    *a) Ensure the two foam gaskets are correctly located on top of
    the heater.*
    b) Adjust the control cables as described in Section 16.
    *c) Top up the radiator coolant level, while bleeding the heater, as
    described in Section 4.*

20 Heater assembly - dismantling and reassembly

1 Unscrew the two heater radiator screws, and pull out the radiator
(Fig. 2.14).

2 Using a knife, cut through the two foam gaskets at the heater casing
joint.
3 Prise the two motor retaining clamps outward (Fig. 2.15).
4 Remove any retaining clips holding the two heater halves together,
then prise up the retaining strap tangs while pulling the two casing
halves apart (Fig. 2.16). Position the heater with the coolant valves
downwards for this operation.
5 Lift out the blower motor, remove the three centre cover plates and
lift out the two flap valves.
6 Prise off the two valve controls (Fig. 2.17).
7 Press the valve controls into position, ensuring that the notches on
the distribution valve gears are aligned (Fig. 2.18B).
8 Install the control valves (Fig. 2.18A) and position the three centre
cover plates.

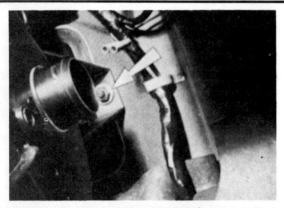

Fig. 2.13. Unscrew the two heater retaining nuts (one each side) (Sec. 19)

Fig. 2.14. Remove the two heater radiator screws (Sec. 20)

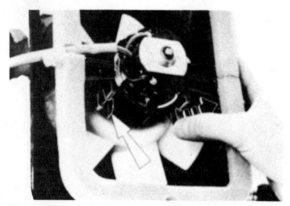

Fig. 2.15. Unclip the heater motor retaining clamps (Sec. 20)

Fig. 2.16. Prise off the heater retaining strap (Sec. 20)

Fig. 2.17. Prise off the heater valve controls (Sec. 20)

Fig. 2.18. Refit the control valves (A) and align the control notches (B)
(Sec. 20)

9   Fit the heater motor in its location and fit the two heater halves together, locating the valve spindles in the housing (Fig. 2.19).
10 Refit the retaining strap, and fit additional spring clips as required. These clips are available from a Ford dealer.
11 Spring the motor clamps into position, refit the heater radiator and secure with the two screws.
12 Position the two foam gaskets carefully on the housing.

21 Heater radiator - removal and refitting

1   In addition to removing the heater radiator as in Section 20, it can be removed without completely removing the heater.
2   Refer to Section 19, and carry out the work described in paragraphs 1 to 9 inclusive.
3   Undo and remove the screws retaining the heater radiator, and pull out the radiator (Fig. 2.14).
4   Refitting is the reversal of this procedure.

Fig. 2.19. Refit the two halves, aligning the valve spindles (Sec. 20)

22 Fascia vents - removal and refitting

1   Should it become necessary to remove the fascia vents, they must be removed, piece by piece, and new ones obtained for refitting.
2   Remove the two screws and pull down the appropriate dash lower trim panel.
3   Pull the hose off the back of the vent.
4   Using a screwdriver, prise out the nozzle insert, taking care not to

damage the fascia (Fig. 2.20A).
5   Prise out the knurled control ring and cut the retaining link with a pair of side cutters (Fig. 2.20B).
6   Push out the four spring clips (Fig. 2.20C) and pull out the vent nozzle (Fig. 2.20D).
7   Press the new vent nozzle into the fascia until the clips engage.
8   Refit the vent hose and the dash lower trim panel.

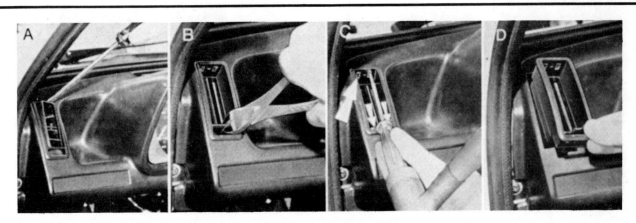

Fig. 2.20. Removing the fascia vent (Sec. 22)

See overleaf for 'Fault diagnosis - cooling system' and 'Fault diagnosis - heating system'

23 Fault diagnosis - cooling system

Symptom	Reason/s	Remedy
Overheating	Insufficient water in cooling system	Top up radiator.
	Drive belt slipping (accompanied by a shrieking noise on rapid engine acceleration)	Tighten belt to recommended tension or replace if worn.
	Fan temperature probe not functioning	To check, connect leads together and switch on ignition, when fan should operate. Replace if faulty.
	Fan motor broken	Fit new motor.
	Radiator core blocked or radiator grille restricted	Reverse flush radiator, remove obstructions.
	Bottom water hose collapsed, impeding flow	Remove and fit new hose.
	Thermostat not opening properly	Remove and fit new thermostat.
	Ignition advance and retard incorrectly set (accompanied by loss of power, and perhaps, misfiring)	Check and reset ignition timing.
	Carburettor incorrectly adjusted (mixture too weak)	Tune carburettor.
	Exhaust system partially blocked	Check exhaust pipe for constrictive dents and blockages.
	Oil level in sump too low	Top up sump to full mark on dipstick.
	Blown cylinder head gasket (water/steam being forced down the radiator overflow pipe under pressure)	Remove cylinder head, fit new gasket.
	Engine not yet run-in	Run-in slowly and carefully.
	Brakes binding	Check and adjust brakes if necessary.
Underheating	Thermostat jammed open	Remove and renew thermostat.
	Incorrect thermostat fitted allowing premature opening of valve	Remove and replace with new thermostat which opens at a higher temperature.
	Thermostat missing	Check and fit correct thermostat.
Loss of cooling water	Loose clips on water hoses	Check and tighten clips if necessary.
	Top, bottom, or by-pass water hoses perished and leaking	Check and replace any faulty hoses.
	Radiator gasket leaking	Remove radiator and repair.
	Thermostat gasket leaking	Inspect and renew gasket.
	Radiator pressure cap spring worn or seal ineffective	Renew radiator pressure cap.
	Blown cylinder head gasket (pressure in system forcing water/steam down over-flow pipe)	Remove cylinder head and fit new gasket.
	Cylinder wall or head cracked	Dismantle engine, despatch to engineering works for repair.

24 Fault diagnosis - heating system

Symptom	Reason/s	Remedy
Insufficient heat	Refer to Section 23, 'Underheating'	
	Kink in heater hose	Re-route to remove kink.
	Wrongly adjusted cable	Adjust, as described in Section 16.
	Heater radiator blocked	Reverse flush.
	Low engine coolant level	Top up coolant.
Heater blower not working	Blower switch broken or disconnected	Check and rectify as necessary.
	Blower fuse (No 2) blown	Check and replace if necessary.
Inadequate output from vents or floor level	Wrongly adjusted cable	Adjust, as described in Section 16.
	Disconnected vent hose/s	Check and rectify.
	Carpet obstructing outlet	Refit carpet.

Chapter 3 Carburation;
fuel, exhaust and emission control systems

Contents

Specifications

Fuel pump

Type	Mechanical, driven from camshaft
Delivery pressure	3.2 to 5.1 lb/in^2 (0.22 to 0.35 kg/cm^2)

Fuel tank

Capacity	7.5 Imp galls (9.0 US galls/34 litres)

Fuel filter ... ...   Nylon mesh located in fuel pump

Air cleaner ... ...   Replaceable paper element type

Carburettor

Type:

960 and 1100 cc	Motorcraft single venturi manual choke
1300 and 1600 cc	Weber dual venturi, electric choke

Motorcraft (Ford) carburettor specification

	960 cc	1100 cc
Throttle barrel diameter	1.26 in (32 mm)	1.26 in (32 mm)
Venturi diameter	0.91 in (23 mm)	0.94 in (24 mm)
Main jet :		
low compression	112	
high compression	110	122
Float level	1.14 $\pm$ 0.03 in	1.22 $\pm$ 0.03 in
	(29 $\pm$ 0.75 mm)	(31 $\pm$ 0.75 mm)
Accelerator pump stroke	0.08 $\pm$ 0.005 in (2.0 $\pm$ 0.13 mm)	
Choke plate pull down	0.12 $\pm$ 0.01 in (3.0 $\pm$ 0.25 mm)	
Mixture % CO	1.25 $\pm$ 0.5	
Idle speed	750 - 850 rpm	
Fast idle	1000 - 1200 rpm	1400 - 1600 rpm

Weber carburettor specification

	1300 cc	1600 cc
Throttle barrel diameter:		
primary	1.26 in (32 mm)	1.26 in (32 mm)
secondary	1.26 in (32 mm)	1.26 in (32 mm)
Venturi diamter:		
primary	0.87 in (22 mm)	0.87 in (22 mm)
secondary	0.87 in (22 mm)	0.87 in (22 mm)
Mainjets:		
primary	107	100 (105 for California)
secondary	105	105 (100 for California)
Air correction jet:		
primary	230	250
secondary	165	250

Weber carburettor

	1300 cc	1600 cc
Emulsion tube:		
primary	F22	F22
secondary	F30	F22
Idling jet:		
primary	50	60
secondary	55	60
Float level	1.38 in (35 mm)	1.34 in (34 mm)
Vacuum pull down	0.21 - 0.23 in (5.2 - 5.8 mm)	0.18 - 0.22 in (4.5 - 5.5 mm)
Choke phasing	0.09 - 0.11 in (2.25 - 2.75 mm)	0.07 - 0.09 in (1.75 - 2.25 mm)
Idling speed	775 - 825 rpm	825 - 875 rpm
Fast idle speed	2000 rpm	1800 rpm
Mixture % CO	1.5 ± 0.25	See engine decal

1 General description

The fuel system comprises four basic components. These are the fuel tank with level indicator, the fuel pump, the carburettor and its controls, and the air cleaner. A number of additional components are fitted in certain territories, with the aim of reducing unwanted vapour and exhaust emissions. These are covered in more detail in Section 24.

The fuel tank is located under the floor pan beneath the rear seats. The filler neck protrudes through the left-hand side of the vehicle, while the combined outlet pipe and fuel level indicator sender unit is located on the right-hand side of the tank. A ventilation or breather pipe is located on the top of the tank.

The fuel pump is located on the rear of the cylinder block, and is mechanically driven by an eccentric on the camshaft. The pump incorporates a nylon mesh filter accessible beneath the top cover.

The carburettor may be either of the Motorcraft (Ford) single venturi type, with cable operated accelerator and choke controls, or of the Weber dual venturi type with cable operated accelerator and electric choke.

The normal air cleaner has a renewable paper element, and an adjustable intake spout, or a spout with an internal flap valve which may be set for summer(s) or winter(w) use.

2 Air cleaner - removal and refitting

1 Disconnect the earth lead from the battery.
2 Remove the three bolts connecting the air cleaner stays to the rocker cover, manifold and cylinder head, and disconnect the breather hose.
3 Remove the air cleaner and take out the element as described in the following Section.
4 Refitting is the reverse of this procedure. Adjust the air cleaner spout or flap to the summer or winter position, as appropriate.

3 Air cleaner element - removal and refitting

1 Disconnect the earth lead from the battery.
2 Remove the centre securing screw, undo the five clips and lift off the air cleaner lid.
3 Lift out the element and clean by directing a jet of compressed air from the centre outwards, holding the jet at least 5 in (127 mm) away from the element. Tap out any loose dust.
4 Renew the element if there are any signs of splitting or cracking, and in any case after 18,000 miles (30,000 km).
5 Carefully wipe any dust from the air cleaner body, ensuring that none enters the carburettor.
6 Refitting is the reverse of this procedure.

4 Fuel pump - general

1 The mechanical pump is located at the rear of the cylinder block, and driven by the camshaft. It is not recommended that this pump be dismantled for repair other than cleaning as described in Section 6.
2 Should a fault occur with the pump, it must be discarded and a new or exchange unit obtained.
3 To test the pump, first confirm that all fuel lines and joints are in good repair and not leaking. Disconnect the fuel pipe at the carburettor inlet joint, and the high tension (thick black) lead to the coil,

and with a suitable container or large rag in position to catch the ejected fuel, turn the engine over. A good spurt of petrol should emerge from the end of the pipe every second revolution.

5 Fuel pump - removal and refitting

1 Disconnect the earth lead from the battery.
2 Remove the inlet and outlet pipes at the pump and tape or plug the ends to stop loss of petrol or entry of dirt. Note that crimped type hose clamps should be cut off and replaced with screw type.
3 Undo and remove the two bolts and spring washers that hold the pump to the cylinder block.
4 Lift away the pump (photo) and clean off all traces of the old gasket.
5 Refitting is the reverse of this procedure, noting the following points:

   a) Before connecting the inlet pipe, move the end to a position lower than the fuel tank. As soon as fuel syphons out, reconnect the pipe.
   b) Disconnect the carburettor inlet pipe, and turn the engine over to prime the pump. As soon as fuel flows, reconnect the pipe.

6 Fuel pump - cleaning

1 Detach the fuel inlet pipe and tape or plug the end.
2 Undo and remove the centre screw and 'O' ring and lift off the sediment cap, filter and seal (photo).
3 Thoroughly clean the sediment cap, filter and pumping chamber using a paintbrush and clean petrol to remove any sediment.
4 Reassembly is the reverse of this procedure, taking care not to over-tighten the screw as this could distort the cap or damage the body.
5 Finally, run the engine to check for leaks.

7 Fuel tank - removal and refitting

1 Disconnect the battery earth lead.
2 Using a length of flexible tubing, syphon as much fuel out of the tank as possible.
3 Jack-up the rear of the car and suitably support it for access beneath.
4 Disconnect the fuel feed pipe at the tank.
5 Disconnect the electrical leads from the sender unit.
6 While supporting the weight of the tank, unscrew and remove the four retaining bolts.
7 Remove the tank (and guard, where applicable), leaving the fuel filler pipe in position.
8 If it is necessary to remove the sender unit, this can be unscrewed from the tank using the appropriate Ford tool. Alternatively a suitable C-spanner or drift can probably be used, but great care should be taken that the flange is not damaged and that there is no danger from sparks if a hammer has to be resorted to.
9 Taking care not to damage the sealing washer, prise out the tank-to-filler pipe seal.
10 Refit the filler pipe seal, using a new seal, if there is any doubt about the condition of the old one.
11 Refit the sender unit using a new seal as the original one will almost certainly be damaged.
12 The remainder of the refitting procedure is the reverse of removal. A smear of grease on the tank filler pipe exterior will aid its fitment.

5.4 Lifting off the fuel pump

6.2 Lifting off the fuel pump cover

8 Fuel tank - cleaning and repair

1   With time it is likely that sediment will collect in the bottom of the fuel tank. Condensation, resulting in rust and other impurities will usually be found in the fuel tank of any car more than three or four years old.
2   When the tank is removed it should be vigorously flushed out with hot water and detergent and, if facilities are available, steam cleaned.
3   Never weld, solder or bring a naked light close to an empty fuel tank, unless at least two hours has elapsed since it has been cleaned as described in the previous paragraph.

9 Accelerator cable - removal, refitting and adjustment

1   Disconnect the earth lead from the battery.
2   From inside the car, remove the two crosshead screws and lower the lower dash trim panel.
3   Pull the grommet from the accelerator pedal (Fig. 3.1), pull the inner cable through and unhook it from the accelerator pedal.
4   Using a suitable punch, knock out the bulkhead grommet (Fig. 3.1). This will destroy the grommet, and release the outer cable.
5   Refer to Section 2 and remove the air cleaner.
6   Slide the clip from the inner cable end, and prise off the cable from the throttle shaft ball.
7   Using a suitable screwdriver, carefully prise out the cable retaining clip (Fig. 3.2). Depress the four pegs on the retainer, and pull the retainer from the mounting bracket (photo).

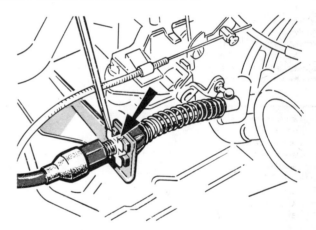

Fig. 3.2. Prise out the accelerator cable retaining clip (Sec. 9)

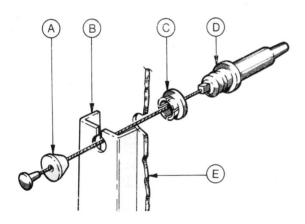

Fig. 3.1. Accelerator cable and pedal (Sec. 9)

A   Grommet D   Outer cable
B   Pedal   E   Bulkhead
C   Grommet

9.7 Pulling out the accelerator cable retainer

8   Refitting is the reverse of this procedure.

Adjustment

9   With the air cleaner removed, jam the accelerator pedal in the fully open position, using a suitable length of wood against the seat, or a heavy weight.
10   Wind back the adjusting sleeve at the carburettor until the carburettor linkage is just in the fully open position.
11   Release the pedal, then check to ensure that full throttle can be obtained.
12   Refit the air cleaner as described in Section 2.

10 Accelerator pedal - removal and refitting

1   Disconnect the earth lead from the battery.
2   From inside the car, remove the two crosshead screws and lower the lower dash trim panel.
3   Pull the grommet from the accelerator pedal (Fig. 3.1), pull the inner cable through and unhook it from the accelerator pedal.
4   Unscrew and remove the two nuts securing the accelerator pedal (photo) and remove the pedal.
5   Refitting is the reverse of this procedure, after which the accelerator cable adjustment should be checked, as described in Section 9.

11 Choke cable - removal, refitting and adjustment

1   Disconnect the earth lead from the battery.

10.4 Remove the accelerator pedal bracket nuts

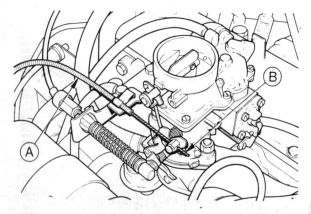

Fig. 3.3. Remove the inner (B) and outer (A) choke cable (Sec. 11)

2   Refer to Section 2 and remove the air cleaner.
3   Undo the screw securing the inner choke cable, and carefully prise out the spring clip retaining the outer cable (Fig. 3.3).
4   Pull the cable clear of the carburettor and attach a length of string to the cable end. Remove the bulkhead grommet.
5   From inside the car, remove the three retaining screws and the lower steering column shroud.
6   Slacken the single cable clamp bolt, and remove the choke cable from the steering column.
7   Carefully pull the cable and draw-cord through into the car, and untie the draw-cord.
8   When refitting, use the draw-cord to pull the choke cable through into the engine compartment. Refit the choke cable to the steering column, and refit the column shroud.

Adjustment

9   Remove the slack from the outer cable and secure it with the spring clip.
10   Pull the choke knob approximately ¼ in (6 mm) from the dash, then remove the slack from the inner cable and with the choke plate fully open, tighten the clamp screw.
11   Refer to Section 2 and refit the air cleaner. Reconnect the battery.

12 Carburettor - dismantling and reassembly - general

1   With time the component parts of the carburettor will wear and petrol consumption will increase. The diameter of the drillings and jets may alter due to erosion and air and fuel leaks may develop around the spindles and other moving parts. Because of the high degree of precision involved, it is best to purchase an exchange rebuilt carburettor. This is one of the few instances where it is better to take the latter course rather than rebuild the component itself.
2   It may be necessary to partially dismantle the carburettor to clear a blocked jet or renew a gasket. Providing care is taken there is no reason why the carburettor may not be completely reconditioned at home, but ensure a full repair kit can be obtained before you strip the carburettor down. **Never** poke out jets with wire but to clean them blow them out with compressed air or with air from a car tyre pump.

13 Carburettor (Ford) - description

The carburettor is of the single venturi downdraught type, incorporating 'by-pass' idling, main, power valve and accelerator pump systems. A manual, cable operated choke is fitted, and the float chamber is externally vented.

Provision is made for throttle speed adjustment, but the mixture control screw is protected by a 'tamper-proof' plastic plug which has to be destroyed to be removed. Replacement plugs can only be obtained by authorised workshops. The reason for this is to prevent adjustment of the mixture setting being carried out by persons not equipped with the necessary CO meter (exhaust gas analyser). The mixture is carefully set during production, to give the specified CO level after the initial running-in period.

The carburettor comprises two castings, the upper and lower bodies. The upper body incorporates the float chamber cover and pivot brackets, fuel inlet components, choke plate and the main and power valve system, idling system and accelerator pump discharge nozzle.

The lower body incorporates the float chamber, the throttle barrel and venturi, throttle valve components, adjustment screws, accelerator pump and distributor vacuum connection.

14 Carburettor (Ford) - adjustments

1   With the exception of the slow and fast idle adjustments, all of the following items can be carried out with the carburettor either on the bench or in the car.

a) Slow running adjustment

2   In view of the increasing awareness of the dangers of exhaust pollution, it is recommended that the slow running (idling) setting is made using a CO meter (exhaust gas analyser). With the engine at normal operating temperature and the throttle speed screw set to give the

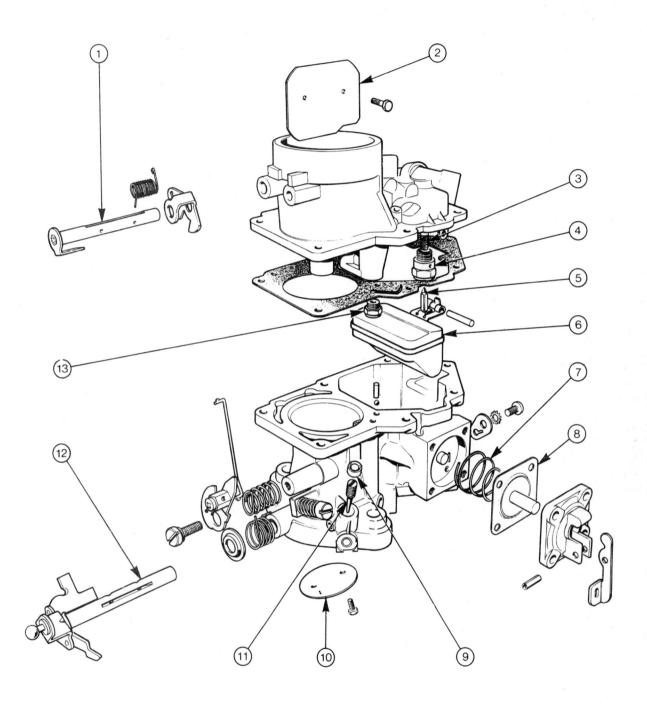

Fig. 3.4. Ford carburettor components (Sec. 13)

1	Choke spindle	8	Accelerator pump diaphragm
2	Choke plate	9	'Tamper-proof' plug
3	Fuel inlet filter	10	Throttle plate
4	Needle valve housing	11	Mixture screw
5	Needle valve	12	Throttle spindle
6	Float	13	Main jet
7	Pump return spring		

specified idling speed, connect the analyser and check that the CO level is within the Specifications. If it is well outside the specification, consideration should be given to the general age and condition of the carburettor, with a view to fitting a new or exchange unit.

3   Where an exhaust gas analyser is not available, a device such as 'Colortune' may be used as an approximate check on mixture setting. If any doubt then exists, it is suggested that you seek the advice of an authorised workshop.

4   To check the slow running speed, first ensure that the choke and accelerator cables are correctly adjusted, Sections 9 and 11. Adjust the idle speed by turning the adjusting screw (Fig. 3.5).

b) Fast idle adjustment

5   Check and adjust the slow idle speed, item a) above, and the choke plate pull down, item c) below.

6   With the engine warmed up, hold the choke plate fully open, operate the choke linkage as far as possible (about 1/3 of its travel) and check the fast idle speed.

7   To adjust the fast idle, bend the tag (Fig. 3.6) the required amount.

c) Choke plate pull down

8   Rotate the choke lever on the carburettor until the choke plate is fully closed.

9   Open the choke plate against the spring pressure up to its stop, then insert a gauge rod or twist drill of the specified size as shown in Fig. 3.7. Bend the adjusting tag as necessary to give the correct dimension between the choke plate and the carburettor.

d) Accelerator pump

10 Unscrew the throttle speed screw until it clears the linkage.

11 Depress the accelerator pump diaphragm plunger fully and then check the clearance between the end of the plunger and the operating lever (Fig. 3.8) using a gauge rod or twist drill of the specified size.

12 If necessary, bend the operating rod at the 'U' bend to give the correct clearance. Reset the slow idle speed, item (a) above.

e) Float level

13 Remove the air cleaner and disconnect the choke cable.

14 Disconnect the fuel inlet pipe and the vent pipe from the carburettor.

15 Remove the upper body securing screws, lift the upper body away, disengaging the choke link at the same time. As the upper body is withdrawn, the accelerator pump discharge valve will be exposed and if the throttle linkage is actuated, it is possible for the valve and weight to be ejected. These components will cause serious damage to the engine if they should fall down the carburettor throat.

16 Hold the carburettor upper body vertically so that the float hangs downward.

17 Measure the distance between the bottom of the float to the mating face of the upper body. (Fig. 3.9). The distance should be as specified. Note that the gasket **must** be removed.

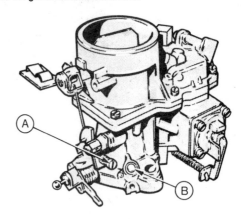

Fig. 3.5. Ford carburettor throttle stop screw (A) and 'tamper-proof' plug (B) (Sec. 14a)

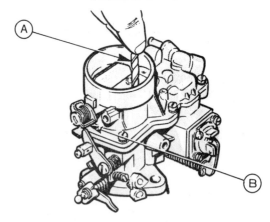

Fig. 3.7. Insert twist drill (A) and adjust pull down tag (B) (Sec. 14c)

Fig. 3.6. Hold open choke plate (B) and adjust fast idle tag (A) (Sec.14b)

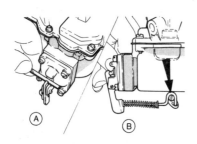

Fig. 3.8. Insert twist drill (A) and bend 'U' link (B) (Sec. 14d)

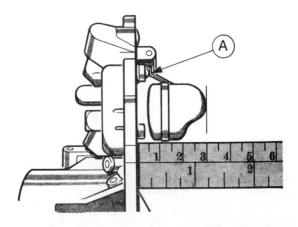

Fig. 3.9. Adjust float level by bending tag (A) (Sec. 14e)

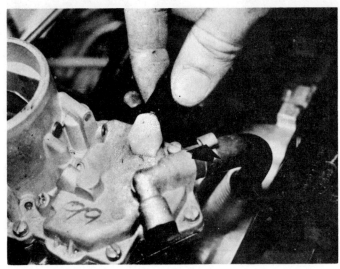

15.5 Crimp type fuel hose clamp

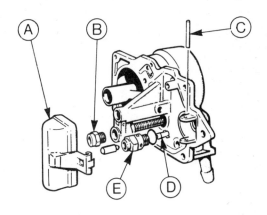

Fig. 3.10. Upper body components (Sec. 16)

A Float	D Inlet fuel filter
B Main jet	E Needle valve housing
C Float pin	

18 Adjust as required by bending the tag 'A' in Fig. 3.9.
19 Reassembly is the reverse of dismantling.

15 Carburettor (Ford) - removal and refitting

1 Open the bonnet, disconnect the earth lead from the battery and remove the air cleaner as described in Section 2.
2 Pull off the retaining clip and prise the accelerator cable off the throttle lever ball.
3 Slacken the inner choke cable clamp screw and prise out the outer cable retaining clip. Free the choke cables from the carburettor.
4 Pull off the distributor vacuum pipe and the fuel vent pipe.
5 If a crimp type clamp is fitted to the fuel inlet pipe (photo), it should be cut off, and a screw type clamp fitted. If a screw type clamp is fitted, slacken the screw, then pull off the fuel feed pipe.
6 Remove the two nuts that secure the carburettor flange and remove the nuts and spring washers.
7 Carefully lift away the carburettor and its gasket, remembering that the float chamber is still full of petrol.
8 Refitting is the reverse of this procedure noting the following points:

 a) *Remove all traces of the old carburettor gasket, clean the mating flanges and fit a new gasket.*
 b) *Check for correct adjustment of the accelerator and choke cables as described in Sections 9 and 11.*

16 Carburettor (Ford) - dismantling, inspection and reassembly

1 Clean the exterior of the carburettor with a water soluble solvent such as 'Jizer.' Clear a suitable area of the workbench in order to lay out the components as they are removed. Refer to Fig. 3.4 as necessary.
2 Unscrew the seven retaining screws and lift off the upper body, disconnecting the choke link.
3 Remove the pivot pin and withdraw the float and fuel inlet needle valve (Fig. 3.10).
4 Unscrew the needle valve seat and remove it together with the filter screen.
5 Remove the main jet.
6 Invert the lower body to eject the accelerator pump ball valve and weight.
7 Do not dismantle the choke valve plate or spindle unless absolutely necessary.
8 Remove the accelerator pump cover and disengage the cover from the operating link. Withdraw the diaphragm and return spring.
9 Do not dismantle the throttle valve plate unless absolutely essential.
10 Unscrew and remove the throttle speed screw.
11 It is not normally suggested that the mixture control screw is

removed unless full workshop facilities including an exhaust gas analyser are available, and a new 'tamper-proof' plug can be obtained.
12 To remove the 'tamper-proof' plug, obtain a long self-tapping screw of suitable diameter to screw through the centre of the plug. The screw should 'bottom' on the mixture screw, and then force out the plug.
13 With the carburettor now completely dismantled, wash all components in clean fuel and renew any components which are worn. Should the choke or throttle valve plate spindles have worn in the carburettor body, then the carburettor should be renewed complete.
14 Blow through all jets and passages with air from a foot pump. **Never** probe jets with a piece of wire since this will damage the jet.
15 Obtain a repair kit which will contain all the necessary gaskets for reassembly.
16 Reassembly is the reverse of the above procedure, noting the following points:

 a) *The accelerator pump spring has its smaller diameter outwards.*
 b) *Check and adjust the float level, as described in Section 14 e).*
 c) *When refitting the upper body, hold the choke mechanism fully closed. The cranked end of the choke link should be at the bottom.*
 d) *Check and adjust the choke plate pull down, as described in Section 14 c).*
 e) *Check and adjust the accelerator pump stroke, as described in Section 14 d).*

17 Carburettor (Weber) - description

The carburettor is of the dual venturi downdraught type, incorporating 'by-pass' idling, main, power valve and accelerator pump systems. An electrically heated automatic choke is fitted, and the float chamber is internally vented.

A connection for the distributor vacuum pipe is provided. Provision is made for throttle speed adjustment, but the mixture control screw is protected by a 'tamper-proof' plastic plug which has to be destroyed to be removed. Replacement plugs can only be obtained by authorised workshops. The reason for this is to prevent adjustment of the mixture setting being carried out by persons not equipped with the necessary CO meter (exhaust gas analyser). The mixture is carefully set during production, to give the specified CO level after the initial running-in period.

The carburettor body comprises two castings which form the upper and lower bodies. The upper incorporates the float chamber cover, float pivot brackets, fuel inlet union, gauze filter, spring-loaded needle valve, twin air intakes, choke plates and the section of the power valve controlled by vacuum.

Incorporated in the lower body is the float chamber, accelerator pump, two throttle barrels and integral main venturis, throttle plates,

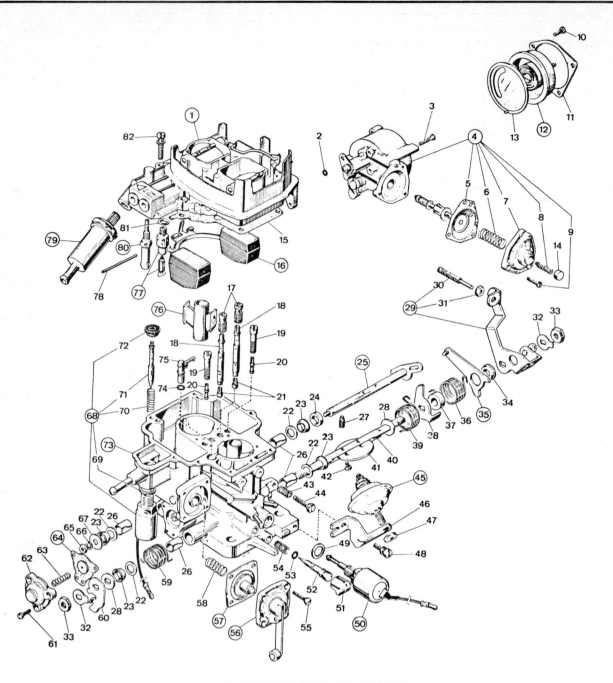

Fig. 3.11. Weber carburettor components

1 Upper body	22 Washer	43 Spring	63 Spring
2 O-ring	23 Bush	44 Adjusting screw	64 Diaphragm
3 Screw	24 Spacer	45 Dash pot (USA only)	65 Nut
4 Automatic choke assy.	25 Secondary shaft	46 Bracket (USA only)	66 Washer
5 Diaphragm	26 Bushes	47 Nut (USA only)	67 Washer
6 Spring	27 Adjusting screw	48 Screw (USA only)	68 External Vent. Sol.
7 Cover	28 Washer	49 Washer (USA only)	(USA only)
8 Adjusting screw	29 Throttle lever assy.	50 Idle cut-off valve	69 Gasket (USA only)
9 Screw	30 Idle adjusting screw	(USA only)	70 Spring (USA only)
10 Screw	31 Locknut	51 Screw cup	71 Spindle (USA only)
11 Locking ring	32 Washer	52 Adjusting screw (idle)	72 Seating valve (USA only)
12 Housing	33 Nut	53 O-ring	73 Carb. body
13 Heat shield	34 Bush	54 Spring	74 Gasket
14 Plug	35 Lever	55 Screw	75 Pump jet
15 Gasket	36 Spring	56 Cover	76 Venturi
16 Float	37 Spacer	57 Diaphragm	77 Needle valve
17 Air correction jets	38 Control lever	58 Spring	78 Float pivot
18 Emulsion tube	39 Spring	59 Return spring	79 Filter
19 Idle jet holder	40 Primary shaft	60 Cam plate	80 Return fuel line
20 Idle jet	41 Throttle valve	61 Screw	81 Gasket
21 Main jets	42 Screw	62 Cover	82 Screw

spindles, levers, jets and the petrol power valve.

The throttle plate opening is in a preset sequence so that the primary starts to open first and is then followed by the secondary in such a manner that both plates reach full throttle position at the same time.

All the carburation systems are located in the lower body and the main progression systems operate in both barrels, whilst the idling and the power valve systems operate in the primary barrel only and the full load enrichment system in the secondary barrel.

The accelerator pump discharges fuel into the primary barrel.

A connection for the vacuum required to control the distributor advance/retard vacuum unit is located on the lower body.

18 Carburettor (Weber) - adjustments

1   With the exception of the slow and fast idle adjustments, all of the following items can be carried out with the carburettor either on the bench or fitted to the engine.

a) Slow running adjustment

2   Refer to Section 14 a) for details, and Fig. 3.12 for the adjusting screw. Ensure that the engine fan is operating by pulling the two wires from the sensor, and connecting the wires with a 'jumper' lead.

b) Fast idle adjustment

3   Open the bonnet and remove the air cleaner, as described in Section 2.
4   Run the engine until the normal running temperature is reached. Hold the throttle partly open, then close the choke plates by hand and release the throttle.
5   The throttle mechanism will hold the choke mechanism at the fast idle position. Release the choke plates, which should return to the open position.

6   If the choke plates do not fully open, then either the engine has not fully warmed up, or the electric choke is faulty.
7   **Without** touching the throttle, start the engine and check the fast idle speed against the figure given in the Specifications.
8   To adjust the fast idle speed, slacken the locknut and screw the adjuster (Fig. 3.13) in or out as required.
9   Tighten the locknut and refit the air cleaner.

c) Vacuum pull-down

10   With the air cleaner removed, as described in Section 2, pull the wire off the electric choke.
11   Remove the three retaining screws and lift off the automatic choke outer housing with the bi-metallic spring. Lift off the internal heat shield.
12   Fit an elastic band to the choke plate lever, and position it to hold the choke plates closed (Fig. 3.14). Open the throttle to allow the choke plates to close fully.
13   Using a suitable screwdriver, push the choke diaphragm open (Fig. 3.14), then measure the clearance between the choke plate and the carburettor body, using a gauge rod or twist drill of the specified size (Fig. 3.15).
14   To adjust the opening, remove the plug and screw the adjusting screw in or out as required (Fig. 3.15).
15   Adjust the choke phasing, item d).
16   Refit the heat shield and the choke housing, Section 20. Reconnect the electric choke wire and the air cleaner as described in Section 2.

d) Choke phasing

17   Adjust the vacuum pull down, item c) above.
18   Hold the throttle partly open, and position the fast idle adjusting screw on the centre step of the fast idle cam. Release the throttle to hold the cam in this position.
19   Push the choke plates down until the cam jams against the fast idle screw.

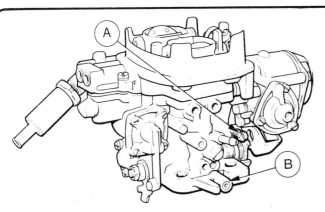

Fig. 3.12. Weber carburettor throttle stop screw (A) and 'tamper-proof' plug (B) (Sec. 18a)

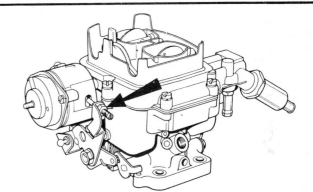

Fig. 3.13. Fast idle adjuster (Sec. 18b)

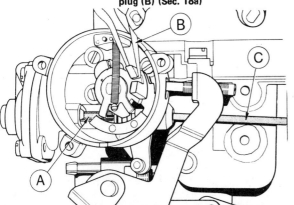

Fig. 3.14. Hold choke open with a rubber band (B) and push the diaphragm rod (A) with a small screwdriver (C) (Sec. 18c)

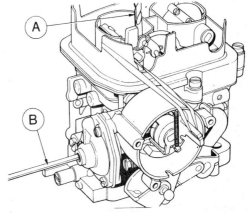

Fig. 3.15. Insert a twist drill (A) and adjust the pull down (B) (Sec. 18c)

20 Measure the clearance between the choke plate and the carburettor body, using a gauge rod or twist drill of the specified size, as shown in Fig. 3.15.
21 Bend the tag (Fig. 3.16) as required to give the correct clearance.
22 Refit the heat shield and the choke housing, Section 20. Reconnect the electric choke wire and the air cleaner, Section 2.

e) Float level

23 Refer to Section 2 and remove the air cleaner assembly.
24 Detach the fuel supply pipe and plug the end to stop dirt ingress.
25 If a crimp type clamp is fitted to the fuel inlet pipe, it should be cut off and a screw type clamp used for refitting.
26 Pull off the electric choke cable.
27 Undo and remove the screws and spring washers that secure the upper body to the lower body. Lift away the upper body, holding the fast idle adjusting screw clear of the choke housing.
28 Carefully examine the float for signs of puncture which may be tested by inserting in warm water and watching for air bubbles.
29 Inspect the float arm for signs of fracture, damage or bending and, if satisfactory, hold the upper body in the vertical position with the float hanging down as shown in Fig. 3.17.
30 Measure the distance between the bottom of the float and the gasket on the upper body and adjust if necessary, to the dimensions given in the Specifications at the beginning of this Chapter. Adjustment is made at the tab which rests against the needle valve.
31 Reassemble the carburettor upper body, which is the reverse sequence to removal.

19 Carburettor (Weber) - removal and refitting

The procedure is very similar to that described for the Ford carburettor, Section 15, except that the manual choke cable is replaced by an electric choke wire, and four nuts are used to secure the unit to the manifold.

20 Carburettor (Weber) - dismantling, inspection and reassembly

1   Before dismantling wash the exterior of the carburettor and wipe dry using a non-fluffy rag. Select a clean area of workbench and lay several layers of newspaper on the top. Obtain several small containers for putting some of the small parts in, which could be easily lost. Whenever a part is to be removed look at it first so that it may be refitted in its original position. As each part is removed place it in order along one edge of the newspaper so that by using this method reassembly is made easier.
2   All parts of the carburettor are shown in Fig. 3.11.
3   Unscrew and remove the fuel filter from the upper body.
4   Undo and remove the six screws and spring washers that retain the upper body to the lower body. Hold the fast idle adjusting screw clear of the automatic choke housing and lift away the upper body and gasket.
5   Carefully extract the float pivot pin and lift out the float assembly followed by the needle valve.
6   Using a box spanner unscrew the needle valve carrier.
7   Undo and remove the three screws and spring washers that secure the spring loaded power valve diaphragm cover. Lift away the cover and spring.
8   Undo and remove the four screws and spring washers that secure the accelerator pump cover to the lower body. Lift away the cover gasket, diaphragm and spring.
9   Undo the two screws that secure each choke plate to the shaft. Lift away the choke plates. Remove the burrs from the threaded holes and then withdraw the shafts.
10 Obtain a selection of screwdrivers with the ends in good condition and square so that the jets may be removed without damage.
11 Unscrew the idling jets and combined main/air correction jets from the lower body, noting the respective sizes and locations of each jet. Remove the accelerator pump jet and its 'O' ring (Fig. 3.18).
12 *Federal vehicles only.* Unscrew and remove the enrichment valve from inside the lower body, and the fuel bowl vent solenoid from the side, where applicable.
13 It is not normally suggested that the mixture control screw is removed unless full workshop facilities, including an exhaust gas analyser are available, and a new 'tamper-proof' plug can be obtained.

14 To remove the 'tamper-proof' plug, obtain a long self-tapping screw of suitable diameter to screw through the centre of the plug. The screw should 'bottom' on the mixture screw, and then force out the plug.
15 Unhook the secondary throttle return spring from the secondary throttle control lever and then unscrew the nut from the primary throttle shaft. Remove the throttle control lever, fast idle lever, washer, secondary throttle control lever, secondary throttle return spring, slow running stop lever, spring and washer from the spindle.
16 Unscrew and remove the nut, spring washer and plain washers from the secondary throttle shaft.
17 Undo the two screws that secure each throttle plate to the shaft. Lift away the two throttle plates. Remove the burrs from the threaded holes and then withdraw the shafts.

Automatic choke dismantling

18 Remove the three screws and detach the automatic choke housing with the bi-metallic spring (Fig. 3.19). Lift off the internal heat shield.
19 Undo and remove the three screws securing the automatic choke to the carburettor. Disconnect the choke link from the housing and lift off the housing.
20 Remove the three screws securing the pull down diaphragm cover (refer to Fig. 3.11) and lift off the cover, spring and diaphragm and operating rod assembly.
21 Dismantling is now complete and all parts should be thoroughly washed and cleaned in petrol. Remove any sediment in the float chamber and drillings but take care not to scratch the fine drillings whilst doing so. Remove all traces of old gaskets using a sharp knife.
22 Clean the jets and passageways using clean, dry compressed air. Check the float assembly for signs of damage or leaking. Inspect the power valve and pump diaphragms and gaskets for splits or deterioration. Examine the mixture screw, needle valve seat and throttle spindle for signs of wear. Renew parts as necessary.
23 Insert the choke spindle in its bore, locate the choke plate in the shaft with the minus (−) sign uppermost. Secure the choke plates in position with two screws each. Peen over the threaded ends to lock.

Automatic choke reassembly

24 Refit the pull down diaphragm and operating rod assembly, spring and cover. Ensure the diaphragm is flat and tighten the three securing screws.
25 Reconnect the automatic choke link, position the 'O' ring (item 15 in Fig. 3.11), refit the choke housing and secure it with three screws.
26 Refer to Section 18, and adjust the vacuum pull down and choke phasing.
27 Refit the internal heat shield with the peg located in the notch in the housing. Connect the bi-metallic spring to the choke lever and loosely fit the three retaining screws. Align the mark on the outer housing with the centre (Index) mark on the choke housing (Fig. 3.20), then tighten the screws. For 1300 cc engines, align with the **lean** mark.
28 Slide the throttle shafts into their appropriate bores and fit the throttle plates into the shafts so that the 78° mark is towards the base of the lower body. Secure the throttle plates with two screws each and peen over the ends to stop them working loose.
29 Fit the plain and spring washers to the secondary throttle shaft and secure with the nut.
30 Refit the washer, primary spring, throttle stop lever, secondary spring, spring, secondary throttle lever, washer, fast idle lever and throttle operating lever to the primary throttle shaft and secure with the nut. Reconnect the secondary throttle spring.
31 If removed, refit the mixture control screw.
32 Refit the 'O' ring and accelerator pump jet to the lower body.
33 Refit the idling jets and the combined main/air correction jets to the lower body in their original positions. If in doubt, refer to the Specifications, noting that the secondary jets are located nearest the choke housing and throttle linkage.
34 *Federal vehicles only.* Refit the enrichment valve and the fuel bowl vent solenoid to the lower body, where applicable.
35 Refit the accelerator pump and power valve diaphragm components (Fig. 3.21), ensure the diaphragms are flat and tighten the screws.
36 Using a box spanner screw in the needle valve housing. A new fibre washer should always be fitted under the housing.
37 Fit the needle valve into the housing (make sure it is the correct way up). Offer up the float to the pivot bracket and retain in position with the pivot pin.

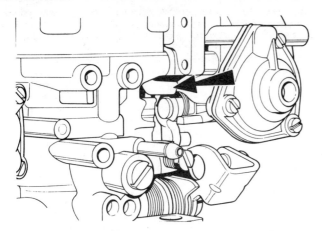

Fig. 3.16. Choke phasing adjusting tag (Sec. 18d)

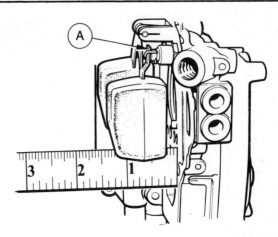

Fig. 3.17. Adjust the float level by bending the tag (A) (Sec. 18e)

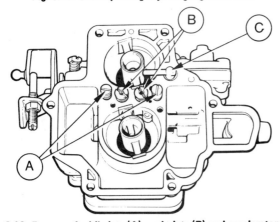

Fig. 3.18. Remove the idle jets (A), main jets (B) and accelerator pump jet (C) (Sec. 30)

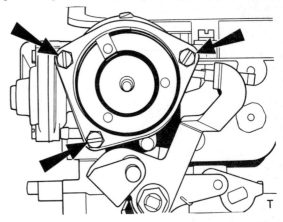

Fig. 3.19. Remove the choke housing securing screws (Sec. 20)

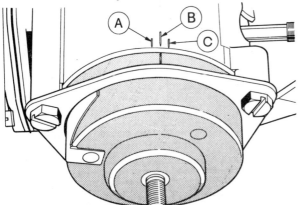

Fig. 3.20. Align the centre mark (B).
A is the rich position, C the lean position (Sec. 20)

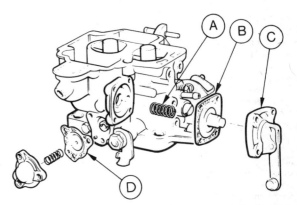

Fig. 3.21. Refit the accelerator pump spring (A) diaphragm (B) and cover (C) and the power valve diaphragm (D) spring and cover (Sec. 20)

38 Refer to Section 18 and check the float level setting.
39 Hold the fast idle adjusting screw clear and refit the upper body to the lower body. Release the fast idle lever and tighten the six screws.
40 Refit the fuel inlet filter.
41 When the carburettor has been refitted to the engine, refer to Section 18 and adjust the fast idle speed, and slow idle speed.
42 If the mixture screw has been disturbed, it should only be adjusted using a CO meter (exhaust gas analyser). Set the mixture to give the specified CO reading, fit a new 'tamper-proof' plug and tap it flush with its housing.

21 Exhaust system - general description

1 The exhaust system is a single piece with a rear muffler, running from the exhaust manifold flange at the front of the engine, under the engine and rear axle.
2 The system is suspended from the floor pan by two rubber insulators (photo) both located behind the muffler.
3 At regular intervals, the system should be checked for corrosion, joint leakage, the condition and security of the insulators and tightness of the joints.

22 Exhaust system - renewal

Note: If only the front pipe or rear muffler is to be renewed, it is important to make the sawcut described in paragraph 6 in the right place. In addition, a service sleeve and U-clamps will be required to connect the two parts of the system.

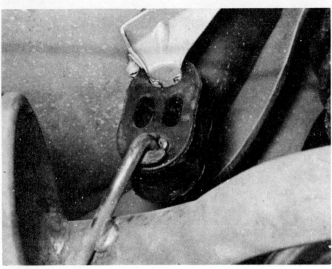

21.2 Exhaust pipe mounting insulators

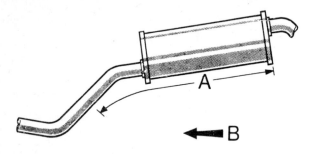

Fig. 3.22. Cut the exhaust pipe at point (A). (B - front of vehicle) (Sec. 22)

1   Disconnect the earth lead from the battery.
2   If possible, raise the car on a ramp or place it over an inspection pit. Alternatively, jack up the car and support it securely to obtain the maximum amount of working room underneath.
3   Unscrew the two bolts securing the exhaust pipe to the manifold and lower the front of the pipe.
4   From under the car, remove the two rubber insulators from behind the muffler and remove the exhaust pipe.
5   With the exhaust pipe on the bench or floor slacken the U-clamps and disconnect the two halves at the service joint where fitted.
6   If the exhaust pipe is still in a single piece, and it is required to renew either the front pipe or the rear muffler, carefully cut the pipe at 90° at the point shown (Fig. 3.22). If the muffler is being renewed, dimension A should be 21.2 in (540 mm). If the front pipe is being renewed, dimension A should be 20.4 in (518 mm).
7   Measure 1.8 in (45 mm) from the cut end, and scribe a line. Slide the service sleeve up to the scribed line on one pipe and position the two U-clamps.
8   Push the other pipe into the service sleeve, but do not tighten the U-clamps.
9   Position the exhaust pipe under the car, then loosely fit the mounting flange to the exhaust manifold.
10   Refit the rear insulators.
11   Align the exhaust system, ensuring that there is a minimum clearance of 1 in (25 mm) between any part of the system and the body or body components.
12   Tighten the U-clamps and exhaust manifold bolts to 30 lbf ft (4.0 kgf m) and lower the car to the ground.

23 Emission control - general

In any engine, there are a large number of gases emitted into the atmosphere.

This pollution occurs in three ways: (i) blow-by gas (unburned mixture) which leaks past the piston rings during the compression stroke and into the engine crankcase; (ii) fuel vapour caused by evaporation of fuel stored in the fuel tank and carburettor; (iii) exhaust gas discharged as the normal products of combustion through the vehicle exhaust pipe.

In some operating territories, the emission control equipment which is fitted is designed to reduce atmospheric pollution to minimal levels without affecting engine performance or economy of running more than is absolutely necessary.

It is emphasised that the efficiency of any emission control system depends in part on the state of tune of the basic engine components - ignition, valve clearances, carburettor settings, and these must always be maintained as described in the appropriate Chapters of this manual.

24 Emission control components - description

1   Some or all of the following items may be fitted to the Fiesta. The exact line-up will depend to a large extent on local legal requirements.

a) Positive crankcase ventilation (PCV)

2   The PCV system operates by drawing in air and mixing it with the vapours which have escaped past the piston rings (blow-by vapours). This mixture is then drawn into the combustion chamber through an oil separator and PCV valve. Refer also to Chapter 1, Section 25.

b) Thermostatically controlled air cleaner

3   This type of air cleaner ensures a constant temperature of the intake air so that fuel atomisation within the carburettor takes place using air at the correct temperature. This is effected by a duct system which draws in fresh air, or pre-heated air from a heat shroud around the engine exhaust manifold.
4   Operation of the system can be summarised as follows:
When the engine is cold, heated air is directed from the exhaust manifold into the air cleaner, but as the engine warms up cold air is progressively mixed with this warm air to maintain a carburettor air temperature of 105 to 130°F (40.5 to 76.8°C). At high ambient temperatures the hot air intake is closed off completely.
The mixing of air is regulated by a vacuum operated valve on the air cleaner inlet duct, which is controlled by a bi-metal temperature sensor inside the air cleaner.

c) Deceleration valve

5   During deceleration, this valve allows an additional flow of air/fuel mixture into the inlet manifold. This improves cylinder combustion and lowers hydro-carbon emission in the exhaust gases.
6   The valve is mounted on the inlet manifold, and consists of a spring loaded diaphragm, a control valve and two ports. During idling, acceleration and cruising, the spring holds the control valve shut, (Fig. 3.23). During deceleration however, the high inlet manifold vacuum is stronger than the spring pressure, and opens the valve. This allows a quantity of air/fuel mixture to by-pass the carburettor throttle plates, and enables completion of the combustion process (Fig. 3.24).
7   When the engine is cold, manifold vacuum may be applied to the underside of the diaphragm by PVS (item g) below), thus cutting out the operation of the deceleration valve (Fig. 3.23).

d) Evaporative emission control

8   The components of this system are shown diagrammatically in Fig. 3.25. The three way control valve allows fuel vapour from the tank to flow to the carbon canister. The carbon-filled canister has the function of absorbing excess fuel vapour from the tank, and releasing it to the carburettor when the engine is running.
9   During tank filling, the spring loaded valve remains closed against the vapour pressure. This build up of pressure causes a vapour lock at the top of the tank. Once the filler cap is replaced, the fuel and vapour in the tank expand if the air temperature rises. This causes an increase of pressure, which opens the control valve and allows excess vapour to pass into the carbon canister, where it is absorbed.
10   Excess fuel vapour from the carburettor is also fed into the carbon canister for absorption (Fig. 3.26). Once the engine is running, fresh air entering the canister 'purges' the fuel vapour from the carbon granules, and feeds it to the air cleaner, from where it passes into the engine.

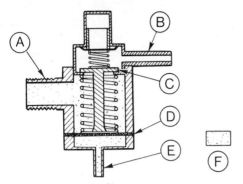

Fig. 3.23. Deceleration valve closed (engine idling, accelerating or
cruising, or cold) (Sec. 24c)

A Outlet into manifold
B Inlet from carburettor
C Valve (closed)
D Diaphragm
E Vacuum connection from PVS
F Manifold vacuum

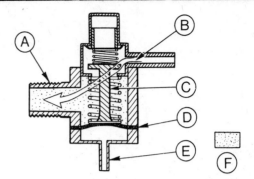

Fig. 3.24. Deceleration valve open (engine decelerating, warm)
(Sec. 24c)

A Outlet into manifold
B Inlet from carburettor
C Valve (open)
D Diaphragm
E Connection from PVS (open
   to atmosphere)
F Manifold vacuum

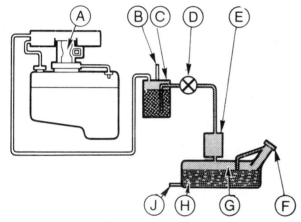

Fig. 3.25. Typical evaporative emission system (Sec. 24d)

A Carburettor (internally vented)
B Canister vent
C Carbon canister
D Spring loaded three way valve
E Fuel/vapour separator
F Filler cap
G Expansion void
H Fuel tank
J Fuel line connection

e) Spark delay valve (SDV)

11 For good driveability, vacuum advance of the spark is required
under part throttle conditions to allow time for the air/fuel mixture to
burn. Unfortunately, the distributor vacuum advance operates much
more quickly than the enriching of the air/fuel mixture, leading to
erratic combustion.

12 To overcome this, a spark delay valve is fitted into the vacuum line.
This valve (Fig. 3.27) allows unrestricted flow of air (vacuum) in one
direction, while impeding the flow through an orifice in the other
direction. This will slow the rate of distributor vacuum advance to
match more closely the rate of air/fuel mixture enrichment.

13 To enable the SDV to be taken into or out of the system as the
engine temperature changes, a PVS (item g) below) may be used.

f) Exhaust gas recirculation (EGR)

14 This sytem is designed to reintroduce small amounts of exhaust
gas into the combustion cycle. This reduces the generation of oxides of
nitrogen (NOx) by firstly reducing the volume of air/fuel mixture
entering the cylinders, and secondly by reducing the peak cylinder
working temperature.

15 Fig. 3.28 shows the operation of the EGR valve, while Fig. 3.29
shows a typical layout. The vacuum line restrictor and reservoir
'dampen out' the rise and fall of vacuum in the system to improve
driveability. The PVS (item g) below) cuts out the EGR valve until the
engine has reached its working temperature.

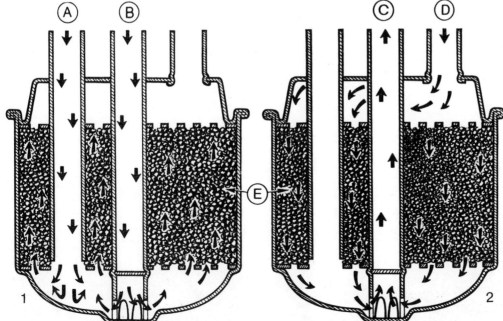

Fig. 3.26. Carbon canister (Sec. 24d)

1 Vapour storage
   (engine off)
2 Purge condition
   (engine running)
A Vapour from tank
B Vapour from
   carburettor
C Vapour to engine
D Air from
   atmosphere
E Carbon granules

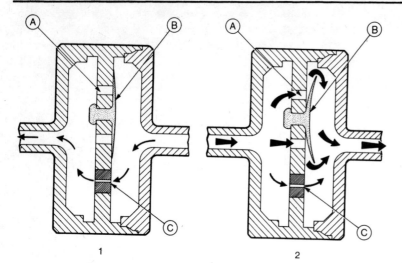

Fig. 3.27. Spark delay valve (SDV) (Sec. 24e)

1 Restricted flow	A Check valve drillings
2 Unrestricted flow	B Check valve
	C Orifice

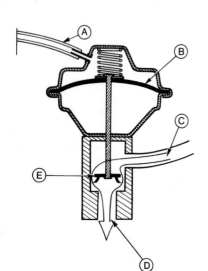

Fig. 3.28. Exhaust gas recirculation (EGR) valve (Sec. 24f)

A Vacuum supply	D Exhaust gas to inlet
B Diaphragm	manifold
C Exhaust gas supply	E Valve

g) Ported vacuum switch (PVS)

16 A ported vacuum switch (PVS) is basically a small temperature operated valve mounted in the engine cooling system. The switch consists of a wax sensor, which expands as the temperature rises, and operates a valve pushrod.

17 Two types of PVS may be fitted. The two port type used with EGR system contains a ball valve which is closed when the sensor is cold (Fig. 3.30) but opens as the engine warms, allowing manifold vacuum to bring the EGR valve into operation.

18 The three port type of PVS may be used with a deceleration valve or a spark delay valve. In this type, the middle port is connected to either the upper port (cold engine) or the lower port (hot engine).

19 When used in conjunction with a deceleration valve (item c) above) the middle port to the deceleration valve is connected to the inlet manifold vacuum (engine cold, Fig. 3.31) or to the atmosphere (engine hot, Fig. 3.32). With the engine cold, the vacuum from the PVS keeps the valve closed, only allowing it to come into operation as the engine warms up.

20 When used in conjunction with a SDV (item e) above), the middle port from the inlet manifold vacuum is connected direct to the distributor (engine cold, Fig. 3.31) or to the SDV (engine hot, Fig. 3.32) and then to the distributor. With the engine cold, the SDV is bypassed, only coming into operation as the engine warms up.

h) Air injection system (AIS) or thermactor

21 This system is designed to reduce the hydrocarbon and carbon monoxide content of the exhaust gases by continuing the oxidation of unburnt gases after they leave the combustion chamber. This is achieved by using an engine driven air pump to inject fresh air into the hot

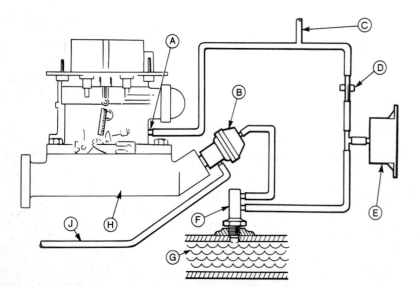

Fig. 3.29. Typical EGR system (Sec. 24f)

A   Vacuum take-off
B   EGR valve
C   Vacuum to distributor
D   Vacuum line restrictor (where fitted)
E   Vacuum line reservoir (where fitted)
F   Two part PVS
G   Cooling system
H   Inlet manifold
J   Exhaust gas supply

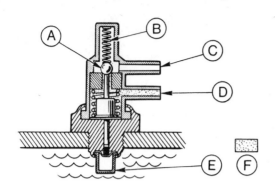

Fig. 3.30. Two port PVS - closed (engine cold) (Sec. 24g)

A Ball valve
B Return spring
C EGR valve connection
D Vacuum supply
E Wax sensor
F Inlet manifold vacuum

exhaust stream after it leaves the combustion chamber. This air mixes with the hot exhaust gases and promotes further oxidation, thus reducing their concentration and converting some of them into carbon dioxide and water (Fig. 3.33).

22 The air pump draws in air through an impeller type, centrifugal fan and exhausts it from the exhaust manifold through a vacuum controlled air bypass valve and check valve. Under normal conditions thermactor air passes straight through the bypass valve, but during deceleration, when there is a high level of intake manifold vacuum, the diaphragm check valve operates to shut off the thermactor air to the air supply check valve and exhaust it to atmosphere. The air supply check valve is a non-return valve which will allow thermactor air to pass to the exhaust manifold but will not allow exhaust gases to flow in the reverse direction.

i) Catalytic converter

23 On some models a catalytic converter is incorporated in the exhaust system. The converter comprises a ceramic honeycomb-like core housed in a stainless steel pipe. The core is coated with a platinum and palladium catalyst which converts unburned carbon monoxide and hydrocarbons into carbon dioxide and water by a chemical reaction.

24 Because of the great heat generated within the converter, it is protected by a heat shield.

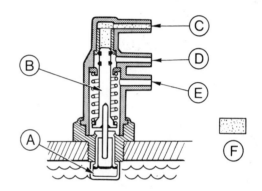

Fig. 3.31. Three port PVS (engine cold) (Sec. 24g)

A Wax sensor
B Plunger (lower position)
C Connection from vacuum (when used with deceleration valve) or to distributor (when used with SDV)
D Connection to deceleration valve or from vacuum (when used with SDV)
E Blocked off by plunger
F Manifold vacuum

Fig. 3.32. Three port PVS (engine hot) (Sec. 24g)

A Wax sensor
B Plunger (upper position)
C Blocked off by plunger
D Connection to deceleration valve or from vacuum (when used with SDV)
E To atmosphere (when used with deceleration valve) or to SDV

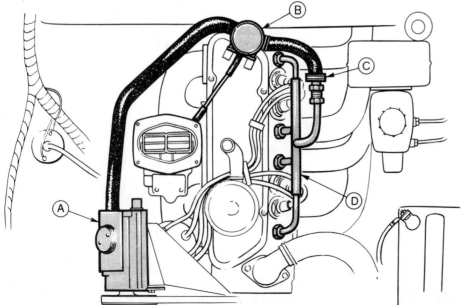

Fig. 3.33. Typical AIS system (Sec. 24h)

A Air pump
B By-pass valve
C Check valve
D Air injection manifold

25 Emission control - warning

1   Before making any adjustment or alteration to the carburettor or emission control systems, the owner is advised to make himself aware of any Federal, State or Provincial laws which may be contravened by making any such adjustment or alteration.

2   Setting dimensions and specifications are given in this Chapter where relevant to adjustment procedure. Where these differ from those given on the engine tune-up decal, the decal information should be assumed to be correct.

3   Where the use of special test equipment is called for (eg, exhaust gas CO analyser, engine tachometer etc), and this equipment is not available, any setting or calibration should be regarded as a temporary measure only and should be rechecked by a suitably equipped Ford dealer or carburation/emission control specialist at the earliest opportunity.

4   Before attempting any carburettor adjustments, first ascertain that the following items are serviceable or correctly set:

  a) *All vacuum hoses and connections.*
  b) *Ignition system.*
  c) *Spark plugs.*
  d) *Ignition initial advance.*

5   If satisfactory adjustment cannot be obtained check the following points:

  a) *Carburettor fuel level.*
  b) *Crankcase ventilation system.*
  c) *Valve clearance.*
  d) *Engine compression.*
  e) *Idle mixture.*

26 Emission control components - maintenance and testing

1   In view of the special test equipment and procedures there is little that can be done in the way of maintenance and testing for the emission control system. In the event of a suspected malfunction of the system, check the security and condition of all vacuum and electrical connections then, where applicable, refer to the following paragraphs for further information.

2   In addition, whenever working on any of these systems, make a **careful** note of any electrical or vacuum line connections before removing them.

a) Positive crankcase ventilation (PCV)

3   Remove all the hoses and components of the system and clean them in paraffin or petrol. Ensure that all hoses are free from any obstruction and are in a serviceable condition. Where applicable, similarly clean the crankcase breather cap and shake it dry. Renew parts as necessary then refit them to the car.

b) Thermostatically controlled air cleaner

Note: These checks should be carried out at a temperature of at least 60°F (16°C).

4   Check that the valve is open (cold air entry) when the engine is switched off. Start the engine and check that the valve closes when idling (except where engine is hot). If either condition does not happen, check that the valve is not binding or sticking, then move to paragraph 5.

5   With the air cleaner cover in position, start the engine and observe the valve. If the valve does not start to open within 5 minutes, check the temperature inside the air cleaner. If above 75°F (24°C), the temperature sensor is at fault. If below 75°F (24°C), run the engine for a further 5 minutes. If the valve has still not opened, renew the sensor.

c) Deceleration valve

6   Connect a vacuum gauge in the line to the deceleration valve from the inlet manifold. Disconnect and plug the PVS connection (Fig. 3.34).

7   Start the engine, run it at 3000 rpm for two to three seconds, then release the throttle while observing the vacuum gauge. As the throttle is released, the vacuum gauge reading will rise to a maximum, then reduce to zero. The time for this reduction should be 2½ to 3½ seconds.

8   If the time is outside these limits, remove the plug from the top of the deceleration valve and screw the adjuster in (to decrease) or out (to increase), between the limits shown in Fig. 3.35. Refit the plug, reconnect the PVS hose and remove the vacuum gauge.

9   If the 'timing' adjusted above is still too long, and the idle speed is too high, disconnect the inlet vacuum hose and plug the valve inlet. If the idle speed remains high, the fault lies elsewhere. If, however, the idle speed falls to normal, repair or renew the deceleration valve (Fig. 3.36).

10 If the 'timing' is too short, insert a small screwdriver through the bottom cover and lift the diaphragm. If the engine speed increases to 1300 - 1600 rpm, repair or renew the valve (Fig. 3.36). If the engine speed does not increase, check the hose to the carburettor, and the air/fuel metering jets in the carburettor for blockage.

d) Evaporative emission control

11 The charcoal canister is located on the right-hand dash panel in the engine compartment. To remove it, disconnect the two hoses, then remove the three nuts securing the canister bracket to the dash panel. Remove the canister and bracket. Refitting is the reverse of the removal procedure.

e) Spark delay valve

12 Note which way round the valve is fitted, then remove it from the car to test its operation. Fit the valve into the test circuit shown (Fig. 3.37) with the black side towards the vacuum source.

13 Close the on/off valve and apply a vacuum of 10 in (250 mm) of mercury with the hand pump. Open the valve and note the time taken for the gauge 'A' to reach 8 in (200 mm) of mercury. If less than six seconds or more than fourteen seconds, the valve is faulty.

14 Refit the valve to the car. The valve is marked 'CARB' and 'DIST'. If fitted the reverse way, it acts as a spark **sustain** valve (SSV).

f) Exhaust gas recirculation

15 To test the valve, connect a hand operated vacuum pump to the vacuum supply pipe and pump to achieve 8 in (200 mm) of mercury. The EGR valve should hold this vacuum for at least thirty seconds. Release the vacuum, start the engine and run up to the normal operating temperature. With the engine idling, operate the hand pump to achieve 8 in (200 mm) of mercury. If the valve is operating correctly, the idle should become slower and lumpy. No change in idle speed indicates a faulty valve.

g) Ported vacuum switch

16 Connect a hand operated vacuum pump to the middle (3 port PVS) or lower (2 port PVS) port of the PVS valve to be tested. Connect vacuum gauge(s) to the other port(s). With the engine at least 18°F (10°C) below the PVS operating temperature, operate the pump to give a vacuum of 10 in (250 mm) of mercury. If the PVS is functioning correctly, there should be a vacuum of 10 in (250 mm) at the upper port of a three port switch, and zero at the upper port of a two port, and lower port of a three port switch.

17 Warm the engine up to its operating temperature, and repeat the test. In this condition, the upper port of a three port switch should be zero, while the upper port of a two port and the lower port of a three port switch should be 10 in (250 mm). In all cases, the measured vacuum should hold for at least 10 seconds.

h) Air injection system (AIS) or Thermactor

18 Apart from checking the condition of the drive belt and pipe connections, and checking the pump drive belt tension, there is little that can be done without the use of special test equipment. Drive belt tension should be checked using a special tension gauge, the tension reading being as given in Chapter 2. However, this is approximately equal to ½ in (13 mm) of belt movement between the longest pulley run under moderate hand pressure.

i) Catalytic converter

19 No special maintenance of the converter is required, except to change it at the specified service intervals. It can however, be damaged by the use of leaded fuels, engine misfiring, excessive richness of the carburettor mixture, incorrect operation of the AIS, or running out of fuel.

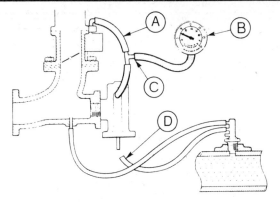

Fig. 3.34. Testing the deceleration valve (Sec. 26c)

A Air/fuel supply hose   C T-piece
B Vacuum gauge   D PVS vacuum hose (disconnected)

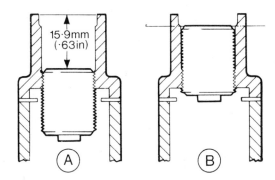

Fig. 3.35. Deceleration valve adjusting limits (Sec. 26c)

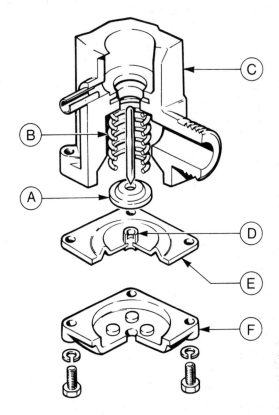

Fig. 3.36. Deceleration valve components (Sec. 26c)

A Spring seat   D Valve tip cup (note position)
B Spring   E Diaphragm
C Body   F Bottom cover

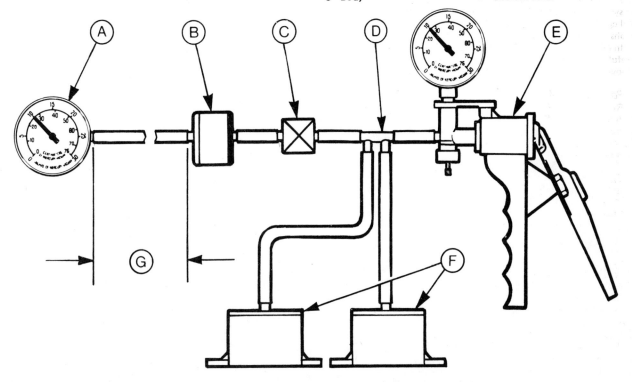

Fig. 3.37. SDV valve test circuit (Sec. 26e)

A Vacuum gauge   C On/off valve   E Hand vacuum pump   G 24 in (600 mm)
B SDV   D T-piece   F Vacuum reservoir (EGR type)

27 Fault diagnosis - fuel system and carburation

Symptom	Cause	Remedy
Fuel consumption excessive Note that this may also be due to an emission control system fault (see below)	Air cleaner choked and dirty giving rich mixture	Remove, clean and replace air cleaner element.
	Fuel leaking from carburettors, fuel pumps, or fuel lines	Check for and eliminate fuel leaks. Tighten fuel line union nuts.
	Float chamber flooding	Check and adjust float level.
	Generally worn carburettor	Remove, overhaul and replace.
	Distributor condenser faulty	Remove and fit new unit.
	Balance weights or vacuum advance mechanism in distributor faulty.	Remove and overhaul distributor.
	Carburettor incorrectly adjusted mixture too rich	Tune and adjust carburettor.
	Idling speed too high	Adjust idling speed.
	Faulty choke operation	Check and correct.
	Contact breaker gap incorrect	Check and reset gap.
	Valve clearances incorrect	Check cam followers to valve stem clearance and adjust as necessary.
	Incorrectly set spark plugs	Remove, clean and re-gap.
	Tyre under-inflated	Check tyre pressure and inflate as necessary.
	Wrong spark plugs fitted	Remove and replace with correct units.
	Brakes dragging	Check and adjust brakes.
Insufficient fuel delivery or weak mixture	Petrol tank air vent restricted	Remove petrol cap and clean out air vent.
	Partially clogged filters in pump and carburettor	Remove and clean filters. Remove and clean out float chamber and needle valve assembly.
	Incorrectly seating valves in fuel pump	Remove, and fit new fuel pump.
	Fuel pump diaphragm leaking or damaged	Remove, and fit new fuel pump.
	Gasket in fuel pump damaged	Remove, and fit new fuel pump.
	Fuel pump valves sticking due to petrol gumming	Remove and thoroughly clean fuel pump.
	Too little fuel in tank (prevalent when climbing)	Refill tank.
	Pipe connections loose	Tighten all joints.
	Splits in fuel pipe	Replace pipe(s).
	Inlet manifold to block or carburettor gasket leaking	Tighten joint or renew gasket as necessary.

28 Fault diagnosis - emission control systems

The following is a list for guidance only, since a combination of faults may produce symptoms which are difficult to trace. It is therefore essential that a Ford dealer or emission control specialist is consulted in the event of problems occurring.

Symptom	Check/correct
Engine fumes	Clogged PCV valve or split or collapsed hoses.
Fuel odour	Choked carbon canister or damaged hoses.
Exhaust fumes	AIS drive belt slack, AIS pump defective, AIS pressure relief valve faulty, hoses damaged. Damaged or clogged catalytic converter.
Poor starting	Thermostatic air cleaner faulty, static ignition timing.
Engine stalling at idle - cold	PCV valve, slow idle setting, deceleration valve, fast idle speed, EGR system, static ignition timing.
Engine stalling at idle - hot	PCV valve, air cleaner, slow idle setting, deceleration valve, EGR system, static ignition timing.
Engine stalling at drive away	Air cleaner, EGR system, static ignition timing, vacuum advance, SDV
Poor idle quality - cold	PCV valve, air cleaner, slow idle setting, fast idle speed, deceleration valve, EGR system, static ignition timing.
Poor idle quality - hot	PCV valve, air cleaner, slow idle setting, EGR system, static ignition timing.
High idle speed	Slow idle setting, fast idle speed, deceleration valve, static ignition timing.
Excessive CO emission	Slow idle setting, deceleration valve, static ignition timing.
Hesitation/flat spots - acceleration	Air cleaner, EGR system, static ignition timing, automatic advance mechanism, SDV.
Hesitation /flat spots - at low speed	PCV valve, slow idle setting, deceleration valve, EGR system, static ignition timing, automatic advance mechanism.
High fuel consumption	Air cleaner, EGR system, static ignition timing, automatic advance mechanism (also refer to Section 27).
Loss of power	Air cleaner, EGR system, static ignition timing, automatic advance mechanism.
Overheating	Static ignition timing.
Detonation	Air cleaner, static ignition timing.

Chapter 4 Ignition system

Contents

Specifications

Fiesta (except USA)
Spark plugs

	950 and 1100 cc	1300 cc
Type	AGRF 22	AGR 12
Gap	0.024 in (0.6 mm)	0.024 in (0.6 mm)

Coil

Type	Oil filled low voltage	Oil filled low voltage
Primary resistance	0.95 to 1.60 ohms	0.95 to 1.60 ohms
Secondary resistance	5000 to 9300 ohms	5000 to 9300 ohms
Output	31 KV	31 KV

Distributor

Automatic advance	Mechanical and vacuum	Mechanical and vacuum
Rotation	Anticlockwise viewed from top	Anticlockwise viewed from top
Contact breaker points gap		
Bosch	0.018 in (0.45 mm)	0.018 in (0.45 mm)
Ford	0.025 in (0.64 mm)	0.025 in (0.64 mm)
Dwell angle	48° to 52°	48° to 52°
Static advance (initial)	10° BTDC	6° BTDC
Firing order	1 - 2 - 4 - 3	1 - 2 - 4 - 3

Condenser

Capacity		
Bosch	0.18 - 0.26 mfd	0.18 - 0.26 mfd
Ford	0.21 - 0.25 mfd	0.21 - 0.25 mfd

Fiesta (USA)
Spark plugs ... ...

	1600 cc
	Refer to engine decal for type and gap

Coil

Type	Oil filled low voltage
Primary resistance	1.3 to 1.6 ohms
Secondary resistance	7000 to 9000 ohms

Distributor

Rotation	Anticlockwise viewed from top
Rotor air gap maximum drop	7.5 KV
Ignition timing	Refer to engine decal
Firing order	1 - 2 - 4 - 3

Torque wrench setting

	lb f ft	kg f m
Spark plugs	13	1.75

1 General description - conventional distributor - except USA

In order that the engine can run correctly it is necessary for an electrical spark to ignite the fuel/air mixture in the combustion chamber at exactly the right moment in relation to engine speed and load. The ignition system is based on feeding low tension voltage from the battery to the coil where it is converted into high tension voltage. The high tension voltage is powerful enough to jump the spark plug gap in the cylinders many times a second under high compression pressures, providing that the system is in good condition and that all adjustments are correct.

The ignition system is divided into two circuits, low tension and high tension.

The low tension circuit (sometimes known as the primary) consists of the battery lead to the ignition switch, ballast resistor lead from the ignition switch to the low tension or primary coil winding (terminal 15 or +), and the lead from the low tension coil winding (terminal 1 or −) to the contact breaker points and condenser in the distributor.

The high tension circuit consists of the high tension or secondary coil winding, the heavy ignition lead from the centre of the coil to the centre of the distributor cap, the rotor arm, the spark plug leads and spark plugs.

The system functions in the following manner (Fig. 4.1). Low tension voltage is changed in the coil into high tension voltage by the opening of the contact breaker point in the low tension circuit. High tension voltage is then fed via the carbon brush in the centre of the distributor cap to the rotor arm of the distributor, and each time it comes in line with one of the four metal segments in the cap, which are connected to the spark plug leads, the opening of the contact breaker points causes the high tension voltage to build up, jump the gap from the rotor arm to the appropriate metal segment and so via the spark plug lead to the spark plug, where it finally jumps the spark plug gap before going to earth.

The ignition is advanced and retarded automatically, to ensure the spark occurs at just the right instant for the particular load at the prevailing engine speed.

The ignition advance is controlled both mechanically and by a vacuum operated system. The mechanical governor comprises two weights, which move out from the distributor shaft as the engine speed rises due to centrifugal force. As they move outwards they rotate the cam relative to the distributor shaft, and so advance the spark. The weights are held in position by two light springs and it is the tension of the springs which is largely responsible for correct spark advancement.

The vacuum consists of a diaphragm, one side of which is connected via a small bore tube to the carburettor, and the other side to the contact breaker plate. Depression in the inlet manifold and carburettor, which varies with the engine speed and throttle opening, causes the diaphragm to move, so moving the contact breaker plate, and advancing the spark. A spring within the vacuum unit returns the breaker plate to the normal position when the amount of manifold depression is reduced.

The wiring harness includes a high resistance wire in the ignition coil feed circuit and it is very important that only a 'ballast resistor' type ignition coil is used. The starter solenoid has an extra terminal so that a wire from the solenoid to the coil supplies voltage direct to the coil when the starter motor is operated (Fig. 4.2). The ballast resistor wire is therefore by-passed and the battery voltage is fed to the ignition system, so giving easier starting.

One of two makes of distributor may be fitted to the Fiesta. These are the Ford, identified by a black distributor cap and an internal condenser, and the Bosch, identified by a red cap and an externally mounted condenser.

On some models where an FM radio is fitted, a 'screening can' is fitted around the distributor and each spark plug to suppress interference. These are easily removable for access.

2 General description - breakerless distributor - USA

The component parts and layout of the breakerless ignition system are shown in Fig. 4.3.

When the ignition switch is on, the ignition primary circuit is energized. When the distributor armature 'teeth' or 'spokes' approach the magnetic coil assembly, a voltage is induced which signals the

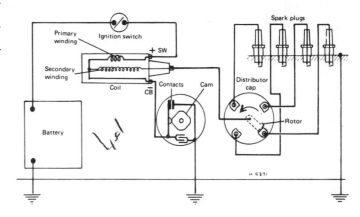

Fig. 4.1. Ignition system theoretical wiring diagram (Sec. 1)

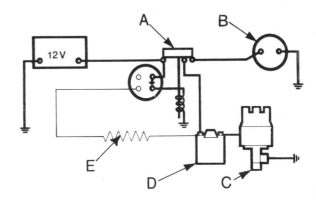

Fig. 4.2. Ignition switch in 'start' position (Sec. 1)

A Starter solenoid   D Ignition coil
B Starter motor   E Ballast resistor wire
C Distributor

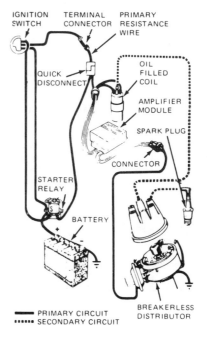

Fig. 4.3. Typical breakerless ignition system (Sec. 2)

amplifier to turn off the coil primary current. A timing circuit in the amplifier module turns on the coil current after the coil field has collapsed.

When on, current flows from the battery through the ignition switch, through the coil primary winding, through the amplifier module and then to ground. When the current is off, the magnetic field in the ignition coil collapses, inducing a high voltage in the coil secondary winding. This is conducted to the distributor cap where the rotor directs it to the appropriate spark plug. This process is repeated for each power stroke of the car engine.

The distributor is fitted with devices to control the actual point of ignition according to the engine speed and load. As the engine speed increases two centrifugal weights move outwards and alter the position of the armature in relation to the distributor shaft to advance the spark slightly. As engine load increases (for example when climbing hills or accelerating), a reduction in intake manifold depression causes the base plate assembly to move slightly in the opposite direction (clockwise) under the action of the spring in the vacuum unit, thus retarding the spark slightly and tending to counteract the centrifugal advance. Under light loading conditions (for example at moderate steady speeds) the comparatively high intake manifold depression on the vacuum advance diaphragm causes the baseplate assembly to move in a counterclockwise direction to give a larger amount of spark advance.

For most practical do-it-yourself purposes ignition timing is carried out as for conventional ignition systems. However, a monolithic timing system is incorporated, and this has a timing receptacle mounted in the left rear of the cylinder block for use with an electronic probe. This latter system can only be used with special electronic equipment, and checks using it are beyond the scope of this manual.

Fault finding on the breakerless ignition system, which cannot be rectified by substitution of parts or cleaning/tightening connections, etc, should be entrusted to a suitably equipped Ford garage since special test procedures and equipment are required.

3   Contact breaker points - adjustment

1   To adjust the contact breaker points to the correct gap, first release the two clips securing the distributor cap to the distributor body, and lift away the cap. Clean the cap inside and out with a dry cloth. It is unlikely that the four segments will be badly burned or scored, but if they are the cap will have to be renewed.
2   Inspect the carbon brush contact located in the top of the cap to ensure that it is not broken and stands proud of the plastic surface.
3   Lift away the rotor arm and check the contact spring on the top of the rotor arm. It must be clean and have adequate tension to ensure good contact.
4   Gently prise the contact breaker points open to examine the condition of their faces. If they are rough, pitted or dirty it will be necessary to remove them and fit new points.
5   Presuming the points are satisfactory, or that they have been cleaned or renewed, measure the gap between the points with feeler gauges by turning the crankshaft until the heel of the breaker arm is on the highest point of the cam. The gap should be as given in the Specifications (photo).
6   If the gap varies from that specified, slacken the contact plate securing screw/s, Bosch distributor 1 screw, Ford distributor 2 screws.
7   Adjust the contact gap by moving the fixed point as required. When the gap is correct, tighten the securing screw/s and recheck the gap.
8   Refit the rotor arm and distributor cap. Retain in position with the two clips.

4   Contact breaker points - removal and refitting

1   If the contact breaker points are burnt, pitted or badly worn, they must be renewed. The contact faces are specially treated, and should not be re-surfaced.
2   Release the two clips securing the distributor cap to the body, and lift away the cap.
3   Lift off the rotor arm by pulling it straight up from the top of the cam spindle.
4   *Bosch:* Pull off the low tension lead, remove the retaining screw and lift out the contact breaker assembly (Fig. 4.4).
5   *Ford:* Slacken the lead securing screw and slide off the two forked ends. Remove the two screws and lift out the contact breaker

3.5 Checking the distributor points gap

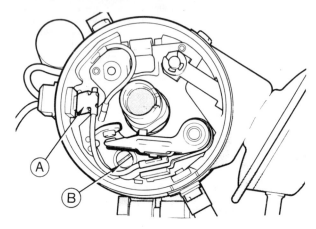

Fig. 4.4. Bosch distributor. Pull off LT lead (A) and remove points retaining screw (B) (Sec. 4)

Fig. 4.5. Ford distributor. Slacken screw (B), pull off the leads and remove the points retaining screws (A) (Sec. 4)

assembly (Fig. 4.5)..
6   Take care not to drop the retaining screws into the distributor, as the distributor must then be removed.
7   Refitting is the reverse procedure to removal. Smear a trace of grease onto the cam to lubricate the cam follower, then reset the gap, as described in Section 3.

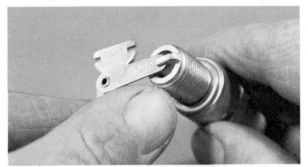

Measuring plug gap. A feeler gauge of the correct size (see ignition system specifications) should have a slight 'drag' when slid between the electrodes. Adjust gap if necessary

Adjusting plug gap. The plug gap is adjusted by bending the earth electrode inwards, or outwards, as necessary until the correct clearance is obtained. Note the use of the correct tool

Normal. Grey-brown deposits lightly coated core nose. Gap increasing by around 0.001 in (0.025 mm) per 1000 miles (1600 km). Plugs ideally suited to engine and engine in good condition

Carbon fouling. Dry, black, sooty deposits. Will cause weak spark and eventually misfire. Fault: over-rich fuel mixture. Check: carburettor mixture settings, float level and jet sizes; choke operation and cleanliness of air filter. Plugs can be re-used after cleaning

Oil fouling. Wet, oily deposits. Will cause weak spark and eventually misfire. Fault: worn bores/piston rings or valve guides; sometimes occurs (temporarily) during running-in period. Plugs can be re-used after thorough cleaning

Overheating. Electrodes have glazed appearance, core nose very white - few deposits. Fault: plug overheating. Check: plug value, ignition timing, fuel octane rating (too low) and fuel mixture (too weak). Discard plugs and cure fault immediately

Electrode damage. Electrodes burned away; core nose has burned, glazed appearance. Fault: initial pre-ignition. Check: for 'Overheating' but may be more severe. Discard plugs and remedy fault before piston or valve damage occurs

Split core nose (may appear initially as a crack). Damage is self-evident, but cracks will only show after cleaning. Fault: pre-ignition or wrong gap-setting technique. Check: ignition timing, cooling system, fuel octane rating (too low) and fuel mixture (too weak). Discard plugs, rectify fault immediately

5 Condenser - removal, testing and refitting

1   The purpose of the condenser (sometimes known as a capacitor) is to ensure that when the contact breaker points open there is no sparking across them which would waste voltage and cause wear.

2   The condenser is fitted in parallel with the contact breaker points. If it develops a short circuit, it will cause ignition failure as the contact breaker points will be prevented from correctly interrupting the low tension circuit.

3   If the engine becomes very difficult to start or begins to miss after several miles of running and the breaker points show signs of excessive burning, then the condition of the condenser must be suspect. One further test can be made by separating the points by hand with the ignition switched on. If this is accompanied by a bright flash, it is indicative that the condenser has failed.

4   Without special test equipment the only safe way to diagnose condenser trouble is to replace a suspected unit with a new one and note if there is any improvement.

5   To remove the condenser from the distributor take off the distributor cap and rotor arm.

6   *Bosch:* Release the condenser cable from the side of the distributor body and then undo and remove the screw that secures the condenser to the side of the distributor body. Lift away the condenser.

7   *Ford:* Slacken the self-tapping screw holding the condenser lead and low tension lead to the contact breaker points. Slide out the forked terminal on the end of the condenser low tension lead. Undo and remove the condenser retaining screw and remove the condenser from the breaker plate.

8   To refit the condenser, simply reverse the order of removal.

6 Distributor - lubrication

1   It is important that the distributor cam is lubricated with petroleum jelly or grease at 6000 miles (10000 km) or 6 monthly intervals. Also the automatic timing control weights and cam spindle are lubricated with engine oil.

2   Great care should be taken not to use too much lubricant as any excess that finds its way onto the contact breaker points could cause burning and misfiring.

3   To gain access to the cam spindle, lift away the distributor cap and rotor arm. Apply no more than two drops of engine oil onto the felt pad. This will run down the spindle when the engine is hot and lubricate the bearings.

4   To lubricate the automatic timing control allow a few drops of oil to pass through the holes in the contact breaker base plate through which the four sided cam emerges. Apply not more than one drop of oil to the pivot post of the moving contact breaker point. Wipe away excess oil and refit the rotor arm and distributor cap.

7 Distributor - removal

1   To remove the distributor from the engine, mark the four spark plug leads so that they may be refitted to the correct plugs and pull off the four spark plugs lead connectors.

2   Disconnect the high tension lead from the centre of the distributor cap by gripping the end cap and pulling. Also disconnect the low tension lead.

3   Pull off the rubber union holding the vacuum pipe to the distributor vacuum advance housing. Refer to the note in paragraph 5.

4   Remove the bolt which holds the distributor clamp plate to the engine and lift out the distributor (photo).

5   **Note:** If it is not wished to disturb the timing, turn the crankshaft until the timing marks are in line and the rotor arm is pointing to number one spark plug segment in the distributor cap. Mark the position of the rotor in relation to the distributor body. This will facilitate refitting the distributor providing the crankshaft is not moved whilst the distributor is away from the engine.

8 Distributor (breakerless) - dismantling and reassembly

1   With this type of distributor, only the cap and rotor arm are

7.4 Lifting out the distributor

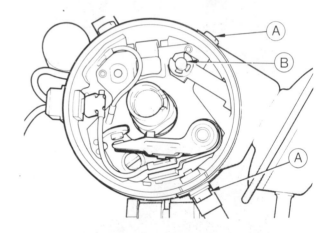

Fig. 4.6. Remove 'U' shaped clip (B), unscrew vacuum unit screws (A) and remove vacuum unit (Sec. 9)

renewable. In the event of failure, the complete unit will have to be renewed.

9 Distributor (Bosch) - dismantling and reassembly

1   The Bosch distributor is partly sealed, and only those components located above the base plate can be renewed (Fig. 4.7). These are the distributor cap, rotor arm, contact breaker points, condenser and vacuum unit. The skew gear at the bottom end of the shaft cannot be renewed.

2   With the distributor on the bench, release the two spring clips retaining the cap and lift away the cap.

3   Pull the rotor arm off the distributor cam spindle.

4   Remove the contact breaker points, as described in Section 3.

5   Unscrew and remove the condenser securing screw and lift away the condenser and connector.

6   Next carefully remove the 'U' shaped clip from the pull rod of the vacuum unit (Fig. 4.6).

7   Undo and remove the two screws that secure the vacuum unit to the side of the distributor body. Lift away the vacuum unit.

8   Undo and remove the screws that secure the distributor cap spring clip retainer to the side of the distributor body. Lift away the two clips and retainers.

9   Reassembly is the reverse of this procedure. Refer to Section 3 and adjust the contact breaker points.

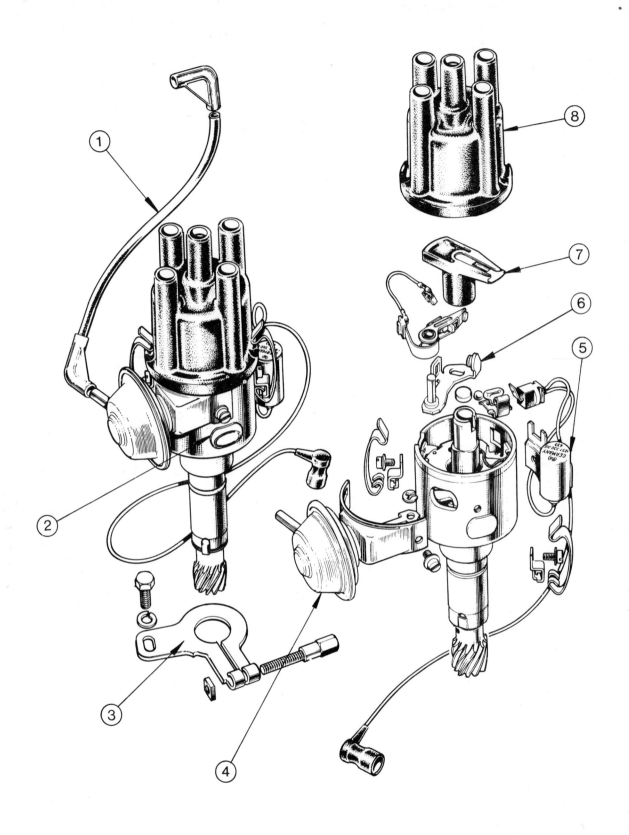

Fig. 4.7. Bosch distributor (Sec. 9)

1 Vacuum supply pipe	3 Distributor clamp plate	5 Condenser	7 Rotor arm
2 Distributor body	4 Vacuum unit	6 Fixed contact point	8 Distributor cap

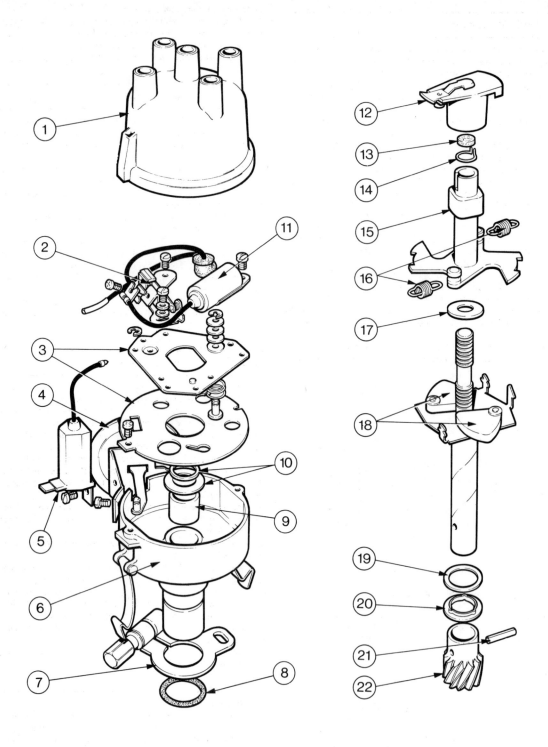

Fig. 4.8. Ford distributor (Sec. 10)

1	Distributor cap	6	Distributor body	12	Rotor arm	18	Governor weights
2	Contact points assembly	7	Distributor clamp plate	13	Felt wick	19	Spacer
3	Base plate assembly	8	Seal	14	Spring clip	20	Washer
4	Vacuum unit	9	Bush	15	Cam spindle	21	Spring pin
5	Radio suppressor (where applicable)	10	Thrust washers	16	Advance springs	22	Drive gear
		11	Condenser	17	Washer		

10 Distributor (Ford) - dismantling

1   With the distributor on the bench, release the two spring clips
retaining the cap and lift away the cap (Fig. 4.8).
2   Pull the rotor arm off the distributor cam spindle.
3   Next prise off the small circlip from the vacuum unit pivot post.
4   Take out the two screws that hold the breaker plate to the distributor
body and lift away.
5   Undo and remove the condenser retaining screw and lift away the
condenser.
6   Take off the circlip, flat washer and wave washers from the pivot
post. Separate the two plates by bringing the holding down screw
through the keyhole slot in the lower plate. Be careful not to lose the
spring now left on the pivot post (Fig. 4.9).
7   Pull the low tension wire and grommet from the lower plate.
8   Undo the two screws holding the vacuum unit to the body. Take off
the unit.
9   The mechanical advance is next removed but first make a careful
note of the assembly particularly which spring fits which post and the
position of the advance springs. The best method of doing this is to
make a sketch. Fig. 4.10 shows an **example** only.
10 Prise off the plastic bump stop, and remove the advance springs.
11 Dismantle the spindle by taking out the felt pad in the top of the
spindle. Expand the exposed circlip and take it out.
12 Now mark which slot in the mechanical advance plate is occupied by
the advance stop which stands up from the action plate, and lift the
cam from the spindle.
13 It is only necessary to remove the spindle and lower plate if it is
excessively worn. If this is the case, with a suitable diameter parallel pin

punch tap out the gear lock pin.
14 The gear may now be drawn off the shaft with a universal puller. If
there are no means of holding the legs these must be bound together
with wire to stop them springing apart during removal.
15 Finally withdraw the shaft from the distributor body.

11 Distributor - inspection and repair

1   Check the contact breaker points for wear, as described in Section 4.
Check the distributor cap for signs of tracking indicated by a thin black
line between the segments. Renew the cap if any signs of tracking are
found.
2   If the metal portion of the rotor arm is badly burned or loose, renew
the arm. If only slightly burned clean the end with a fine file. Check that
the contact spring has adequate pressure and the bearing surface is clean
and in good condition.
3   Check that the carbon brush in the distributor cap is unbroken and
stands proud of its holder.
4   Examine the centrifugal weights and pivots for wear and the advance
springs for slackness. They can best be checked by comparing with new
parts. If they are slack they must be renewed.
5   Check the points assembly for fit on the breaker plate, and the cam
follower for wear.
6   Examine the fit of the spindle in the distributor body. If there is
excessive side movement it will be necessary to either fit a new bush or
obtain a new body.

12 Distributor (Ford) - reassembly

1   Reassembly is a straightforward reversal of the dismantling process
but there are several points which must be noted.
2   Lubricate with engine oil the balance weights and other parts of the
mechanical advance mechanism, the distributor shaft and the portion of
the shaft on which the cam bears, during assembly. Do not oil excessively
but ensure these parts are adequately lubricated.
3   When fitting the spindle, first refit the thrust washers below the
lower breaker plate before inserting into the distributor body. Next fit
the wave washer at the lower end and refit the drive gear. Secure it
with a new pin.
4   Assemble the upper and lower spindle with the advance stop
in the correct slot (the one which was marked) in the mechanical
advance plate.
5   After assembling the advance weights and springs, check that they
move freely without binding.
6   Before assembling the breaker plates make sure that the nylon
bearing studs are correctly located in their holes in the upper breaker
plate, and the small earth spring is fitted on the pivot post (Fig. 4.9).
7   As the upper breaker plate is being refitted pass the holding down
stud through the keyhole slot in the lower plate.
8   Hold the upper plate in position and refit the wave washers, flat
washer and circlip (Fig. 4.9).
9   When all is assembled reset the contact breaker points, as described
in Section 3.

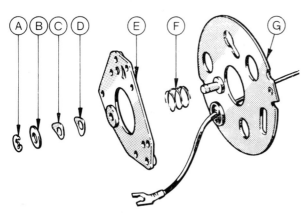

Fig. 4.9. Base plate assembly (Sec. 10)

A   Circlip   E   Upper plate
B   Washer   F   Earth spring
C   Wave washer   G   Lower plate
D   Wave washer

13 Distributor - refitting

1   If a new shaft or gear has not been fitted (ie, the original parts are
still being used), it will not be necessary to retime the ignition.
2   Insert the distributor into its location with the vacuum advance
assembly to the rear.
3   Notice that the rotor arm rotates as the gears mesh. The rotor arm
must settle in exactly the same direction that it was in before the
distributor was removed. To do this lift out the assembly far enough
to rotate the shaft one tooth at a time lowering it home to check the
direction of the rotor arm. When it points in the desired direction with
the assembly fully home fit the distributor clamp plate bolt and plain
washer.
4   With the distributor assembly fitted reconnect the low tension lead.
Reconnect the HT lead to the centre of the distributor cap and refit the
rubber union of the vacuum pipe which runs from the inlet manifold to
the side of the vacuum advance unit.
5   If the engine has been disturbed, refer to Section 15.

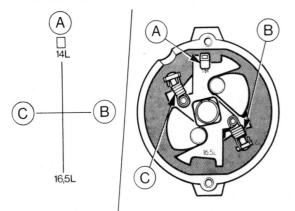

Fig. 4.10. Sketch of cam plate and advance spring location (Sec. 10)

A   Bump stop   B   Thin spring   C   Thick spring

14 Spark plugs and HT leads

1   The correct functioning of the spark plugs is vital for the correct running and efficiency of the engine.

2   At the specified intervals, the plugs should be removed, examined, cleaned, and if worn excessively, renewed. The condition of the spark plugs will also tell much about the overall condition of the engine (see page 87).

3   The plugs fitted as standard are as listed in Specifications at the beginning of this Chapter. If the tip and insulator nose are covered with hard black looking deposits, then this is indicative that the mixture is too rich. Should the plug be black and oily, then it is likely that the engine is fairly worn, as well as the mixture being too rich.

4   If the insulator nose of the spark plug is clean and white, with no deposits, this is indicative of a weak mixture, or too hot a plug (a hot plug transfers heat away from the electrode slowly - a cold plug transfers it away quickly).

5   If the insulator nose is covered with light tan to greyish brown deposits, then the mixture is correct and it is likely that the engine is in good condition.

6   If there are any traces of long brown tapering stains on the outside of the white portion of the plug, then the plug will have to be renewed, as this shows that there is a faulty joint between the plug body and the insulator, and compression is being allowed to leak away.

7   This spark plug gap is of considerable importance, as, if it is too large or too small, the size of the spark and its efficiency will be seriously impaired. The spark plug gap should be set to the figure given in the Specifications at the beginning of this Chapter.

8   To set it, measure the gap with a feeler gauge, and then bend open, or close, the outer plug electrode until the correct gap is achieved. The centre electrode should never be bent as this may crack the insulation and cause plug failure if nothing worse.

9   When refitting the plugs refit the leads from the distributor in the correct firing order which is 1, 2, 4, 3 (No. 1 cylinder being the one nearest the crankshaft pulley).

10 The plug leads require no routine attention other than being kept clean and wiped over regularly.

11 At intervals of 6000 miles (10000 km) or 6 months, however, remove the leads from the plugs and distributor (one at a time) and make sure no water has found its way onto the connections. Take care that the plug lead end fitting only is pulled; do not pull the leads or they may become detached from the end fitting.

15 Ignition timing (when refitting the distributor)

1   When a new gear or shaft has been fitted, or the engine has been rotated, or if a new assembly is being fitted, it will be necessary to retime the ignition. Carry it out this way.

2   Look up the initial advance (static) for the particular model in the Specifications at the beginning of this Chapter.

3   Turn the engine until No. 1 piston is coming up to TDC on the compression stroke. This can be checked by removing No. 1 spark plug and feeling the pressure being developed in the cylinder or by removing the rocker cover and noting when both inlet and exhaust valves are closed.

4   If this check is not made it is very easy to set the timing 180° out.

5   The engine can be turned by one of three methods. Either by using an 'inching' device, found in certain types of proprietary test equipment, or a suitable socket and ratchet on the crankshaft pulley bolt, or by engaging top gear and edging the car along.

6   Continue turning the engine until the appropriate timing mark on the crankshaft pulley is in line with the pointer (photo).

Breakerless distributor

7   Position the distributor in the block with one of the armature 'spokes' aligned as shown in Fig. 4.11 and the rotor in the No. 1 firing position (ie. as if aligned with the No. 1 spark plug lead terminal in the distributor cap).

All models

8   Continue turning the engine until the appropriate timing mark on the crankshaft pulley is in line with the pointer (photo). Now, with the vacuum advance unit pointing to the rear of the engine and the

15.6/8 Aligning the timing notch on the crankshaft pulley with the appropriate mark on the timing cover

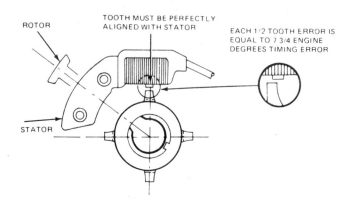

Fig. 4.11. Armature position for distributor (breakerless) installation (Sec. 15)

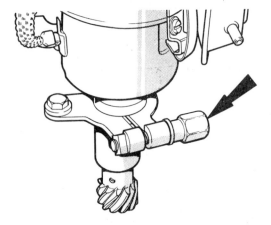

Fig. 4.12. Distributor clamp pinch bolt (Sec. 15)

rotor arm in the same position as was noted before removal, insert the distributor into its location. Notice that the rotor arm rotates as the gears mesh. Lift out the distributor far enough to rotate the shaft one tooth at a time, lowering it home to check the direction of the rotor arm. When it points in the desired direction with the assembly fully home fit the distributor clamp plate, bolt and plain washer.

9   Slacken the clamp plate pinch bolt (Fig. 4.12) and carefully turn the distributor body until the contact breaker points are just opening when the rotor is pointing to the contact in the distributor cap which is connected to No. 1 spark plug. A convenient way is to put a mark on the outside of the distributor body in line with the segment in the

cover, so that it shows when the cover is removed.

10 If this position cannot be reached, check that the drive gear has meshed on the correct tooth by lifting out the distributor once more. If necessary, rotate the driveshaft gear one tooth and try again.

11 Tighten the pinch bolt enough to hold the distributor, but do not overtighten.

12 Set in this way, the timing should be approximately correct but small adjustments may have to be made following a road test, or with a timing light, Section 16.

13 The setting of a distributor including the amount of vacuum and mechanical advance can only be accurately carried out on an electrical tester. Alterations to the vacuum advance shims or tension on the mechanical advance unit springs will change the characteristics of the unit.

16 Ignition timing (using a timing light)

1 Look up the initial (static) advance for the particular model in the Specifications at the beginning of this Chapter. Locate the appropriate mark on the timing chain cover and the crankshaft pulley (photo 15.6) and highlight them with a white chalk or a paint mark.

2 Disconnect the vacuum line from the distributor, and temporarily plug the line.

3 Connect a proprietary ignition timing light in accordance with the manufacturer's instructions to No. 1 spark plug lead, then run the engine until warm. Allow the engine to idle, shine the timing light onto the timing cover and note the position of the white line with respect to the timing pointer. If the line and pointer do not coincide, stop the engine, slacken the distributor clamp bolt, run the engine again and position the distributor until the timing marks do coincide. **Note:** If the timing marks cannot be made to coincide, or if the engine will not start and the ignition timing is suspected as being incorrect, refer to Section 15 to ensure that the distributor is correctly positioned.

4 Having set the timing, stop the engine and tighten the distributor clamp bolt, then run the engine up to 2500 rpm (approx) and check that the timing advances (indicating that the centrifugal advance is operating).

5 Stop the engine, unplug and reconnect the distributor vacuum line then again run the engine up to 2500 rpm (approx) and check that a greater amount of advance is obtained than at paragraph 4 (indicating that the vacuum advance is operating).

6 If a satisfactory result is not obtained in the tests at paragraphs 4 and 5, further investigation of the distributor should be carried out.

7 On completion of any testing, ensure that all test connections are removed.

17 Ignition system - fault diagnosis

By far the majority of breakdown and running troubles are caused by faults in the ignition system either in the low tension or high tension circuits.

There are two main symptoms indicating faults. Either the engine will not start or fire, or the engine is difficult to start and misfires. If it is a regular misfire, (ie. the engine is running on only two or three cylinders), the fault is almost sure to be in the secondary or high tension circuit. If the misfiring is intermittent the fault could be in either the high or low tension circuits. If the car stops suddenly, or will not start at all, it is likely that the fault is in the low tension circuit. Loss of power and overheating, apart from faulty carburation settings, are normally due to faults in the distributor or to incorrect ignition timing.

Engine fails to start

1 If the engine fails to start and the car was running normally when it was last used, first check there is fuel in the petrol tank. If the engine turns over normally on the starter motor and the battery is evidently well charged, then the fault may be in either the high or low tension circuits. First check the HT circuit. **Note:** If the battery is known to be fully charged, and the ignition light comes on, and the starter motor fails to turn the engine **check the tightness of the leads on the battery terminals** and also the secureness of the earth lead to its **connection to the body.** It is quite common for the leads to have worked loose, even if they look and feel secure. If one of the battery terminal posts gets very hot when trying to work the starter motor this is a sure indication of a faulty connection to that terminal.

2 One of the commonest reasons for bad starting is wet or damp spark plug leads and distributor. Remove the distributor cap. If condensation is visible internally dry the cap with a rag and also wipe over the leads. Refit the cap.

3 If the engine still fails to start, check that voltage is reaching the plugs by disconnecting each plug lead in turn at the spark plug end, and holding the end of the cable about 3/16 inch (5 mm) away from the cylinder block. Spin the engine on the starter motor.

4 Sparking between the end of the cable and the block should be fairly strong with a strong regular blue spark. (Hold the lead with rubber to avoid electric shocks). If voltage is reaching the plugs, then remove them and clean and regap them. The engine should now start.

5 If there is no spark at the plug leads, take off the HT lead from the centre of the distributor cap and hold it to the block as before. Spin the engine on the starter once more. A rapid succession of blue sparks between the end of the lead and the block indicate that the coil is in order and that the distributor cap is cracked, the rotor arm is faulty, or the carbon brush in the top of the distributor cap is not making good contact with the spring on the rotor arm. Possibly, the points are in bad condition. Clean and reset them as described in this Chapter, Section 3.

6 If there are no sparks from the end of the lead from the coil, check the connections at the coil end of the lead. If it is in order start checking the low tension circuit.

7 Use a 12v voltmeter or a 12v bulb and two lengths of wire. With the ignition switched on and the points open, test between the low tension wire to the coil (it is marked 15 or +) and earth. No reading indicates a break in the supply from the ignition switch. Check the connections at the switch to see if any are loose. Refit them and the engine should run. A reading shows a faulty coil or condenser, or broken lead between the coil and the distributor.

8 Take the condenser wire off the points assembly and with the points open test between the moving point and earth. If there now is a reading then the fault is in the condenser. Fit a new one and the fault is cleared.

9 With no reading from the moving point to earth, take a reading between earth and the — or 1 terminal of the coil. A reading here shows a broken wire which will need to be renewed between the coil and distributor. No reading confirms that the coil has failed and must be renewed, after which the engine will run once more. Remember to refit the condenser wire to the points assembly. For these tests it is sufficient to separate the points with a piece of dry paper while testing with the points open.

Engine misfires

10 If the engine misfires regularly run it at a fast idling speed. Pull off each of the plug caps in turn and listen to the note of the engine. Hold the plug cap in a dry cloth or with a rubber glove as additional protection against a shock from HT supply.

11 No difference in engine running will be noticed when the lead from the defective circuit is removed. Removing the lead from one of the good cylinders will accentuate the misfire.

12 Remove it about 3/16 inch (5 mm) away from the block. Re-start the engine. If the sparking is fairly strong and regular, the fault must lie in the spark plug.

13 The plug may be loose, the insulation may be cracked, or the points may have burnt away giving too wide a gap for the spark to jump. Worse still, one of the points may have broken off. Either renew the plug, or clean it, reset the gap, and then test it.

14 If there is no spark at the end of the plug lead, or if it is weak and intermittent, check the ignition lead from the distributor to the plug. If the insulation is cracked or perished, renew the lead. Check the connections at the distributor cap.

15 If there is still no spark, examine the distributor cap carefully for tracking. This can be recognised by a very thin black line running between two or more electrodes, or between an electrode and some other part of the distributor. These lines are paths which now conduct electricity across the cap thus letting it run to earth. The only answer is a new distributor cap.

16 Apart from the ignition timing being incorrect, other causes of misfiring have already been dealt with under the Section dealing with the failure of the engine to start. To recap, these are that:

a) The coil may be faulty giving an intermittent misfire;
b) There may be a damaged wire or loose connection in the low tension circuit;
c) The condenser may be faulty; or

*d) There may be a mechanical fault in the distributor (broken
     driving spindle or contact breaker spring).*

17 If the ignition timing is too far retarded, it should be noted that the engine will tend to overheat, and there will be quite noticeable drop in power. If the engine is overheating and the power is down, and the ignition timing is correct, then the carburettor should be checked, as it is likely that this is where the fault lies.

Chapter 5 Clutch

Contents

Specifications

Clutch type	Single dry plate, diaphragm spring

Actuation ... ... Cable

Size

960 and 1100 cc	6.5 in (165 mm)
1300 cc and 1600 cc	7.5 in (190 mm)

Lining thickness

All models	0.12 in (3.05 mm)

Torque wrench settings

	lbf ft	kgf m
Gearbox to engine flange bolts	30	4.0
Pressure plate to flywheel	7	1.0

1 General description

All models covered by this manual are fitted with a single diaphragm spring clutch. The unit comprises a steel cover which is dowelled and bolted to the rear face of the flywheel and contains the pressure plate, diaphragm spring and fulcrum rings (Fig. 5.1).

The clutch driven plate (disc) is free to slide along the splined gearbox input shaft and is held in position between the flywheel and the pressure plate by the pressure of the pressure plate spring. Friction lining material is riveted to the driven plate and it has a spring cushioned hub to absorb transmission shocks and to help ensure a smooth take off.

The circular diaphragm spring is mounted on shoulder pins and held in place in the cover by two fulcrum rings. The spring is also held to the pressure plate by three spring steel clips which are riveted in position.

The clutch is actuated by a cable controlled by the clutch pedal. The clutch release mechanism consists of a release fork and bearing which are in permanent contact with the release fingers on the pressure plate assembly. There should therefore never be any free-play at the release fork. Wear of the friction material in the clutch is adjusted by means of a cable adjuster at the clutch pedal. When the pedal is released, the cable tension is applied by the tension spring (Fig. 5.1). When the pedal is depressed, the pawl on the pedal engages in a tooth on the toothed segment. As the clutch disc wears, the toothed segment is pulled round by the tension spring.

Depressing the clutch pedal actuates the clutch release arm by means of the cable. The release arm pushes the release bearing forward to bear against the release fingers so moving the centre of the diaphragm two annular rings which act as fulcrum points. As the centre of the spring is pushed in, the outside of the spring is pushed out, so moving the pressure plate backward and disengaging the pressure plate from the driven plate.

When the clutch pedal is released, the diaphragm spring forces the pressure plate into contact with the friction linings on the driven plate and at the same time pushes it a fraction of an inch forward on its splines. The driven plate is now firmly sandwiched between the pressure plate and the flywheel, so the drive is taken up.

2 Clutch - removal

1 To remove the clutch it is necessary to disconnect the engine and transmission assembly. This can be done by either removing the engine and transmission complete, and then separating them on the bench (Chapter 1), or by removing the transmission only (Chapter 6).
2 Remove the clutch assembly by unscrewing the six bolts holding the pressure plate assembly to the rear face of the flywheel. Unscrew the bolts diagonally, half a turn at a time, to prevent distortion to the cover flange.
3 With all the bolts and spring washers removed lift the clutch assembly off the locating dowels (photo). The driven plate (clutch disc) may fall out at this stage as it is not attached to either the clutch cover assembly or the flywheel.

3 Clutch - overhaul

1 It is not practical to dismantle the pressure plate assembly. If a new clutch driven plate is being fitted it is false economy not to renew the release bearing at the same time. This will preclude having to renew it at a later date when wear on the clutch lining is very small.
2 If the pressure plate assembly requires renewal (see Section 5) an exchange unit must be purchased. This will have been accurately set up and balanced to very fine limits.

4 Clutch - inspection

1 Examine the clutch driven plate friction lining for wear and loose rivets and the plate for rim distortion, cracks, broken hub springs, and worn splines. The surface of the friction linings may be highly glazed, but as long as the clutch material pattern can be clearly seen this is

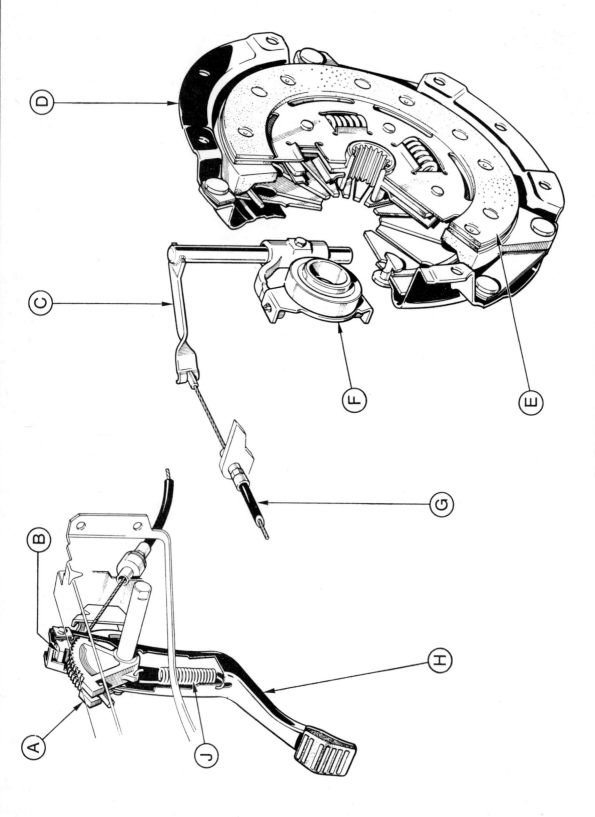

Fig. 5.1. Clutch assembly (Sec. 1)

A Toothed segment
B Pawl
C Release arm

D Clutch pressure plate
E Clutch disc
F Release forked bearing

G Clutch cable
H Clutch pedal
J Tension spring

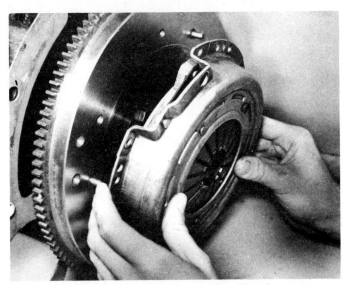

2.3 Removing the clutch pressure plate assembly (Sec. 2)

Fig. 5.2. Refitting and centralising the clutch disc (Sec. 5)

Fig. 5.3. Remove the release arm bolt (Sec. 6)

satisfactory. Compare the amount of lining wear with a new clutch driven plate at the stores in your local garage, and if the linings are more than three quarters worn renew the driven plate.

2   It is always best to renew the clutch driven plate as an assembly to preclude further trouble, but, if it is wished to merely renew the linings, the rivets should be drilled out and not knocked out with a punch. The manufacturers do not advise that only the linings are renewed and personal experience dictates that it is far more satisfact-ory to renew the driven plate complete than to try and economise by

fitting only new friction linings.

3   Check the machined faces of the flywheel and the pressure plate. If either is grooved it should be machined until smooth or renewed.

4   If the pressure plate is cracked or split it is essential that an exchange unit is fitted, also if the pressure of the diaphragm spring is suspect.

5   Check the release bearing for smoothness of operation. There should be no harshness and no slackness in it. It should spin reasonably freely bearing in mind it has been pre-packed with grease.

5   Clutch - refitting

1   It is important that no oil or grease gets onto the clutch driven plate friction linings, or the pressure plate and flywheel faces. It is advisable to refit the clutch with clean hands and to wipe down the pressure plate and flywheel faces with a clean dry rag before reassembly begins.

2   Place the clutch driven plate against the flywheel, ensuring that it is the correct way round. The flywheel side of the clutch driven plate is smooth (Fig. 5.2). If the driven plate is fitted the wrong way round, it will be quite impossible to operate the clutch.

3   Refit the clutch cover assembly loosely on the dowels. Refit the six bolts and spring washers, and tighten them finger tight so that the clutch driven plate is gripped but can still be moved.

4   The clutch driven plate must now be centralised so that when the engine and gearbox are mated, the gearbox input shaft splines will pass through the splines in the centre of the driven plate hub.

5   Centralisation can be carried out quite easily by inserting a round bar or long screwdriver through the hole in the centre of the clutch, so that the end of the bar rests in the small hole in the end of the crank-shaft. Ideally an old input shaft should be used (Fig. 5.2).

6   Using the hole in the end of the crankshaft as a fulcrum, moving the bar sideways or up and down will move the clutch driven plate in the necessary direction to achieve centralisation.

7   Centralisation is easily judged by removing the bar and moving the driven plate hub in relation to the hole in the centre of the clutch cover diaphragm spring. When the hub appears exactly in the centre of the hole all is correct. Alternatively, the input shaft will centre the clutch hub exactly obviating the need for visual alignment.

8   Tighten the clutch bolts firmly in a diagonal sequence to ensure that the cover plate is pulled down evenly and without distortion of the flange. Finally tighten the bolts down to the specified torque.

6   Clutch release bearing - renewal

1   With the gearbox and engine separated to provide access to the clutch, attention can be given to the release bearing located in the bellhousing, over the input shaft.

2   The release bearing is an important component and unless it is nearly new it is a mistake not to renew it during an overhaul of the clutch.

3   To remove the release bearing, first remove the bolt securing the release arm (Fig. 5.3) and pull out the shaft.

4   The release fork and bearing can then be pulled off the input shaft.

5   To free the bearing from the release fork, simply unhook it (photo).

6   Refitting is a reversal of this procedure.

7   Clutch cable - renewal

1   To disconnect the clutch cable from the release arm, depress and release the cable (Fig. 5.4). Using a pair of pliers, unhook the cable end from the release arm.

2   Remove the two screws from the lower dash trim panel, bend back the metal tabs and remove the panel.

3   Pull the clutch pedal upwards and rotate the toothed segment forwards against the pull of the tension spring.

4   Unhook the clutch cable from the toothed segment, and allow the segment to swivel back (Fig. 5.5A).

5   Pull the cable forwards through the gap between the pedal and the adjusting device, and remove it from the engine compartment.

6   To refit the clutch cable, hook one end into the car and through the gap between the pedal and the adjusting device.

7   Pull the clutch pedal upwards to disengage the pawl, and swing the

6.5 Unhooking the release fork from the bearing (Sec. 6)

Fig. 5.6. Removing the toothed segment and tension spring (Sec. 8)

Fig. 5.7. Removing the automatic adjustment pawl

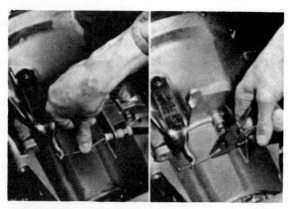

Fig. 5.4. Disconnecting the clutch cable from the release arm (Sec. 7)

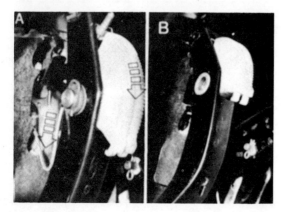

Fig. 5.5. Disconnecting the clutch cable (A) and removing the pedal (B) (Sec. 7 and 8)

8 Clutch pedal and ratchet - removal and refitting

1   Unhook both ends of the clutch cable, but do not fully remove it. Refer to Section 7, paragraphs 1 to 5 inclusive.
2   Pull the spring clip from the pedal shaft (Fig. 5.5A), pull the complete pedal assembly sideways off its shafts (Fig. 5.5B).
3   Remove the two toothed segment bushes and lift out the segment and tension spring (Fig. 5.6).
4   Remove one of the spring clips and pull out the pawl retaining shaft. Lift out the pawl and its tension spring (Fig. 5.7).
5   Refitting is the reverse of the removal procedure, but a new spring clip should be used on the pedal shaft for safety's sake, and a little general purpose grease applied to the pedal pivot. Also, if there is wear in the pivot bush, a new bush should be fitted.
6   Finally refit the cable ends as described in Section 7, paragraphs 6 to 9 inclusive.

9 Fault diagnosis

There are four main faults to which the clutch and release mechanism are prone. They may occur by themselves, or in conjunction with any of the other faults. They are clutch squeal, slip, spin and judder.

Clutch squeal - diagnosis and remedy
1   If, on taking up the drive or when changing gear, the clutch squeals, this is indicative of a badly worn clutch release bearing.
2   As well as regular wear due to normal use, wear of the clutch release bearing is much accentuated if the clutch is ridden or held down for

toothed segment forwards.
8   Hook the clutch cable into the segment, and allow the segment to move backwards.
9   Finally, operate the clutch pedal two or three times, checking that the adjusting device is operating correctly, and refit the lower dash trim panel.

long periods in gear, with the engine running. To minimise wear of this component the car should always be taken out of gear at traffic lights and for similar hold ups.

3   The clutch release bearing is not an expensive item, but is difficult to get at.

Clutch slip - diagnosis and remedy

4   Clutch slip is a self-evident condition which occurs when the clutch driven plate is badly worn, oil or grease have got onto the flywheel or pressure plate faces, or the pressure plate itself is faulty.

5   The reason for clutch slip is that due to one of the faults mentioned above, there is either insufficient pressure from the pressure plate, or insufficient friction from the driven plate to ensure solid drive.

6   If small amounts of oil get into the clutch, they will be burnt off under the heat of the clutch engagement, and in the process, gradually darken the linings. Excessive oil on the clutch will burn off leaving a carbon deposit which can cause quite bad slip, or fierceness, spin and judder.

7   If clutch slip is suspected, and confirmation of this condition is required, there are several tests which can be made.

8   With the engine in second or third gear and pulling lightly sudden depression of the accelerator pedal may cause the engine to increase its speed without any increase in road speed. Easing off on the accelerator will then give a definite drop in engine speed without the car slowing.

9   In extreme cases of clutch slip the engine will race under normal acceleration conditions.

10 The remedy is to renew the defective part, and if applicable, to trace and rectify the oil leak.

Clutch spin - diagnosis and remedy

11 Clutch spin is a condition which occurs when there is an obstruction in the clutch, either in the gearbox input shaft or in the operating lever itself, or oil may have partially burnt off the clutch lining and have left a resinous deposit which is causing the clutch disc to stick to the pressure plate or flywheel.

12 The reason for clutch spin is that due to any, or a combination of, the faults just listed, the clutch pressure plate is not completely freeing from the driven plate even with the clutch pedal fully depressed.

13 If clutch spin is suspected, the condition can be confirmed by the following faults. Extreme difficulty in engaging first gear from rest, difficulty in changing gear, and very sudden take up of the clutch drive at the fully depressed end of the clutch pedal travel as the clutch is released.

14 Check that the clutch adjusting device is working properly.

15 If these points are checked and found to be in order then the fault lies internally in the clutch, and it will be necessary to remove the clutch for examination.

Clutch judder - diagnosis and cure

16 Clutch judder is a self-evident condition which occurs when the gearbox or engine mountings are loose or too flexible, when there is oil on the face of the clutch friction plate, or when the clutch pressure plate has been incorrectly adjusted.

17 The reason for clutch judder is that due to one of the faults just listed, the clutch pressure plate is not freeing smoothly from the driven plate and is snatching.

18 Clutch judder normally occurs when the clutch pedal is released in first or reverse gears, and the whole car shudders as it moves backward or forward.

Chapter 6 Transmission

Contents

Specifications

Type	Four forward gears with synchromesh, one reverse gear	

Ratios
	960 cc, 1100 cc and 1300 cc	1600 cc
First gear	3.58 : 1	3.58 : 1
Second gear	2.05 : 1	2.05 : 1
Third gear	1.35 : 1	1.30 : 1
Top gear	0.96 : 1	0.88 : 1
Reverse gear	3.77 : 1	

Final drive ratios
	Standard	Optional
960 cc		
low compression	3.84 : 1	4.06 : 1
high compression	4.06 : 1	4.29 : 1
1100 cc	4.06 : 1	—
1300 cc	3.84 : 1	—
1600 cc	3.58 : 1	—

Speedometer driven gear
Number of teeth:

with 135SR x 12 tyres	21
with 145SR x 12 and 155SR x 12 tyres	20

Oil capacity	5 pints (2.8 litres)

Oil type	SAE 80 hypoid

Torque wrench settings
	lbf ft	kgf m
Gearbox to engine flange bolts	30	4.0
Gearbox to crossmember bolts	65	9.0
Small housing section to large housing section	18	2.5
Small housing section cover plate	7.2	1.0
Gear lever retaining nut	22	3.0
Final drive gear to housing	60	8.3
Gear lever housing to floor pan	6.5	0.9
Selector rod stabiliser Allen key	39	5.5

1 General description

1 The complete transmission assembly consists of the clutch, gearbox, final drive or differential assembly, the gear linkage and selector mechanism and the driveshafts. The clutch and driveshafts are dealt with in separate Chapters. This Chapter covers the remaining items which, with the exception of the gear linkage, are contained within the gearbox casing. This casing is made in two halves from a light alloy. Fig. 6.1 is a cutaway view of the gearbox, showing the driveshafts fitted to the 1100 cc variant.

2 The gearbox consists of two shafts, the input shaft, and the output or main shaft. The helically cut forward gears on the two shafts are in constant mesh (Fig. 6.2), the gears being engaged through blocker ring synchromesh units. The reverse gear has straight cut teeth, and drives the toothed 1st/2nd gear synchroniser hub on the output shaft through an idler gear.

3 Power from the output shaft is transmitted to the drive gear which is bolted to the differential carrier (Fig. 6.2). Rotation of the differential rotates the pinion gears and side gears, and so power is fed to the driveshafts.

4 Transverse movement of the gear lever rotates the gear linkage

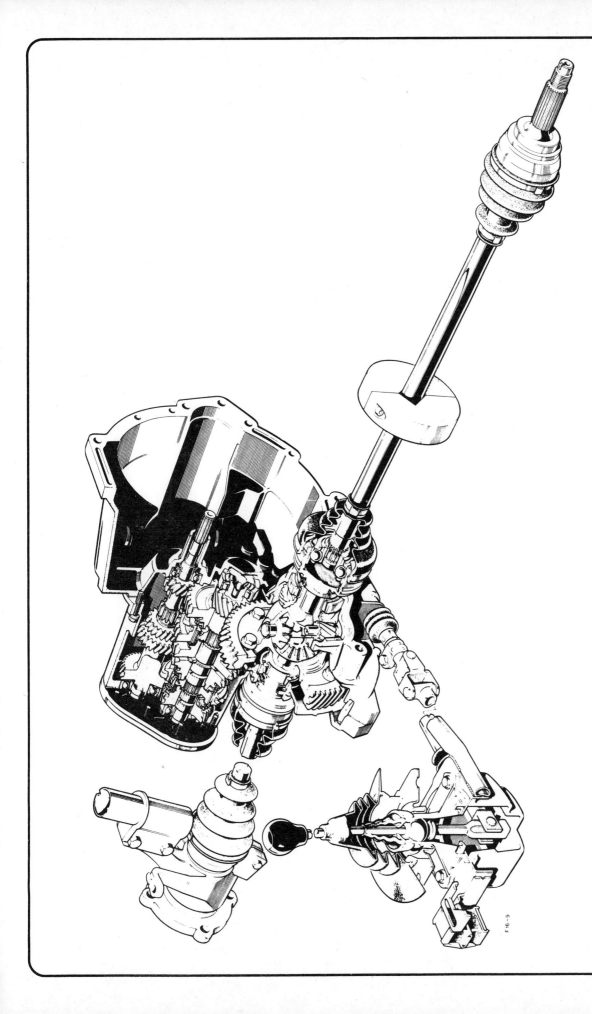

F·16 - 9

Fig. 6.1. Cutaway view of transmission with 1100 cc driveshaft (Sec. 1)

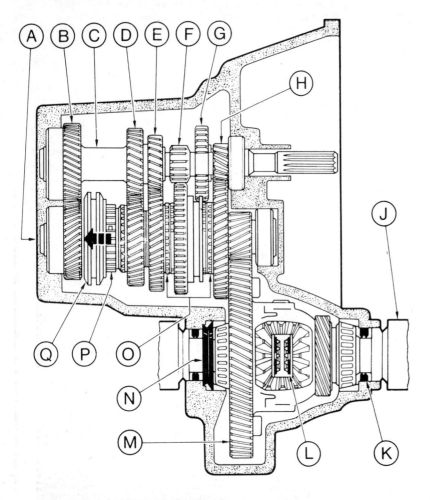

Fig. 6.2. Transmission and differential gear (Sec. 1)

A   Output shaft (mainshaft)
B   4th gear pair
C   Input shaft
D   3rd gear pair
E   2nd gear pair
F   Reverse gear pair
G   Reverse idler gear
H   1st gear pair
J   Driveshaft joint (right-hand)
K   Oil seal
L   Driveshaft circlip
M   Differential gear
N   Sprung thrust washers
O   1st/2nd synchroniser assembly
P   3rd/4th synchroniser assembly
Q   3rd/4th selector sleeve in 4th gear

Fig. 6.3. Unscrew the speedometer cable (sec. 2)

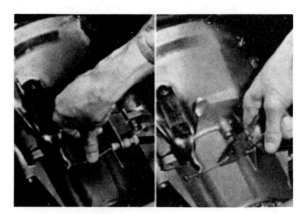

Fig. 6.4. Unhooking the clutch cable (Sec. 2)

shaft. This rotary movement rotates an internal guide shaft. A cam on the guide shaft then engages with either the 1st/2nd selector fork, the 3rd/4th selector fork or the reverse idler gear lever. Longitudinal movement of the gear lever pushes or pulls the gear linkage shaft, which moves the guide shaft. The cam on the guide shaft then moves the selected fork, and engages the synchromesh. A blocker plate with a spring loaded interlock pin prevents engagement of more than one gear.

2   Transmission - removal

1   The transmission can be removed from the vehicle as a unit with the engine, as described in Chapter 1, or as a separate item.

2   When removing the transmission alone, the bolts holding the engine to its crossmember have to be removed. In order to support the weight of the engine, it will be necessary to have an engine hoist available. If this is not possible, a strong jack may be employed. In addition, the vehicle will have to be raised far enough to allow comfortable working room under the vehicle.

3   Before commencing operations, select 4th gear to make gearshift adjustment easier when refitting.

4   Open the bonnet and disconnect the battery cables.

5   Unscrew and remove the speedometer cable from the engine compartment (Fig. 6.3).

6   Press down on the clutch cable (Fig. 6.4) and unhook the cable

from the release arm. Pull the cable through its bracket.

7   Jack up the front of the vehicle to a comfortable height, and fit axle stands.

8   Support the weight of the engine by either fitting slings around the engine and using a hoist, or by placing a jack under the sump, using a block of wood between the sump and the jack.

9   Remove the four upper engine to transmission flange bolts from above (Fig. 6.5).

10 Unscrew the gear selector pinch bolt and disconnect the selector rod (Fig. 6.6). Unhook the selector rod spring.

11 Slacken both stabiliser bar inner locknuts, slacken the outer locknut and unscrew the Allen key from the transmission housing (Fig. 6.7).

12 Remove the split pin and castellated nut from each of the two track rod outer ends, and separate the balljoints (Fig. 6.8).

13 Remove the left-hand track control arm from the body mounting, and detach the balljoint from the pivot bearing at the outer end (Fig. 6.9).

14 Disconnect the left-hand driveshaft joint from the transmission by inserting a large screwdriver between the gearbox and the joint. Knock the screwdriver down with the heel of the hand, while pulling the wheel and driveshaft outwards (Fig. 6.10). **Note:** As soon as this joint is disconnected, the transmission oil will leak out, so be ready with a drain tray!

15 Suspend the driveshaft with wire to avoid undue strain on the outer joint.

Fig. 6.5. Removing the four upper flange bolts (Sec. 2)

Fig. 6.6. Disconnect the selector rod (Sec. 2)

Fig. 6.7. Slacken the inner stabiliser nuts and unscrew the Allen screw (Sec. 2)

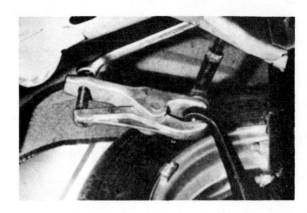

Fig. 6.8. Disconnecting the track rod end (Sec. 2)

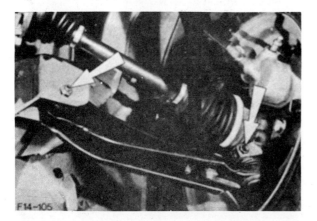

Fig. 6.9. Remove the left-hand track control arm (right-hand is similar) (Sec. 2)

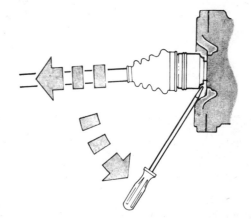

Fig. 6.10. Disconnecting the left-hand driveshaft (Sec. 2)

16 Place a suitable plug in position (Fig. 6.11) to avoid displacement of the drive pinions.

17 Remove the right-hand track control arm from the body mounting, and detach the balljoint from the pivot bearing at the outer end (Fig. 6.9).

18 *1300/1600 cc models.* Unscrew and remove the Allen screws around the driveshaft joint at the centre of the right-hand driveshaft. Suspend the driveshaft from the floor pan to prevent undue strain on the outer joint.

19 Unscrew the nuts securing the right-hand driveshaft centre bearing bracket to the engine and remove the bracket.

20 Using a large screwdriver between the transmission casing and the universal joint, tap out the joint.

21 *960 cc and 1100 cc models.* Using a large screwdriver between the transmission casing and the joint, tap out the right-hand driveshaft (Fig. 6.12). Suspend the driveshaft from the floor pan to prevent undue strain on the outer joint.

22 *All models.* Disconnect the starter motor cables, remove the two bolts and lift out the starter motor.

23 Unscrew the two lower engine to transmission flange bolts, remove the three engine to transmission crossmember mounting bolts and lift out the transmission.

---

3 Transmission - dismantling

1 Place the complete unit on a firm bench or table and ensure that you have the following equipment available, in addition to the normal range of spanners, sockets and so on.

a) *Good quality circlip pliers, internal and external.*
b) *Hide, rubber or copper headed mallet, at least 2 lb (0.15 kg).*
c) *Suitable drifts.*
d) *Small containers for needle rollers circlips and so on (an egg box can be very useful!)*
e) *Engineers vice mounted on a firm bench.*
f) *A selection of metal tubing.*

2 Read the whole of this Section, referring to Fig. 6.14 before starting work.

3 Unscrew and remove the bolt holding the clutch release bearing fork to the operating arm (photo) and lift out the arm.

4 Slide the clutch release bearing off the input shaft splines.

5 Unscrew the selector shaft locking pin retainer, and lift out the spring and locking pin (Fig. 6.13).

6 Remove the eight bolts and lift off the transmission housing cover (photo).

7 Ease off the two large circlips retaining the input and output shafts (photo).

8 Remove the bolts holding the two halves of the casing and lift off the smaller half (photo). It may be necessary to tap the housing *gently* with a mallet to free the two halves.

9 Lift out the magnetic disc (Fig. 6.15), taking care not to drop it as it might shatter.

10 Lift out the selector fork guide shaft (Fig. 6.16), and remove the selector forks.

11 Remove the shift locking plate, and the guide shaft spring (Fig. 6.17).

12 Lift the input shaft, output shaft and reverse idler gear as an assembly (Fig. 6.18). Place the shafts to one side for subsequent dismantling and reassembly.

13 Lift the complete differential gear from the housing (photo), and place it to one side for subsequent overhaul.

14 At this stage all the major components have been removed from the transmission casing. This leaves a number of bearings and oil seals,

Fig. 6.11. Position a plug to secure the differential pinions (Sec. 2)

Fig. 6.12. Disconnecting the right-hand driveshaft (Sec. 2).

3.3 Removing the clutch release bearing fork to the operating arm

Fig. 6.13. Remove the retainer (A), spring (B) and selector locking pin (C) (Sec. 3)

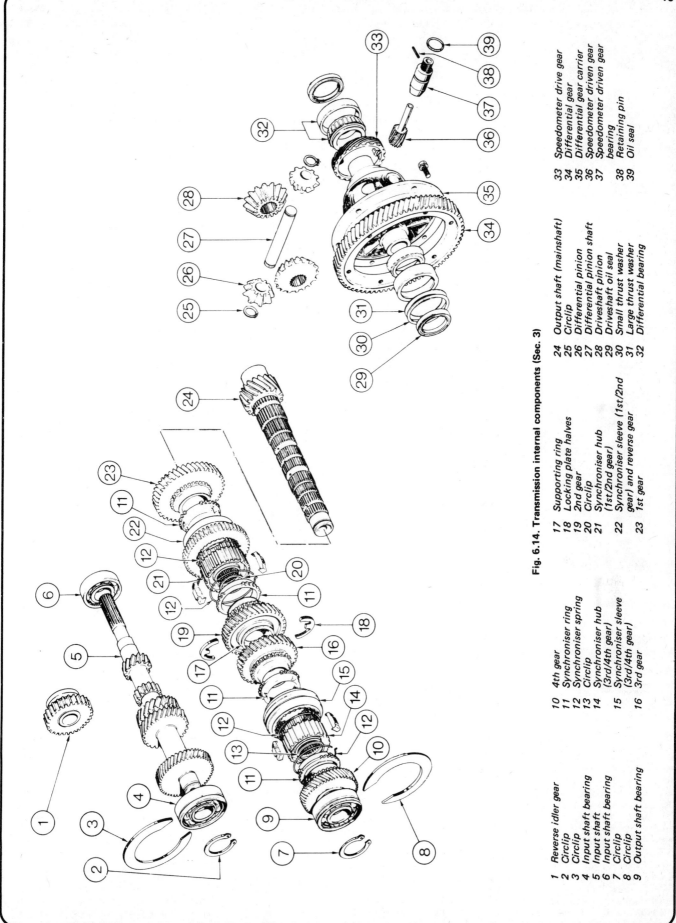

Fig. 6.14. Transmission internal components (Sec. 3)

1 Reverse idler gear
2 Circlip
3 Circlip
4 Input shaft bearing
5 Input shaft
6 Input shaft bearing
7 Circlip
8 Circlip
9 Output shaft bearing

10 4th gear
11 Synchroniser ring
12 Synchroniser spring
13 Circlip
14 Synchroniser hub (3rd/4th gear)
15 Synchroniser sleeve (3rd/4th gear)
16 3rd gear

17 Supporting ring
18 Locking plate halves
19 2nd gear
20 Circlip
21 Synchroniser hub (1st/2nd gear)
22 Synchroniser sleeve (1st/2nd gear) and reverse gear
23 1st gear

24 Output shaft (mainshaft)
25 Circlip
26 Differential pinion
27 Differential pinion shaft
28 Differential pinion
29 Driveshaft oil seal
30 Small thrust washer
31 Large thrust washer
32 Differential bearing

33 Speedometer drive gear
34 Differential gear
35 Differential gear carrier
36 Speedometer driven gear
37 Speedometer driven gear bearing
38 Retaining pin
39 Oil seal

3.6 Removing the transmission cover plate

3.7 Ease off the input and mainshaft circlips

3.8 Lifting off the smaller housing half

Fig. 6.15. Removing the magnetic disc (Sec. 3)

Fig. 6.16. Lifting out the selector fork guide shaft (Sec. 3)

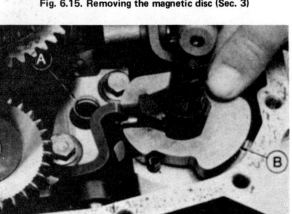

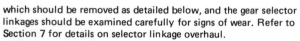

Fig. 6.17. Remove the guide shaft spring (A) and locking plate (B) (Sec. 3)

Fig. 6.18. Lifting out the input shaft, output shaft (mainshaft) and reverse idler gear (Sec. 3)

which should be removed as detailed below, and the gear selector linkages should be examined carefully for signs of wear. Refer to Section 7 for details on selector linkage overhaul.

15 To remove the output shaft bearing from the larger casing, it is necessary to break the inner bearing cage, and remove and discard the rollers. Pull out the oil slinger with a pair of pliers, destroying it if necessary (photo).

16 Removal of the outer bearing race entails the **careful** use of levers to ease the race out in stages. Use small blocks of wood between the levers and the casing to avoid damaging the casing.

17 To remove the input shaft oil seal, pass a screwdriver through the recess in the housing, and tap out the seal (Fig. 6.19).

18 Prise out the differential gear oil seal from outside the larger casing, using a screwdriver.

19 Again from outside the casing, drive out the differential gear bearing race using a suitable drift.

20 Again using a screwdriver, prise the second differential gear oil seal out of the smaller casing half.

21 From outside the smaller casing, use a suitable drift to tap out the bearing race and the two spring washers. These washers, as well as the bearing race, will have to be renewed on reassembly.

---

4   Mainshaft - dismantling and reassembly

1   When overhauling the mainshaft, it is a good plan to allow plenty of space on the bench or table for laying out the parts in the order in which they are removed. This and Fig. 6.22 will make reassembly that

3.13 Removing the differential gear assembly

3.15 Remove the mainshaft bearing oil slinger

Fig. 6.19. Knock out the input shaft oil seal (A) with a screwdriver (B) (Sec. 3)

4.3 Removing the mainshaft bearing circlip

Fig. 6.20. Pulling off the mainshaft bearing using the bearing outer circlip (Sec. 4)

much easier.

2 Where applicable, parts should be 'rocked' for excessive movement on the shaft before actual removal.

3 Using suitable circlip pliers, expand and remove the bearing retaining circlip (photo).

4 Refit the outer bearing circlip, removed in Section 3, paragraph 7. Fit a two legged puller, and pull off the bearing (Fig. 6.20).

5 Slide off the fourth gear (photo).

6 Using a pair of circlip pliers, expand and remove the 3rd/top synchroniser assembly retainer (photo).

7 Remove the synchroniser ring, synchroniser assembly and second synchroniser ring.

8 Slide off the 3rd gear (photo).

9 Lift off the 2nd gear supporting ring (photo) and slide out the locking plate halves (photo).

10 Slide off the 2nd gear (photo).

11 Using circlip pliers, expand and remove the 1st/2nd synchroniser circlip (photo).

12 Remove the synchroniser ring, synchroniser and reverse gear assembly (photo) and second synchroniser ring.

13 Slide off the 1st gear.

14 If a new synchroniser assembly is being fitted it is necessary to take it to pieces first to clean off all preservatives. Paragraphs 16 and 17 also apply if the assembly has been accidentally dismantled.

15 To dismantle an assembly for cleaning slide the synchroniser sleeve off the splined hub and clean all the preservative from the blocker bars, spring rings, the hub itself and the sleeve (Fig. 6.21).

16 Oil the components lightly and then fit the sleeve to the hub. Note the three slots in the hub and fit a blocker bar in each.

17 Fit the two springs, one on the front and one on the rear face of the inside of the synchroniser sleeve under the blocker bars with the tagged end of each spring locating in the 'U' section of the same bar.

4.5 Sliding off the 4th gear

4.6 Removing the 3rd/top synchroniser circlip

4.8 Sliding off the 3rd gear

4.9A Lifting off the 2nd gear supporting ring ...

4.9B ... and sliding out the locking plates

4.10 Sliding off the 2nd gear

4.11 Removing the 1st/2nd synchroniser circlip

4.12 Slide off the 1st/2nd synchroniser and reverse gear assembly

One spring must be put on anti-clockwise, and one clockwise when viewed from the side (see Fig. 6.23). When either side of the assembly is viewed face on, the direction of rotation of the springs should then appear the same.

18 After inspecting all components, and renewing where necessary, all parts should be cleaned, and lightly oiled with transmission oil before reassembly.

19 Slide on the 1st gear, with the cone facing upwards (photo).

20 Refit the reverse gear assembly, complete with synchroniser rings, with the selector fork groove downwards.

21 Fit the 1st/2nd synchroniser circlip.

22 Slide on the second gear with the cone facing downwards, then slide in the locking plate halves, and fit the retaining ring.

23 Slide on the 3rd gear with the cone facing upwards.

24 Refit the 3rd/4th synchroniser assembly complete with synchroniser rings.

25 Refit the 3rd/4th synchroniser retaining circlip.

26 Select a piece of tubing to fit around the mainshaft and onto the bearing inner race. Fit the bearing with the external circlip groove

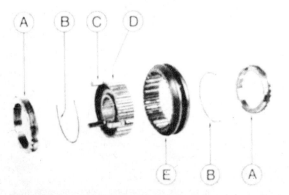

Fig. 6.21. Synchroniser rings (A), retaining spring (B), blocker bars (C), synchroniser hub (D) and synchroniser sleeve (E) (Sec. 4)

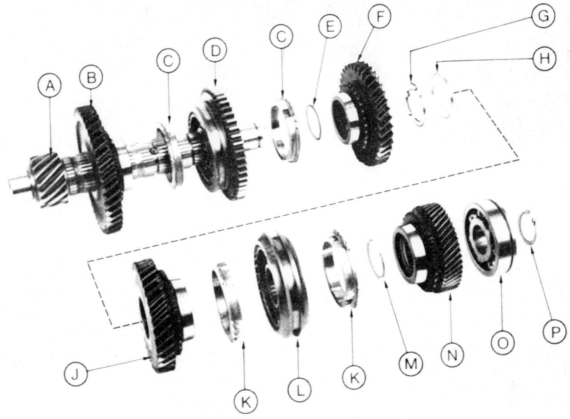

Fig. 6.22. Mainshaft (output shaft) components (Sec. 4)

A   Mainshaft and drive gear
B   1st gear
C   1st/2nd synchroniser rings
D   1st/2nd synchroniser assembly
    with reverse gear

E   Circlip
F   2nd gear
G   Locking plate halves
H   Supporting ring

J   3rd gear
K   3rd/4th synchroniser rings
L   3rd/4th synchromesh assembly
M   Circlip

N   4th gear
O   Mainshaft bearing
P   Circlip

Fig. 6.23. Locate the tagged end of each spring in the same bar (Sec. 4)

4.19 Correct positioning of 1st gear

4.26 Refitting the mainshaft bearing

upwards, and tap it onto the end of the shaft (photo). Refit the retaining circlip.

5   Input shaft - dismantling and reassembly

1   The input shaft is a one piece casting which cannot be dismantled. It is, however, a good plan to renew the two roller bearings (photo) as a matter of course when overhauling the transmission.
2   To remove the larger bearing, first expand and remove the retaining circlip (photo).
3   Refit the outer bearing circlip, removed in Section 3, paragraph 7. Fit a two legged puller, and pull off the bearing, fitting the legs around the outer circlip.
4   Again using a two legged puller, remove the smaller roller bearing.

5   Select a suitable diameter tubing to fit over the input shaft and onto the bearing inner races. Tap each bearing in turn onto the shaft, noting that the external circlip groove on the larger bearing should face away from the gears.
6   Finally, fit the larger bearing retaining circlip.

6   Differential gear - dismantling and reassembly

1   Since the pinion bearings in the differential gear are not pre-loaded, and the complete gear depth of mesh is controlled by the two spring washers in the casing, it is not beyond the scope of the home mechanic to overhaul the gear (Fig. 6.24). The only special tools required are a fairly heavy two legged puller, and a pair of external circlip pliers.

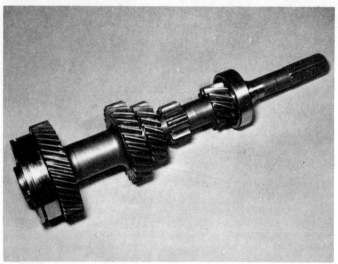

5.1 Input shaft complete with two bearings

5.2 Removing the larger input shaft bearing circlip

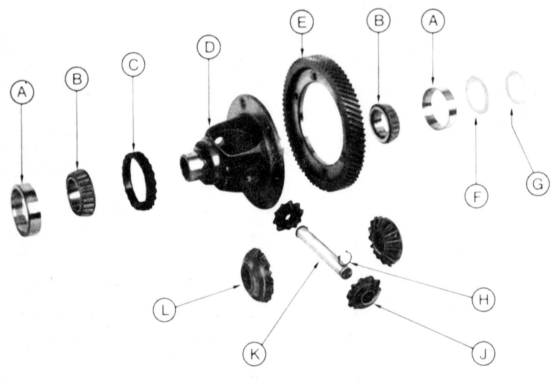

Fig. 6.24. Differential assembly (Sec. 6)

A Outer bearing track	D Differential gear carrier	G Small thrust washer	K Differential
B Roller bearing	E Differential gear	H Circlip	L Driveshaft pinions
C Speedometer drive gear	F Large thrust washer	J Differential pinion	

2 Firstly, remove any plugs fitted during the transmission removal.
3 Rotate the differential drive pinion gears and shaft. This will have the effect of pushing the two driveshaft pinions sideways out of the casing.
4 Using the circlip pliers, expand and remove one of the differential shaft circlips (Fig. 6.25). Tap out the shaft, and at the same time lift out the pinion drive gears.
5 Using the two-legged puller, pull off the two taper bearing races. Lift off the speedometer drive gear.
6 Unscrew and remove the six bolts holding the differential gear to the casing. Tap off the gear using a soft faced mallet (copper or rubber).
7 Examine the gears for wear and renew as required, as described in Section 9.

8 Fit the differential gear to the casing with the recess towards the casing (Fig. 6.26). Fit six new bolts and tighten them diagonally and progressively to draw on the differential gear.
9 Position the speedometer drive gear onto its shoulder on the differential casing.
10 Place the differential gear on the protected jaws of a partly opened vice. Using a suitable diameter piece of tubing, fit the two taper bearing races with their larger diameters facing the differential casing.
11 Pass the differential pinion shaft into the casing, through the drive pinions (Fig. 6.27) and out of the casing. Secure the shaft with its retaining circlip.
12 Fit the two driveshaft pinions to the drive pinion teeth, then

Fig. 6.25. Removing the pinion shaft circlip (Sec. 6)

Fig. 6.26. Fit the differential gear with the recess towards the casing (Sec. 6)

Fig. 6.27. Fitting the differential pinion shaft (Sec. 6)

Fig. 6.28. Twist the driveshaft pinions into the housing (Sec. 6)

twist them into the housing (Fig. 6.28).

13 Find suitable diameter plastic or wooden plugs, and pass them through the casing and into the driveshaft pinions. A discarded driveshaft end is obviously ideal for this. The purpose of this plug is to hold the driveshaft pinions in the correct position when refitting the transmission. Failure to do this will lead to problems.

7 Selector mechanism - removal and refitting

1 Unscrew the two bolts retaining the selector lever mechanism (photo) and lift out the mechanism (photo). It may be necessary to twist the guide shaft to disengage the lever ends.

2 Lift out the guide shaft and cam assembly (photo).

3 If required, prise off the spring clip and slide the reverse relay lever (photo) from its pivot.

4 Pull the rubber gaiter off the end of the control shaft, and unscrew the Allen key holding the selector gate to the control shaft (photo).

5 Using a suitable diameter drift, tap the control shaft out of the casing. Lever out the control shaft oil seal from outside the casing.

6 Fit a new control shaft oil seal from outside the casing, and gently tap it home.

7 Slide the control shaft into the casing and through the selector gate, and tap it fully home. Tighten the Allen screw, and fit a new rubber gaiter.

8 If it has been dismantled, refit the selector levers to the retainer plate, and fit the spring clips (Fig. 6.29).

9 If it has been removed, refit the reverse relay lever to its pivot, and retain it with the spring clip.

10 Refit the guide shaft and cam assembly, ensuring it is correctly sealed.

11 Refit the selector lever mechanism, and tighten the two retaining plate bolts (Fig. 6.30).

8 Speedometer driven gear - removal and refitting

1 On this transmission, the speedometer driven gear can be removed with the transmission in the vehicle if wear or damage are suspected. If the transmission is dismantled, the gear can be examined (photo), and then renewed if necessary.

2 Using a pair of pliers, prise out the bearing retaining pin from the outside of the casing.

3 Withdraw the bearing together with the driven gear, then pull the gear from the bearing.

4 Check the bearing oil seal for damage, and renew it if necessary.

5 Push the gear shaft into its bearing.

6 Refit the gear and bearing assembly, and gently tap in the locking pin (Fig. 6.31).

9 Transmission - examination and renovation

1 It is assumed that the transmission has been dismantled for reasons of excessive noise, lack of synchromesh, or failure to stay in gear. Anything more drastic such as total failure, seizure or a cracked gearcase would be better dealt with by obtaining an exchange unit.

2 Examine all gears for excessively worn, chipped or damaged teeth. Any such gears should be renewed. It will usually be found that if a tooth on a gear is damaged, the corresponding gear on the other shaft will also be damaged.

3 Inspect all transmission casing threads for damage and, if evident, the hole will have to be drilled oversize, a new thread cut and a new bolt obtained.

4 Check all bearings for wear by holding the inner track and turning the outer track. Any roughness, or sideways movement indicates wear. Normally, they should be renewed on a transmission that is being rebuilt.

5 Check all synchroniser rings for wear on the bearing surface which should have clearly defined oil reservoir grooves. If these are smooth or obviously uneven, renewal is essential. Also, when fitted to their mating cones, there should be no rock.

6 The sliding hubs are also subject to wear and should be closely examined. Check that the blocker bars are neither sloppy nor difficult to move. If there is any rock or backlash between the synchroniser hub and sleeve the whole assembly will have to be

7.1A Selector mechanism retaining bolts

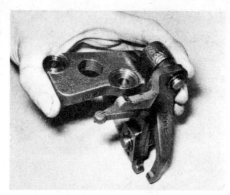

7.1B Selector mechanism removed

7.2 Lifting out the guide shaft and cam assembly

7.3 Reverse relay lever and retaining clip

7.4 Selector gate retaining screw

Fig. 6.29. Selector lever spring clips (Sec. 7)

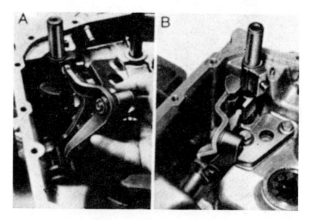

Fig. 6.30. Fitting the selector levers (A) and retaining bolts (B) (Sec. 7)

renewed as the parts are not individually available.

7   Check that the splines on the input shaft are not badly worn where the clutch disc slides along the shaft.

8   Inspect the reverse idler shaft and ensure that it has a smooth surface with no signs of pitting or scoring.

9   Check the differential pinion gears for signs of excess wear and backlash, and renew the gears as a set if necessary.

10 Examine the selector forks where they rub against the grooves in the edge of the synchroniser sleeves. If possible compare the selector forks with new units to determine the extent of wear. Renew them if necessary.

11 Inspect the selector mechanism components for excessive wear and sloppy linkages. Look particularly for elongated holes or worn operating rods, and renew if necessary.

10 Transmission - reassembly

1   Thoroughly clean the transmission casing halves and end cover, removing any loose metal particles. Examine all bearing and oil seal apertures, and **carefully** remove any burrs using a screwdriver. Remove all old gasket parts and clean the mating faces. Care should be taken during these operations not to remove any of the casing metal since, firstly, this will allow oil leaks at the joints, and secondly, any metal splinters will damage the internal transmission components.

2   Insert the smaller spring washer into the smaller housing half with the outer diameter facing the housing, then the larger washer with the outer diameter facing the bearing race (photo).

3   Insert the outer bearing race with the smaller internal diameter facing the housing (photo), and hold it in position with one **light** blow

8.1 Speedometer driven gear in transmission case

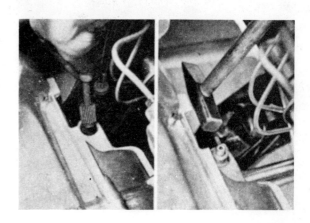

Fig. 6.31. Refitting the speedometer driven gear and locking pin (Sec. 8)

10.2 Refitting the differential spring thrust washers

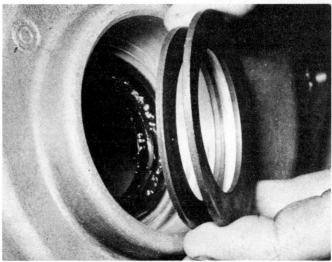

10.3 Refitting the differential bearing outer race

10.8 Correct location of input shaft oil seal

of a pin punch on the edge of the housing.

4   From outside the bearing case, insert a new oil seal and tap it into its location, using a piece of wood to spread the load evenly.

5   Place the larger casing half on a firm bench with the clutch bell-housing downwards.

6   Insert the differential gear outer bearing race with the smaller internal diameter facing the larger housing half. Tap it into position, taking care not to damage the bearing face.

7   From outside the casing, insert a new oil seal and tap it into its seating, using a piece of wood to spread the load evenly.

8   Fit a new input shaft oil seal into the casing ensuring it is fully located in its seat (photo).

9   Insert a new oil slinger into the output shaft bearing housing (Fig. 6.32).

10 Position a new output shaft bearing into its housing, and tap it fully home using the **outer** race only (photo). Once installed, the bearing should be staked, using a pin punch, by **lightly** burring the edges of the housing.

11 Insert the differential assembly into the casing, with the large gear uppermost.

12 Place the reverse idler gear on its shaft, and hold it at the top of the shaft using the reverse relay lever (Fig. 6.33).

13 Hold the input and output shafts together, with their gears in mesh, and carefully lower the pair of shafts into their locations in the housing (photo). While lowering the shafts, allow the reverse idler gear to drop downwards as in the photo. It may be necessary to

Fig. 6.32. Inserting the output shaft oil slinger (Sec. 10)

10.10 Correct location of output (main) shaft bearing and oil slinger

Fig. 6.33. Slide on the reverse idler gear, and hold it with the relay lever (Sec. 10)

10.13 Refitting the input and main shafts

10.14 Correct fitting of the shift locking plate

twist the shafts slightly to enable the output shaft gear to mesh with the large differential gear.
14 Refit the shift locking plate (photo) and the guide shaft spring (Fig. 6.34).
15 Refit the selector forks and guide shaft, with the longer shaft pin downwards (Fig. 6.34).
16 For subsequent selector lever adjustment, twist the external control shaft clockwise to select 4th gear.
17 Carefully clean all metal particles from the magnetic disc and insert it into its recess (photo).

Fig. 6.34. Fitting the guide shaft spring (arrowed) and guide shaft with selector forks (Sec. 10)

10.17 Location of magnetic disc in larger housing half

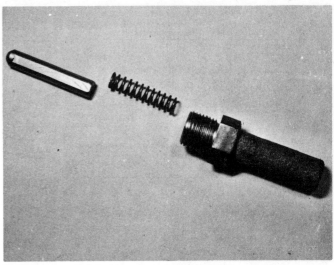
10.21 Selector shaft locking pin, spring and retainer

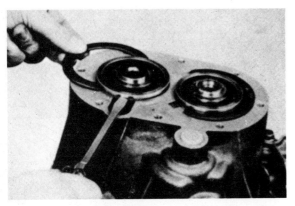
Fig. 6.35. Fitting the shaft retaining circips (Sec. 10)

10.22 Refitting the clutch release bearing arm into the fork

Fig. 6.36. Fitting the gasket around the circlips (Sec.10)

18 Fit a new gasket to the larger housing half and refit the smaller housing half. Be careful not to dislodge the magnetic disc. Tighten the bolts to the **correct** torque, as overtightening could strip the threads in the light metal casing.
19 Using a screwdriver in the input and output shaft bearing circlip grooves, raise the shafts sufficiently to slide on the two circlips (Fig. 6.35).
20 Twist the circlips as necessary to accommodate the gasket (Fig. 6.36), fit a new gasket, refit the housing cover and tighten its retaining bolts, to the **correct** torque.
21 Refit the selector shaft locking pin, spring and retaining nut (photo).

22 Slide the clutch release bearing onto the input shaft splines, refit the release arm and shaft (photo) and secure them with the retaining bolt.

11 Transmission - refitting

1 Refitting the transmission to the car will, of course, depend on the method of removal. If it was removed together with the engine, it should be reassembled and refitted as described in Chapter 1. If removed on its own, the following procedure should be followed.
2 Before installing the transmission, lightly grease the splines on the driveshafts and differential gear, ensuring that the drive pinions are not displaced. Refit the locating plugs. Also, check that the clutch driven plate is correctly aligned, as described in Chapter 5, and that the engine backplate is correctly installed on its two dowels.
3 When installing the transmission, it may be helpful to have an assistant with a spanner on the crankshaft pulley bolt, turning the crankshaft slightly to assist in aligning the input shaft splines with those in the clutch driven plate. **Do not** allow the weight of the transmission to hang from the input shaft at any stage.
4 Refit the transmission, and lightly tighten the two lower engine to transmission flange bolts.
5 Use two drifts to align the holes in the engine crossmember, and fit three **new** self-locking bolts. Tighten these and the two lower flange

bolts to the **correct** torque. Note that if any of these flange bolts are overtightened, it could result in stripped threads in the transmission casing. This means that the transmission will have to be removed again, and the holes drilled and tapped to accept oversize bolts, or where possible, longer bolts fitted with spring washers and nuts.

6 Refit the starter motor with its two bolts and reconnect the cables.

7 *960 cc and 1100 cc models.* Fit a **new** circlip to the right-hand driveshaft end (Fig. 6.37), remove the plug from the transmission casing, and insert the driveshaft. Using a suitable screwdriver placed against the joint weld, tap the driveshaft fully home until the circlip engages (Fig. 6.37). If there is no weld, use a plastic or rubber mallet to drive the shaft home.

8 *1300 cc and 1600 cc models.* Fit a **new** circlip to the right-hand driveshaft end (Fig. 6.37), remove the plug from the transmission casing, and insert the driveshaft. Using a suitable screwdriver placed against the universal joint flange, tap the joint home until the circlip engages (Fig. 6.37).

9 Refit the driveshaft centre bearing bracket to the engine, and secure it with the three nuts and washers.

10 Reassemble the centre driveshaft joint and secure with the Allen screws.

11 *All models.* Refit the right-hand track control arm to the body mounting with the bolt facing forward. It may be necessary to use a suitable drift to align the bush with its mounting holes. Refit the outer balljoint and tighten the clamp bolt (Fig. 6.9).

12 Fit a **new** circlip to the left-hand driveshaft end and refit the driveshaft as described in paragraph 7.

13 Refit the left-hand track control arm to the body mounting and the outer end clamp (Fig. 6.9).

14 Refit the two track rod outer ends, tighten the castellated nuts and secure with **new** split pins.

15 Refit the transmission stabiliser bar and tighten the Allen screw into the transmission housing, taking care not to overtighten (Fig. 6.7). Tighten the locknut against the stabiliser bar bush. Screw the other

inner nut against its bracket and finally tighten the outer locknut.

16 Refit the gear selector rod to the transmission control rod and tighten the clamp bolt. Adjust the linkage as detailed in Section 14. Refit the selector rod spring (Fig. 6.38).

17 Refill the transmission with the specified grade of oil (Fig. 6.39).

18 With the engine crossmember bolts now fitted, the weight of the engine can now be released from the hoist or jack, and the vehicle lowered to the ground.

19 Refit and tighten the four top transmission to engine flange bolts.

20 Pass the clutch cable through its bracket, ensuring that the end is correctly located. Using a pair of pliers, hook the inner cable into the release arm (Fig. 6.40).

21 Refit the speedometer cable and tighten the knurled retaining nut.

22 Reconnect the battery and close the bonnet.

12 Selector linkage - removal and refitting

1 Before removing the gear selector linkage, engage 4th gear. This is so that the linkage adjustment can be carried out when refitting.

2 Unscrew and remove the gear lever knob, and pull off the gaiter (Fig. 6.41).

3 Unhook the selector rod spring from the floor pan and remove it (Fig. 6.38).

4 Slacken the selector rod pinch bolt at the transmission, and pull off.

5 Slacken the outer stabiliser bar locknut from the crossmember bracket. Slacken the inner locknut from the stabiliser bar bush then screw the other inner locknut up to the locknut at the bush.

6 Unscrew the Allen screw from the transmission housing, pull it through the bush and lower the stabiliser bar.

7 Unscrew the two nuts holding the gear lever housing to the floor pan, then lower and remove the complete linkage.

8 Refitting is the reverse of this procedure, noting the following points:

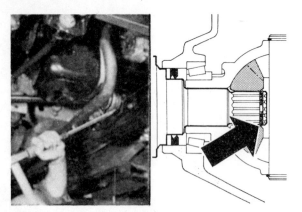

Fig. 6.37. Tapping in the driveshaft until the circlip (arrowed) engages (Sec. 11)

Fig. 6.38. Fitting the selector rod spring (Sec. 11)

Fig. 6.39. Transmission oil filler and level plug (Sec. 11)

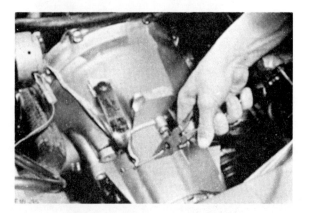

Fig. 6.40. Fitting the clutch cable (Sec. 11)

a) *Do not overtighten the stabiliser bar Allen screw in the transmission housing.*

b) *Do not fully tighten the gear lever housing to floor pan nuts until after fitting the stabiliser bar.*

c) *Adjust the gearshift linkage as described in Section 14.*

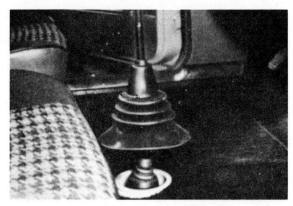

Fig. 6.41. Pull off the gear lever gaiter (Sec. 12)

13 Selector linkage - overhaul

1   The complete linkage assembly is shown in Fig. 6.42.

2   Unscrew the four nuts and bolts holding the two housing halves together, pull off the lower housing gaiter and withdraw the selector rod and gaiter through the base plate aperture (Fig. 6.43).

3   Drill out the rivet holding the selector rod to the gear lever and remove the plastic bushes. Remove the guide plate and selector rod gaiter.

4   With the bottom of the gear lever held in a soft jawed vice, prise off the rubber spring retaining circlip (Fig. 6.44), then lift off the rubber spring, bearing cup and upper housing half.

5   Refit the upper housing half to the gear lever, followed by the bearing cup and rubber spring. It will then be necessary to depress the rubber spring clear of the circlip groove. Fit a **new** circlip.

6   Slide the gaiter onto the selector rod (Fig. 6.42), then fit the guide plate to the upper housing half (Fig. 6.45).

7   Fit two new plastic bushes to the gear lever lower end, then fit the selector rod yoke. Note that the selector rod will point towards the front of the car, while the gear lever is bent towards the rear (Fig. 6.42).

8   Fit a new rivet and use a suitable diameter punch to knock down the end of the rivet securely.

9   Lubricate the gear lever guide in the selector housings, and the guide plate with graphite grease.

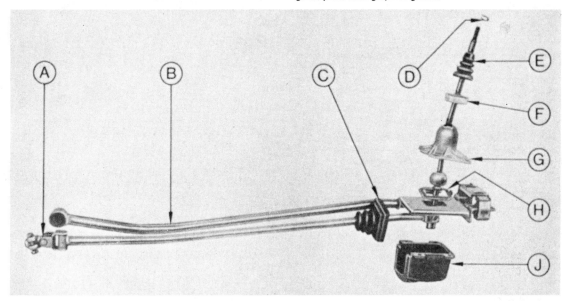

Fig. 6.42. Selector linkage components (Sec. 13)

A Selector rod	D Circlip	G Upper housing half
B Stabiliser rod	E Rubber spring	H Guide plate
C Gaiter	F Bearing cap	J Lower housing half

Fig. 6.43. Withdrawing the selector rod and gaiter through the base plate (Sec. 13)

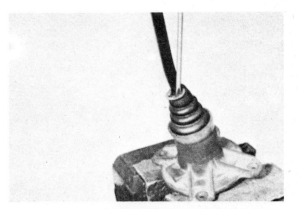

Fig. 6.44. Prising off the rubber spring circlip (Sec. 13)

Fig. 6.45. Fitting the guide plate (Sec. 13)

10 Pass the selector rod and gaiter through the baseplate aperture then secure the housing halves to the baseplate with four nuts and bolts. Note that the upper housing and guideplate assembly must be fitted so that the bevelled corners of the guideplate will face the front of the vehicle.
11 Examine the condition of the stabiliser bar bush, and of the gear lever housing insulating rubbers, and renew them if they are worn or damaged.

14 Selector linkage - adjustment

1   To carry out this operation, requires the use of a drift of 0.16 in (4 mm) diameter, a drift to fit the hole in the transmission control shaft and a wooden spanner.
2   The spacer can be manufactured from any available wood, to the dimensions shown in Fig. 6.46C. The dimension given as 70 should be accurate, while the other dimensions are only suggested. Note that the dimensions are in millimetres.

Approximate Imperial equivalent are:
15 mm - 0.6 in   20 mm - 0,8 in   50 mm - 2.0 in
70 mm - 2.75 in   105 mm - 4.0 in

3   From inside the car, select 4th gear, then jack up the front of the car and fit stands.
4   Slacken the clamp bolt securing the selector rod to the control rod (Fig. 6.46A).

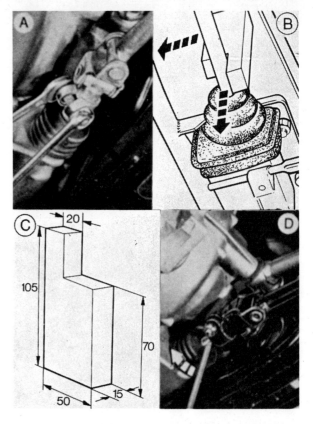

Fig. 6.46. Adjusting the gear selector linkage (Sec. 14)

5   Pull the selector rod and gear lever downwards until the holes in the end of the gear lever and the lower gear lever housing are aligned. Insert the 0.16 in (4 mm) diameter pin to lock the gear lever in this position (Fig. 6.46B).
6   Pull the selector rod down and to the right (Fig. 6.46B) and wedge the spacer in the position shown.
7   Using a suitable drift, rotate the control rod clockwise (Fig. 6.46D) and push it into the transmission housing. Tighten the clamp bolt in this position.

15 Fault diagnosis

Symptom	Reason/s	Remedy
Weak or ineffective synchromesh	Synchronising cones worn, split or damaged	Dismantle and overhaul gearbox. Fit new gear wheels and synchronising cones.
	Baulk ring synchromesh dogs worn, or damaged	Dismantle and overhaul gearbox. Fit new baulk ring synchromesh.
Jumps out of gear	Broken gearchange fork rod spring	Dismantle and replace the spring.
	Gearbox coupling dogs badly worn	Dismantle gearbox. Fit new coupling dogs.
	Selector fork rod groove badly worn	Fit new selector fork rod.
Excessive noise	Incorrect grade of oil in gearbox or oil level too low	Drain, refill or top up gearbox with correct grade of oil.
	Bush or needle roller bearings worn or damaged	Dismantle and overhaul gearbox. Renew bearings.
	Gear teeth excessively worn or damaged	Dismantle, overhaul gearbox. Renew gear wheels.
	Differential thrust washers worn allowing excessive end play	Dismantle and overhaul gearbox. Renew thrust washers.
Excessive difficulty in engaging gear	Linkage out of adjustment	Adjust linkage.
	Clutch cable not adjusting	Check operation of adjuster. Renew cable if no further adjustment available.
	Refer to Chapter 5, Section 9 for Clutch Fault Diagnosis.	

Chapter 7 Braking system

Contents

Specifications

General

Type	Dual line hydraulic, split diagonally front and rear Servo assistance on certain models
Front brakes	Disc, self-adjusting
Rear brakes	Drum, self-adjusting
Handbrake (parking brake)	Cable operated to rear wheels

Front brakes

Disc diameter - inner	5.0 in (148 mm)
- outer	8.7 in (221 mm)
Disc thickness - nominal	0.39 in (10.0 mm)
- minimum	0.34 in (8.7 mm)
Disc runout (total)	0.006 in (0.15 mm)
Wheel cylinder piston diameter	1.89 in (48 mm)
Disc pad material - 960 cc and 1100 cc	Mintex M175
- 1300 cc and 1600 cc	Don 237

Rear brakes

Drum diameter	7.00 in (178 mm)
Shoe width	1.18 in (30 mm)
Wheel cylinder diameter - 960 cc and 1100 cc	0.59 in (15 mm)
- 1300 cc and 1600 cc	0.69 in (17.5 mm)
Lining material	Mintex M79/1
Brake fluid specification	SAM-6C-9101-A or C

Torque wrench settings

	lb f ft	kg f m
Caliper to front suspension unit	40	5.5
Rear backplate to axle housing	17	2.3
Hydraulic unions	9	1.3
Bleed valves - sufficient to seal	8 max	1.0 max
Pressure control valve to bracket	17	2.3

1 General description

Disc brakes are fitted to the front wheels of all models together with single leading shoe drum brakes at the rear. The mechanically operated handbrake works on the rear wheels only.

The front brakes are of the rotating disc and floating caliper type, with one caliper per disc. Each caliper contains one piston and two friction pads, which on application of the footbrake pinch the disc rotating between them (Fig. 7.1).

Application of the footbrake creates hydraulic pressure in the master cylinder and fluid from the cylinder travels via metal and flexible pipes to the wheel cylinder. This pressure pushes the piston, and thus the inner pad against the disc, while the opposite reaction pulls the piston housing, and thus the outer pad against the disc.

Two seals are fitted to the operating cylinder, the outer seal prevents moisture and dirt entering the cylinder, while the inner seal which is retained in a groove inside the cylinder, prevents fluid leakage.

As the friction pads wear so the piston moves further out of the cylinder and the level of fluid in the hydraulic reservoir drops. Disc pad wear is therefore taken up automatically and eliminates the need for periodic adjustment by the owner.

The rear drum brakes each have one wheel cylinder operating two shoes (Fig. 7.2). Hydraulic pressure from the master cylinder is conveyed along metal and flexible pipes to the wheel cylinder. Two opposed pistons in the wheel cylinder thus move outwards against the brake shoes, forcing them into contact with the inside face of the drum. As the rear brake shoes wear the footbrake operates a

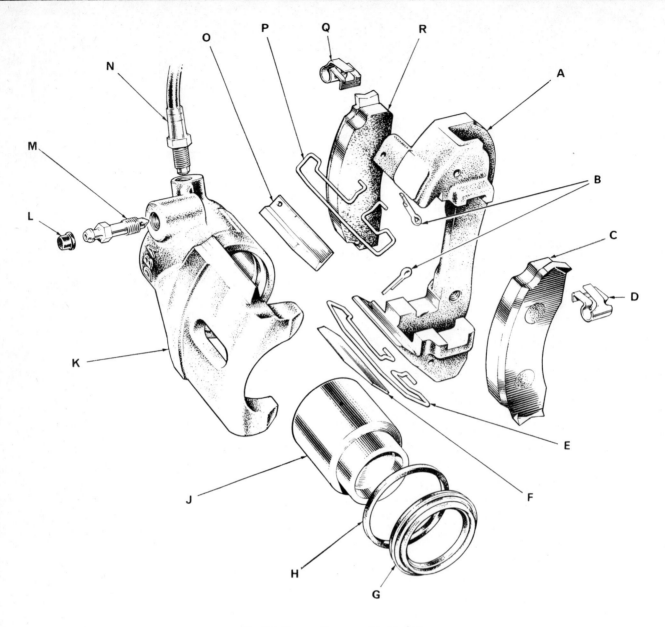

Fig. 7.1. Front caliper assembly (Sec. 1)

A Pad housing	F Retaining key	K Piston housing	O Retaining key
B Retaining pins	G Piston bellows	L Dust cap	P Tension spring
C Inner brake pad	H Piston seal	M Bleed nipple	Q Anti-rattle clip
D Anti-rattle clip	J Piston	N Flexible hose	R Outer brake pad
E Tension spring			

self-adjusting mechanism in the rear brakes thus eliminating the need to adjust the rear brakes individually.

The master cylinder is mounted on the left-hand side of the engine compartment on left-hand drive cars, and on the right on right-hand drive cars. When a servo unit is fitted to right-hand drive vehicles however, the servo unit and master cylinder are located on the left-hand side and are operated by a connecting linkage.

All models have a dual line braking system with a separate circuit for the right-hand front/left-hand rear brakes, and another for the left-hand front/right-hand rear brakes (Fig. 7.3). If failure of any of the hydraulic pipes occurs half the braking system still operates. Servo assistance in this condition is still available.

On some models a warning light is fitted on the facia which illuminates should either circuit fail. The bulb is connected to a pressure differential switch within the master cylinder. On models for certain markets, a pressure control valve is fitted in the hydraulic line. This valve 'senses' sudden braking, and controls the pressure to the rear

brakes, to prevent them from locking up when the car is unladen.

All models use a floor mounted handbrake (parking brake) lever located between the front seats. A cable runs from the lever through an equaliser on the rear axle to the handbrake backplate. A transverse cable runs from the equaliser to the right-hand rear brake. The longitudinal cable incorporates a manual adjuster.

2 Front disc pads - inspection and renewal

1   The design of the front caliper makes it difficult to determine the amount of wear on the disc pads without the use of a special tool or removal of the piston housing as described below.
2   The special tool needed can be obtained from your Ford dealer under the number 12-002, pad wear checking gauge (Fig. 7.4).
3   To check the inner pad thickness, hold the tool with the shaft touching the disc and the lower part of its housing touching the inner

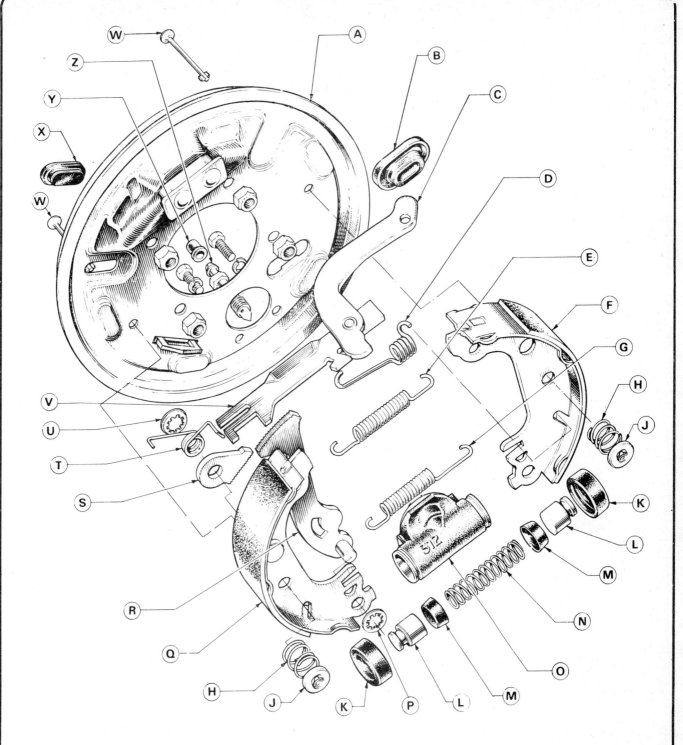

Fig. 7.2. Rear brake assembly (Sec. 1)

A	Back plate	K	Piston boot	S	Small ratchet
B	Rubber gaiter	L	Hydraulic piston	T	Ratchet spring
C	Handbrake operating lever	M	Piston seal	U	Spring clip
D	Lever return spring	N	Piston spring	V	Spacer strut
E	Shoe retracting spring	O	Wheel cylinder	W	Hold down pin
F	Trailing brake shoe	P	Spring clip	X	Inspection plug
G	Shoe retracting spring	Q	Leading shoe	Y	Dust cap
H	Hold down spring	R	Large ratchet	Z	Bleed nipple
J	Hold down washer				

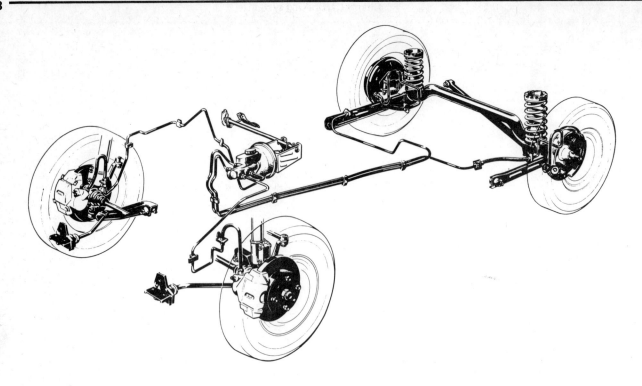

Fig. 7.3. Right-hand drive brake pipe layout (with servo unit) (Sec. 1)

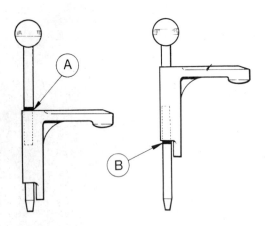

Fig. 7.4. Pad wear gauge 12-002 showing inner (A) and outer (B) pad wear indicating bands (Sec. 2)

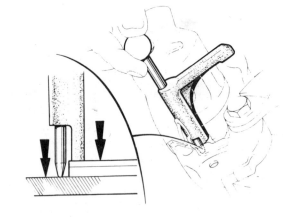

Fig. 7.5. Checking the inner brake pad (sec. 2)

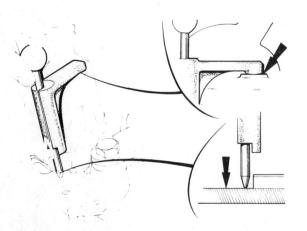

Fig. 7.6. Checking the outer brake pad (Sec. 2)

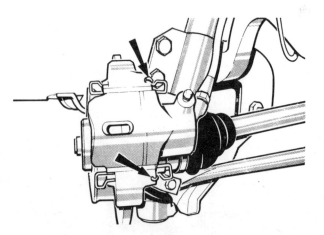

Fig. 7.7. Remove the key retaining pins (Sec. 2)

brake pad (Fig. 7.5).

4   To check the outer pad thickness, hold the tool with the shaft touching the disc and the arm on the housing touching the boss on the piston housing (Fig. 7.6).

5   If either of the indicating bands shown in Fig. 7.4 is visible outside the housing, both disc pads should be renewed. Note that disc pads are supplied in sets of four so that all the front wheel pads should be renewed at the same time.

6   Apply the handbrake, slacken the roadwheel bolts, jack up the front of the car and place on firmly based axle stands. Remove the front wheel.

7   Remove and discard the two key retaining pins (Fig. 7.7).

8   Push firmly against the piston housing to relieve the spring pressure, and slide out the retaining keys (photo).

9   Lift away the piston housing (photo) and hang it securely using a piece of wire, ensuring that the flexible hose is not strained.

10 Inspect the amount of friction material left on the pads. The pads must be renewed when the thickness of the friction material has been reduced to a minimum of 0.06 in (1.5 mm).

11 To renew the pads, ease out the pads and anti-rattle springs.

12 Carefully clean the disc, anti-rattle springs and keys to ensure they are free from dirt, grease or rust.

Note: Great care must be taken that none of the brake pad dust is inhaled since this contains asbestos.

13 Fit new pads and anti-rattle clips (photo) into the housing. The clips are fitted to the top of the pads.

14 If the fluid level in the master cylinder reservoir is high, when the pistons are moved into their respective bores to accommodate new pads the level could rise sufficiently for the fluid to overflow. Place absorbent cloth around the reservoir or syphon a little fluid out so preventing paintwork damage being caused by the hydraulic fluid. Push the piston into the bore as required, using a piece of wood.

15 Fit the piston housing, push firmly against the housing and slide in the retaining keys (Fig. 7.8) until the retaining pin holes align. Fit **new** retaining pins from the disc side of the housing, and bend over the ends.

16 Refit the roadwheel and lower the car. Tighten the wheel bolts securely.

17 To correctly seat the pistons pump the brake pedal several times and finally top up the hydraulic fluid level in the master cylinder reservoir as necessary.

---

3   Front brake caliper - removal and refitting

Note: *Always use new bolts when refitting the caliper disc pad housing. The latest standard of bolt carries the number 10.9 on the bolt head, and is available as a Ford replacement (part no. E800627 - S100)*

1   The front brake caliper on the Fiesta consists of two halves, the piston housing and the disc pad housing. The more usual repair to be carried out is removal of the piston housing to overhaul it as described in paragraph 2 onwards. If, however, the complete assembly is to be removed, carry out those items in paragraphs 2, 3 and 7. Refitting is contained in paragraphs 8 to 13.

2   Apply the handbrake, slacken the roadwheel bolts and jack up the front of the car. Place the car on firmly based axle stands and remove the front wheel.

3   Unscrew the flexible hose from the piston housing and tape the end to prevent excessive loss of fluid and the entry of dirt.

4   Remove and discard the two key retaining pins (Fig. 7.7).

5   Push firmly against the piston housing to relieve the spring pressure, and slide out the retaining keys (photo 2.8).

6   Lift away the piston housing (photo 2.9).

7   To remove the disc pad housing, unscrew the two retaining bolts (Fig. 7.9) and withdraw the housing.

8   To refit the disc pad housing, slide it into position, taking care not to damage the pad material on the edge of the disc. Refit and tighten the two retaining bolts (Fig. 7.9).

9   Using a suitable piece of wood, carefully push the operating piston

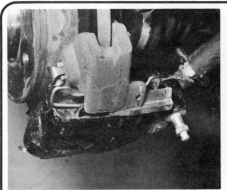
2.8 Sliding out the retaining key

2.9 Lifting off the piston housing

2.13 New pads fitted, with anti-rattle clips at the top

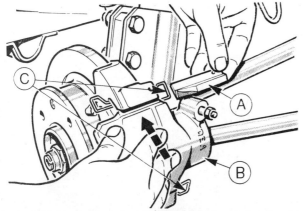
Fig. 7.8. Pushing the piston housing (B) against the tension of springs (C) and inserting the retaining key (A) (Sec. 2)

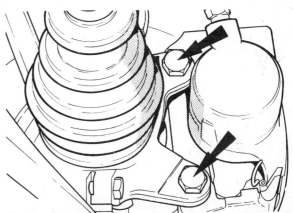
Fig. 7.9. Unscrew the disc pad housing retaining bolts (Sec. 2)

fully into the housing.

10 Fit the piston housing, push firmly against the housing and slide in the retaining keys (Fig. 7.8) until the retaining pin holes align. Fit **new** retaining pins from the disc side of the housing and bend over the ends.

11 Refit the flexible hose, taking care not to damage the threads, and tighten to the correct torque.

12 Once the caliper has been refitted, the braking system must be bled, Section 12.

13 Refit the front wheel/s and lower the car. Tighten the wheel bolts.

4 Front brake caliper - overhaul

1 If the complete caliper assembly has been removed, it should be dismantled as described in Section 3, paragraphs 4 to 6 inclusive.

2 Pull the rubber bellows from the operating piston (Fig. 7.10) and discard it.

3 Apply low air pressure to the brake fluid inlet and blow out the operating piston. Remove the piston seal and discard it.

4 Unscrew and remove the piston housing bleed valve.

5 Thoroughly wash all parts in methylated spirits or clean hydraulic fluid. During reassembly new rubber seals must be fitted, these should be well lubricated with clean hydraulic fluid.

6 Inspect the piston and bore for signs of wear, score marks or damage and, if evident, new parts should be obtained ready for fitting or a new caliper obtained.

7 Fit a new piston seal to its groove in the piston housing.

8 Lubricate the piston with clean brake fluid, slide it fully into the bore, taking care not to dislodge the piston seal.

9 Fit a new piston bellows carefully to its locations around the piston and the piston housing.

10 Refit the bleed valve, and tighten it securely, but not overtight.

5 Front brake disc - removal and refitting

1 Apply the handbrake, slacken the roadwheel bolts and jack up the front of the car. Place the car on firmly based axle stands and remove the front wheel.

2 Remove the two caliper retaining bolts (Fig. 7.9) and slide the complete caliper assembly forward off the disc. Using a suitable length of wire, firmly suspend the caliper so that the flexible hose is not strained.

3 Remove the single crosshead retaining screw and lift off the brake disc (Fig. 7.11).

4 Thoroughly clean the disc and inspect for signs of deep scoring, cracks or excessive corrosion. If these are evident, the discs may be reground, but no more than a maximum of 0.06 in (1.53 mm) may be removed. It is however, preferable to fit new discs if at all possible.

5 Before refitting the disc, ensure that the mating faces of the disc and hub are clean and free from burrs.

6 Refit the disc and tighten the securing screw.

7 Slide the caliper assembly onto the disc, taking care not to damage the pad material.

8 Refit and secure the two caliper retaining bolts.

9 If a dial indicator gauge is available, it is advisable to check the disc for runout. The measurement should be taken as near to the edge of the worn yet smooth part of the disc as possible, and must not exceed 0.006 in (0.15 mm). If the figure obtained is found to be excessive, check the mating surfaces of the disc and hub for dirt or damage and check the bearing and cups for excessive wear or damage, Chapter 9.

10 If a dial indicator gauge is not available the runout can be checked by means of a feeler gauge placed between the casting of the caliper and the disc. Establish a reasonably tight fit with the feeler gauge between the top of the casting and the disc and rotate the disc and hub. Any high or low spots will immediately become obvious by extra tightness or looseness of the fit of the feeler gauge. The amount of runout can be checked by adding or subtracting feeler gauges as necessary.

11 Once the disc runout has been checked and found to be correct, refit the front wheel and lower the car to the ground. Tighten the road-wheel bolts.

6 Drum brake shoes - inspection and renewal

1 After high mileages, it will be necessary to fit new shoes and linings. Refitting new brake linings to shoes is not considered economic, or possible, without the use of special equipment. However, if the services of a local garage or workshop having brake relining equipment are available then there is no reason why the original shoes should not be relined successfully. Ensure that the correct specification linings are fitted to the shoes.

2 Bonded linings are fitted to all Fiestas in production, and it is suggested that replacement shoes are also of the bonded type. The reason for this is that the wear on a bonded lining can be checked on the edge, while riveted linings cannot be.

3 To check the rear brake linings for wear, prise out the rubber plug from the rear of the brake backplate (Fig. 7.12). There should be a minimum of 0.06 in (1.5 mm) of lining material, and this can be determined by shining a lamp through the backplate aperture. Refit the plug after inspection.

4 If the linings need to be renewed, chock the front wheels, jack up the rear of the car and place on firmly based axle stands. Remove the rear roadwheel.

5 Fully release the handbrake, then pull out the spring clip and remove the clevis pin connecting the handbrake cable to its operating arm (Fig. 7.13).

6 Using a suitable screwdriver, prise out the dust cap in the centre of the hub. Remove and discard the split pin and lift off the nut retainer.

7 Unscrew the retaining nut, and remove the washer and outer bearing race. Slide the hub and brake drum assembly off the spindle (photo). It may be necessary to use a soft-faced hammer on the outer circumference of the drum if it is sticking.

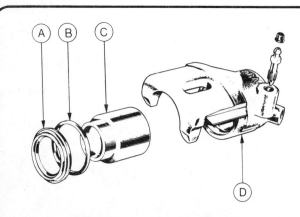

Fig. 7.10. Piston components (Sec. 4)

A *Rubber bellows*   C *Piston*
B *Piston seal*   D *Piston housing*

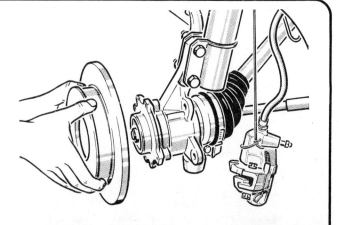

Fig. 7.11. Lifting off the front brake disc (Sec. 5)

6.7 Removing the rear brake drum

6.9 Right-hand rear brake shoe and springs

6.10 Brake shoe holding down spring (trailing shoe shown)

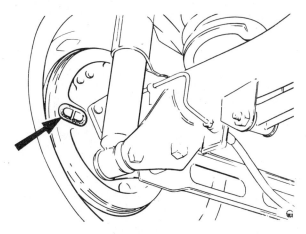

Fig. 7.12. Prise out the rubber brake inspecting plug (Sec. 6)

Fig. 7.13. Pull out the spring clip (D) and clevis pin (A) to disconnect the handbrake lever (C) from the clevis (B) (Sec. 6)

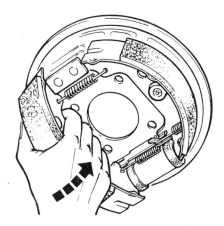

Fig. 7.14. Twisting off the leading shoe (Sec. 6)

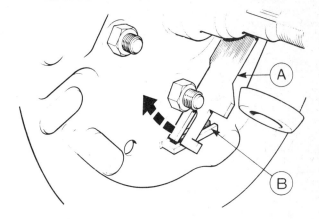

Fig. 7.15. Disconnecting the spacer strut (A) from its slot (B) (Sec. 6)

8   The bonded brake linings should be renewed once they have worn to a thickness of 0.06 in (1.5 mm). If riveted linings have been fitted, they should be renewed as soon as the rivet heads are flush with the lining material.

9   Note the size and location of the two retracting springs linking the two brake shoes (photo). The leading shoe is the shoe whose moving edge (touching the wheel cylinder) faces the drum in its normal rotation. In this photo, the lower shoe is the leading one.

10 Depress the leading shoe holding down spring (photo) and rotate its retaining washer through 90° to disengage it from the pin secured to the backplate. Lift away the washer and spring.

11 Twist the leading shoe outwards and upwards away from the backplate (Fig. 7.14). Remove the shoe retracting springs and the shoe.

12 Remove the trailing shoe holding down spring and washer as described in paragraph 10.

13 Slide the lower end of the spacer strut from the slot in the backplate (Fig. 7.15). Lift out the brake shoe, withdrawing the handbrake operating lever from the backplate.

14 Secure the wheel cylinder pistons by wrapping a length of soft wire or a strong elastic band around the cylinder. **Do not** operate the footbrake, as this will eject the pistons.

15 To dismantle the leading shoe assembly, prise off and discard the two spring clips, and remove the two ratchet arms and springs.

16 To dismantle the trailing shoe assembly, twist the spacer strut upwards and remove the strut, spring and handbrake operating lever.

17 Thoroughly clean all traces of dust from the shoes, backplates and brake drums using a stiff brush. It is recommended that compressed

air is not used as it blows up dust which **should not be inhaled.** Brake dust can cause judder, or squeal and, therefore, it is important to clean out as described.

18 Check that the piston is free in the cylinder, that the rubber dust covers are undamaged and in position, and that there are no hydraulic leaks.

19 Prior to reassembly smear a trace of brake lubricant on the shoe support pads, brake shoe pivots, and on the ratchet wheel face and threads. Wolfrakote TOP Paste is the most suitable lubricant for this purpose.

20 With the drum and hub assembly removed, it is advisable to examine

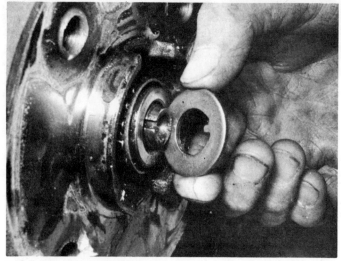

6.29 Refitting the tabbed washer

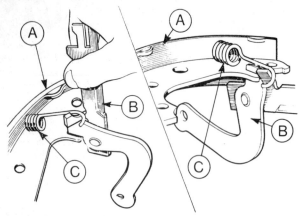

Fig. 7.16. Fit return spring (C) and spacer strut/handbrake lever (B) to brake shoe (A) then lever downwards (Sec. 6)

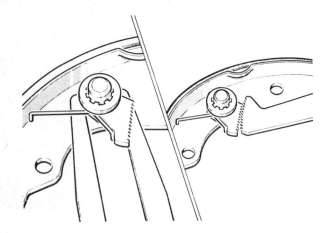

Fig. 7.17. Assemble the smaller ratchet using feeler blades, then engage the two ratchets (Sec. 6)

6.30 New split pin fitted through the nut retainer

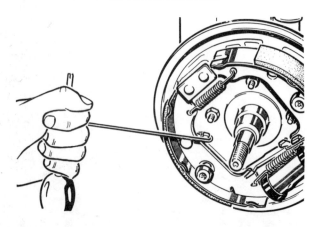

Fig. 7.18. Pulling the small ratchet back (Sec. 6)

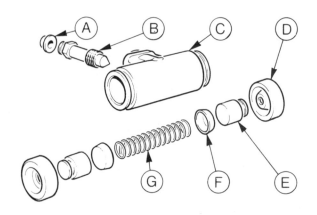

Fig. 7.19. Rear wheel cylinder components (Sec. 7)

A   Dust cap   E   Piston
B   Bleed nipple   F   Piston seal
C   Wheel cylinder   G   Spring
D   Dust cover

the bearings and oil seals for wear or damage, and renew them as detailed in Chapter 9, Section 11.

21 Fit the handbrake lever return spring to the trailing shoe, insert the spacer strut/handbrake lever and twist downwards (Fig. 7.16).

22 To reassemble the leading shoe, place the smaller ratchet on its post with two 0.008 in (0.2 mm) feeler blades under the ratchet (Fig. 7.17). Refit the return spring then press on a new retaining clip. Check that the ratchet rotates and returns freely.

23 Fit the larger ratchet to the brake shoe and press on a new retaining clip. Position the two ratchets with an overlap (Fig. 7.17).

24 Feed the handbrake lever through the backplate and fit the trailing shoe against its pivot point and the wheel cylinder piston. Secure the shoe to the backplate with the hold down spring and washer. Rotate the washer 90° to lock in position (photo 6.7). Locate the end of the spacer strut in its slot in the backplate.

25 Fit the stronger retracting spring between the two brake shoes, locate the leading shoe into the pivot point and twist it downwards against the backplate. Locate the other end against the wheel cylinder piston. Check that the larger ratchet slot engages with the spacer strut.

26 Fit the leading shoe hold down spring, then fit the weaker retracting spring between the two shoes using a suitable pair of pliers.

27 Using a suitable length of wire approximately 0.06 in (1.5 mm) diameter, make a small hook and pull the spring loaded ratchet back against its spring (Fig. 7.18).

28 Refit the handbrake operating lever gaiter against the backplate, and reconnect the cable, clevis pin and spring pin (Fig. 7.13).

29 Refit the brake drum and hub assembly. Slide in the outer bearing race and tabbed washer (photo).

30 Refit the retaining nut, and tighten it to a torque of 27 lb f ft (3.7 kg f m) while turning the brake drum. Slacken the nut 90°, to give the correct endfloat, then fit the nut retainer and a new split pin (photo). Bend up the ends of the split pin, and tap the dust cover fully home.

31 Refit the roadwheel, lower the car to the ground and tighten the wheel bolts.

32 Depress the brake pedal several times to bring the shoes into correct adjustment. Finally, road test the car to ensure correct operation of the brakes.

7 Drum brake wheel cylinder - removal, overhaul and refitting

1 Refer to Section 6 and remove the brake drum and shoes. Clean down the rear of the backplate using a stiff brush. Place a quantity of rag under the backplate to catch any hydraulic fluid that may issue from the open pipe or wheel cylinder.

2 Wipe the top of the brake master cylinder reservoir and unscrew the cap. Place a piece of polythene sheet over the top of the reservoir and refit the cap.

3 Using an open ended spanner carefully unscrew the hydraulic pipe connection union at the rear of the wheel cylinder. To prevent dirt entering, tape over the end of the pipe.

4 Unscrew the two retaining bolts from the rear of the backplate and remove the cylinder.

5 Unscrew and remove the brake bleed nipple.

6 Pull off the two rubber dust covers, and pull out the pistons (Fig. 7.19).

7 Slide out the piston seals, and remove the spring.

8 Inspect the cylinder bore for score marks caused by impurities in the hydraulic fluid. If any are found the cylinder and pistons will require renewal together, as a replacement unit.

9 If the cylinder bore is sound thoroughly clean it out with fresh hydraulic fluid.

10 Reassembly and refitting are a reversal of the above procedure, noting the following points:

  i)   Always use new seals and dust covers.
  ii) Lubricate the seals with hydraulic fluid and insert them carefully, larger diameter first, into the bore.
  iii) After refitting is complete, bleed the brakes, as described in Section 12.

8 Drum brake backplate - removal and refitting

1 Refer to Section 6 and remove the brake drum and shoes.

2 Refer to Section 7 and remove the wheel cylinder.

3 Remove the four retaining nuts and lift off the backplate.

4 When refitting the backplate, note the natural run of the brake fluid pipe, and refit the backplate accordingly.

5 Tighten the four retaining nuts, then refit the wheel cylinder, brake shoes and drum, Sections 6 and 7.

9 Master cylinder - removal and refitting

1 Apply the handbrake and chock the front wheels. Drain the fluid from the master cylinder reservoir and master cylinder by attaching a plastic bleed tube to one of the front brake bleed screws. Undo the screw one turn and then pump the fluid out into a clean glass container by means of the brake pedal. Hold the brake pedal against the floor at the end of each stroke and tighten the bleed screw. When the pedal has returned to its normal position loosen the bleed screw and repeat the process. The above sequence should now be carried out on one of the rear brake bleed screws.

2 Wipe the area around the union nuts on the side of the master cylinder body (photo) and, using an open ended spanner, undo the union nuts. Tape over the ends of the pipes to stop dirt entering.

3 Where applicable, pull off the pressure differential switch wire.

4 On models without a servo, unscrew the two screws and pull down

9.2 Right-hand drive brake master cylinder and servo unit

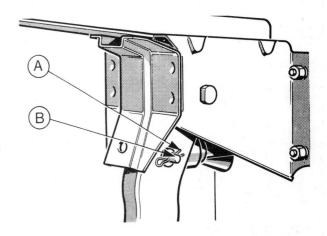

Fig. 7.20. Pull out the spring clip (A) and remove the clevis (B) (Sec. 9)

the lower dash trim panel. Withdraw the spring clip (Fig. 7.20) and pull out the clevis pin and bushes from the pedal.

5 Undo and remove the two nuts and spring washers that secure the master cylinder taking care not to damage the servo unit and ensure that no hydraulic fluid is allowed to drip onto the paintwork.

6 Refitting the master cylinder is the reverse sequence to removal. Always start the union nuts before finally tightening the master cylinder nuts. It will be necessary to bleed the complete hydraulic system; full details will be found in Section 12.

10 Master cylinder - overhaul

If a new master cylinder is to be fitted, it will be necessary to lubricate the seals before fitting to the car as they have a protective coating when originally assembled. Remove the blanking plugs from the hydraulic pipe union seatings. Inject clean hydraulic fluid into the master cylinder and operate the primary piston several times so that the fluid spreads over all the internal working surfaces.

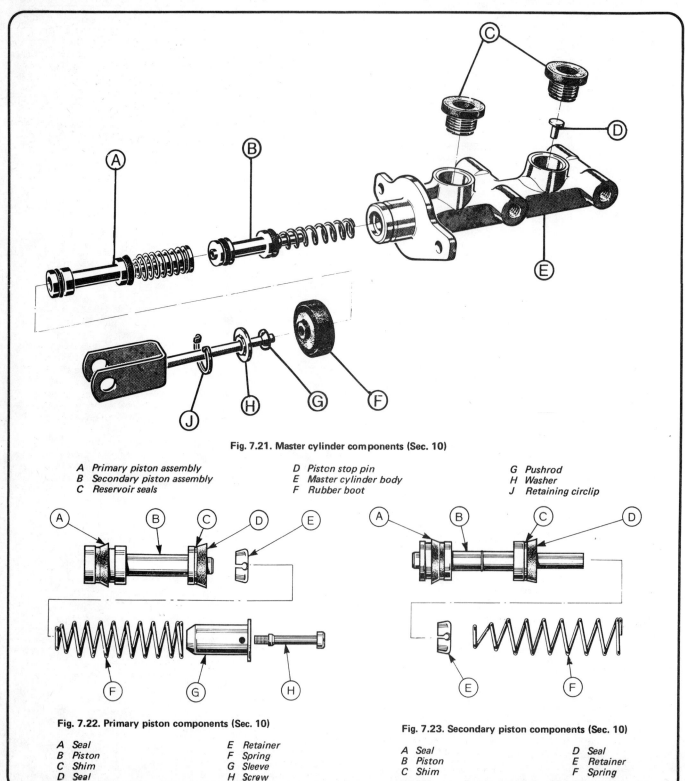

Fig. 7.21. Master cylinder components (Sec. 10)

A   Primary piston assembly   D   Piston stop pin   G   Pushrod
B   Secondary piston assembly   E   Master cylinder body   H   Washer
C   Reservoir seals   F   Rubber boot   J   Retaining circlip

Fig. 7.22. Primary piston components (Sec. 10)

A   Seal   E   Retainer
B   Piston   F   Spring
C   Shim   G   Sleeve
D   Seal   H   Screw

Fig. 7.23. Secondary piston components (Sec. 10)

A   Seal   D   Seal
B   Piston   E   Retainer
C   Shim   F   Spring

If the master cylinder is to be dismantled after removal, proceed as follows:

1   The component parts are shown in Fig. 7.21.

2   Before dismantling, wipe the exterior of the master cylinder and reservoir clean. Pull off the reservoir and lever out the two rubber seals.

3   Push in the operating rod to release the spring pressure, and lift out the piston stop pin (Fig. 7.21).

4   Pull the rubber boot back along the operating rod, then use a pair of thin nosed pliers to remove the rod retaining circlip. Lift out the rod with the circlip, washer and boot. Pull off and discard the boot.

5   Remove the primary piston assembly and lay to one side.

6   Lightly tap the master cylinder against a wooden base to shake out the secondary piston assembly.

7   To dismantle the primary piston, remove the screw (Fig. 7.22) and withdraw the sleeve, spring, retainer, seal and shim. Using a small screwdriver, lever off the second seal taking care not to damage the piston.

8   To dismantle the secondary piston (Fig. 7.23), pull off the spring, retainer, seal and shim. Use a small screwdriver to lever off the second seal, taking care not to damage the piston.

9   Thoroughly wash all parts in either methylated spirits or clean approved hydraulic fluid and place in order ready for inspection.

10 Examine the bore of the master cylinder carefully for any signs of scoring, ridges or corrosion and, if it is found to be smooth all over, new seals can be fitted. If there is any doubt as to the condition of the bore, then a new assembly must be obtained.

11 If examination of the seals shows them to be apparently oversize or very loose on their seats, suspect oil contamination in the system. Oil will swell these rubber seals, and if one is found to be swollen it is reasonable to assume that all seals in the braking system will require attention.

12 Before reassembly again wash all parts in methylated spirits or clean approved hydraulic fluid. **Do not** use any other type of oil or cleaning fluid or the seals will be damaged.

13 Reassembly is the reverse of this procedure, noting the following points:

Dip all seals in clean hydraulic fluid before fitting.
Seal lips **must** *face in the direction shown in Figs. 7.22 and 7.23.*
Lubricate the cylinder bore with clean hydraulic fluid before inserting the piston assemblies.

11 Flexible hoses - inspection, removal and refitting

1   Inspect the condition of the flexible hydraulic hoses leading from the front wings to the brake calipers, and also from the body to the brackets on the rear axle casing. If they are swollen, damaged or chafed, they must be renewed.

2   Undo the locknuts at both ends of the flexible hoses and then holding the hexagon nut on the flexible hose steady undo the other union and remove the flexible hose and washer.

3   Refitting is a reversal of the removal procedure, but carefully check that all the securing brackets are in a sound condition and that the locknuts are tight.

4   After refitment, the braking system must be bled, Section 12.

12 Bleeding the hydraulic system

1   Removal of all the air from the hydraulic system is essential to the correct working of the braking system, and before undertaking this, examine the fluid reservoir cap to ensure that both vent holes, one on top and the second underneath but not in line, are clear. Check the level of fluid and top-up if required.

2   Check all brake line unions and connections for possible seepage, and at the same time check the condition of the rubber hoses, which may be perished.

3   If the condition of the wheel cylinders is in doubt, check for possible signs of fluid leakage.

4   If there is any possibility of incorrect fluid having been put into the system, drain all the fluid out and flush through with methylated spirits. Renew all piston seals and cups since these will be affected and could possibly fail under pressure.

5   Gather together a clean jar, an 18 in (450 mm) length of plastic or

12.6 Fit a length of tubing then unscrew the bleed nipple

rubber tubing which fits tightly over the bleed nipple, and a tin of the correct brake fluid.

6   Clean the dirt from around the left-hand front caliper bleed nipple, pull off the dust cap and push on the length of tubing (photo).

7   Place the other end of the tube in the jar and add about ¾ in (20 mm) of brake fluid — just enough to cover the end of the tube. Now raise the jar and support it at least 12 in (300 mm) above the bleed nipple. Slacken the bleed screw about half a turn, then have an assistant depress and release the brake pedal.

8   As the pedal is depressed, brake fluid and/or air should be pumped into the jar. If not, unscrew the bleed valve further until this happens. Continue depressing and releasing the brake pedal, pausing for about 3 seconds between each stroke, until no more bubbles can be seen coming from the tube, then tighten the bleed nipple (with the pedal released), remove the rubber tube and refit the dust cap. At intervals make certain that the reservoir is kept topped up, otherwise air will enter at this point again.

9   Repeat the operations of paragraphs 6 to 8 on the other front brake.

10 On vehicles which have a brake pressure control valve, repeat the operations of paragraphs 6 to 8 on the upper bleed nipple; then similarly bleed the lower nipple.

11 Repeat the bleeding operations on each rear drum brake. **Note** *On models with a brake pressure control valve, this valve may operate if the pedal is depressed too quickly. This is indicated by an appreciable resistance to pedal effort and, should it occur, the pedal should be released for approximately 10 seconds before the bleeding operation is repeated.*

12 When completed, check the level of the fluid in the reservoir and then check the feel of the brake pedal, which should be firm and free from any 'spongy' action, which is normally associated with air in the system.

13 Pressure control valve - description, removal and refitting

1   This valve is a deceleration sensing valve fitted as a legal requirement in certain territories. On heavy braking, the front of the car dips, thus reducing the weight over the rear wheels and making it easier to lock the rear brakes. As the car brakes, a ball is thrown forward against a spring, and reduces, and finally stops, the flow of fluid to the rear brakes. The ball stays in the closed position until the car has slowed sufficiently for the spring to force the ball off its seat and allow fluid to flow to the rear brakes.

2   The valve itself cannot be serviced, and should be renewed if faulty.

3   Remove the master cylinder reservoir cap, place a piece of polythene over the neck and refit the cap.

4   Unscrew the four pressure lines from the valve and tape the ends to prevent loss of fluid and entry of dirt.

5   Undo and remove the two mounting bolts and nuts from the bracket, in front of the right-hand rear wheel, and remove the valve.

6 Refit the valve to its bracket, and screw on the nuts a few turns.
7 Refit the four brake line unions to their respective locations:

a) *From left front brake to upper port on side of valve (next to bleed nipple).*
b) *From right front brake to lower port on side of valve (next to bleed nipple).*
c) *From upper port on front of valve to right rear brake.*
d) *From lower port on front of valve to left rear brake.*

8 Tighten the two mounting bolts.
9 Remove the piece of polythene from the master cylinder reservoir, and bleed the brakes, Section 12.

14 Servo unit (brake booster) - description

On some variants, a vacuum servo unit is fitted into the brake hydraulic circuit in series with the master cylinder, to provide assistance to the driver when the brake pedal is depressed. This reduces the effort required by the driver to operate the brakes under all braking conditions.

The unit operates by vacuum obtained from the induction manifold and comprises basically a booster diaphragm and check valve. The servo unit and hydraulic master cylinder are connected together so that the servo unit piston rod acts as the master cylinder pushrod. The driver's braking effort is transmitted through another pushrod, and a linkage on right-hand drive vehicles, to the servo unit piston and its built-in control system. The servo unit piston does not fit tightly into the cylinder but has a strong diaphragm to keep its edges in constant contact with the the cylinder wall, so assuring an airtight seal between the two parts. The forward chamber is held under vacuum conditions created in the inlet manifold of the engine and, during periods when the brake pedal is not in use, the controls open a passage to the rear chamber so placing it under vacuum conditions as well. When the brake pedal is depressed, the vacuum passage to the rear chamber is cut off and the chamber exposed to atmospheric pressure. The consequent rush of air pushes the servo piston forward in the vacuum chamber and operates the main pushrod to the master cylinder.

The controls are designed so that assistance is given under all conditions and, when the brakes are not required, vacuum in the rear chamber is established when the brake pedal is released. All air from the atmosphere entering the rear chamber is passed through a small air filter.

Under normal operating conditions the vacuum servo unit is very reliable and does not require overhaul except at very high mileages. In this case it is far better to obtain a service exchange unit, rather than repair the original unit.

15 Servo unit - removal and refitting

1 Slacken the clip securing the vacuum hose to the servo unit, and

pull off the hose.
2 Remove the master cylinder, Section 9.
3 *Left-hand drive variants:* Remove the two crosshead screws and pull down the lower dash trim panel. Withdraw the spring clip (Fig. 7.20), and pull out the clevis pin and bushes from the pedal.
4 *Right-hand drive variants:* From inside the engine compartment, withdraw the spring clip and pull out the clevis pin from the servo unit pushrod.
5 Undo and remove the four nuts and spring washers that secure the servo unit, and remove the unit.
6 Refitting is the reverse of this procedure. It will then be necessary to bleed the brakes, Section 12.

16 Brake pedal and linkage - removal, overhaul and refitting

1 On all left-hand drive variants, and right-hand drive variants without a servo unit, the brake pedal pushrod is also the master cylinder or servo unit pushrod as applicable. On right-hand drive vehicles with a servo unit, the brake pedal pushrod is connected to the servo pushrod through a connecting linkage (Fig. 7.24).
2 On all right-hand drive variants, the clutch and brake pedal box must be removed to remove the brake pedal. This is not necessary on left-hand drive cars.

Left-hand drive brake pedal
3 Pull off the spring clip and withdraw the pushrod clevis pin from the brake pedal.
4 Remove the retaining clip, then pull the pedal shaft and clutch pedal sideways, releasing the pedal, pedal bushes, flat washers and wave washer.

Right-hand drive brake pedal
5 Refer to Chapter 5, Section 7 and disconnect the clutch cable from the pedal.
6 From inside the engine compartment, unscrew and remove the four nuts securing the pedal box to the bulkhead.
7 Unscrew the two crosshead screws and pull down the lower dash trim panel.
8 Make a note of the connections and pull the two wires from the brake light switch (Fig. 7.25).
9 Pull off the spring clip and withdraw the pushrod clevis pin. Unscrew the pedal box retaining bolt (Fig. 7.25) and pull the pedal box assembly rearward.
10 Remove the retaining clip, then pull the pedal shaft and clutch pedal sideways, releasing the brake pedal, pedal bushes, flat washers and wave washer (Fig. 7.26).

Right-hand drive servo connecting linkage
11 Remove the spring clip and clevis pin from the pedal pushrod at the connecting linkage (Fig. 7.27).
12 Remove the spring clip and clevis pin from the servo unit pushrod.

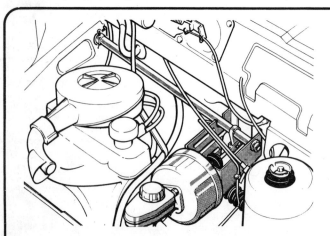

Fig. 7.24 Right-hand drive servo unit and connecting linkage (Sec. 16)

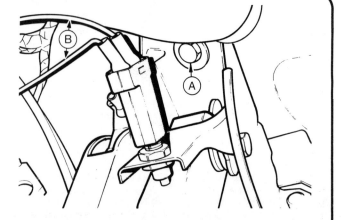

Fig. 7.25. Remove the two brake light switch wires (B) and unscrew the pedal box screw (A) (Sec. 16)

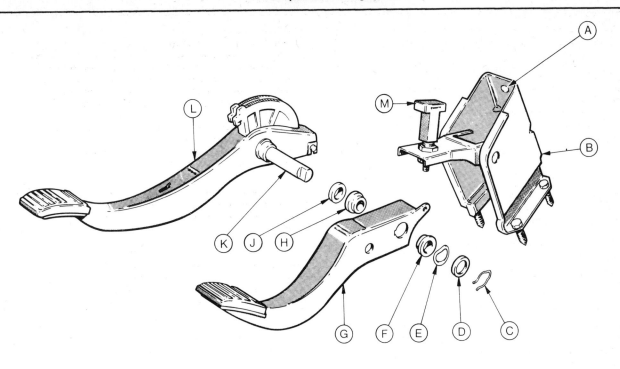

Fig. 7.26. Brake and clutch pedal assembly (Sec. 16)

A *Retaining bolt hole*	D *Flat washer*	G *Brake pedal*
B *Pedal box*	E *Wave washer*	H *Pedal bush*
C *Spring clip*	F *Pedal bush*	J *Flat washer*

K *Pedal shaft*
L *Clutch pedal*
M *Brake light switch*

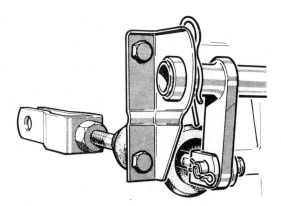

Fig. 7.27. Brake pedal connecting linkage for right-hand drive cars with a servo unit (Sec. 16)

13 Pull off the cross-shaft spring clip (Fig. 7.27), then push the cross-shaft to one side. Disengage it from its end housing, and lift and remove it. Remove the cross-shaft mounting bushes.

All variants
14 Examine all bushes, clevis pins and spring clips for wear, damage or deterioration, and renew as necessary.
15 Refitting is the reverse of this procedure.

17 Handbrake - adjustment

1 Adjustment of the handbrake is normally automatically carried out by the action of the rear brake automatic adjusters. When new components have been fitted or where the handbrake cable has stretched, then the following operations should be carried out.
2 Chock the front wheels, jack-up the rear of the car and support on firmly based axle stands. Release the handbrake.
3 Slide under the car and check that the cables follow their correct runs and are correctly fitted in their guides (Fig. 7.29). The cable

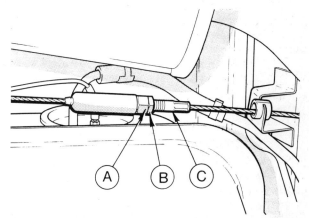

Fig. 7.28. Slacken the locknut (B) and turn the adjuster (A) to remove the slack from the cable (C) (Sec. 17)

guides must be kept well greased at all times.
4 Slacken the adjuster locknut and unscrew the adjuster (Fig. 7.28). Tighten the adjuster until all the cable slack has been removed and the handbrake levers begin to move.
5 From the point where the levers begin to move, tighten the adjuster three complete turns, then tighten the locknut.
6 Finally remove the stands and lower the car to the ground.

18 Handbrake lever - removal and refitting

1 Chock the front wheels, jack-up the rear of the car and support on firmly based axle stands. Release the handbrake.
2 Working inside the car remove the carpeting from around the area of the handbrake lever.
3 Remove the split pin and withdraw the clevis pin that connects the cable to the lower end of the handbrake lever (Fig. 7.30).
4 Undo and remove the two bolts that secure the handbrake lever assembly to the floor. Lift away the lever assembly.
5 Refitting the lever assembly is the reverse sequence to removal.

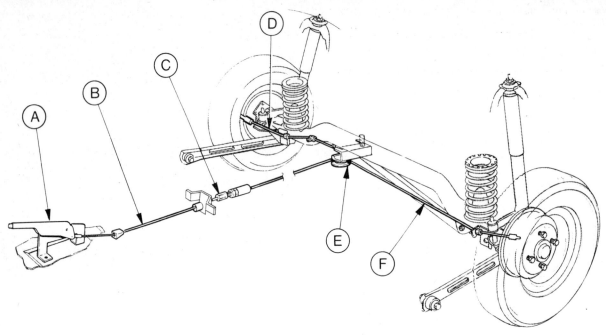

Fig. 7.29. Handbrake cables (Sec. 17 and 19)

A   Handbrake lever   C   Cable adjuster   E   Equaliser
B   Primary cable   D   Transverse cable   F   Rear cable

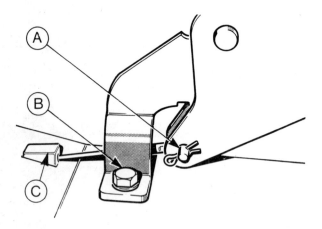

Fig. 7.30. Handbrake lever (Sec. 18 and 19)

A   Clevis spring pin   C   Cable guide
B   Handbrake

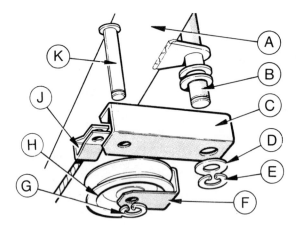

Fig. 7.31. Handbrake cable equaliser (Sec. 19)

A   Axle tube   F   Cable guide
B   Pivot rod   G   Spring clip
C   Equaliser bracket   H   Cable roller
D   Washer   J   Transverse cable clevis
E   Spring clip   K   Clevis pin

The following additional points should be noted:

a) *Apply some grease to the primary cable clevis pin.*
b) *Adjust the cable as described in Section 17.*

19 Handbrake cables - removal and refitting

Primary cable
1   Chock the front wheels, jack up the rear of the car and support on firmly based axle stands. Release the handbrake.
2   Remove the carpet from around the handbrake lever, withdraw the split pin and the clevis pin that retains the cable (Fig. 7.30).
3   Slacken the adjuster locknut (Fig. 7.28) and unscrew the adjuster from the cable.

4   Using a soft-faced hammer, tap the cable guide down through the floor, and remove the cable.
5   Refitting the primary cable is the reverse sequence to removal but the following additional points should be noted:

a) *Apply some grease to the cable guides and insert the cable. Also lubricate the front clevis pin.*
b) *Refer to Section 17 and adjust the primary cable.*

Rear cable
6   Chock the front wheels, jack up the rear of the car and support on firmly based axle stands. Release the handbrake.
7   Slacken the adjuster locknut (Fig. 7.28) and unscrew the adjuster from the primary cable.
8   Remove the spring clip from the cable roller clevis pin (Fig. 7.31) and remove the cable roller and guide.

9   Remove the spring clip and clevis pin from the left-hand rear brake handbrake lever, and remove the cable.
10 Refitting the cable is the reverse sequence to removal but the following additional points should be noted:

a) *Apply some grease to the pulley and pivot pin, the threaded end of the cable and the clevis pin.*
b) *Adjust the cable as described in Section 17.*

Transverse cable

11 Chock the front wheels, jack up the rear of the car and support on firmly based axle stands. Release the handbrake.
12 Remove the spring clip and clevis pin from the right-hand rear brake handbrake cable.
13 Remove the spring clip from the cable roller clevis pin (Fig. 7.31), and remove the clevis pin and transverse cable clevis.
14 Refitting is the reverse sequence to removal but the following additional points should be noted:

a) *Apply some grease to the cable guide (photo) and two clevis pins.*
b) *Check the primary cable adjustment as described in Section 17.*

19.14 Apply grease to the transverse cable guide

20 Fault diagnosis

Before diagnosing faults from the following chart, check that any braking irregularities are not caused by:

1   *Uneven and incorrect tyre pressures.*
2   *Incorrect 'mix' of radial and crossply tyres.*
3   *Wear in the steering mechanism.*
4   *Defects in the suspension and dampers.*
5   *Misalignment of the bodyframe.*

Symptom	Reason/s
Pedal travels a long way before the brakes operate	Brake shoes set too far from the drums (auto. adjusters seized).
Stopping ability poor, even though pedal pressure is firm	Linings, discs or drums badly worn or scored. One or more wheel hydraulic cylinders seized, resulting in some brake shoes not pressing against the drums (or pads against discs). Brake linings contaminated with oil. Wrong type of linings fittings (too hard). Brake shoes wrongly assembled. Servo unit not functioning.
Car veers to one side when the brakes are applied	Brake pads or linings on one side are contaminated with oil. Hydraulic wheel cylinder(s) on one side partially or fully seized. A mixture of lining materials fitted between sides. Brake discs not matched. Unequal wear between sides caused by partially seized wheel cylinders.
Pedal feels spongy when the brakes are applied	Air is present in the hydraulic system.
Pedal feels springy when the brakes are applied	Brake linings not bedded into the drums (after fitting new ones). Master cylinder or brake backplate mounting bolts loose. Severe wear in brake drums causing distortion when brakes are applied. Discs out of true.
Pedal travels right down with little or no resistance and brakes are virtually non-operative	Leak in hydraulic system resulting in lack of pressure for operating wheel cylinders. If no signs of leakage are apparent the master cylinder internal seals are failing to sustain pressure.
Binding, juddering, overheating	One or a combination of reasons given in the foregoing Sections.

Chapter 8 Electrical system

Contents

Specifications

System type	12 volt, negative earth (ground)

Battery

Type	12 volt, lead acid
Capacity - 960 cc	27 amp hour
1100 cc	45 amp hour
1300 cc	45 amp hour
1600 cc	54 amp hour (35 amp hour, USA)

Note: *A battery of higher capacity may be fitted for some markets, or as an option*

Specific gravity, charged	1.27 to 1.29 at 25°C (77°F)

Starter motor (Lucas)

Type	M 35 J
Number of brushes	4
Minimum brush length	0.32 in (8 mm)
Brush spring force	6.16 lb (2.8 kg)
Minimum commutator thickness	0.03 in (2.05 mm)
Maximum current draw	365 amps

Starter motor (Bosch)

	0.5 PS	0.7 PS
Number of brushes	4	4
Minimum brush length	0.39 in (10 mm)	0.39 in (10 mm)
Brush spring force	2.0 to 2.7 lb (0.9 to 1.3 kg)	2.0 to 2.7 lb (0.9 to 1.3 kg)
Minimum commutator diameter	1.29 in (32.8 mm)	1.29 in (32.8 mm)
Maximum current draw	305 amp	380 amp

Starter motor (Femsa)

Number of brushes	2
Minimum brush length	0.47 in (12 mm)
Brush spring force	1.54 to 3.08 lb (0.7 to 1.4 kg)
Minimum commutator diameter	1.18 in (30 mm)
Maximum current draw	325 amp

Alternator (Lucas)

	15 ACR	17 ACR	18 ACR
Nominal output at 13.5 volt (6000 rpm)	28 amp	35 amp	45 amp
Maximum continuous speed (rpm)	15,000	15,000	15,000
Stator winding resistance per phase	0.198 ohm	0.133 ohm	0.092 ohm
Rotor winding resistance at 20°C (68°F)	3.35 ohm ± 5%	3.25 ohm ± 5%	3.25 ohm ± 5%
Minimum brush length	0.2 in (5 mm)	0.2 in (5 mm)	0.2 in (5 mm)
Regulating voltage, 4000 rpm, 3 to 7 amp load	14.2 to 14.6 volt	14.2 to 14.6 volt	14.2 to 14.6 volt

Alternator (Bosch)

	G1-28A	K1-45A
Nominal output at 13.5 volt (6000 rpm)	28 amp	45 amp
Maximum continuous speed (rpm)	15,000	15,000
Stator winding resistance per phase	0.2 ohm	0.1 ohm
Rotor winding resistance at 20°C (68°F)	4.0 ohm	4.0 ohm
Minimum brush length	0.2 in (5 mm)	0.2 in (5 mm)
Regulating voltage, 4000 rpm, 3 to 7 amp load	13.7 to 14.5 volt	13.7 to 14.5 volt

Alternator (Femsa)

	ALT-12N	ALS-12N
Nominal output at 13.5 volt (6000 rpm)	32 amp	45 amp
Maximum continuous speed (rpm)	15,000	15,000
Stator winding resistance per phase	0.17 ohm	0.09 ohm
Rotor winding resistance at 20°C (68°F)	4.0 ohm	4.5 ohm
Minimum brush length	0.3 in (7 mm)	0.3 in (7 mm)
Regulating voltage, 4000 rpm, 3 to 7 amp load	13.7 to 14.5 volt	13.7 to 14.5 volt

Windscreen wipers

Front	Two speed electric, self-parking
Rear (where fitted)	Single speed electric, self-parking

Bulb chart

	Quantity	Size	Fitting
Headlamp - Halogen	2	55/60 watt	clip ring
Tungsten	2	45/50 watt	clip ring
Side light (parking lamp)	2	4 watt	bayonet
Stop/rear light	2	21/5 watt	bayonet
Reversing light (back-up lamp)	1	21 watt	bayonet
License plate light	2	4 watt	bayonet
Direction indicators - front	2	21 watt	bayonet
rear	2	21 watt	bayonet
side	2	4 watt	bayonet
Warning lights - instruments	5	1.3 watt	push in
switches	-	1.3 watt	push in
Panel illumination lights	3 or 4	2.6 watt	push in
Clock illumination	2	1.4 watt	bayonet
Cigarette lighter	1	1.4 watt	bayonet
Glove compartment	1	1 watt	push in
Interior light	1	10 watt	bayonet

Fuses (not USA)

Main fuse box below facia

Fuse No.	Rating	Circuits protected
1	8 amp	Interior light, hazard flashers, horn, clock, cigarette lighter, glove box light
2	16 amp	Stop lights, heater motor, engine fan, direction indicators, reversing light, windscreen washers
3	8 amp	Wiper motor, instruments, brake warning system, rear screen wash/wipe system
4	8 amp	LH side light, RH rear light, rear fog lamp
5	8 amp	RH side light, LH rear light, instrument illumination, license plate light, clock light, cigarette lighter illumination
6	8 amp	Main beam, headlamps
7	8 amp	Dipped beam headlamps

Fuses (USA)

Main fuse box below facia	Fuse No.	Rating	Circuits protected
...	1	16 amp	Cigarette lighter, horn, interior lamp. flasher lights, stop light
	2	8 amp	Windshield washer, seat belt control, heater blower, back up (reversing) lamp
	3	8 amp	Wiper motor, brake warning system, instrument cluster, exhaust emission system, wiper/washer system, heated rear window (backlight)
	4	8 amp	RH tail lamp, RH side marker, license plate lamp
	5	8 amp	Instrument illumination, LH tail lamp, LH side marker
	6	8 amp	High beam
	7	8 amp	Low beam
	8	8 amp	Cooling fan switch

Other fuses

Bracket next to pedal box under facia		
	16 amp	Heated rear window
	2 amp	Radio supply

Torque wrench settings

									lb f ft	kg f m
Alternator pulley nut	...	...	...	...	...	...	...	...	25 to 29	3.5 to 4.0
Alternator mounting bolts	...	...	...	...	...	...	...		15 to 18	2.1 to 2.5
Alternator mounting bracket	...	...	...	...	...	...	...		20 to 25	2.8 to 3.5
Starter motor retaining bolts	...	...	...	...	...	...	...		20 to 25	2.8 to 3.5

1 General description

The major components of the 12 volt negative earth system comprise a 12 volt battery, an alternator (driven from the crankshaft pulley), and a starter motor.

The battery supplies a steady amount of current for the ignition, lighting and other electrical circuits and provides a reserve of power when the current consumed by the electrical equipment exceeds that being produced by the alternator.

The alternator has its own regulator which ensures a high output if the battery is in a low state of charge and the demand from the electrical equipment is high, and a low output if the battery is fully charged and there is little demand from the electrical equipment.

When fitting electrical accessories to cars with a negative earth system it is important, if they contain silicone diodes or transistors, that they are connected correctly; otherwise serious damage may result to the components concerned. Items such as radios, tape players, electronic ignition systems, electronic tachometer, automatic dipping etc, should all be checked for correct polarity.

It is important that the battery positive lead is always disconnected if the battery is to be boost charged, also if body repairs are to be carried out using electric welding equipment - the alternator must be disconnected otherwise serious damage can be caused. Whenever the battery has to be disconnected it must always be reconnected with the negative terminal earthed. Whenever working on electrical equipment, it is a good idea to disconnect the battery earth lead. Do not forget to reset the clock once the battery has been reconnected.

2 Battery - removal and refitting

1 The battery is on a carrier fitted to the valance of the engine compartment. It should be removed once every three months for cleaning and testing. Disconnect the positive and then the negative leads from the battery terminals by undoing and removing the plated nuts and bolts. Note that two cables are attached to the positive terminal.

2 Unscrew and remove the bolt, and plain washer that secures the battery clamp plate to the carrier. Lift away the clamp plate. Carefully lift the battery from its carrier holding it vertically to ensure that none of the electrolyte is spilled.

3 Refitting is a direct reversal of this procedure. **Note:** Refit the negative lead before the positive lead and smear the terminals with petroleum jelly to prevent corrosion. **Never** use an ordinary grease.

3 Battery - maintenance and inspection

1 Normal weekly battery maintenance consists of checking the electrolyte level of each cell to ensure that the separators are covered by ¼ inch (6 mm) of electrolyte. If the level has fallen top-up the battery using distilled water only. Do not overfill. If a battery is overfilled or any electrolyte spilled, immediately wipe away and neutralize as electrolyte attacks and corrodes any metal it comes

into contact with very rapidly.

2 If the battery has the Auto-fil device fitted, a special topping-up sequence is required. The white balls in the Auto-fil battery are part of the automatic topping up device which ensures correct electrolyte level. The vent chamber should remain in position at all times except when topping-up or taking specific gravity readings. If the electrolyte level in any of the cells is below the bottom of the filling tube top-up as follows:

   a) *Lift off the vent chamber cover.*
   b) *With the battery level, pour distilled water into the trough until all the filling tubes are full.*
   c) *Immediately refit the cover to allow the water in the trough and tubes to flow into the cells. Each cell will automatically receive the correct amount of water.*

3 As well as keeping the terminals clean and covered with petroleum jelly, the top of the battery, and especially the top of the cells, should be kept clean and dry. This helps prevent corrosion and ensures that the battery does not become partially discharged by leakage through dampness and dirt.

4 Once every three months remove the battery and inspect the battery securing bolts, the battery clamp plate, tray, and battery leads for corrosion (white fluffy deposits on the metal which are brittle to touch). If any corrosion is found, clean off the deposits with ammonia and paint over the clean metal with an anti-rust/anti-acid paint.

5 At the same time inspect the battery case for cracks. If a crack is found, clean and plug it with one of the proprietary compounds marketed for this purpose. If leakage through the crack has been excessive then it will be necessary to refill the appropriate cell with fresh electrolyte as detailed later. Cracks are frequently caused to the top of the battery case by pouring in distilled water in the middle of winter *after* instead of *before* a run. This gives the water no chance to mix with the electrolyte and so the former freezes and splits the battery case.

6 If topping-up the battery becomes excessive and the case has been inspected for cracks that could cause leakage, but none are found, the battery is being overcharged and the voltage regulator will have to be checked by an automobile electrician.

7 With the battery on the bench at the three monthly interval check, measure the specific gravity with a hydrometer to determine the state of charge and condition of the electrolyte. There should be very little variation between the different cells and if variation in excess of 0.025 is present it will be due to either:

   a) *Loss of electrolyte from the battery at some time caused by spillage or a leak resulting in a drop in the specific gravity of the electrolyte, when the deficiency was replaced with distilled water instead of fresh electrolyte.*
   b) *An internal short circuit caused by buckling of the plates or a similar malady pointing to the likelihood of total battery failure in the near future.*

8 The specific gravity of the electrolyte for fully charged conditions at the electrolyte temperature indicated, is listed in Table A. The

specific gravity of a fully discharged battery at different temperatures of the electrolyte is given in Table B.

Table A
Specific Gravity - Battery Fully Charged
1.268 at 100°F or 38°C electrolyte temperature
1.272 at 90°F or 32°C electrolyte temperature
1.276 at 80°F or 27°C electrolyte temperature
1.280 at 70°F or 21°C electrolyte temperature
1.284 at 60°F or 16°C electrolyte temperature
1.288 at 50°F or 10°C electrolyte temperature
1.292 at 40°F or 4°C electrolyte temperature
1.296 at 30°F or -1.5°C electrolyte temperature

Table B
Specific Gravity - Battery Fully Discharged
1.098 at 100°F or 38°C electrolyte temperature
1.102 at 90°F or 32°C electrolyte temperature
1.106 at 80°F or 27°C electrolyte temperature
1.110 at 70°F or 21°C electrolyte temperature
1.114 at 60°F or 16°C electrolyte temperature
1.118 at 50°F or 10°C electrolyte temperature
1.122 at 40°F or 4°C electrolyte temperature
1.126 at 30°F or -1.5°C electrolyte temperature

4   Battery - eleotrolyte replenishment

1   If the battery is in a fully charged state and one of the cells maintains a specific gravity reading which is 0.025 or more lower than the others, and where possible a check of each cell has been made with a voltmeter to check for short circuits (a four to seven second test should give a steady reading of between 12 to 18 volts) then it is likely that electrolyte has been lost from the cell with the low reading.

2   Top-up the cell with a solution of 1 part sulphuric acid to 2.5 parts of water. If the cell is already fully topped-up draw some electrolyte out of it with a hydrometer.

3   When mixing the sulphuric acid and water **never add water to sulphuric acid** - always pour the acid slowly onto the water in a glass container. **If water is added to sulphuric acid it will explode.**

4   Continue to top-up the cell with the freshly made electrolyte and then recharge the battery and check the hydrometer readings.

5   Battery - charging

1   In winter time when heavy demand is placed upon the battery, such as when starting from cold, and most electrical equipment is continually in use, it is a good idea to occasionally have the battery fully charged from an external source at the rate of 3.5 to 4 amps.

2   Continue to charge the battery at this rate until no further rise in specific gravity is noted over a four hour period.

3   Alternatively, a trickle charger charging at the rate of 1.5 amps can be safely used overnight.

4   Specially rapid 'boost' charges which are claimed to restore the power of the battery in 1 to 2 hours are not recommended as they can cause serious damage to the battery plates through over-heating.

5   While charging the battery, note that the temperature of the electrolyte should never exceed 100°F (37.8°C).

6   Alternator - general

The alternator may be of Lucas, Bosch or Femsa manufacture according to the production source (Fig. 8.1).

The main advantage of the alternator over its predecessor, the dynamo, lies in its ability to provide a high charge at low revolutions.

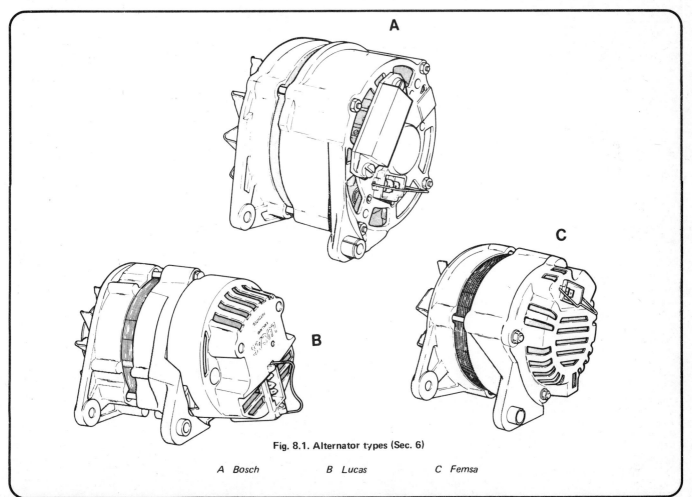

Fig. 8.1. Alternator types (Sec. 6)

A Bosch   *B Lucas*   *C Femsa*

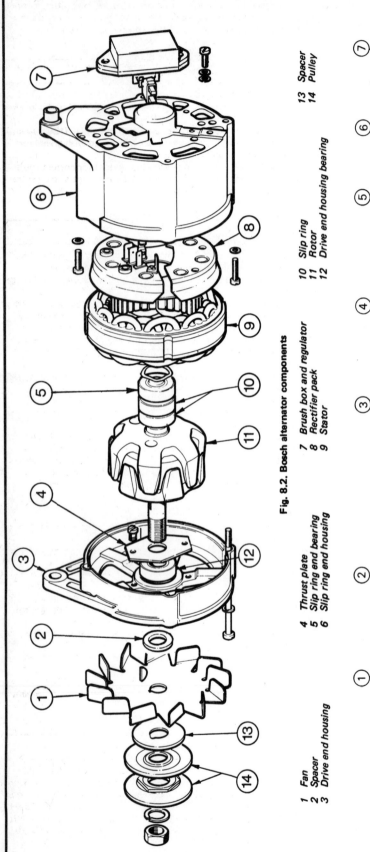

Fig. 8.2. Bosch alternator components

1	Fan	4	Thrust plate	7	Brush box and regulator	10	Slip ring	13	Spacer
2	Spacer	5	Slip ring end bearing	8	Rectifier pack	11	Rotor	14	Pulley
3	Drive end housing	6	Slip ring end housing	9	Stator	12	Drive end housing bearing		

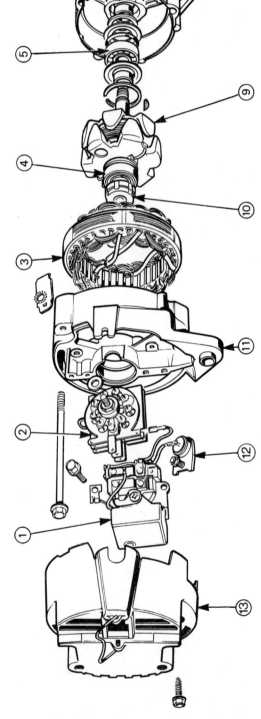

Fig. 8.3. Lucas alternator components

1	Regulator	4	Slip ring end bearing	7	Pulley	10	Slip ring	12	Surge protection diode
2	Rectifier pack	5	Drive end bearing	8	Fan	11	Slip ring end housing	13	End cover
3	Stator	6	Drive end housing	9	Rotor				

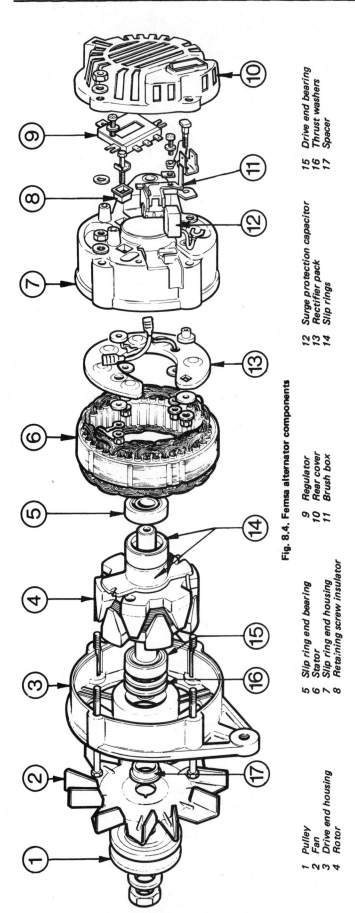

Fig. 8.4. Femsa alternator components

1 Pulley
2 Fan
3 Drive end housing
4 Rotor

5 Slip ring end bearing
6 Stator
7 Slip ring end housing
8 Retaining screw insulator

9 Regulator
10 Rear cover
11 Brush box

12 Surge protection capacitor
13 Rectifier pack
14 Slip rings

15 Drive end bearing
16 Thrust washers
17 Spacer

Driving slowly in heavy traffic with a dynamo invariably means no charge is reaching the battery. In similar conditions even with the wiper, heater, lights and perhaps radio switched on the alternator will ensure a charge reaches the battery.

7 Alternator - routine maintenance

1   The equipment has been designed for the minimum amount of maintenance in service, the only items subject to wear being the brushes and bearings.
2   Brushes should be examined after about 75,000 miles (120,000 km) and renewed if necessary. The bearings are prepacked with grease for life, and should not require further attention.
3   Check the fan belt every 3,000 miles (5,000 km) for correct adjustment which should be 0.5 inch (13 mm) total movement at the centre of the longest run between pulleys.

8 Alternator - special procedures

Whenever the electrical system of the car is being attended to, and external means of starting the engine are used, there are certain precautions that must be taken otherwise serious and expensive damage can result.
1   Always make sure that the negative terminal of the battery is earthed. If the terminal connections are accidentally reversed or if the battery has been reverse charged the alternator diodes will be damaged.
2   The output terminal on the alternator marked 'BAT' or 'B+' must never be earthed but should always be connected directly to the positive terminal of the battery.
3   Whenever the alternator is to be removed or when disconnecting the terminals of the alternator circuit, always disconnect the battery terminal earth first.
4   The alternator must never be operated without the battery to alternator cable connected.
5   If the battery is to be charged by external means always disconnect both battery cables before the external charger is connected.
6   Should it be necessary to use a booster charger or booster battery to start the engine always double check that the negative cable is connected to negative terminal and the positive cable to positive terminal.

9 Alternator - removal and refitting

1   Disconnect the battery leads.
2   Note the terminal connections at the rear of the alternator and disconnect the plug or multipin connector.
3   Undo and remove the alternator adjustment arm bolt (photo) slacken the alternator mounting bolts and push the alternator inwards towards the engine. Lift away the fan belt from the pulley.
4   Remove the remaining two mounting bolts and carefully lift the alternator away from the car (photo).
5   Take care not to knock or drop the alternator otherwise this can cause irreparable damage.
6   Refitting the alternator is the reverse sequence to removal.
7   Adjust the fan belt so that it has 0.5 inch (13 mm) total movement at the centre of the longest run between pulleys.

10 Alternator - fault diagnosis and repair

Due to the specialist knowledge and equipment required to test or service an alternator it is recommended that if the performance is suspect the car be taken to an automobile electrician who will have the facilities for such work. Because of this recommendation, information is limited to the inspection and renewal of the brushes. Should the alternator not charge or the system be suspect the following points may be checked before seeking further assistance:

1   *Check the fan belt tension, as described in Section 7.*
2   *Check the battery, as described in Section 3.*
3   *Check all electrical cable connections for cleanliness and security.*

9.3 Unscrew the alternator adjusting arm bolts ...

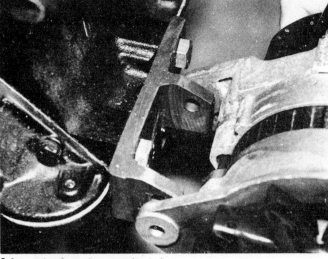

9.4 ... and remove the mounting bolts

Fig. 8.5. Lucas brush retaining screws (Sec. 11)

Fig. 8.7. Bosch regulator retaining screws (Sec. 12)

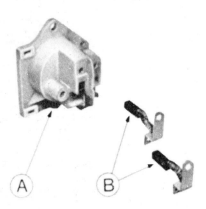

Fig. 8.6. Lucas brush box (A) and brushes (B) (Sec. 11)

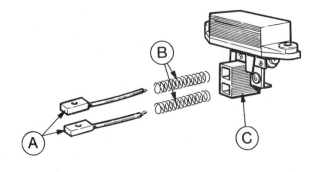

Fig. 8.8. Bosch brushes (A), brush springs (B) and brush box (C) (Sec. 12)

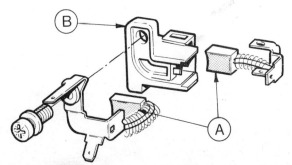

Fig. 8.9. Femsa brushes (A) and brush box (B) (Sec. 13)

11 Alternator brushes (Lucas) - inspection, removal and refitting

1   Undo and remove the two screws and washers securing the end cover.

2   To inspect the brushes correctly the brush holder mountings should be removed complete by undoing the two bolts and disconnecting the 'Lucar' connection to the diode plates.

3   With the brush holder moulding removed and the brush assemblies still in position check that they protrude from the face of the moulding by at least 0.2 inches (5 mm). Also check that when depressed, the

spring pressure is 7 to 10 ozs, when the end of the brush is flush with the face of the brush moulding. To be done with any accuracy this requires a push type spring gauge.

4   Should either of the foregoing requirements not be fulfilled the spring assemblies should be renewed (Fig. 8.5).

5   This can be done by simply removing the holding screws of each assembly and renewing them (Fig. 8.6).

6   With the brush holder moulding removed the slip rings on the face end of the rotor are exposed. These can be cleaned with a petrol soaked cloth and any signs of burning may be removed very carefully with with fine glass paper. On no account should any other abrasive be used or any attempt at machining be made.

7   When the brushes are refitted they should slide smoothly in their holders. Any sticking tendency may first be rectified by wiping with a petrol soaked cloth or, if this fails, by carefully polishing with a very fine file where any binding marks may appear.

8   Reassemble in the reverse order of dismantling. Ensure that leads which may have been connected to any of the screws are reconnected correctly.

12 Alternator brushes (Bosch) - inspection, removal and refitting

1   Undo and remove the two screws, spring and plain washers that secure the brush box to the rear of the brush end housing (Fig. 8.7). Lift away the brush box.

2   Check that the carbon brushes are able to slide smoothly in their guides without any sign of binding.

3   Measure the length of brushes and if they have worn down to 0.2 in (5 mm) or less, they must be renewed.

4   Hold the brush wire with a pair of engineer's pliers and unsolder it from the brush box. Lift away the two brushes and springs (Fig. 8.8).

5   Insert the new brushes and check to make sure that they are free to move in their guides. If they bind, lightly polish with a very fine file.

6   Solder the brush wire ends to the brush box taking care that no solder is allowed to pass to the stranded wire.

7   Whenever new brushes are fitted new springs should also be fitted.

8   Refitting the brush box is the reverse sequence to removal.

13 Alternator brushes (Femsa) - inspection, removal and refitting

1   Disconnect the two wires from the brush box.

2   Remove the crosshead retaining screw then withdraw the brush box.

3   Check that the carbon brushes are able to slide smoothly in their guides without any sign of binding.

4   Measure the amount by which the brushes protrude from the brush box. If this is less than 0.3 inch (7 mm), obtain and fit new brushes (Fig. 8.9).

5   Refitting the brush box is a straightforward reversal of the removal procedure.

14 Starter motor - general description

The starter motor fitted to engines covered by this manual may be either of the inertia or pre-engaged type.

The pre-engaged type is recognisable by the solenoid assembly mounted on the motor body.

The principle of operation of the inertia type starter motor is as follows: When the ignition is switched on and the switch operated, current flows from the battery to the starter motor solenoid switch which causes it to become energised. Its internal plunger moves inwards and closes an internal switch so allowing full starting current to flow from the battery to the starter motor. This causes a powerful magnetic field to be induced into the field coils which causes the armature to rotate.

Mounted on helical splines is the drive pinion which, because of the sudden rotation of the armature shaft and so into engagement with the flywheel ring gear. The engine crankshaft will then be rotated until the engine starts to operate on its own, and at this point, the drive pinion is thrown out of mesh with the flywheel ring gear.

The method of engagement on the pre-engaged starter differs considerably in that the drive pinion is brought into mesh with the starter ring gear before the main starter current is applied.

When the ignition is switched on, current flows from the battery to the solenoid which is mounted on the top of the starter motor. The plunger in the solenoid moves inwards so causing a centrally pivoted engagement lever to move in such a manner that the forked end pushes the drive pinion into mesh with the starter ring gear. When the solenoid reaches the end of its travel, it closes an internal contact and full starting current flows to the starter field coils. The armature is then able to rotate the crankshaft so starting the engine.

A special one way clutch is fitted to the starter drive pinion so that when the engine just fires and starts to operate on its own, it does not drive the starter motor.

15 Starter motor (inertia) - testing on engine

1   If the starter motor fails to operate, then check the condition of the battery by turning on the headlamps. If they glow brightly for several seconds and then gradually dim, the battery is in an uncharged condition.

2   If the headlamps continue to glow brightly and it is obvious that the battery is in good condition then check the tightness of the battery terminal to its connection on the body frame. Check the tightness of the connections at the relay switch and at the starter motor. Check the wiring with a voltmeter for breaks or shorts.

3   If the wiring is in order then check the starter motor switch is operating. To do this, connect a length of **heavy** cable, or metal rod across the two solenoid terminals (photo). If it is working, the starter motor will be heard to 'click', as it tries to rotate. Alternatively, check it with a voltmeter.

4   If the battery is fully charged, the wiring in order, and the switch working but the starter motor fails to operate, then it will have to be removed from the car for examination. Before this is done, however, ensure that the starter pinion has not jammed in mesh with the flywheel. Check by turning the square end of the armature shaft with a spanner. This will free the pinion if it is stuck in engagement with the flywheel teeth.

16 Starter motor (inertia) - removal and refitting

1   Disconnect the positive and then the negative terminals from the battery. Also disconnect the starter motor cable from the terminal on the starter motor end cover.

2   Undo and remove the bolts and spring washers which secure the starter motor to the clutch and flywheel housing. Lift the starter motor away by manipulating the drive gear out from the ring gear area and then from the engine compartment (photo).

3   Refitting is the reverse procedure to removal. Make sure that the starter motor cable, when secured in position by its terminal, does not touch any part of the body or power unit which could damage the insulation.

17 Starter motor (inertia) - dismantling, overhaul and reassembly

1   Clamp the starter motor in a vice fitted with soft protective jaws.

2   To dismantle the starter motor drive, first use a press to push the retainer clear of the circlip which can then be removed. Lift away the retainer and mainspring.

3   Slide the remaining parts with a rotary action of the armature shaft.

4   It is most important that the drive gear is completely free from oil, grease and dirt. With the drive gear removed, clean all parts thoroughly in paraffin. **Under no circumstances oil the drive components.** Lubrication of the drive components could easily cause the pinion to stick.

5   Remove the two screws securing the drive end plate to the yoke. Guide the end plate off the shaft, and lift out the armature.

6   Remove the four screws securing the commutator end plate, and tap the plate clear of the yoke. Pull out the two brushes connected to the field windings, and move the end plate away.

7   If the brushes are worn to 0.32 in (8 mm) or less, they should be renewed. To renew the brushes attached to the field windings, their flexible connectors must be unsoldered and the connectors of new brushes soldered in their place. The other two brushes can be purchased as an assembly, with the terminal post (Fig. 8.11).

8   The brush spring pressure should be approximately 28 ounces (0.8 kg). If it is much less than this, the two brush box rivets should be

15.3 Solenoid terminal location

16.2 Lifting out the starter motor

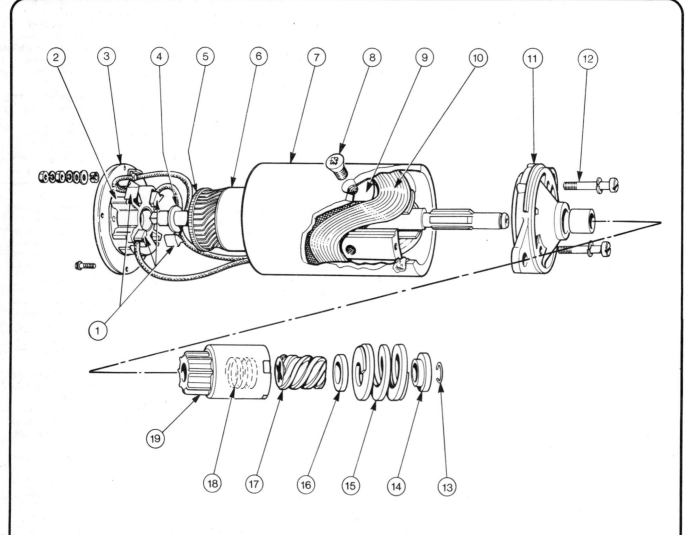

Fig. 8.10. Lucas inertia starter motor (Sec. 17)

1	Brushes	6	Armature	11	Drive end plate	16	Cushion washer
2	Brushbox	7	Main casing (yoke)	12	Retaining screws	17	Screwed sleeve
3	Commutator end plate	8	Pole piece retaining screw	13	'C' clip	18	Anti-drift spring
4	Thrust washer	9	Pole piece	14	Spring cup	19	Drive pinion
5	Commutator	10	Field winding	15	Cushion spring		

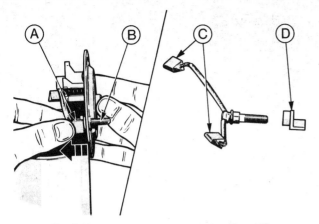

Fig. 8.11. Lucas inertia motor brushes (Sec. 17)

A Insulator   C Brushes
B Terminal stud   D Insulator

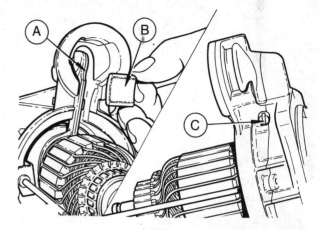

Fig. 8.12. Bosch actuating arm (A), rubber insert (B) and pivot (C) (Sec. 20)

drilled out, and a new brush box fitted.

9 If any of the brushes tend to stick in their holders then wash them with a petrol moistened cloth and, if necessary, lightly polish the sides of the brush with a very fine file until it moves quite freely in its holder.

10 If the surface of the commutator is dirty or blackened, clean it with a petrol dampened rag. If this fails to remove all the burnt areas and spots, then use a piece of glass paper.

11 If the commutator is very badly worn, mount the armature in a lathe and with the lathe turning at high speed, take a very fine cut out of the commutator and finish the surface by polishing with glass paper. **Do not undercut the insulators between the commutator segments.**

12 With the starter motor dismantled, test the four field coils for an open circuit. Connect a 12 volt battery with a 12 volt bulb in one of the leads between the field terminal post and the tapping point of the field coils to which the brushes are connected. An open circuit is proved by the bulb not lighting.

13 If the bulb lights, it does not necessarily mean that the field coils are in order, as there is a possibility that one of the coils will be earthed to the starter yoke or pole shoes. To check this, remove the lead from the brush connector and place it against a clean portion of the starter yoke. If the bulb lights, the field coils are earthing. Renewal of the field coils calls for the use of a wheel operated screwdriver, a soldering iron, caulking and riveting operations and is beyond the scope of the majority of owners. The starter yoke should be taken to a reputable electrical engineering works for new field coils to be fitted. Alternatively purchase an exchange Lucas starter motor.

14 If the armature is damaged, this will be evident after visual inspection. Look for signs of burning, discolouration, and for conductors that have lifted away from the commutator.

15 With the starter motor stripped down, check the condition of the bushes. They should be renewed when they are sufficiently worn to allow visible side movement of the armature shaft.

16 The old bushes are simply driven out with a suitable drift and the new bushes inserted by the same method. As the bushes are of the phosphor bronze type it is essential that they are allowed to stand in engine oil for at least 20 minutes before fitting.

17 Reassembly is the reverse of the above procedure.

18 Starter motor (pre-engaged) - testing on engine

1 If the starter motor fails to operate then check the condition of the battery by turning on the headlamps. If they glow brightly for several seconds and then gradually dim the battery is in an uncharged condition.

2 If the headlights continue to glow brightly and it is obvious that the battery is in good condition, then check the tightness of the battery wiring connections (and in particular the earth lead from the battery terminal to its connection on the body frame). If the positive terminal on the battery becomes hot when an attempt is made to work the starter this is a sure sign of poor connection on the battery terminal. To rectify, remove the terminal, clean the mating faces thoroughly and reconnect. Check the connections on the rear of the starter solenoid. Check the wiring with a voltmeter or test lamp for breaks or shorts.

3 Test the continuity of the solenoid windings by connecting a test lamp circuit comprising a 12 volt battery and low wattage bulb between the 'STA' terminal and the solenoid body. If the two windings are in order the lamp will light. Next connect the test lamp (fitted with a high wattage bulb) between the solenoid main terminals. Energise the solenoid by applying a 12 volt supply between the unmarked Lucar terminal and the solenoid body. The solenoid should be heard to operate and the test bulb light. This indicates full closure of the solenoid contacts.

4 If the battery is fully charged, the wiring in order, the starter/ignition switch working and the starter motor still fails to operate then it will have to be removed from the car for examination. Before this is done ensure that the starter motor pinion has not jammed in mesh with the flywheel by engaging a gear and rocking the car to and fro. This should free the pinion if it is stuck in mesh with the flywheel teeth.

19 Starter motor (pre-engaged) - removal and refitting

Removal is basically identical to that for the inertia type starter motor with the exception of the cables at the rear of the solenoid. Note these connections and then detach the cable terminal from the solenoid.

20 Starter motor (Bosch pre-engaged) - dismantling, overhaul and reassembly

1 Detach the heavy duty cable linking the solenoid 'STA' terminal to the starter motor terminal, by undoing and removing the securing nuts and washers.

2 Undo and remove the screws securing the solenoid to the drive end bracket.

3 Carefully withdraw the solenoid coil unit from the drive end bracket.

4 Lift off the solenoid plunger and return spring from the engagement lever.

Note: On 0.5 PS types, the coil unit and plunger are an integral unit.

5 Remove the two screws securing the commutator end housing centre cap and remove the cap and seal. Using a suitable pair of pliers, pull off the 'C' clip and shims.

6 Unscrew and remove the two nuts or screws and washers and lift off the end housing.

7 With a piece of wire bent into the shape of a hook, lift back each of the brush springs in turn and pull out the brushes. Lift off the brush plate.

8 Pull the drive end housing and armature assembly from the yoke, separating them by tapping gently with a hammer.

9 Remove the rubber insert from the solenoid aperture in the drive end housing. Unscrew the pivot bolt nut and remove the pivot bolt (Fig. 8.12).

10 On starter motors which are held together by studs and nuts, unscrew the studs and remove the stop brackets.

11 Withdraw the armature assembly from the end housing, and unhook the actuating arm.

12 Taking care not to hold the roller clutch in a vice, move the

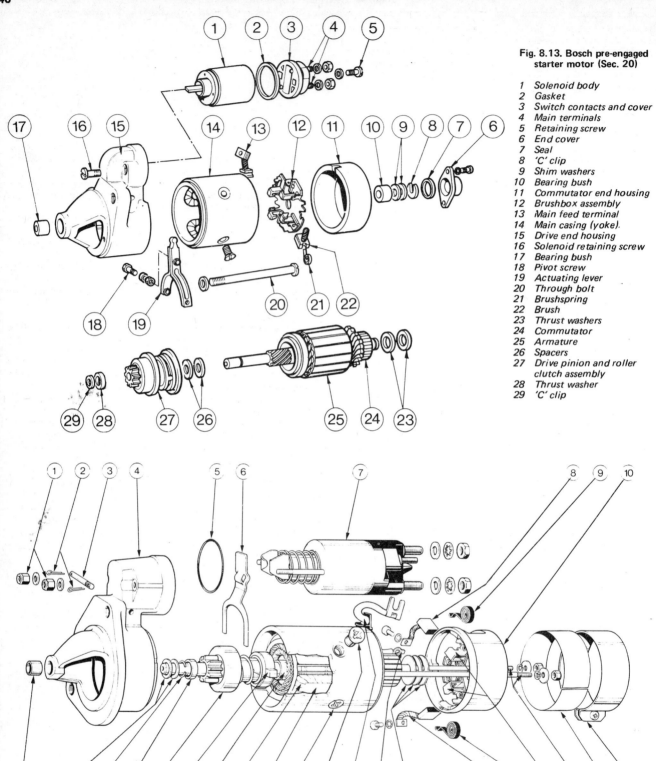

Fig. 8.13. Bosch pre-engaged starter motor (Sec. 20)

1   Solenoid body
2   Gasket
3   Switch contacts and cover
4   Main terminals
5   Retaining screw
6   End cover
7   Seal
8   'C' clip
9   Shim washers
10 Bearing bush
11 Commutator end housing
12 Brushbox assembly
13 Main feed terminal
14 Main casing (yoke).
15 Drive end housing
16 Solenoid retaining screw
17 Bearing bush
18 Pivot screw
19 Actuating lever
20 Through bolt
21 Brushspring
22 Brush
23 Thrust washers
24 Commutator
25 Armature
26 Spacers
27 Drive pinion and roller clutch assembly
28 Thrust washer
29 'C' clip

Fig. 8.14. Femsa pre-engaged starter motor (Sec. 21)

1 Solenoid securing nuts	9 Brush spring	17 Shims	24 Armature
2 Pivot retaining pins	10 Commutator housing	18 Field winding connector	25 Fork locating lugs
3 Pivot pin	11 Brush cover	19 Main feed cable	26 Pinion and roller assembly
4 Drive end housing	12 Seal	20 Pole screw	27 Circlip collar
5 Rubber seal	13 Through studs	21 Main casing (yoke)	28 Circlip
6 Actuating fork	14 Brush holders	22 Pole shoe	29 Shims
7 Solenoid	15 Brush spring	23 Field winding	30 Bearing
8 Positive brush	16 Negative brush		

thrust collar clear of the 'C' clip and remove the clip. Slide the thrust collar and drive pinion assembly off the shaft.

13 If the brushes are worn to 0.39 in (10 mm) or less, they should be renewed. To renew them, the flexible connectors should be cut at their mid point and the new connectors soldered to them. Check for sticking brushes, and clean them if necessary with a petrol moistened cloth.

14 If cleaning the commutator with petrol fails to remove all the burnt areas and spots, then wrap a piece of glass paper around the commutator and rotate the armature.

15 If the commutator is very badly worn, remove the drive gear. Then mount the armature in a lathe and, with the lathe turning at high speed, take a very fine cut out of the commutator and finish the surface by polishing with glass paper. **Do not undercut the insulators between the commutator segments.**

16 With the starter motor dismantled, test the four field coils for an open circuit. Connect a 12 volt battery with a 12 volt bulb in one of the leads between the field terminal post and the tapping point of the field coils to which the brushes are connected. An open circuit is proved by the bulb not lighting.

17 If the bulb lights, it does not necessarily mean that the field coils are in order, as there is a possibility that one of the coils will be earthed to the starter yoke or pole shoes. To check this, remove the lead from the brush connector and place it against a clean portion of the starter yoke. If the bulb lights, the field coils are earthing. Renewal of the field coils calls for the use of a wheel operated screwdriver, a soldering iron, caulking and riveting operations, and is beyond the scope of the majority of owners. The starter yoke should be taken to a reputable electrical engineering works for new field coils to be fitted. Alternatively purchase an exchange starter motor.

18 If the armature is damaged whis will be evident on inspection. Look for signs of burning, discolouring and for conductors that have lifted away from the commutator.

19 If a bearing is worn so allowing excessive side play of the armature shaft, the bearing bush must be renewed. Drift out the old bush with a piece of suitable diameter rod, preferably with a shoulder on it to stop the bush collapsing.

20 Soak a new bush in engine oil for 20 minutes before fitting.

21 As a new bush must not be reamed after fitting, it must be pressed into position using a small mandrel of the same internal diameter as the bush and have a shoulder on it. Place the bush on the mandrel and press it into position using a bench vice.

22 Use a test lamp and battery to test the continuity of the coil winding between terminal 'STA' and a good earth point on the solenoid body. If the light fails to light, the solenoid should be renewed.

23 Whilst the motor is apart, check the operation of the drive clutch. It must provide instantaneous take up of the drive in one direction and rotate easily and smoothly in the opposite direction.

24 Make sure that the drive moves freely on the armature shaft splines without binding or sticking.

25 Reassembly is the reverse of this procedure. The following additional points should be noted:

   a) *Fit the brush plate so that its two cut-outs align with the fixing studs or screws.*
   b) *Fit sufficient shims on the commutator end of the armature shaft before fitting the 'C' clip to remove all endfloat. Add a smear of lithium based grease before fitting the cap.*
   c) *Smear lithium based grease onto the solenoid armature hook, before re-assembly.*

21 Starter motor (Femsa pre-engaged) - dismantling, overhaul and reassembly

1 Slacken the screw securing the brush cover band, and slide the band off the motor. Remove the rubber seal.

2 With a piece of wire bent into the shape of a hook, lift back each of the brush springs in turn and pull out the brushes.

3 Lever the thrust collar back along the armature shaft and prise the circlip from its groove (Fig. 8.15).

4 Remove the two nuts and washers that secure the commutator end housing and pull off the housing. Lift off the shims.

5 Slacken the lower terminal on the solenoid, and slide out the solenoid to motor cable.

6 The actuating arm pivot pin is splined at one end, and must be tapped out from the opposite end with a suitable drift, after removing the split pin.

7 Withdraw the armature assembly from the yoke, allowing the circlip, collar and shims to drop clear. Pull off the yoke.

8 Unclip the starter pinion from the actuating arm (Fig. 8.16) and remove the pinion and arm from the drive end housing.

9 Remove the two securing nuts and washers and remove the solenoid and seal from the drive end housing.

10 If the brushes are worn to 0.47 in (12 mm) or less they should be renewed. Unscrew the two crosshead screws and refit the new brushes. Check for sticking brushes, and clean them if necessary with a petrol moistened cloth.

11 If cleaning the commutator with a petrol moistened rag fails to remove the burnt areas and spots, wrap a piece of glass paper around the commutator and rotate the armature.

12 If this fails to remove all the burnt areas, or if the commutator is very badly worn, mount the armature in a lathe. With the lathe turning at high speed, take a very fine cut off the commutator and finish the surface by polishing with glass paper. **Do not undercut the insulators between the segments.**

13 With the starter motor dismantled, test the four field coils for an open circuit. Connect a 12 volt battery with a 12 volt bulb between the lead from the motor to the solenoid, and the brush connector. An open circuit is proved by the bulb not lighting.

14 If the bulb lights it does not necessarily mean that the field coils are in order, as there is the possibility that one of the coils is earthed

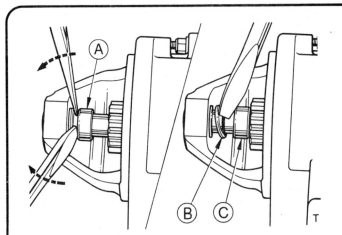

Fig. 8.15. Levering the collar (A) along the shaft to (C) to remove the circlip (B) (Sec. 21)

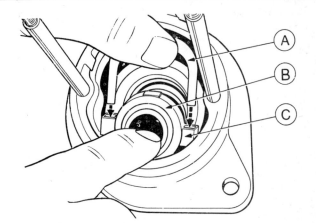

Fig. 8.16. Unclipping the actuating fork (A) from the locating lugs (C) on the pinion assembly (B) (Sec. 21)

to the starter yoke or pole shoes. To check this, remove the test lead
from the brush connector and place it against a clean portion of the
starter yoke. If the bulb lights, the field coils are earthing. Renewal of
the field coils calls for the use of a wheel operated screwdriver, a
soldering iron, caulking and riveting operations, and is beyond the
scope of the majority of owners. The starter yoke should be taken to
a reputable electrical engineering works for new field coils to be fitted.
Alternatively, purchase an exchange starter motor.
15 If the armature is damaged this will be evident on inspection.
Look for signs of burning, discolouration and for conductors to have
lifted away from the commutator.
16 If a bearing is worn so allowing excessive side play of the armature
shaft, the bearing bush must be renewed. To renew the drive end bracket
bush, tap out the bush with a suitable diameter drift. To remove the
commutator end housing bush, select a threaded tap of suitable
diameter and screw it into the bush. Hold the tap in a vice and knock
off the housing, using a block of wood to prevent damage to the
housing.
17 Soak new bushes in engine oil for 20 minutes before fitting.
18 New bushes must be pressed into position using a small mandrel of
the same diameter as the internal diameter of the bush with a shoulder
on it. Place the bush on the mandrel and press into position using a
bench vice.
19 Using a test lamp and battery test the continuity of the solenoid
coils. Connect them between the 'STA' terminal and a good earth
point on the solenoid body. If the lamp fails to light, renew the solenoid.
20 Check the operation of the drive clutch. It must provide instantaneous
take up of the drive in one direction and rotate easily and smoothly in
the opposite direction.
21 Make sure that the drive moves freely on the armature shaft splines
without binding or sticking.
22 Reassembly is the reverse of this procedure. The following
additional points should be noted:

 a) *When fitting the solenoid, the small spade terminal should be to
    the right (Fig. 8.17).*
 b) *Fit shims at the commutator end of the armature shaft to
    remove all endfloat with the end housing fitted.*
 c) *Ensure that the rubber seal under the brush cover band is
    carefully positioned to prevent entry of water.*

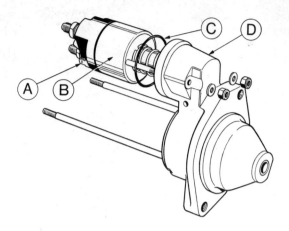

**Fig. 8.17. Fit the solenoid (B) and 'O' ring (C) to the end housing (D)
with the terminal (A) as shown (Sec. 21)**

5   Mark the centre of the front and rear windows (outside if a heated
rear screen is fitted) using a soft wax crayon or masking tape and
position the car at right-angles to the chart so that:

 a) *The vertical centre line and the window markings are exactly in
    line when viewed through the rear window and*
 b) *the horizontal line is at height 'H-X' above the ground.*

6   Each headlamp has two adjusting screws accessible from the engine
compartment (photo). The vertical adjuster is located at the top centre
of the lamp, the horizontal adjuster at a lower corner. Cover the right-
hand headlamp and switch on the main beam.
7   Adjust the horizontal alignment of the left-hand headlamp so that
the intersection of the horizontal and angled light pattern coincides
with the vertical line on the aiming chart.
8   Adjust the vertical alignment so that the light/dark intersection of
the beam pattern coincides with the dotted line on the aiming board.
9   Repeat the procedure for the right headlamp.
10 On completion, switch off the headlamps and clean the crayon
marks from the window.

22 Headlamp bulb and assembly - removal and refitting

1   Disconnect the battery earth lead and from inside the engine
compartment, pull the loom plug off the rear of the headlamp (photo).
2   Pull off the rubber gaiter then squeeze the two arms of the retaining
clip (photo) inwards to release the clip.
3   Lift out the headlamp bulb (photo) taking care not to touch the
bulb glass with the fingers. If it is touched, the bulb should be washed
in methylated spirits and dried with a clean soft cloth.
4   Pull off the side light (parking lamp) plug.
5   Refer to Section 25 and remove the direction indicator assembly.
6   Remove the upper headlamp securing screw, push down on the
clip (photo) and tilt the headlamp forwards to remove it.
7   Refitting is the reverse of the removal procedure. If the
complete headlamp assembly has been removed, it is recommended
that the beam alignment is checked, and adjusted if necessary as
described in Section 23.

23 Headlamp beam-alignment

1   The procedure given in this Section is satisfactory for most
practical purposes, although it is not intended to replace the alignment
procedure used by many dealers and motor factors who would use
beam setting equipment.
2   Refer to Fig. 8.18 which shows a beam setting chart for left-hand
drive vehicles (for right-hand drive vehicles the chart is a mirror image).
3   Position the vehicle on flat, level ground 33 ft (10 m) from a wall
on which the aiming chart is to be fixed. A suitable chart can be drawn
using white chalk on any convenient flat wall such as a garage wall or
door.
4   Bounce the front of the vehicle to ensure that the suspension has
settled and measure the height from the headlamp centre to the ground
(H).

24 Sidelight (parking lamp) bulb - removal and refitting

1   Disconnect the battery earth lead.
2   Twist the bulb holder anti-clockwise and remove it from the rear
of the headlamp (photo).
3   Twist the bulb anti-clockwise to remove it.
4   Refitting is the reverse of the removal procedure, noting that the
holder will only fit in one position.

25 Front direction indicator bulb and assembly - removal and refitting

1   Disconnect the battery earth lead and remove the bulb holder from
the rear of the lamp by twisting anti-clockwise (photo).
2   Remove the bulb by twisting it anti-clockwise.
3   Release the retaining clip next to the radiator, and swing the lamp
assembly outwards.
4   Refitting is the reverse of the removal procedure.

26 Side marker lamps - removal and refitting

1   Disconnect the battery earth lead, and turn the steering on full lock
for ease of access.
2   Pull the bulb holder from the rear of the lamp assembly, and twist
the bulb anti-clockwsie to remove it.
3   To remove the lamp body, press in the two tags and remove it
(Fig. 8.19).
4   Refitting is the reverse of the removal procedure.

22.1 Loom plug at rear of headlamp

22.2 Squeeze the two retaining clip arms

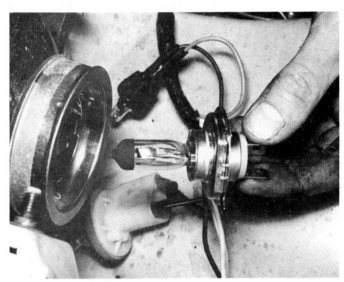

22.3 Lifting out the headlamp bulb

22.6 Unclipping the upper retaining clip

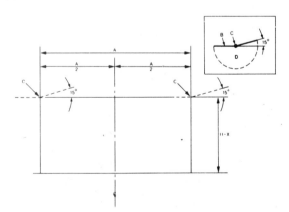

Fig. 8.18. Headlamp beam alignment chart (left-hand drive)

A Distance between headlamp
   centres
B Light/dark boundary
C Dipped beam centre

D Dipped beam pattern
H Height from ground to centre
   of headlamps
X 8 in (20 cm)

23.6 Upper headlamp adjusting screw

24.2 Lifting out the sidelamp bulb holder

25.1 Lifting out the front direction indicator bulb

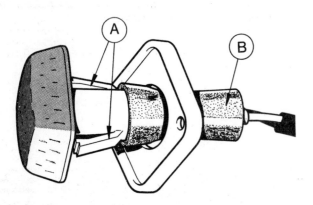

Fig. 8.19. Side marker bulb holder (B) and locating lugs (A) (Sec. 26)

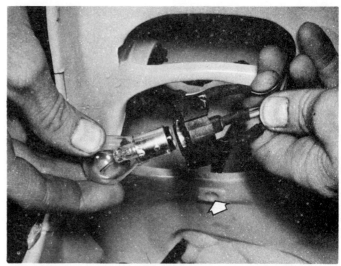

27.2/3 Removing a rear lamp bulb. Trim clip location arrowed

27 Rear lamp bulb and assembly - removal and refitting

1   To gain access to the rear lamps, first remove the spare wheel cover
where appropriate.
2   Using a wide bladed screwdriver, prise the side trim panel retaining
clip from its body location (photo). Pull the trim panel inwards and
downwards to remove it.
3   Pull the appropriate bulb holder from its body location (photo)
and remove the bulb by twisting anti-clockwise.
4   To remove the lamp body, remove the bulb holders, then
unscrew the three retaining nuts (Fig. 8.20).
5   Refitting is the reverse of this procedure, ensuring that the lamp
body sealing gasket is not damaged or distorted.

28 License plate (number plate) lamp assembly - removal and refitting

1   From under the rear bumper, squeeze the two retaining lugs
together, and pull the lamp assembly upwards (photo).
2   To remove the bulb, pull off the lamp cover and lens assembly, and
remove the bulb by turning anti-clockwise.
3   Note the wire connections, and pull them from the lamp body.
4   Refitting is the reverse of this procedure.

29 Screen wiper motor and linkage (front) - removal and refitting

1   Open the bonnet and disconnect the battery earth lead.

2   Pull off the two multi-plugs from the windscreen wiper motor
(photo).
3   Unscrew the three bracket retaining bolts and lift the wiper motor
forward to gain access to the rear.
4   Prise the linkage off the operating arm, and remove the motor.
5   Lift up the cap on the wiper arm (photo), unscrew the retaining
nut and pull off the wiper arm and blade.
6   Remove one of the ignition coil bracket bolts and slacken the
other bolt. Swing the coil downwards, clear of the bonnet lock plate.
7   Remove the six mounting bolts, and lift away the bonnet
lock assembly (Fig. 8.21).
8   Unscrew each wiper spindle retaining nut and remove the
washers. Pull the shafts downwards clear of the bulkhead, and remove
the linkage through the bonnet lock aperture (Fig. 8.22).
9   To dismantle the linkage, prise off the ball joints. To remove
the pivot shaft, remove the circlip, shims, housing and wave washer
(Fig. 8.23).
10 Refitting is the reverse of this procedure, noting the following
points:

  a) Apply a trace of suitable non-setting sealer to the bonnet lock
      plate and wiper motor mounting plate faces before reassembly.
  b) Refit the wiper arms with both motor and arms in the 'parked'
      position.

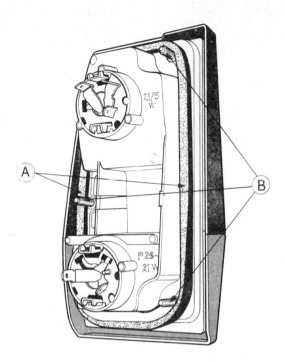

Fig. 8.20. Rear lamp unit gasket (A) and fixing studs (B) (Sec. 27)

30 Screen wiper motor and linkage (rear) - removal and refitting

1   Open the bonnet and disconnect the battery earth lead.
2   Lift the cap on the wiper arm (photo 29.5), unscrew the retaining nut and pull off the wiper arm and blade.
3   Unscrew the pivot shaft nut and remove the washer.
4   Open the rear door, and using a wide bladed screwdriver, prise the door trim retaining clips from the door, and remove the door trim panel.
5   Disconnect the motor multi-plug and remove the earth lead retaining screw.
6   Remove the two bolts retaining the motor retaining bracket (Fig. 8. 24) and lift out the motor.
7   Refitting is the reverse of this procedure, fitting the wiper arms with both the motor and the arm in the 'parked' position.

31 Wiper motor - dismantling and reassembly

Since the individual components of this motor are not available, it is not possible to overhaul it. A new unit must be fitted.

32 Wiper arms and blades - removal and refitting

1   To remove a wiper blade, raise the arm away from the screen and turn the blade to 90° to the arm. Depress the spring clip, and slide the blade down the arm clear of the hook (Fig. 8.25).
2   Slide the blade up the arm, clear of the hook.
3   To renew the rubber, slide out the two inserts (Fig. 8.26) and remove the rubber. Ensure the cut-outs on the inserts face inwards when refitting (Fig. 8.26).
4   To remove the arm, lift the cap, unscrew the retaining nut and lift

28.1 Lifting out the number plate lamp

29.2 Front wiper motor location

29.5 Unscrew the wiper arm retaining nut

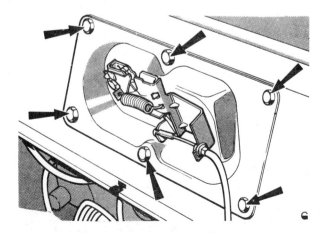

Fig. 8.21. Remove the bonnet lock mounting plate bolts (Sec. 29)

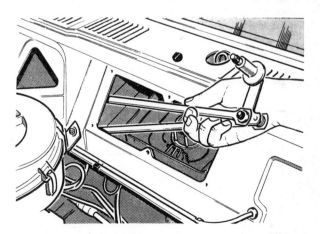

Fig. 8.22. Removing the front wiper linkage (Sec. 29)

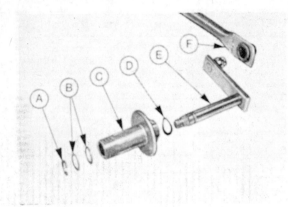

Fig. 8.23. Front wiper pivot shaft assembly (Sec. 29)

A   *Circlip*   D   *Wave washer*
B   *Shim washers*   E   *Pivot shaft*
C   *Bush and housing*   F   *Linkage*

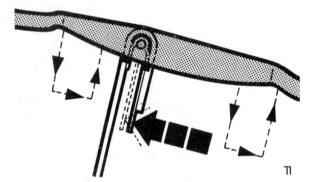

Fig. 8.25. Removing the wiper blade (Sec. 32)

off the arm (photo 29.5). When refitting the arm, ensure both the motor and the arm are in the 'parked' position.

33 Washer nozzles - removal and refitting

Front screen

1   Remove one bolt from the ignition coil mounting bracket, slacken the other bolt and swing the coil downwards clear of the bonnet lock plate.
2   Remove the six bolts and lift off the bonnet lock plate (Fig. 8.21).
3   Carefully prise the nozzle downwards from its location. Use a small screwdriver, taking care not to damage the paintwork. Pull off the washer tube.
4   Refitting is the reverse of this procedure.

Rear screen

5   Open the rear door and pull off the weatherstrip in the area of the nozzle. Pull down the headlining.
6   Pull off the washer tube, then unscrew the nozzle retaining nut.
7   Refitting is the reverse of this procedure.

Headlamp

8   The headlamp washer nozzle is an integral part of the over-rider. Refer to Chapter 10, Section 8 for removal and refitting.
9   To adjust the aim of the headlamp washers, a special tool, number 32-001 is used. If this is not available, the nozzle should be aimed by inserting a small screwdriver into the slots around the nozzle and twisting until the washer jet strikes the centre of the headlamp.

34 Washer pumps (front and rear screen) - removal and refitting

Front screen

1   Open the bonnet and disconnect the battery earth lead.

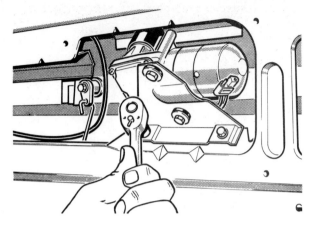

Fig. 8.24. Removing the rear wiper motor (Sec. 30)

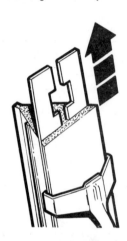

Fig. 8.26. Pulling out the wiper blade inserts (note location of cut-outs) (Sec. 32)

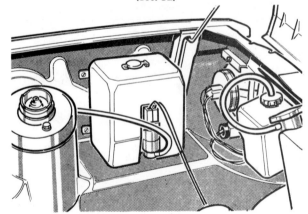

Fig. 8.27. Front screen washer pump location (Sec. 34)

2   Unplug the loom multi-plug from the pump (Fig. 8.27), and pull off the hoses.
3   Unclip the pump from its mounting.
4   Refitting is the reverse of this procedure.

Rear screen

5   Open the bonnet and disconnect the battery earth lead.
6   Open the rear door and remove the spare wheel cover.
7   Unhook the rubber restraining strap (Fig. 8.28) and lift the reservoir from its mounting bracket. Take care not to spill any fluid in the reservoir.
8   Disconnect the loom multi-plug and hoses from the pump and remove the pump.
9   Refitting is the reverse of this procedure.

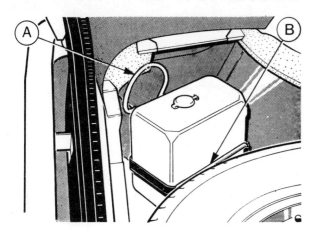

Fig. 8.28. Rear screen washer reservoir (Sec. 34)

A   Washer tube   *B   Rubber retaining strap*

35 Washer pump (headlamp) - removal and refitting

1   Open the bonnet and disconnect the battery earth lead.
2   Disconnect the windscreen washer pump multi-plug.
3   Pull the windscreen washer hose from the washer pump outlet.
4   Remove the reservoir cap and return pipe.
5   Loosen the reservoir bracket clamp bolt.
6   Have a suitable diameter plug handy and pull the hose, connecting the headlamp washer pump to the reservoir, from the pump and plug the hose.
7   Carefully lift the reservoir and windscreen washer pump from the vehicle.
8   Disconnect the headlamp washer pump multi-plug and pull off the outlet hose. Unscrew the two retaining screws, and remove the pump and return pipe. Pull the return pipe from the pump.
9   Refitting is the reverse of this procedure.

36 Horn - fault finding and rectification

1   If the horn works badly or fails completely, check the wiring leading to the horn plug located on the body panel next to the horn itself. Also check that the plug is properly pushed home and is in a clean condition free from corrosion etc.
2   Check that the horn is secure on its mounting and that there is nothing lying on the horn body.
3   If the fault is not an external one, remove the horn and check by substituting a new horn.

37 Fuses

1   If a fuse blows, always trace and rectify the cause before renewing it with one of the same rating.
2   The fuse block is located under the dash panel, to the off side of the steering column.
3   The fuse ratings and circuits protected vary according to model and reference should be made to 'Specifications' Section at the beginning of this Chapter.

38 Instrument cluster - removal and refitting

1   Open the bonnet and disconnect the battery earth lead.
2   Remove the upper steering column shroud retaining screw (where fitted), ease off the upper shroud.
3   Remove the two screws from below the lower dashboard storage space, and lower the trim panel, where fitted.
4   Reach behind the instrument cluster, and disconnect the speedometer cable by pressing the grooved section sideways, and pulling off the cable (photo). If it is not possible to reach the rear of the instrument cluster for any reason, unscrew the cable end from the top of the transmission casing, pull the cable out with the instrument cluster, then

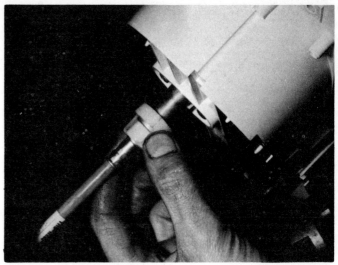

38.4 Removing the speedometer cable

Fig. 8.29. Instrument cluster bezel cut-outs (A) (Sec. 38)

38.6A Unscrewing the panel upper retaining screws

disconnect it from the speedometer.
5   Grip the two cut-outs at the rear of the instrument cluster bezel, and pull off the bezel (Fig. 8.29).
6   Remove the four instrument cluster retaining screws (photo), pull

the cluster out, then disconnect the multi-plug and twist and remove the indicator and brake warning lights. Disconnect the speedometer cable if not done in paragraph 4 (photo).

7   Refitting is the reverse of this procedure, noting the following points:

  a) *To reconnect the speedometer cable, push it onto the speed-ometer until a click is heard. Pull the cable to check it is correctly engaged.*
  b) *After reconnecting the battery, reset the clock where fitted, and check the operation of all gauges and bulbs.*

39 Instrument cluster - dismantling and reassembly

1   Remove the instrument cluster as described in Section 28.
2   To remove any of the instruments or gauges, remove the six lens retaining screws (Fig. 8.30), remove the appropriate nuts or screws from the rear of the cluster, then remove the gauge from the front.
3   To remove the instrument voltage regulator, remove the single crosshead screw (photo) then pull off the regulator.
4   To remove any of the warning or illumination bulbs, twist the appropriate holder anti-clockwise and remove it. Remove the bulb by pulling it from its holder (Fig. 8.31).
5   Reassembly is the reverse of this procedure, taking care not to twist, crimp or damage the printed film on the rear of the cluster.

40 Speedometer cable - renewal

1   Refer to Section 38 and follow paragraphs 1 to 4 inclusive.
2   Unscrew the speedometer cable from the top of the transmission (photo), and remove the strap holding the speedometer cable to the choke cable.
3   Pull out the engine bulkhead grommet, and pull the speedometer cable through the bulkhead.
4   Refitting is the reverse of this procedure. Push the cable onto the speedometer until a click is heard, then pull the cable to check that it is fully engaged.

38.6B 'L' variant instrument cluster

39.3 Instrument voltage regulator

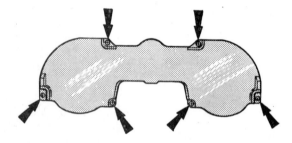

Fig. 8.30. Instrument cluster lens screw locations (Sec. 39)

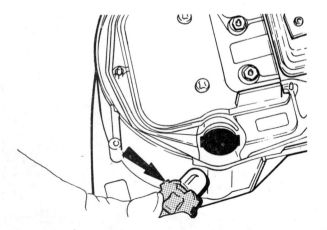

Fig. 8.31. Removing an instrument bulb holder (Sec. 29)

40.2 Speedometer cable at transmission casing

41 Instrument panel switches and warning light bulbs - removal and refitting

1 Open the bonnet and disconnect the earth lead from the battery.
2 *Sport and Ghia models.* It is necessary to remove the switch cover panel, as described below.
3 Open the ashtray, lift it slightly and pull to remove it.
4 Pull off the heater control knobs, remove the four crosshead screws and pull the cover panel forward. Disconnect the multiplug (Fig. 8.32) and remove the panel.
5 *All models.* Using a wad of cloth or paper to protect the switch panel, prise out the required switch with a small screwdriver (Fig. 8.33).
6 Pull off the multiplug or bulb holder from the rear of the switch.
7 To remove the bulb from its holder, pull it clear.
8 Refitting is the reverse of this procedure.

42 Heater controls - removal, refitting and adjustment

These operations are covered in detail in Chapter 2.

43 Cigarette lighter and element - removal and refitting

1 To remove the heating coil, pull out the element, depress the coil to expose the nut, and grip the shaft with a pair of long nosed pliers (Fig. 8.34).
2 Unscrew the locknut and detach the coil.
3 Refitting is the reverse of this procedure.
4 To refit the housing, refer to Section 41, paragraphs 1 to 4 inclusive.
5 Pull the housing and illumination ring from the switch panel or cover panel as appropriate.
6 Refitting is the reverse of this procedure.

44 Clock - removal and refitting

1 Refer to Chapter 10, Section 30 and remove the centre console.
2 Remove the two crosshead screws from the rear of the clock (Fig. 8.35) and lift off the bezel.
3 Pull out the two illumination bulb holders and pull off the two wires.
4 Push out the clock from the rear of the console.
5 To renew the two bulbs, twist them anticlockwise to remove them.
6 Refitting is the reverse of this procedure, not forgetting to reset the clock.

45 Glove compartment light - renewal

1 Pull the bulb from its socket to renew it.
2 If the lamp body is to be renewed, it should be twisted anticlockwise and removed from the rear.

46 Instrument cluster light control - removal and refitting

1 Open the bonnet and disconnect the earth lead from the battery.
2 Remove the three screws from the top of the lower glove compartment on the driver's side.
3 Unscrew the two screws retaining the control knob mounting plate and lift away the plate (Fig. 8.36).
4 Pull off the loom multiplug.
5 Refitting is the reverse of this procedure.

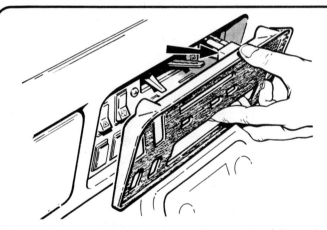

Fig. 8.32. Removing the heater cover panel (Sport and Ghia) (Sec. 41)

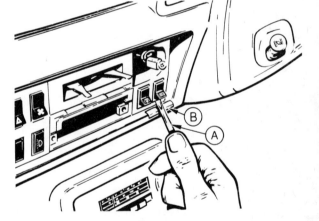

Fig. 8.33. Removing a switch using a screwdriver (A) and paper pad (B) (Sec. 41)

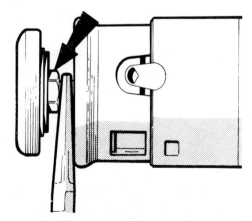

Fig. 8.34. Holding the cigarette lighter shaft to expose the nut (Sec. 43)

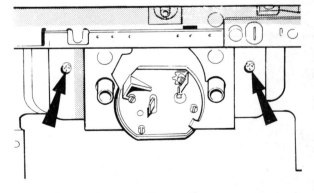

Fig. 8.35. Remove the clock bezel retaining screws (Sec. 44)

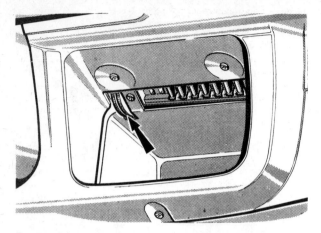

Fig. 8.36. Remove the instrument cluster light control (Sec. 46)

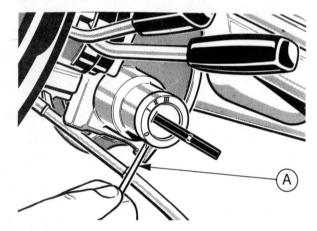

Fig. 8.37. Using a small screwdriver (A) to depress the spring clip (Sec. 48)

51.2 Stop light switch location

47 Steering column switches - removal and refitting

1   Removal procedure for the three steering column switches - multi-function switch, light switch and windscreen wiper/washer switch - is basically the same.
2   Open the bonnet and disconnect the earth lead from the battery.
3   Remove the upper steering column shroud retaining screw (where fitted), ease off the upper shroud.
4   Remove the three screws retaining the lower shroud, and ease the

lower shroud over the choke knob.
5   Remove the appropriate switch retaining screws, disconnect the multiplug then detach the switch from the steering column.
6   Refitting is the reverse of this procedure.

48 Ignition switch - removal and refitting

1   Remove the steering column shrouds, Section 47, paragraphs 2 to 4 inclusive.
2   Insert the ignition key, and turn it to position I (accessories).
3   Insert a small screwdriver through the cutout on the underside of the switch housing (Fig. 8.37).
4   Push inwards against the spring clip, and at the same time pull the ignition key and switch from the housing.
5   Refitting is the reverse of this procedure.

49 Steering column lock - removal and refitting

1   To remove the steering column lock, it is necessary to remove the steering column assembly, to gain access to the two shear-off retaining bolts. Refer to Chapter 9, Section 18.
2   Using a suitable diameter drill remove the headless bolts that clamp the lock to the steering column. Alternatively use a centre punch to rotate the bolts.
3   Lift away the lock assembly and clamp bracket.
4   Refitting the lock assembly is the reverse sequence to removal. Make sure that the pawl enters the steering shaft. It will be necessary to use new shear bolts which must be tightened equally until the heads separate from the shank.

50 Door pillar switches - removal and refitting

1   Open the bonnet and disconnect the earth lead from the battery.
2   Remove the crosshead retaining screw from the appropriate switch.
3   Pull the switch well clear of the door pillar, then pull off the wire.
4   Refitting is the reverse of this procedure.

51 Stop light switch - removal, refitting and adjustment

1   Open the bonnet and disconnect the battery earth lead.
2   Make a note of the correct connections, and pull off the two wires (photo).
3   Remove the retaining nut and lift out the switch.
4   Screw the adjusting nut fully onto the switch, fit the switch to its bracket and loosely fit the locknut.
5   Position the two nuts so that the switch operates at a point between 0.2 and 0.8 in (5.0 and 20.0 mm) of the pedal travel. This measurement should be made at the centre of the brake pedal pad.
6   Tighten the locknut, reconnect the two wires and reconnect the earth lead to the battery.

52 Handbrake (parking brake) warning light switch - removal and refitting

1   The warning light switch is fitted to a bracket at the handbrake operating lever (Fig. 8.38). It may be necessary to remove a front seat to gain access to the fixing screws.
2   Open the bonnet and disconnect the earth lead from the battery.
3   Pull back the carpet around the handbrake lever, and pull off the switch cover.
4   Pull the wire off the switch, and remove the two crosshead retaining screws. Remove the switch.
5   Refitting is the reverse of this procedure.

53 Flasher unit and relays - removal and refitting

1   In the event of failure of a particular piece of equipment always check the connecting wiring, bulbs and fuses before assuming that it is the relay or flasher unit that is at fault. Take the relay or flasher unit

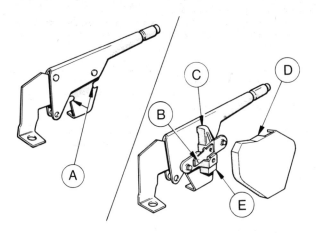

Fig. 8.38. Handbrake warning switch (Sec. 52)

A *Retaining screw cut-outs*   D *Switch cover*
B *Wire connection*   E *Operating plunger*
C *Switch body*

to your dealer for testing or check the circuit by substituting a new component.
2   The flasher unit and relays are located on a bracket welded to the engine bulkhead, inside the car next to the steering column. If more than one unit is removed at any one time, make a careful note of the relay position and associated wiring plug to avoid incorrect reconnection.
3   Open the bonnet and disconnect the earth lead from the battery.
4   Unscrew the two retaining screws and remove the lower dash trim panel on the driver's side.
5   Pull off the loom multiplug and unclip the appropriate unit from the bracket (Fig. 8.39).
6   Refitting is the reverse of this procedure.

54 Interior light and bulb - removal and refitting

1   To remove the bulb, prise the lamp assembly from its location and pull the bulb from the spring clip.

2   To remove the complete lamp, make a note of the connections and pull off the wires.
3   Refitting is the reverse of this procedure.

55 Seat belt/starter interlock system

1   This system is installed on North American cars (not Canada) and is designed to prevent operation of the car unless the front seat belts have been fastened.
2   If either of the front seats is occupied and the seat belts have not been fastened, then, as the ignition key is turned to the 'II' (ignition on) position, a warning lamp will flash and a buzzer will sound.
3   If the warning is ignored, further turning of the key to the start position will not actuate the starter motor.
4   In an emergency, and in the event of a failure in the system, an override switch is located under the bonnet. One depression of the switch will permit one starting sequence of the engine without the front seat belts being fastened.
5   If a fault develops in the system, first check the fuse and then the security of all leads and connections.

56 Radios and tape players - fitting (general)

A radio or tape player is an expensive item to buy and will only give its best performance if fitted properly. It is useless to expect concert hall performance from a unit that is suspended from the dash panel on string with its speaker resting on the back seat or parcel shelf! If you do not wish to do the installation yourself there are many in-car entertainment specialists who can do the fitting for you.

Make sure the unit purchased is of the same polarity as the car, and ensure that units with adjustable polarity are correctly set before commencing installation.

It is difficult to give specific information with regard to fitting, as final positioning of the radio/tape player, speakers and aerial is entirely a matter of personal preference. However, the following paragraphs give guidelines to follow, which are relevant to all installations.

Radios

Most radios are a standardised size of 7 inches wide, by 2 inches deep - this ensures that they will fit into the radio aperture provided in most cars. If your car does not have such an aperture, then the radio

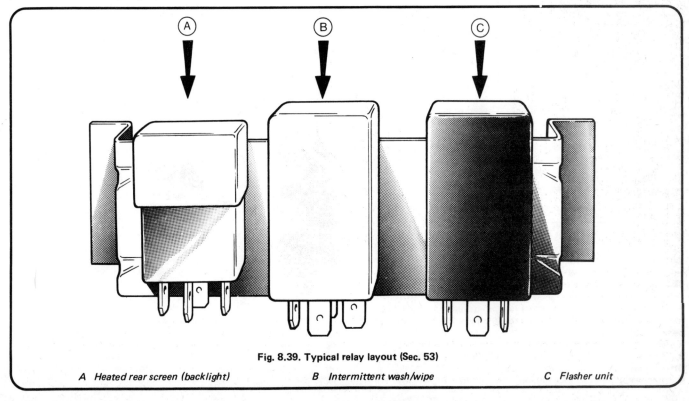

Fig. 8.39. Typical relay layout (Sec. 53)

A *Heated rear screen (backlight)*   B *Intermittent wash/wipe*   C *Flasher unit*

must be fitted in a suitable position either in, or beneath, the dashpanel. Alternatively, a special console can be purchased which will fit between the dashpanel and the floor. These consoles can also be used for additional switches and instrumentation if required. Where no radio aperture is provided, the following points should be borne in mind before deciding exactly where to fit the unit:

a) *The unit must be within easy reach of the driver wearing a seat belt.*

b) *The unit must not be mounted in close proximity to an electronic tachometer, the ignition switch and its wiring, or the flasher unit and associated wiring.*

c) *The unit must be mounted within reach of the aerial lead, and in such a place that the aerial lead will not have to be routed near the components detailed in the preceding paragraph 'b'.*

d) *The unit should not be positioned in a place where it might cause injury to the car occupants in an accident; for instance, under the dashpanel above the driver's or passenger's legs.*

e) *The unit must be fitted really securely.*

Some radios will have mounting brackets provided together with instructions: others will need to be fitted using drilled and slotted metal strips, bent to form mounting brackets - these strips are available from most accessory shops. The unit must be properly earthed, by fitting a separate earthing lead between the casing of the radio and the vehicle frame.

Use the radio manufacturers' instructions when wiring the radio into the vehicle's electrical system. If no instructions are available refer to the relevant wiring diagram to find the location of the radio 'feed' connection in the vehicle's wiring circuit. A 1-2 amp 'in-line' fuse must be fitted in the radio's 'feed' wire - a choke may also be necessary (see next Section).

The type of aerial used, and its fitted position is a matter of personal preference. In general the taller the aerial, the better the reception. It is best to fit a fully retractable aerial - especially, if a mechanical car-wash is used or if you live in an area where cars tend to be vandalised. In this respect electric aerials which are raised and lowered automatically when switching the radio on or off are convenient, but are more likely to give trouble than the manual type.

When choosing a site for the aerial the following points should be considered:

a) *The aerial lead should be as short as possible - this means that the aerial should be mounted at the front of the car.*

b) *The aerial must be mounted as far away from the distributor and HT leads as possible.*

c) *The part of the aerial which protrudes beneath the mounting point must not foul the roadwheels, or anything else.*

d) *If possible the aerial should be positioned so that the coaxial lead does not have to be routed through the engine compartment.*

e) *The plane of the panel on which the aerial is mounted should not be so steeply angled that the aerial cannot be mounted vertically (in relation to the 'end-on' aspect of the car). Most aerials have a small amount of adjustment available.*

Having decided on a mounting position, a relatively large hole will have to be made in the panel. The exact size of the hole will depend upon the specific aerial being fitted, although, generally, the hole required is of ¾ inch (19 mm) diameter. On metal bodied cars, a 'tank-cutter' of the relevant diameter is the best tool to use for making the hole. This tool needs a small diameter pilot hole drilled through the panel, through which, the tool clamping bolt is inserted. On GRP bodied cars, a 'hole-saw' is the best tool to use. Again, this tool will require the drilling of a small pilot hole. When the hole has been made the raw edges should be de-burred with a file and then painted, to prevent corrosion.

Fit the aerial according to the manufacturer's instructions. If the aerial is very tall, or if it protrudes beneath the mounting panel for a considerable distance it is a good idea to fit a stay between the aerial and the vehicle frame. This stay can be manufactured from the slotted and drilled metal strips previously mentioned. The stay should be securely screwed or bolted in place. For best reception it is advisable to fit an earth lead between the aerial and the vehicle frame - this is essential for GRP bodied cars.

It will probably be necessary to drill one or two holes through bodywork panels in order to feed the aerial lead into the interior of the car. Where this is the case ensure that the holes are fitted with rubber grommets to protect the cable, and to stop possible entry of water.

Positioning and fitting of the speaker depends mainly on its type. Generally, the speaker is designed to fit directly into the aperture already provided in the car. Where this is the case, fitting the speaker is just a matter of removing the protective grille from the aperture and screwing or bolting the speaker in place. Take great care not to damage the speaker diaphragm whilst doing this. It is a good idea to fit a 'gasket' between the speaker frame and the mounting panel, in order to prevent vibration - some speakers will already have such a gasket fitted.

If a 'pod' type speaker was supplied with the radio, this can be secured to the mounting panel with self-tapping screws.

When connecting a rear mounted speaker to the radio, the wires should be routed through the vehicle beneath the carpets or floor mats - preferably along the side of the floorpan, where they will not be trodden on by passengers. Make the relevant connections as directed by the radio manufacturer.

By now you will have several yards of additional wiring in the car, use PVC tape to secure this wiring out of harm's way. Do not leave electrical leads dangling. Ensure that all new electrical connections are properly made (wires twisted together will not do) and completely secure.

The radio should now be working, but before you pack away your tools it will be necessary to 'trim' the radio to the aerial. If specific instructions are not provided by the radio manufacturer, proceed as follows. Find a station with a low signal strength on the medium-wave band, slowly turn the trim screw of the radio in, or out, until the loudest reception of the selected station is obtained - the set is then trimmed to the aerial.

Tape players

Fitting instructions for both cartridge and cassette stereo tape players are the same and in general the same rules apply as when fitting a radio. Tape players are not usually prone to electrical interference like radio - although it can occur - so positioning is not so critical. If possible the player should be mounted on an 'even-keel'. Also it must be possible for a driver wearing a seat belt to reach the unit in order to change or turn over tapes.

For the best results from speakers designed to be recessed into a panel, mount them so that the back of the speaker protrudes into an enclosed chamber within the car (eg. door interiors or the boot cavity).

To fit recessed type speakers in the front doors first check that there is sufficient room to mount the speakers in each door without it fouling the latch or window winding mechanism. Hold the speaker against the skin of the door, and draw a line around the periphery of the speaker. With the speaker removed draw a second 'cutting' line, within the first, to allow enough room for the entry of the speaker back, but at the same time providing a broad seat for the speaker flange. When you are sure that the 'cutting-line' is correct, drill a series of holes around its periphery. Pass a hacksaw blade through one of the holes and then cut through the metal between the holes until the centre section of the panel falls out.

De-burr the edges of the hole and then paint the raw metal to prevent corrosion. Cut a corresponding hole in the door trim panel - ensuring that it will be completely covered by the speaker grille. Now drill a hole in the door edge and a corresponding hole in the door surround. These holes are to feed the speaker leads through - so fit grommets. Pass the speaker leads through the door trim, door skin and out through the holes in the side of the door and door surround. Refit the door trim panel and then secure the speaker to the door using self-tapping screws. **Note:** If the speaker is fitted with a shield to prevent water dripping on it, ensure that this shield is at the top.

Pod type speakers can be fastened anywhere offering a corresponding mounting point on each side of the car. Pod speakers sometimes offer a better reproduction quality if they face the rear window - which then acts as a reflector - so it is worthwhile to do a little experimenting before finally fixing the speaker.

57 Radios and tape players - suppression of interference (general)

To eliminate buzzes and other unwanted noises, costs very little and is not as difficult as sometimes thought. With a modicum of common sense and patience and following the instructions in the following paragraphs, interference can be virtually eliminated.

The first cause for concern is the generator. The noise this makes over the radio is like an electric mixer and the noise speeds up when you rev up (if you wish to prove the point, you can remove the drivebelt and try it). The remedy for this is simple; connect a 1.0-3.0 mf capacitor between earth, probably the bolt that holds down the generator base, and the *large* terminal on the dynamo or alternator. This is most important for if you connect it to the small terminal, you will probably damage the generator permanently (see Fig. 8.40).

A second common cause of electrical interference is the ignition system. Here a 1.0 ohm capacitor must be connected between earth and the 'SW' or '+' terminal on the coil (see Fig. 8.41). This may stop the tick-tick-tick sound that comes over the speaker. Next comes the spark itself.

There are several ways of curing interference from the ignition HT system. One is to use carbon film HT leads but these have a tendency to 'snap' inside and you do not know then, why you are firing on only half your cylinders. So the second, and more successful method is to use resistive spark plug caps (see Fig. 8.42) of about 10,000 to 15,000 ohm resistance. If, due to lack of room, these cannot be used, an alternative is to use 'in-line' suppressors (Fig. 8.42) - if the interference is not too bad, you may get away with only one suppressor in the coil to distributor line. If the interference does continue (a 'clacking' noise) then doctor all HT leads.

At this stage it is advisable to check that the radio is well earthed, also the aerial, and to see that the aerial plug is pushed well into the set and that the radio is properly trimmed (see preceding Section). In addition, check that the wire which supplies the power to the set is as short as possible and does not wander all over the car. At this stage it

is a good idea to check that the fuse is of the correct rating. For most sets this will be about 1 to 2 amps.

At this point the more usual causes of interference have been suppressed. If the problem still exists, a look at the causes of interference may help to pinpoint the component generating the stray electrical discharges.

The radio picks up electromagnetic waves in the air; now some are made by radio stations and other broadcasters and some, not wanted, are made by the car. The car made signals are produced by stray electrical discharges floating around the car. Common producers of these signals are electric motors; ie. the windshield wipers, electric screen washers, electric window winders, heater fan or an electric aerial if fitted. Other sources of interference are electric fuel pumps, flashing turn signals, and instruments. The remedy for these cases is shown in Fig. 8.43 for an electric motor whose interference is not too bad and Fig. 8.44 for instrument suppression. Turn signals are not normally suppressed. In recent years, radio manufacturer's have included in the 'live' line of the radio, in addition to the fuse, an 'in-line' choke. If your installation lacks one of these, put one in as shown in Fig. 8.45.

All the foregoing components are available from radio shops or accessory shops. For a transistor radio, a 2A choke should be adequate. If you have an electric clock fitted this should be suppressed by connecting a 0.5 mf capacitor directly across it as shown for a motor in Fig. 8.43.

If after all this, you are still experiencing radio interference, first assess how bad it is, for the human ear can filter out unobtrusive unwanted noises quite easily. But if you are still adamant about eradicating the noise, then continue.

As a first step, a few 'experts' seem to favour a screen between the radio and the engine. This is OK as far as it goes, literally! - for the whole set is screened and if interference can get past that then a small piece of aluminium is not going to stop it.

A more sensible way of screening is to discover if interference is coming down the wires. First, take the live lead; interference can get

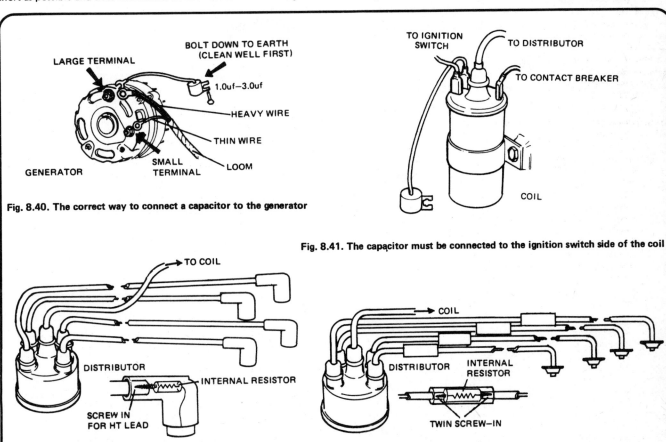

Fig. 8.40. The correct way to connect a capacitor to the generator

Fig. 8.41. The capacitor must be connected to the ignition switch side of the coil

Fig. 8.42. Ignition HT lead suppressors

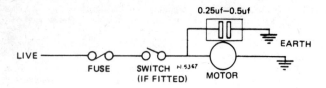

Fig. 8.43. Correct method of suppressing electric motors

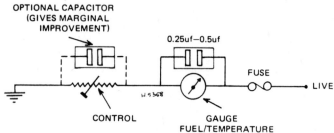

Fig. 8.44. Method of suppressing gauges and their control units

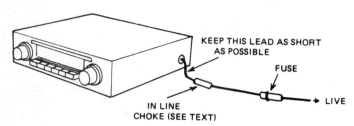

Fig. 8.45. An 'in-line' choke should be fitted into the live supply lead as close to the unit as possible

between the set and the choke (hence the reason for keeping the wires short). One remedy here is to screen the wire and this is done by buying screened wire and fitting that. The loudspeaker lead could be screened also to prevent 'pick-up' getting back to the radio - although this is unlikely.

Without doubt, the worst source of radio interference comes from the ignition HT leads, even if they have been suppressed. The ideal way of suppressing these is to slide screening tubes over the leads themselves. As this is impractical, we can place an aluminium shield over the majority of the lead areas. In a vee- or twin-cam engine, this is relatively easy but for a straight engine the results are not particularly good.

Now for the really impossible cases, here are a few tips to try out. Where metal comes into contact with metal, an electrical disturbance is caused which is why good clean connections are essential. To remove interference due to overlapping or butting panels you must bridge the join with a wide braided earth strap (like that from the frame to the engine/transmission). The most common moving parts that could create noise and should be strapped are, in order of importance:

a) Silencer to frame.
b) Exhaust pipe to engine block and frame.
c) Air cleaner to frame.
d) Front and rear bumpers to frame.
e) Steering column to frame.
f) Hood and trunk lids to frame.
g) Hood frame to frame on soft tops.

These faults are most pronounced when (1) the engine is idling, (2) labouring under load. Although the moving parts are already connected with nuts, bolts, etc., these do tend to rust and corrode, thus creating a high resistance interference source.

If you have a 'ragged' sounding pulse when mobile, this could be wheel or tyre static. This can be cured by buying some anti-static powder and sprinkling it liberally inside the tyres.

If the interference takes the shape of a high pitched screeching noise that changes its note when the car is in motion and only comes now and then, this could be related to the aerial, especially if it is of the telescopic or whip type. This source can be cured quite simply by pushing a small rubber ball on top of the aerial (yes, really!) as this breaks the electric field before it can form; but it would be much better to buy yourself a new aerial of a reputable brand. If, on the other hand, you are getting a loud rushing sound every time you brake, then this is brake static. This effect is most prominent on hot dry days and is cured only by fitting a special kit, which is quite expensive.

In conclusion, it is pointed out that it is relatively easy, and therefore cheap to eliminate 95 per cent of all noises, but to eliminate the final 5 per cent is time and money consuming. It is up to the individual to decide if it is worth it. Please remember also, that you will not get concert hall performance from a cheap radio.

Finally at the beginning of this Section are mentioned tape players; these are not usually affected by interference but in a very bad case, the best remedies are the first three suggestions plus using a 3 - 5 amp choke in the 'live' line and in incurable cases screen the live and speaker wires.

Note: If your car is fitted with electronic ignition, then it is not recommended that either the spark plug resistors nor the ignition coil capacitor be fitted as these may damage the system. Most electronic ignition units have built-up suppression and should, therefore, not cause interference.

58 Fault diagnosis

Symptom	Reason/s
Starter motor fails to turn engine	Battery discharged.
	Battery defective internally.
	Battery terminal leads loose or earth lead not securely attached to body.
	Loose or broken connections in starter motor circuit.
	Starter motor switch or solenoid faulty.
	Starter motor pinion jammed in mesh with flywheel gear ring.
	Starter brushes badly worn, sticking, or brush wires loose.
	Commutator dirty, worn or burnt.
	Starter motor armature faulty.
	Field coils earthed.
Starter motor turns engine very slowly	Battery in discharged condition.
	Starter brushes badly worn, sticking, or brush wires loose.
	Loose wires in starter motor circuit.
Starter motor turns without turning engine	Starter motor pinion sticking on the screwed sleeve.
	Pinion or flywheel gear teeth broken or worn.
Starter motor noisy or excessively rough engagement	Pinion or flywheel gear teeth broken or worn.
	Starter drive main spring broken.
	Starter motor retaining bolts loose.
Battery will not hold charge for more than a few days	Battery defective internally.
	Electrolyte level too low or electrolyte too weak due to leakage.
	Plate separators no longer fully effective.
	Battery plates severely sulphated.
	Fan/alternator belt slipping.
	Battery terminal connections loose or corroded.
	Alternator not charging properly*.
	Short in lighting circuit causing continual battery drain.
	Regulator unit not working correctly.
Ignition light fails to go out, battery runs flat in a few days	Fan belt loose and slipping or broken.
	Brushes worn, sticking, broken or dirty.
	Brush springs weak or broken.
	Alternator faulty*.

If all appears to be well but the alternator is still not charging, take the car to an automobile electrician to check the alternator and regulator.

Failure of individual electrical equipment to function correctly is dealt with alphabetically below. In cases of electrical failure it is always worth checking the obvious, such as blow fuses (particularly if associated equipment has also failed) and loose or broken wires.

Symptom	Reason/s
Fuel gauge gives no reading	Fuel tank empty!
	Electric cable between tank sender unit and gauge earthed or loose.
	Fuel gauge case not earthed.
	Fuel gauge supply cable interrupted.
	Fuel gauge unit broken.
Fuel gauge registers full all the time	Electric cable between tank unit and gauge broken or disconnected.
Horn operates all the time	Horn push either earthed or stuck down.
	Horn cable to horn push earthed.
Horn fails to operate	Blown fuse.
	Cable or cable connection loose, broken or disconnected.
	Horn has an internal fault.
Horn emits intermittent or unsatisfactory noise	Cable connections loose.
	Horn incorrectly adjusted.
Lights do not come on	Blown fuse
	If engine not running, battery discharged.
	Light bulb fitment burnt out or bulbs broken.
	Wire connections loose, disconnected or broken.
	Lights switch shorting or otherwise faulty.
Lights come on but fade out	If engine not running battery discharged.

Symptom	Reason/s
Lights give very poor illumination	Lamp glasses dirty. Reflector tarnished or dirty. Lamps badly out of adjustment. Incorrect bulb with too low wattage fitted. Existing bulbs old and badly discoloured. Electrical wiring too thin not allowing full current to pass.
Lights work erratically - flashing on and off, especially over bumps	Battery terminals or earth connections loose. Lights not earthing properly. Contacts in light switch faulty.
Wiper motor fails to work	Blown fuse. Wire connections loose, disconnected or broken. Brushes badly worn. Armature worn or faulty. Field coils faulty.
Wiper motor works very slowly and takes excessive current	Commutator dirty, greasy or burnt. Drive to spindles too bent or unlubricated. Drive spindle binding or damaged. Armature bearings dry or unaligned. Armature badly worn or faulty.
Wiper motor works slowly and takes little current	Brushes badly worn. Commutator dirty, greasy or burnt. Armature badly worn or faulty.
Wiper motor works but wiper blades remain static	Linkage disengaged or faulty. Drive spindle damaged or worn. Wiper motor gearbox parts badly worn.

The following wire codes and colours are common to all diagrams on pages 157 to 167 inclusive

Wire codes

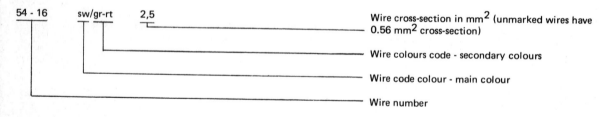

54 - 16	sw/gr-rt	2,5	Wire cross-section in mm^2 (unmarked wires have 0.56 mm^2 cross-section)
			Wire colours code - secondary colours
			Wire code colour - main colour
			Wire number

Wiring colour abbreviations

Code	Wiring colour		Code	Wiring colour
bl	Blue		rs	pink
br	Brown		rt	red
ge	Yellow		sw	black
gr	Grey		vi	violet
gn	Green		ws	white

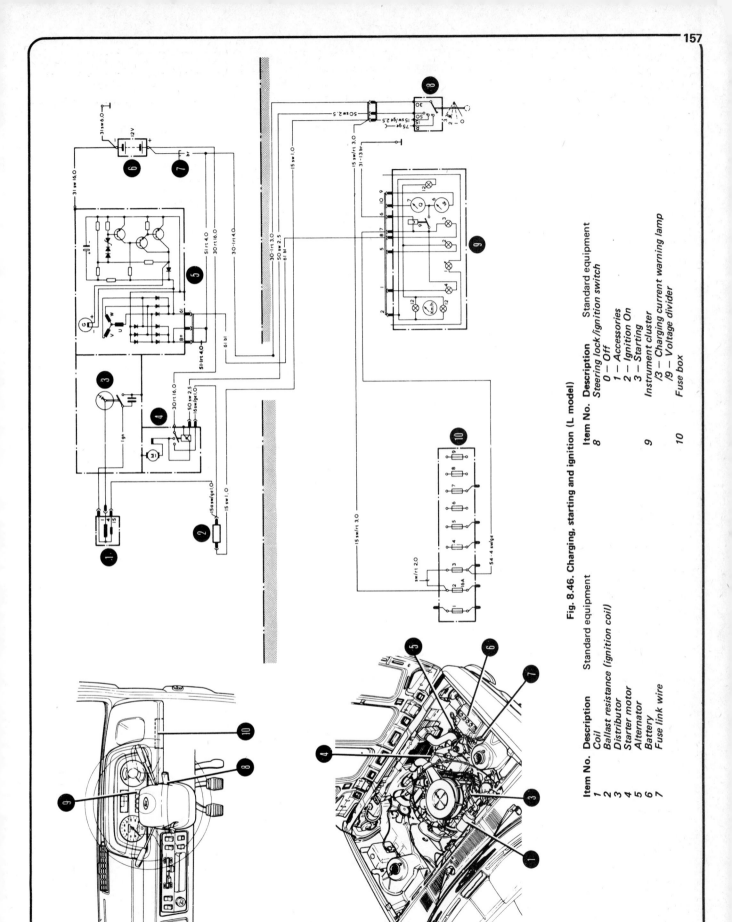

Fig. 8.46. Charging, starting and ignition (L model)

Item No.	Description	Standard equipment
1	Coil	
2	Ballast resistance (ignition coil)	
3	Distributor	
4	Starter motor	
5	Alternator	
6	Battery	
7	Fuse link wire	

Item No.	Description	Standard equipment
8	Steering lock/ignition switch	
	0 – Off	
	1 – Accessories	
	2 – Ignition On	
	3 – Starting	
9	Instrument cluster	
	/3 – Charging current warning lamp	
	/9 – Voltage divider	
10	Fuse box	

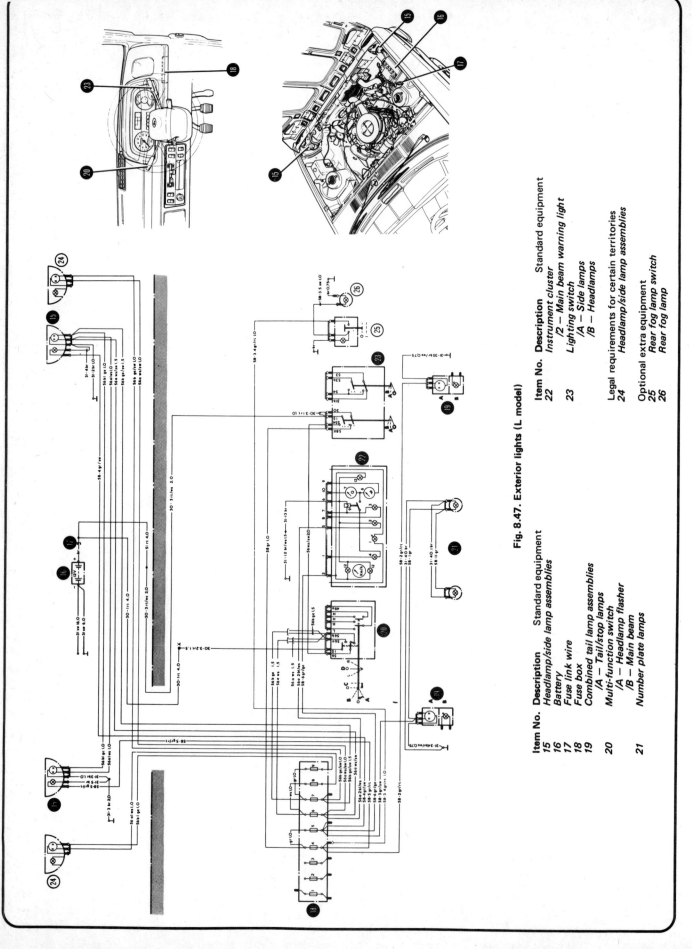

Fig. 8.47. Exterior lights (L model)

Item No.	Description
	Standard equipment
15	Headlamp/side lamp assemblies
16	Battery
17	Fuse link wire
18	Fuse box
19	Combined tail lamp assemblies
	/A – Tail/stop lamps
20	Multi-function switch
	/A – Headlamp flasher
	/B – Main beam
21	Number plate lamps

Item No.	Description
	Standard equipment
22	Instrument cluster
	/2 – Main beam warning light
23	Lighting switch
	/A – Side lamps
	/B – Headlamps
	Legal requirements for certain territories
24	Headlamp/side lamp assemblies
	Optional extra equipment
25	Rear fog lamp switch
26	Rear fog lamp

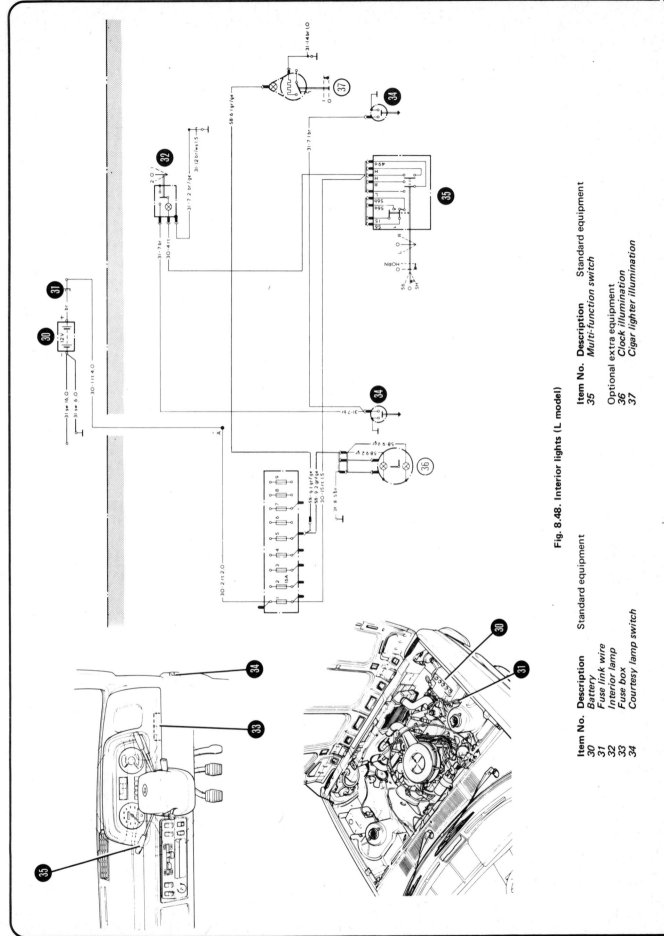

Fig. 8.48. Interior lights (L model)

Item No.	Description	Standard equipment
30	Battery	
31	Fuse link wire	
32	Interior lamp	
33	Fuse box	
34	Courtesy lamp switch	

Item No.	Description	Standard equipment
35	Multi-function switch	

Optional extra equipment
36	Clock illumination	
37	Cigar lighter illumination	

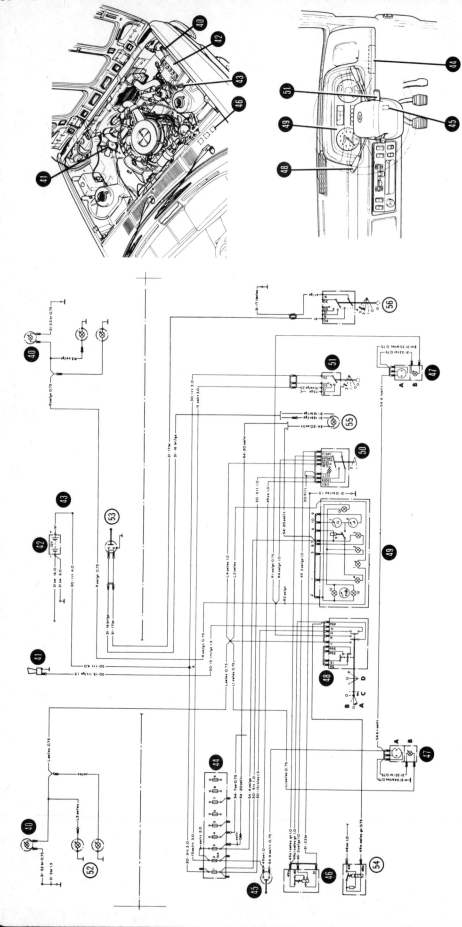

Fig. 8.49. Horn, indicators and hazard lights (L model)

Item No.	Description	Std. equipment	Item No.	Description	Std. equipment	Item No.	Description	Std. equipment
40	Direction indicators - front		49	Instrument cluster			Legal requirements for certain territories	
41	Horn			/1 – Direction indicator warning lamp - green		52	Side repeater indicator lamps	
42	Battery		50	Hazard flasher switch		53	Dual circuit brake warning system switch	
43	Fuse link wire		51	Steering lock/ignition switch		54	Flasher unit (without hazard flasher system)	
44	Fuse box			0 – Off		55	Dual circuit brake warning system lamp	
45	Stop lamp switch			1 – Accessories		56	Steering lock/ignition switch	
46	Flasher unit			2 – Ignition On				
47	Combined tail lamp assemblies			3 – Starting			Optional extra equipment	
	/A – Tail/stop lamps					57	Reversing lamp switch	
	/B – Direction indicators					58	Reversing lamp	
48	Multi function switch							
	/C – Horn							
	/D – Direction indicators							

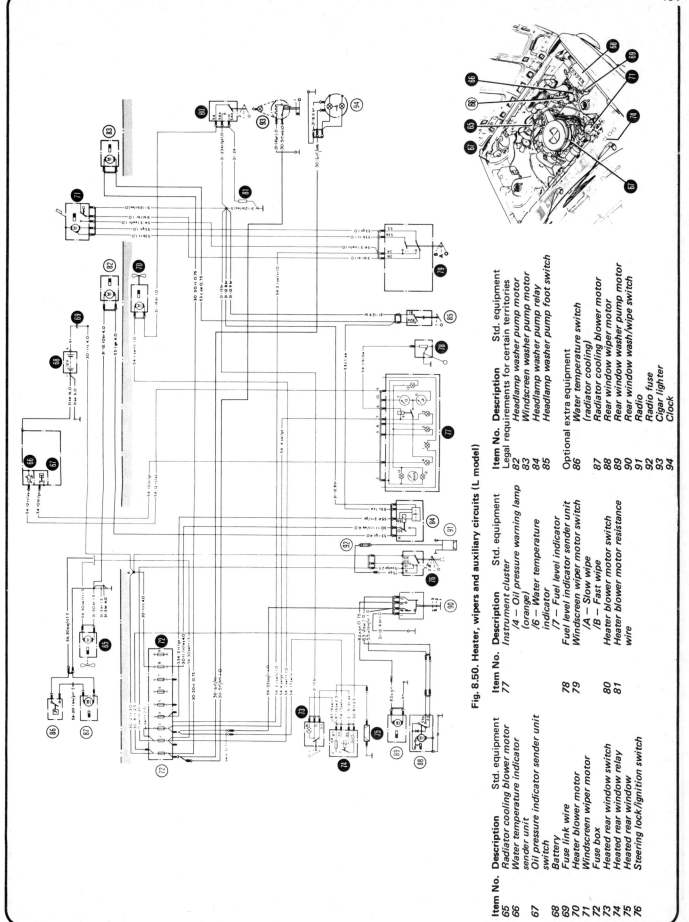

Fig. 8.50. Heater, wipers and auxiliary circuits (L model)

Item No.	Description Std. equipment
65	Radiator cooling blower motor
66	Water temperature indicator
67	Oil pressure indicator sender unit
68	Battery
69	Fuse link wire
70	Heater blower motor
71	Windscreen wiper motor
72	Fuse box
73	Heated rear window switch
74	Heated rear window relay
75	Heated rear window
76	Steering lock/ignition switch

Item No.	Description Std. equipment
77	Instrument cluster
	/4 – Oil pressure warning lamp
	(orange)
	/6 – Water temperature
	indicator
	/7 – Fuel level indicator
78	Fuel level indicator sender unit
79	Windscreen wiper motor switch
	/A – Slow wipe
	/B – Fast wipe
80	Heater blower motor switch
81	Heater blower motor resistance
	wire

Item No.	Description Std. equipment
	Legal requirements for certain territories
82	Headlamp washer pump motor
83	Windscreen washer pump motor
84	Headlamp washer pump relay
85	Headlamp washer pump foot switch
	Optional extra equipment
86	Water temperature switch
	(radiator cooling)
87	Radiator cooling blower motor
88	Rear window wiper motor
89	Rear window washer pump motor
90	Rear window wash/wipe switch
91	Radio
92	Radio fuse
93	Cigar lighter
94	Clock

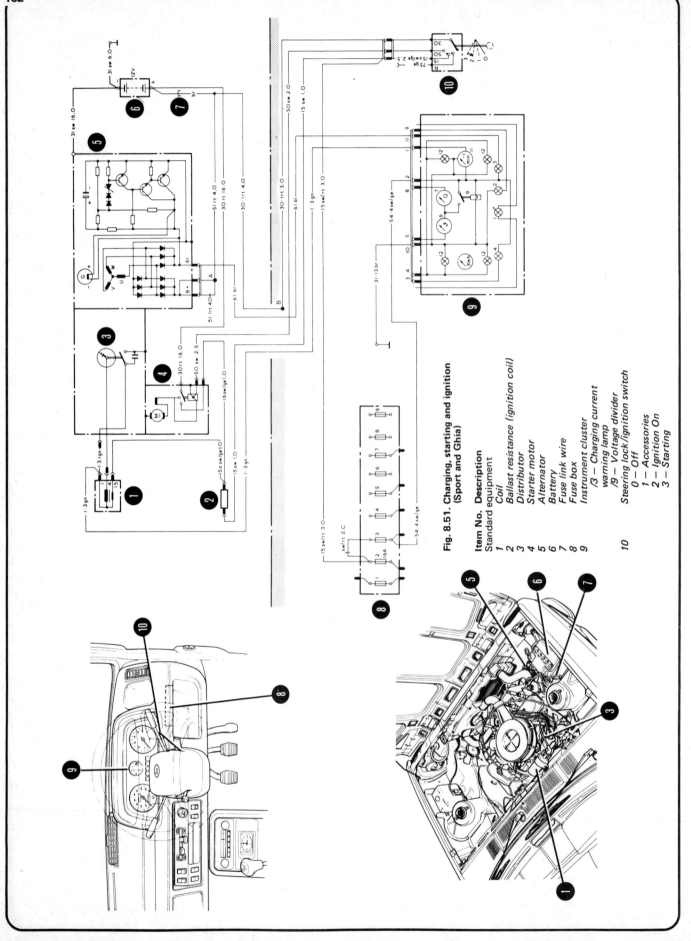

Fig. 8.51. Charging, starting and ignition (Sport and Ghia)

Item No. Description
Standard equipment
1 Coil
2 Ballast resistance (ignition coil)
3 Distributor
4 Starter motor
5 Alternator
6 Battery
7 Fuse link wire
8 Fuse box
9 Instrument cluster
/3 – Charging current warning lamp
/9 – Voltage divider
10 Steering lock/ignition switch
0 – Off
1 – Accessories
2 – Ignition On
3 – Starting

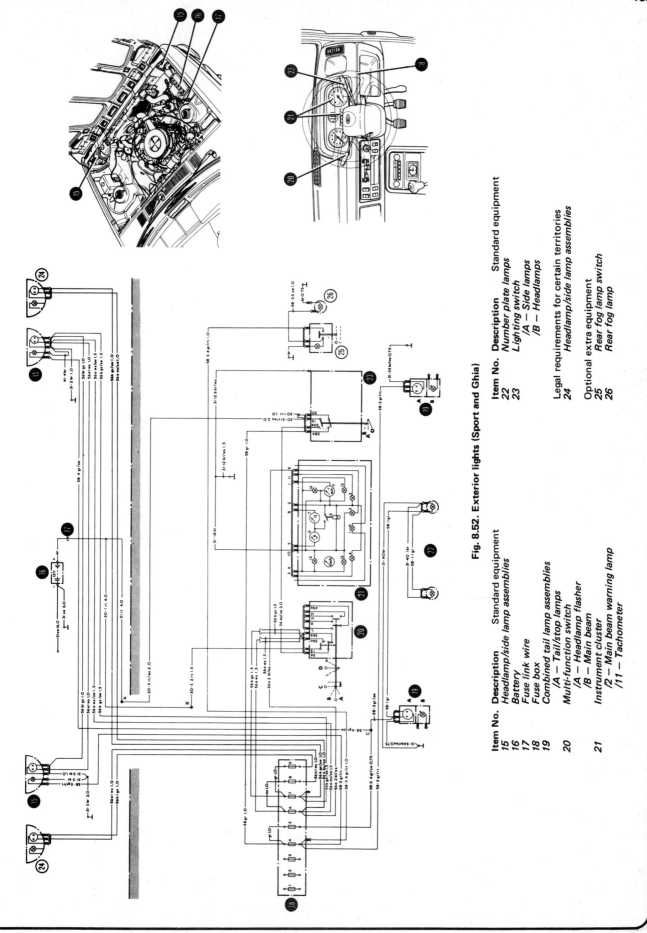

Fig. 8.52. Exterior lights (Sport and Ghia)

Item No.	Description	Standard equipment
15	Headlamp/side lamp assemblies	
16	Battery	
17	Fuse link wire	
18	Fuse box	
19	Combined tail lamp assemblies	
	/A – Tail/stop lamps	
20	Multi-function switch	
	/A – Headlamp flasher	
	/B – Main beam	
21	Instrument cluster	
	/2 – Main beam warning lamp	
	/11 – Tachometer	

Item No.	Description	Standard equipment
22	Number plate lamps	
23	Lighting switch	
	/A – Side lamps	
	/B – Headlamps	

Legal requirements for certain territories

24	Headlamp/side lamp assemblies

Optional extra equipment

25	Rear fog lamp switch
26	Rear fog lamp

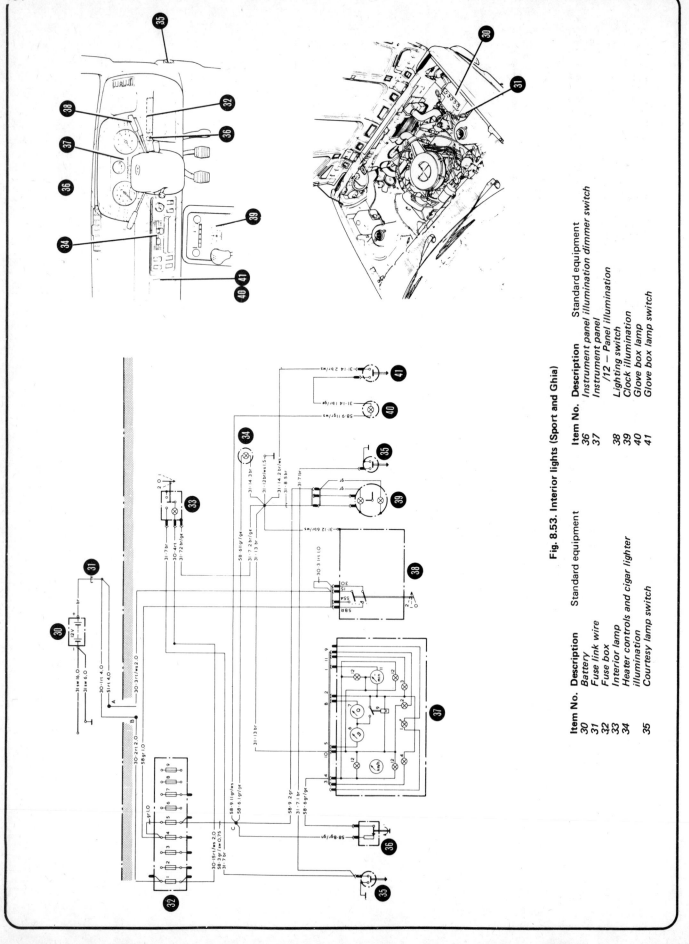

Fig. 8.53. Interior lights (Sport and Ghia)

Item No.	Description	Standard equipment
30	Battery	
31	Fuse link wire	
32	Fuse box	
33	Interior lamp	
34	Heater controls and cigar lighter illumination	
35	Courtesy lamp switch	

Item No.	Description	Standard equipment
36	Instrument panel illumination dimmer switch	
37	Instrument panel /12 – Panel illumination	
38	Lighting switch	
39	Clock illumination	
40	Glove box lamp	
41	Glove box lamp switch	

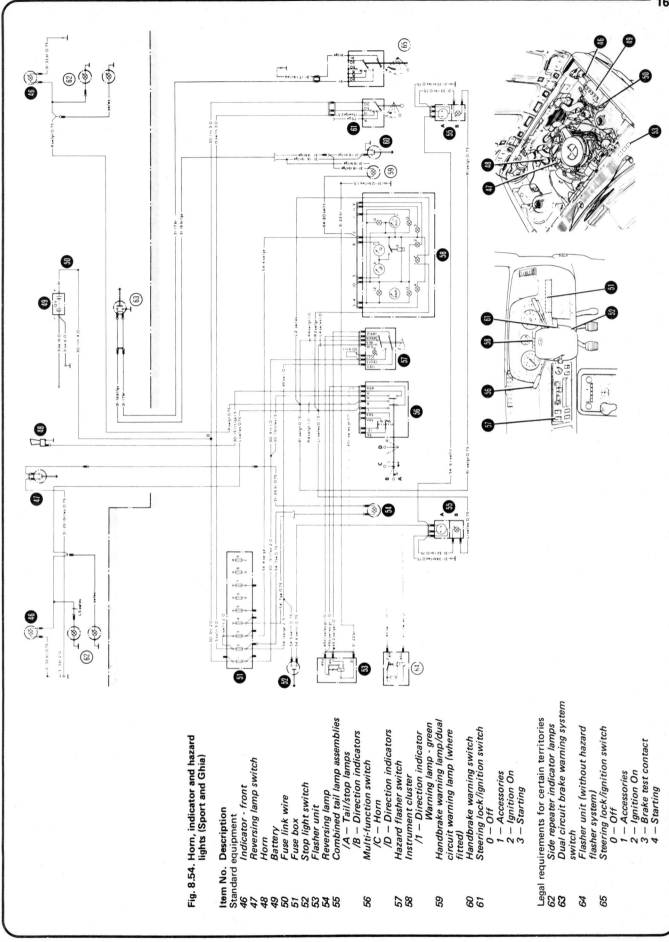

Fig. 8.54. Horn, indicator and hazard lights (Sport and Ghia)

Item No. Description

Standard equipment

46 Indicator - front
47 Reversing lamp switch
48 Horn
49 Battery
50 Fuse link wire
51 Fuse box
52 Stop light switch
53 Flasher unit
54 Reversing lamp
55 Combined tail lamp assemblies
    /A – Tail/stop lamps
    /B – Direction indicators
56 Multi-function switch
    /C – Horn
    /D – Direction indicators
57 Hazard flasher switch
58 Instrument cluster
    /1 – Direction indicator
    Warning lamp - green
59 Handbrake warning lamp/dual
    circuit brake warning lamp (where
    fitted)
60 Handbrake warning switch
61 Steering lock/ignition switch
    0 – Off
    1 – Accessories
    2 – Ignition On
    3 – Starting

Legal requirements for certain territories

62 Side repeater indicator lamps
63 Dual circuit brake warning system
    switch
64 Flasher unit (without hazard
    flasher system)
65 Steering lock/ignition switch
    0 – Off
    1 – Accessories
    2 – Ignition On
    3 – Brake test contact
    4 – Starting

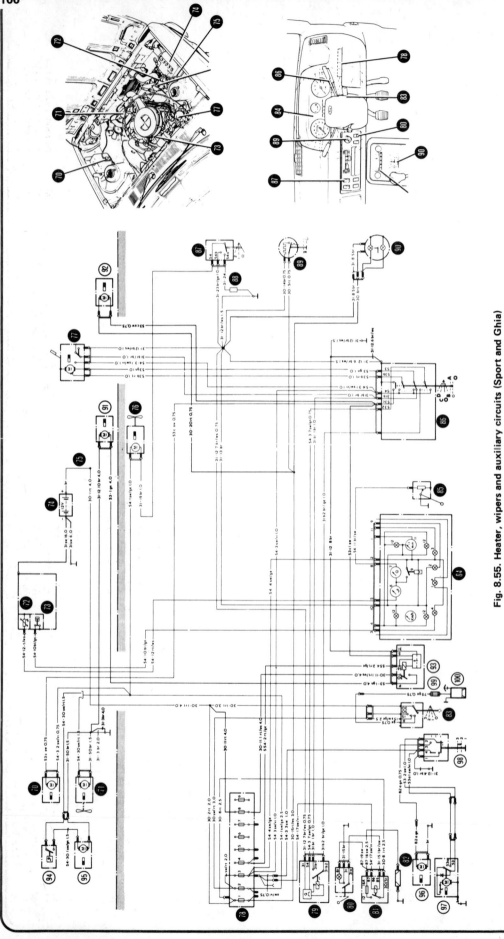

Fig. 8.55. Heater, wipers and auxiliary circuits (Sport and Ghia)

Item No.	Description Std. equipment
70	Windscreen washer pump motor
71	Radiator cooling blower motor
72	Water temperature indicator sender unit
73	Oil pressure indicator sender unit switch
74	Battery
75	Fuse link wire
76	Heater blower motor
77	Windscreen wiper motor
78	Fuse box
79	Windscreen wiper inter-mittent relay

Item No.	Description Std. equipment
80	Heated rear window switch
81	Heated rear window relay
82	Heated rear window
83	Steering lock/ignition switch
84	Instrument cluster
	/4 – Oil pressure warning lamp (orange)
	/6 – Water temperature indicator
	/7 – Fuel level indicator
85	Fuel indicator/sender unit
86	Windscreen washer/wiper motor switch

Item No.	Description Std. equipment
	A – Windscreen washer push switch
	B – Intermittent wipe
	C – Slow wipe
	D – Fast wipe
87	Heater blower motor switch
88	Heater blower motor resistance wire
89	Cigar lighter
90	Clock
91	Legal requirements for certain territories Headlamp washer pump motor

Item No.	Description Std. equipment
92	Windscreen washer pump motor
93	Headlamp washer pump relay
	Optional extra equipment
94	Water temperature switch (radiator fan)
95	Radiator cooling blower motor
96	Rear screen washer pump
97	Rear screen wiper motor
98	Rear screen wash/wipe switch
99	Radio fuse
100	Radio

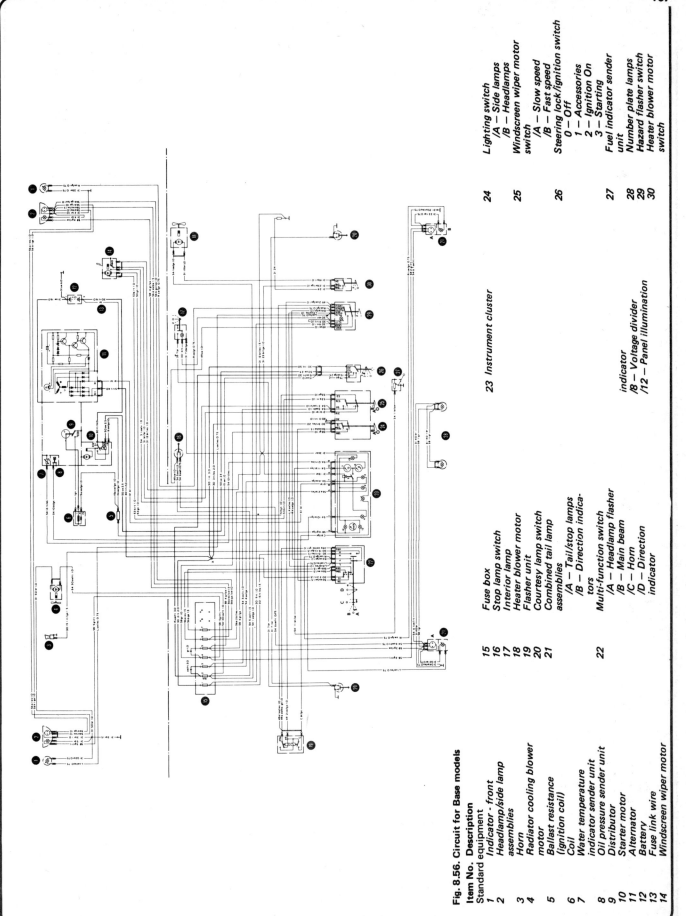

Fig. 8.56. Circuit for Base models

Item No.	Description
	Standard equipment
1	Indicator - front
2	Headlamp/side lamp assemblies
3	Horn
4	Radiator cooling blower motor
5	Ballast resistance (ignition coil)
6	Coil
7	Water temperature indicator sender unit
8	Oil pressure sender unit
9	Distributor
10	Starter motor
11	Alternator
12	Battery
13	Fuse link wire
14	Windscreen wiper motor
15	Fuse box
16	Stop lamp switch
17	Interior lamp
18	Heater blower motor
19	Flasher unit
20	Courtesy lamp switch
21	Combined tail lamp assemblies
	/A – Tail/stop lamps
	/B – Direction indicators
22	Multi-function switch
	/A – Headlamp flasher
	/B – Main beam
	/C – Horn
	/D – Direction indicator
23	Instrument cluster
24	Lighting switch
	/A – Side lamps
	/B – Headlamps
25	Windscreen wiper motor switch
	/A – Slow speed
	/B – Fast speed
26	Steering lock/ignition switch
	0 – Off
	1 – Accesories
	2 – Ignition On
	3 – Starting
27	Fuel indicator sender unit
28	Number plate lamps
29	Hazard flasher switch
30	Heater blower motor switch
	indicator
	/8 – Voltage divider
	/12 – Panel illumination

168

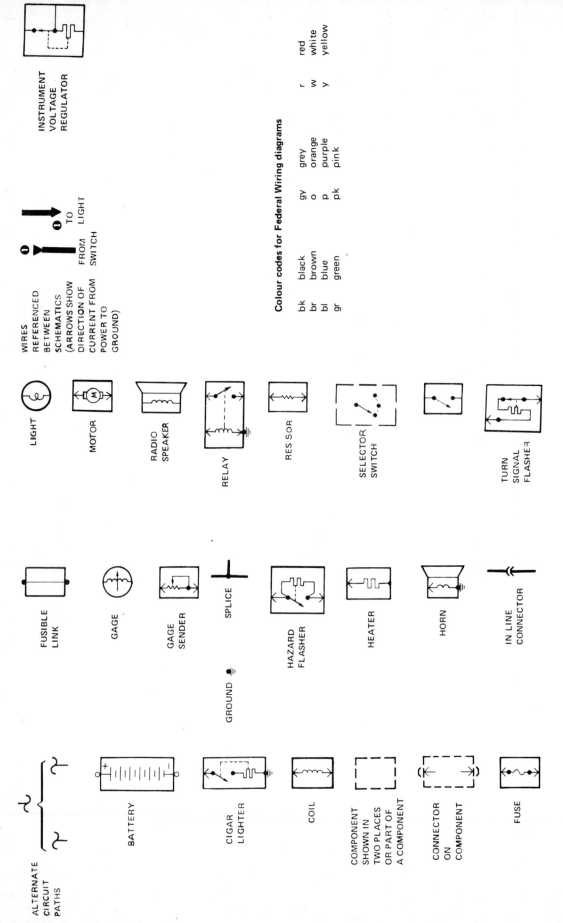

INSTRUMENT VOLTAGE REGULATOR

WIRES REFERENCED BETWEEN SCHEMATICS (ARROWS SHOW DIRECTION OF CURRENT FROM POWER TO GROUND)

TO LIGHT
FROM SWITCH

Colour codes for Federal Wiring diagrams

bk	black	gy	grey	r	red
br	brown	o	orange	w	white
bl	blue	p	purple	y	yellow
gr	green	pk	pink		

LIGHT

MOTOR

RADIO SPEAKER

RELAY

RES SOR

SELECTOR SWITCH

TURN SIGNAL FLASHER

FUSIBLE LINK

GAGE

GAGE SENDER

SPLICE

GROUND

HAZARD FLASHER

HEATER

HORN

IN LINE CONNECTOR

ALTERNATE CIRCUIT PATHS

BATTERY

CIGAR LIGHTER

COIL

COMPONENT SHOWN IN TWO PLACES OR PART OF A COMPONENT

CONNECTOR ON COMPONENT

FUSE

Electrical symbols relating to Federal Wiring diagrams on pages 169 to 179 inclusive

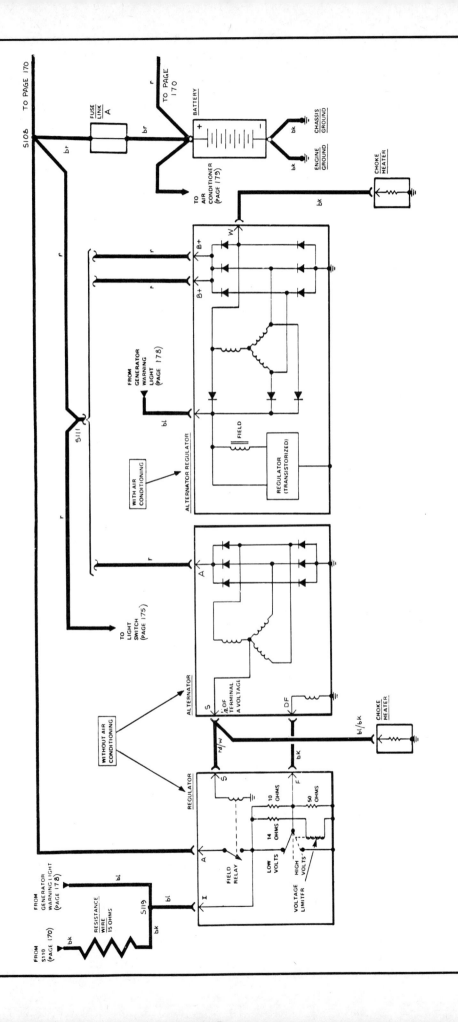

Fig. 8.57. Federal Wiring Diagram: Charge/Start/Ignition/Power Distribution

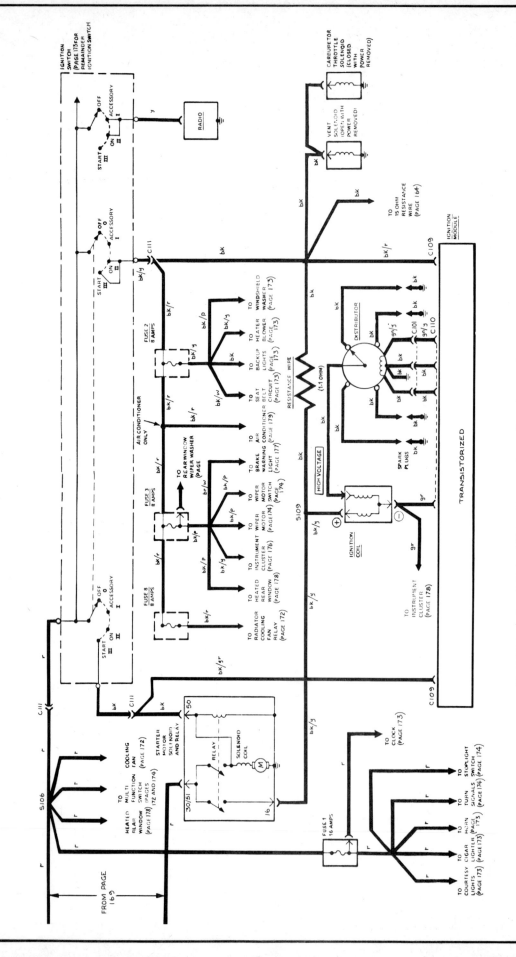

Fig. 8.57. (continued) Federal Wiring Diagram: Charge/Start/Ignition/Power Distribution

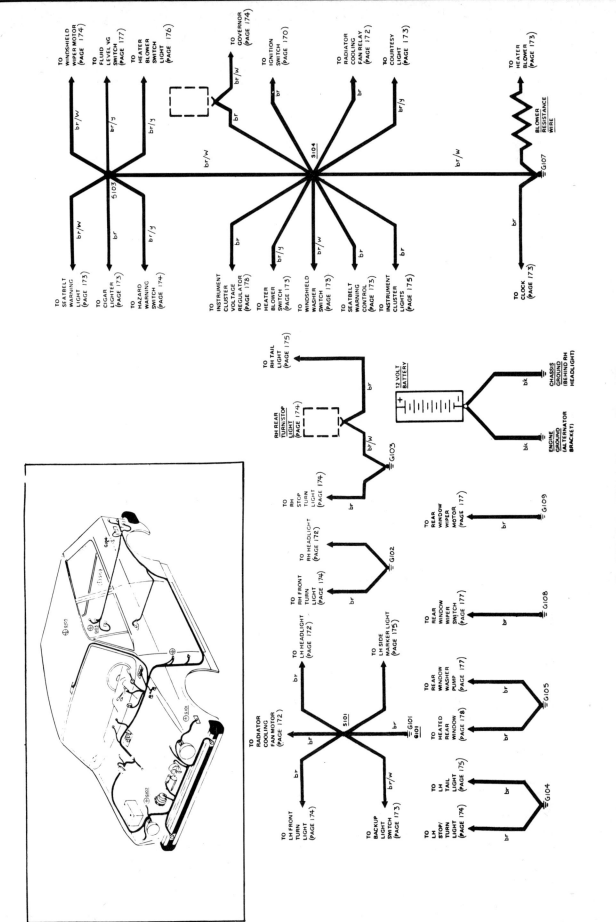

Fig. 8.58. Federal Wiring Diagram: Ground Wires

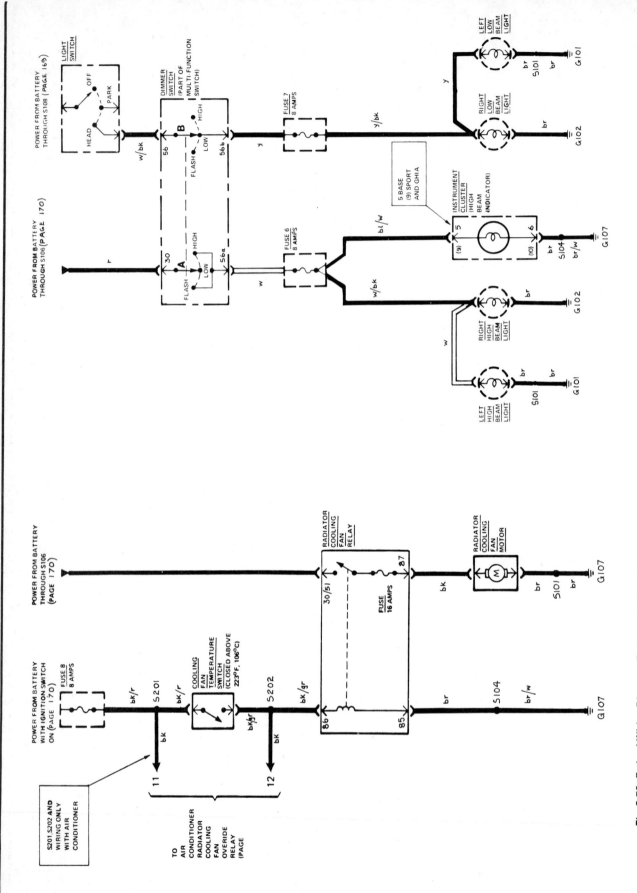

Fig. 8.60. Federal Wiring Diagram: Headlights

Fig. 8.59. Federal Wiring Diagram: Radiator Cooling Fan

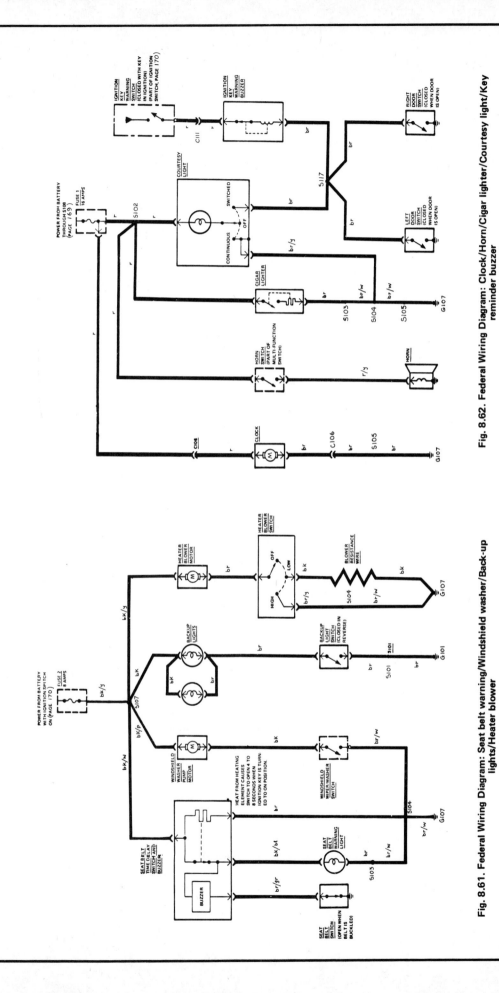

Fig. 8.62. Federal Wiring Diagram: Clock/Horn/Cigar lighter/Courtesy light/Key reminder buzzer

Fig. 8.61. Federal Wiring Diagram: Seat belt warning/Windshield washer/Back-up lights/Heater blower

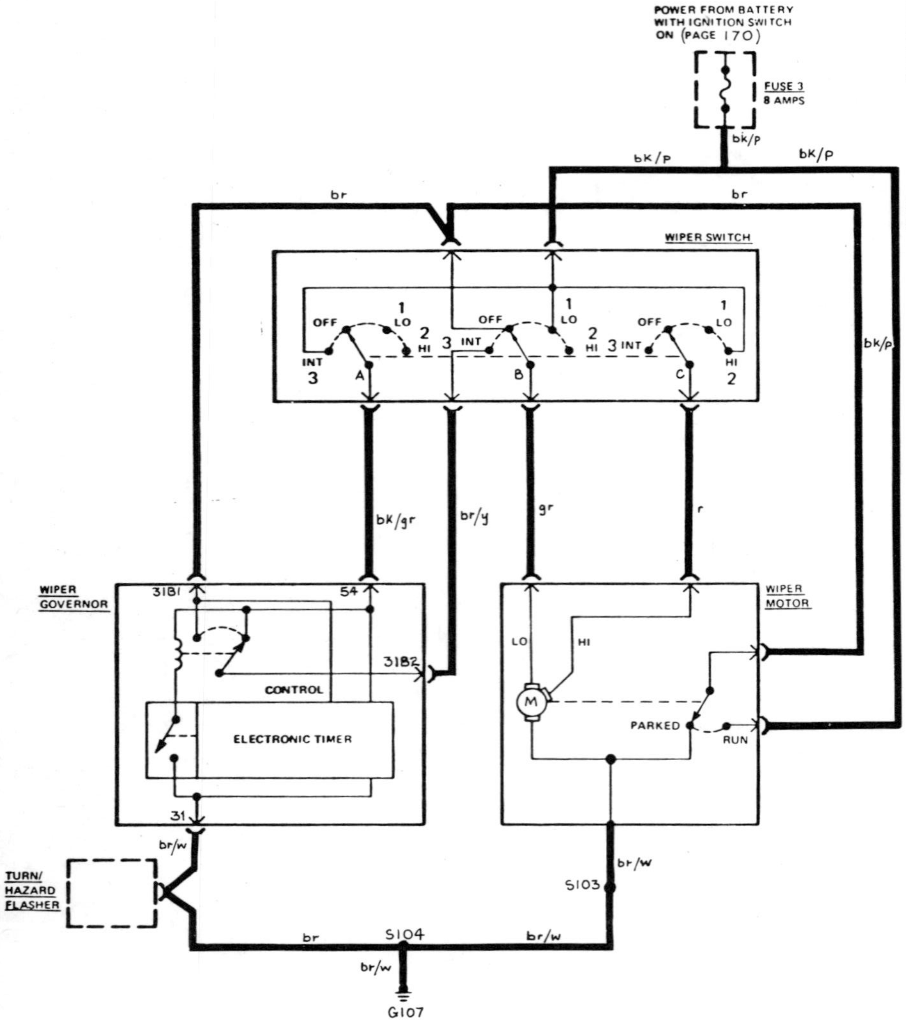

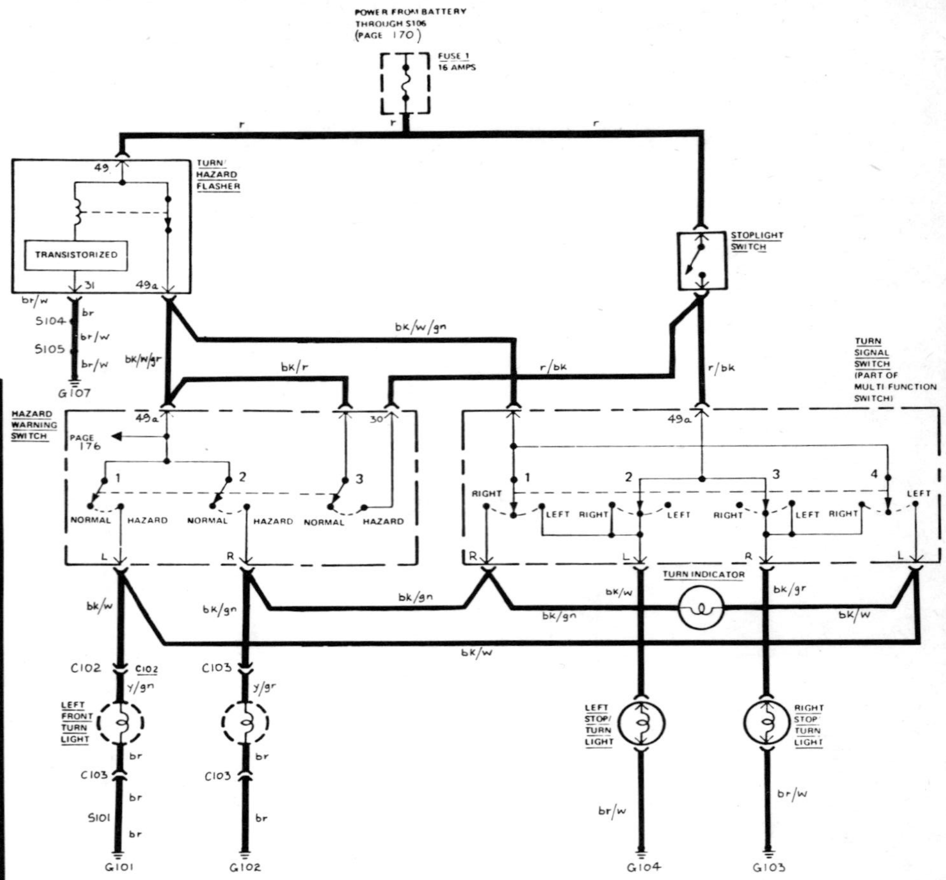

Fig. 8.64. Federal Wiring Diagram: Turn/Stop/Hazard warning lights

Fig. 8.63. Federal Wiring Diagram: Windshield wipers

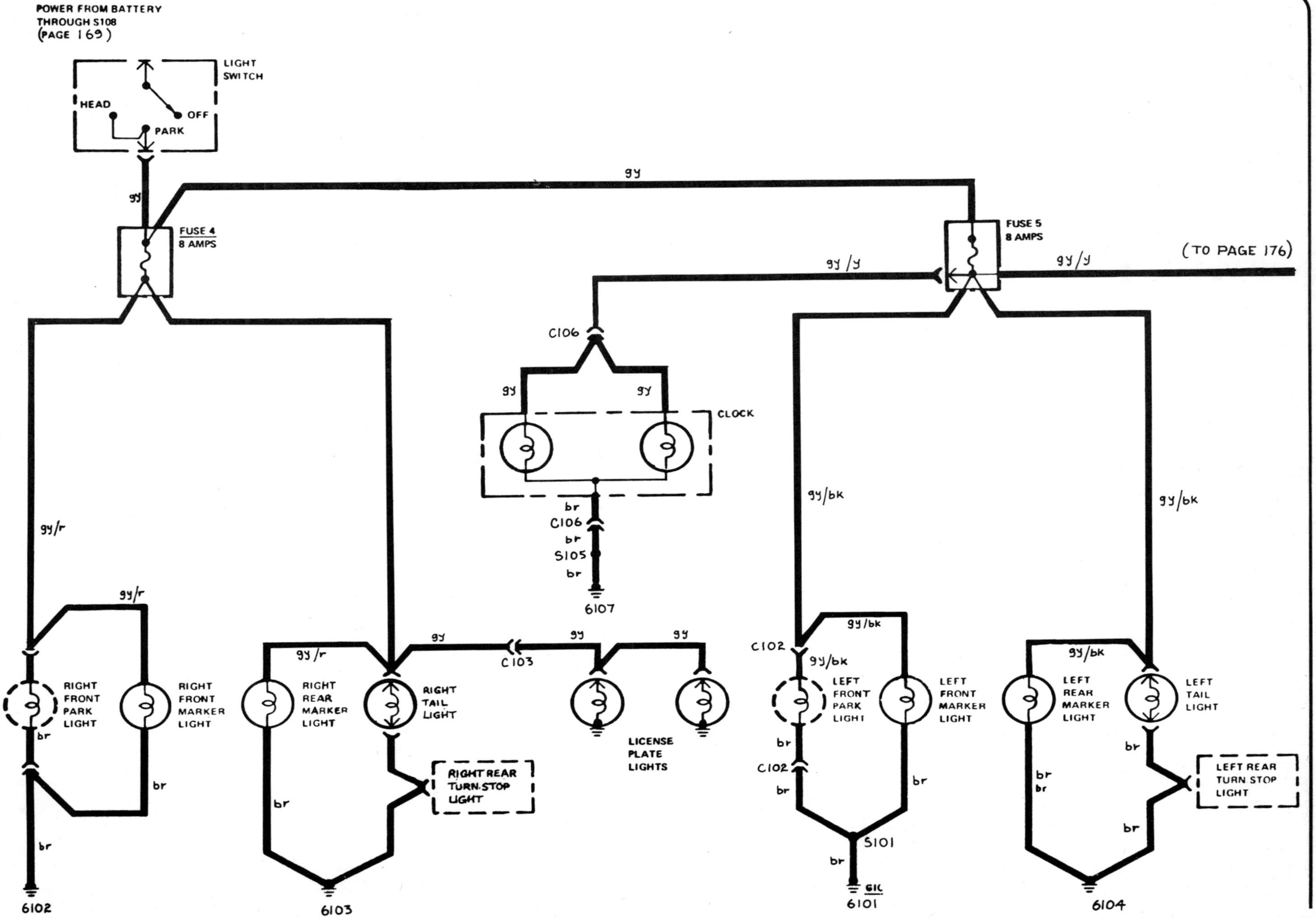

Fig. 8.65. Federal Wiring Diagram: Exterior/Instrument lights

(TO PAGE 176)

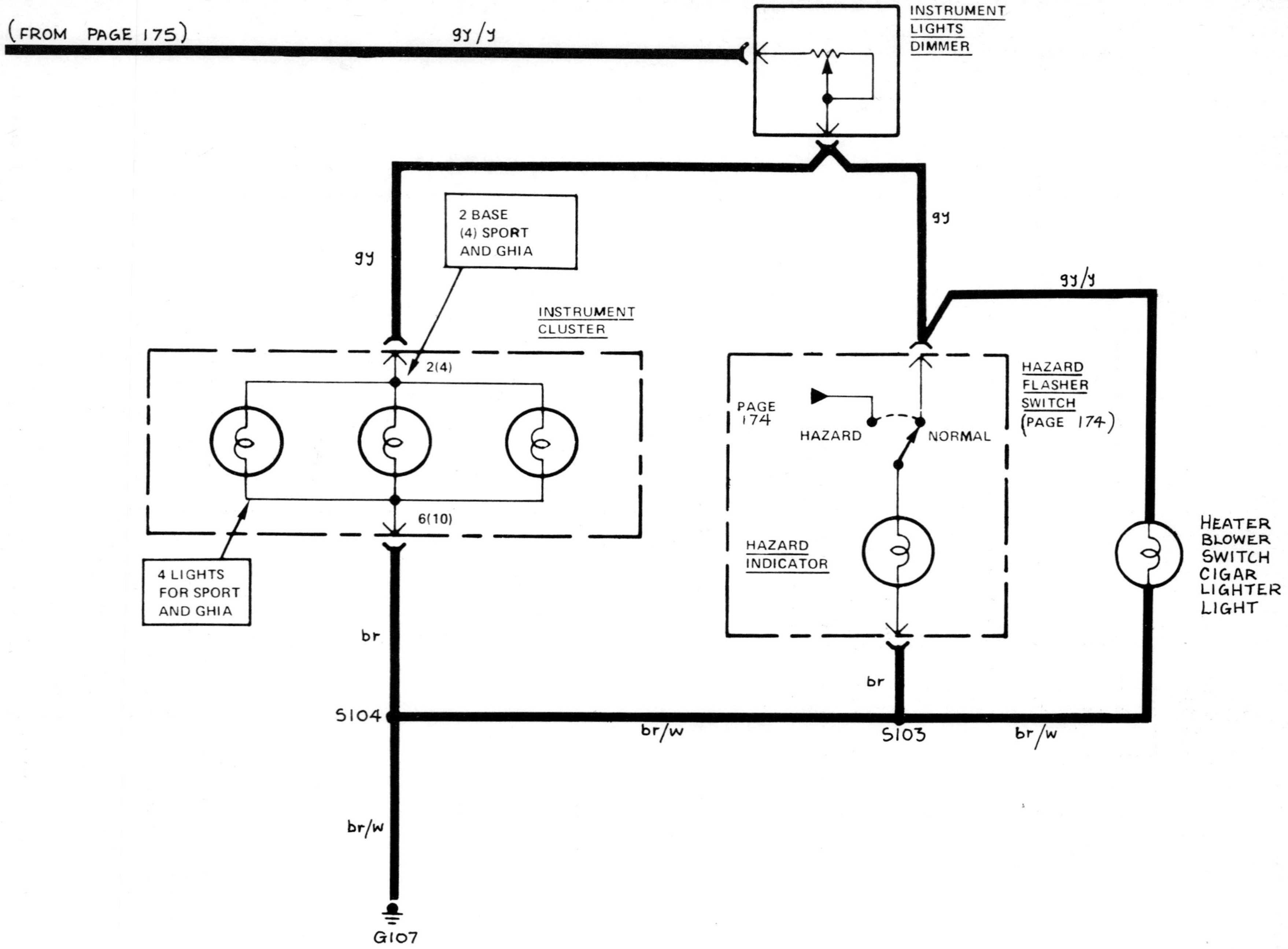

(FROM PAGE 175)

gy/y

INSTRUMENT
LIGHTS
DIMMER

gy

gy

HAZARD
FLASHER
SWITCH
(PAGE 174)

NORMAL

HAZARD

PAGE
174

HAZARD
INDICATOR

gy/y

HEATER
BLOWER
SWITCH
CIGAR
LIGHTER
LIGHT

br/w

br

S105

br/w

INSTRUMENT
CLUSTER

2 BASE
(4) SPORT
AND GHIA

2(4)

gy

6(10)

br

S104

4 LIGHTS
FOR SPORT
AND GHIA

br/w

G107

Fig. 8.65. (continued) Federal Wiring Diagram: Exterior/Instrument lights

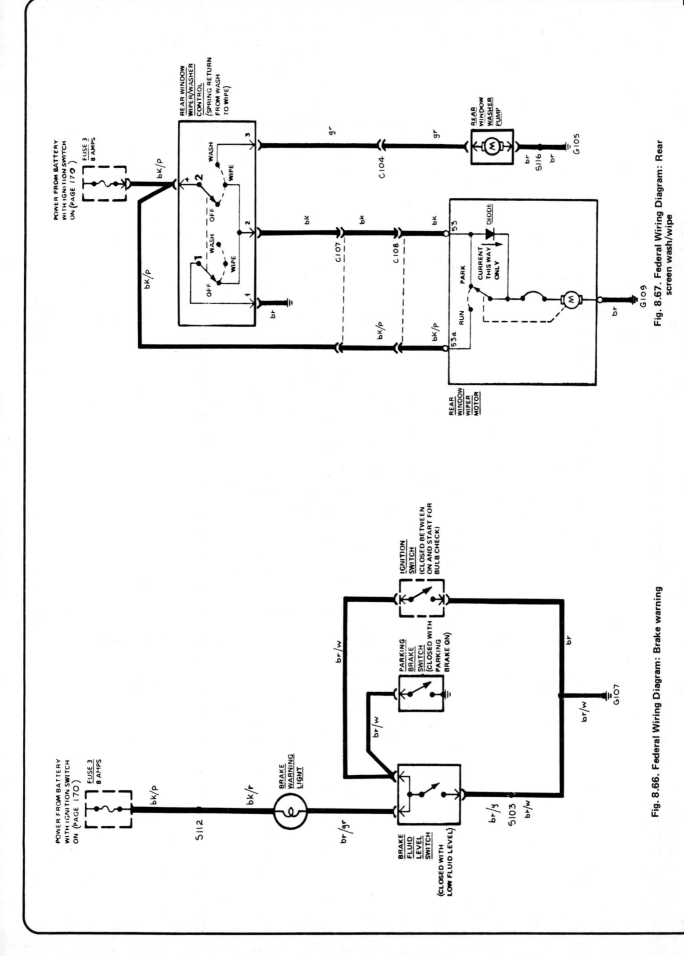

Fig. 8.67. Federal Wiring Diagram: Rear screen wash/wipe

Fig. 8.66. Federal Wiring Diagram: Brake warning

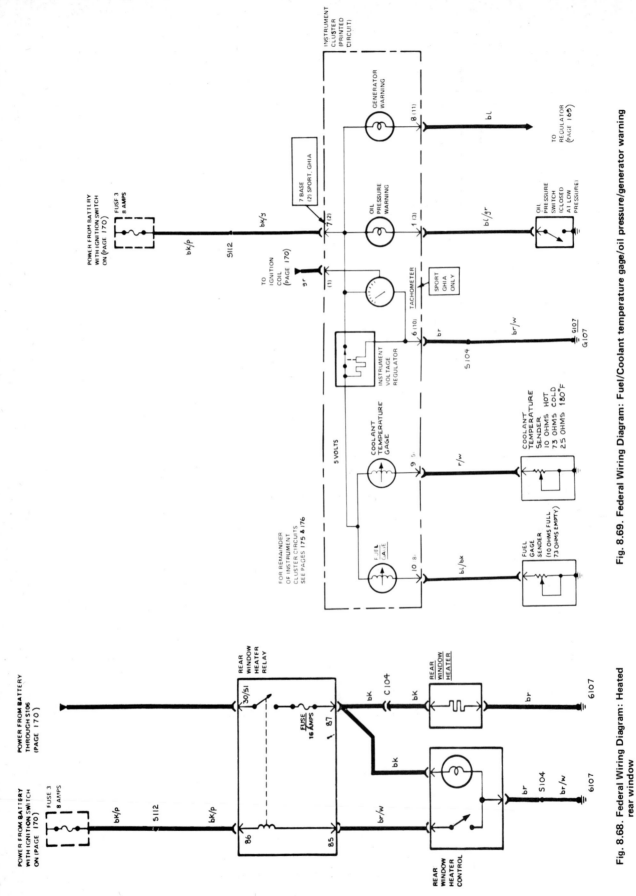

Fig. 8.69. Federal Wiring Diagram: Fuel/Coolant temperature gage/oil pressure/generator warning

Fig. 8.68. Federal Wiring Diagram: Heated rear window

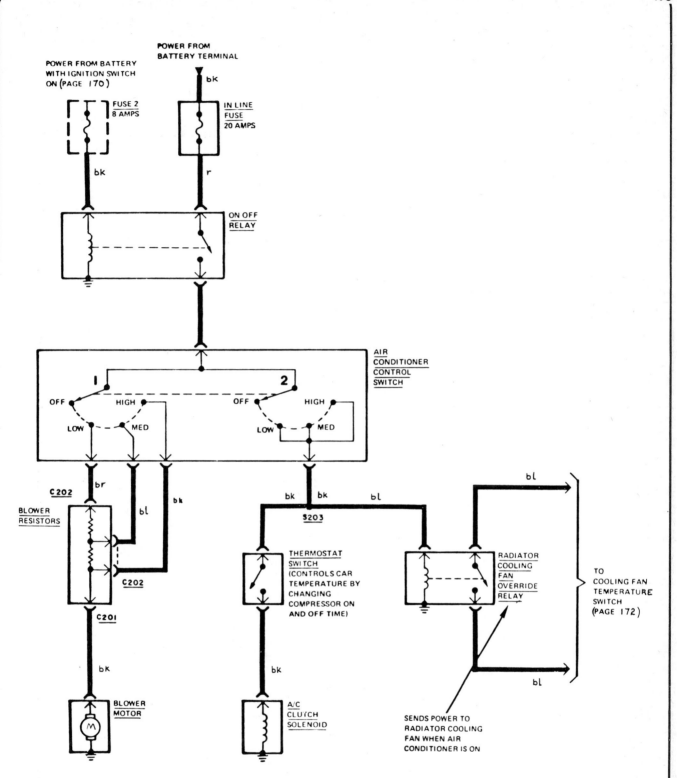

Fig. 8.70. Federal Wiring Diagram: Air conditioner

Chapter 9 Suspension, steering and driveshafts

Contents

Specifications

Front suspension

Type	Independent, MacPherson strut
Lateral control	Track control arms
Longitudinal control	Tie bar
Shock absorbers	Hydraulic, telescopic, double-acting
Spring rating	The spring rating varies according to the vehicle and intended market. When replacements are required, consult a Ford dealer for further information

Rear suspension

Type	Coil spring with two trailing arms and single Panhard rod. Stabiliser bar on certain variants
Shock absorbers	Hydraulic, telescopic, double-acting
Spring rating	The spring rating varies according to the vehicle and intended market. When replacements are required, consult a Ford dealer for further information

Steering gear

Type	Rack and pinion
Lubricant type	SAE 90EP gear oil
Lubricant capacity	0.15 litres (0.25 Imp pint/0.3 US pint)
Steering gear adjustment	By shims
Rack slipper bearing shim thicknesses	0.005, 0.007, 0.010, 0.015, 0.020 in (0.127, 0.19, 0.25, 0.38, 0.50 mm)

Front wheel alignment (unladen)

Castor angle:	
standard	$- 0^\circ 15'$ to $+ 1^\circ 15'$
heavy duty	$- 0^\circ 47'$ to $+ 0^\circ 43'$
Max. difference (side to side)	$1^\circ 15'$
Camber angle:	
standard	$0^\circ 49'$ to $2^\circ 49'$
heavy duty	$0^\circ 46'$ to $2^\circ 46'$
Max. difference (side to side)	$1^\circ 15'$
Toe setting	+ 0.04 in (1.0 mm) (toe-in) to − 0.24 in (6.0 mm) (toe-out)

Wheels

Pressed steel	12 x 4.00 C or 12 x 4.50 C
Aluminium	12 x 4.50 J

Tyres

Size	135SR x 12, 145SR x 12 or 155SR x 12

Pressures	Front	Rear
Load up to 3 persons:		
135SR	27 lbf/in^2 (1.9 kgf/cm^2)	27 lbf/in^2 (1.9 kgf/cm^2)
145SR and 155SR	23 lbf/in^2 (1.6 kgf/cm^2)	26 lbf/in^2 (1.8 kgf/cm^2)

	Front	Rear
Load in excess of 3 persons:		
135SR	31 lbf/in^2 (2.2 kgf/cm^2)	31 lbf/in^2 (2.2 kgf/cm^2)
145SR and 155SR	26 lbf/in^2 (1.8 kgf/cm^2)	28 lbf/in^2 (2.0 kgf/cm^2)

Note 1: These pressures apply to cold tyres
Note 2: Where a tyre chart is affixed to the vehicle , refer to this for pressures

Torque wrench settings

	lbf ft	kgf m
Hub retaining nut	180 to 200	24 to 27
Track control arm inner bush bolt	30 to 33	4.2 to 4.6
Track control arm balljoint pinch bolt	15 to 18	2.1 to 2.5
Balljoint to track control arm	40 to 48	5.6 to 6.6
Front hub to suspension leg bolts	74 to 88	10.2 to 12.2
Tie bar to bracket	32 to 40	4.5 to 5.6
Tie bar bracket to body	30 to 38	4.2 to 5.2
Piston rod nut	30 to 38	4.2 to 5.2
Top mount to body	15 to 18	2.1 to 2.5
Intermediate driveshaft bearing housing to support bracket bolts	13 to 16	1.8 to 2.2
Engine to bearing support bracket bolts	48 to 55	6.5 to 7.5
Panhard rod to body and axle	40 to 48	5.4 to 6.4
Trailing arm to body and axle	40 to 48	5.4 to 6.4
Shock absorber to axle	40 to 48	5.4 to 6.4
Shock absorber to body	18 to 22	2.5 to 3.5
Stabiliser bar to body	15 to 18	2.1 to 2.5
Brake carrier plate ,..	15 to 18	2.1 to 2.5
Steering gear to bulkhead	33 to 37	4.6 to 5.1
Track rod end to steering arm	18 to 22	2.5 to 3.0
Steering coupling to steering rack	33 to 41	4.6 to 5.7
Steering wheel nut	20 to 25	2.8 to 3.4
Track rod locknut	42 to 50	5.8 to 6.9
Pinion bearing cover	13 to 17	1.7 to 2.4
Rock slipper cover	4.5 to 6.7	0.6 to 0.9
Wheel bolts	63 to 85	8.7 to 11.7

1 General description

Each of the independent front suspension MacPherson strut units consists of a vertical strut enclosing a double acting damper surrounded by a coil spring.

The upper end of each strut is secured to the top of the wing valance under the bonnet by rubber mountings.

Bolted to the foot of the suspension leg, is the wheel spindle and hub assembly, which incorporates the rearward facing steering arms. Track rods connect each steering arm to the rack and pinion steering gear.

The lower end of each suspension unit is located by a track control arm. A tie bar is fitted between the outer ends of each track control arm and secured at the front to mountings on the body front member.

A rubber rebound stop is fitted inside each suspension unit thus preventing the spring becoming over-extended and jumping out of its mounting plates. Upward movement of the wheel is limited by the spring becoming fully compressed but this is damped by the addition of a rubber bump stop fitted around the suspension unit piston rod which comes into operation before the spring is fully compressed.

Whenever repairs have been carried out on a suspension unit it is essential to check the wheel alignment as the linkage could be altered which will affect the correct front wheel settings.

Every time the car goes over a bump vertical movement of a front wheel pushes the damper body upwards against the combined resistance of the coil spring and the damper piston.

Hydraulic fluid in the damper is displaced and forced through the compression valve into the space between the inner and outer cylinder. On the downward movement of the suspension, the road spring forces the damper body downwards against the pressure of the hydraulic fluid which is forced back again through the rebound valve. In this way the natural oscillations of the spring are damped out and a comfortable ride is obtained.

The steering gear is of the rack and pinion type and is located on the rear bulkhead by two 'U' shaped clamps. The pinion is connected to the steering column by a flexible coupling.

Turning the steering wheel causes the rack to move in a lateral direction and the trackrods attached to each end of the rack pass this movement to the steering arms on the suspension/axle nuts thereby moving the roadwheels.

One adjustment is possible on the steering gear, namely rack slipper adjustment, but the steering gear must be removed from the car to carry out this adjustment. Adjustment is made by varying the thickness of a shim-pack.

The steering shaft includes a disengagement device, while the steering column contains a convoluted collapsible section which is designed to collapse progressively in the event of impact damage, thus protecting the drive to some degree.

Power output from the transmission is taken by the driveshaft assemblies to the front hub spindle. Each driveshaft consists of three sections:

a) Transmission output shaft and inner constant velocity joint.
b) Inter-connecting (or intermediate) shaft.
c) Front hub spindle and outer constant velocity joint.

On 1300 and 1600 cc models, the right-hand intermediate shaft is further split into two parts, the inner one of which is supported by a ball bearing fixed to the engine block.

At the rear, the axle casing is located by two trailing arms bolted to the body in front of the axle, and a transverse Panhard rod fixed to the floor pan. Locating struts welded to the shock absorber are fixed to the axle casing through rubber bushes, and prevent any tendency for the axle to roll. Certain variants have a rear stabiliser bar to reduce roll of the vehicle on cornering.

Road shocks are absorbed by coil springs, and double acting telescopic shock absorbers fitted between the axle casing and reinforced mountings on the vehicle body. These shock absorbers work on the same principle as those at the front.

2 Front hub bearings - maintenance

1 The front wheel bearings and seals on Fiesta vehicles have been designed to give them an extended service life.
2 To achieve this, all components of the front hub have been designed to close tolerances, and require no adjustment to eliminate free play.
3 At such time as it becomes necessary to renew the bearings, both inner and outer bearings should be renewed at the same time. It is also recommended that only the correct Ford bearings are used.

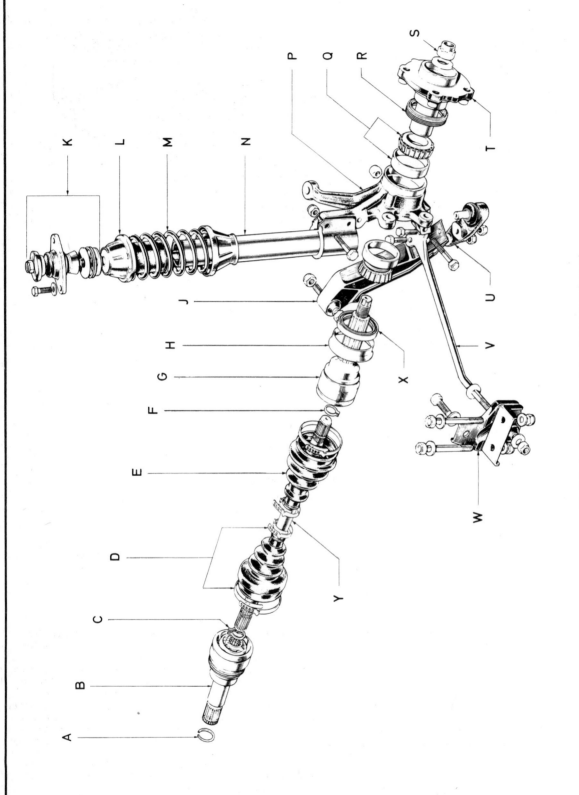

Fig. 9.1. Front axle, suspension and driveshaft (Sec. 1)

A Circlip
B Inner driveshaft
C Circlip
D Bellows clamps
E Bellows

F Circlip
G Outer driveshaft
H Dust shield
J Track control arm
K Top mount assembly

L Upper spring seat
M Spring
N Suspension strut
P Bearing carrier
Q Outer hub bearing

R Grease retainer
S Hub retaining nut
T Hub
U Balljoint
V Tie bar

W Tie bar bracket
X Grease retainer
Y Intermediate driveshaft

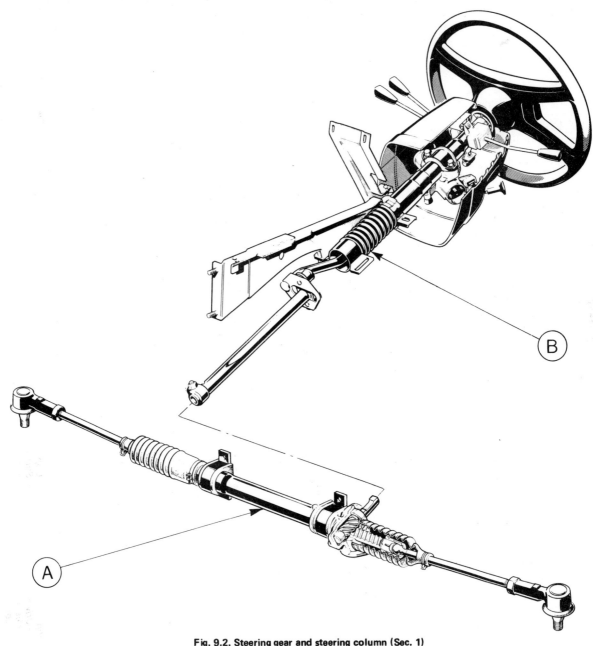

Fig. 9.2. Steering gear and steering column (Sec. 1)

A   Rack assembly   *B   Steering column*

---

3   Front hub bearings and carrier - removal and refitting

---

1   Slacken the roadwheel bolts, jack up the front of the car, fit axle stands and remove the roadwheels. Refit two wheel bolts finger tight.
2   With an assistant **firmly** applying the foot brake, unscrew and remove the hub retaining nut and plain washer. Release the foot brake.
3   From the inner face of the hub, remove the two brake caliper retaining bolts and slide off the caliper assembly. Hang the caliper from a suitable location with a length of wire, ensuring that the brake pipe is not strained.
4   Pull the hub and disc assembly from the bearing carrier, using a suitable two-legged puller if necessary.
5   Remove the split pin and unscrew the castellated nut from the track rod end. Separate the track rod from the bearing carrier (photo) using a proprietary separator or wedges.
6   Unscrew and remove the track control arm inner mounting bolt. Remove the pinch bolt holding the track control arm balljoint to the bearing carrier and separate the balljoint (photo).

7   At this stage it must be decided whether to remove the bearing carrier alone, or complete with the suspension strut. If only the bearings are to be renewed, proceed to paragraph 9.
8   If the bearing carrier is to be renewed the two bolts holding this to the suspension strut will have to be removed (photo). These bolts are tightened in production after the components have been assembled using a special alignment jig. Once these bolts have been removed, they must be renewed with special bolts, identified by two knurled bands on the shank (Fig. 9.4). In addition, the front wheel alignment must be checked, Section 19. If this type of bolt is already fitted, it may be re-used.
9   In order to avoid undue strain on the driveshaft joints, the outer constant velocity joint should be supported, preferably with a length of wire to a suitable body location.
10   If the special bolts referred to in paragraph 8 have not been removed, unscrew and remove the two top suspension mount bolts (photo) and washers.
11   Remove the bearing carrier and, if applicable, the suspension strut, downwards and outwards from the vehicle.

Fig. 9.3. Rear axle and suspension assembly (Sec. 1)

A Trailing arms
B Spring insulator pads
C Shock absorbers

D Stabiliser bar, where fitted
E Springs
F Bump rubbers

G Axle tube
H Panhard rod
J Rear hub and drum assembly

3.5 Separate the track rod ball joint

3.6 Separate the track control arm ball joint

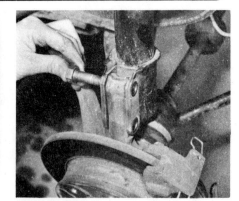

3.8 Removing the bearing carrier retaining bolts

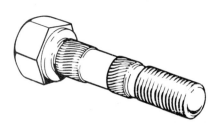

Fig. 9.4. Special bolts for service use (Sec. 3)

3.10 Unscrew the top suspension mount bolts

12 If the bearing carrier is being renewed, it should be discarded. If the bearings only are being renewed, the unit should be placed on a bench with the bearing carrier firmly supported on blocks of wood.

13 Using a suitable pair of pliers, pull the dust shield from its location in the inner side of the bearing carrier.

14 Using a suitable screwdriver, lever out the two grease retainers (one from each side) and discard them.

15 Lift out the roller bearings and examine them and the mating cones for any signs of wear, damage or looseness. If necessary, drift out the bearing cones with a suitable punch.

16 When renewing the bearings, it is recommended that only the correct Ford bearings are used. Always renew both bearing and cone as a matched pair. In general, it is false economy not to renew both bearings, even if one appears satisfactory.

17 Clean the bearing carrier of old grease and examine the bearing cone seats for any signs of burrs. These should be removed by careful use of a fine file.

18 With the bearing carrier firmly supported, tap the new bearing cones **fully** home, using a brass or copper drift.

19 Fully pack the bearing cages and rollers with wheel bearing grease and insert them into their respective cones. Apply grease to the sealing lips of the grease seals and insert the seals into the bearing carrier. Tap the seals **gently** home, using a block of wood.

20 Tap the dust shields into the inner face of the carrier, with the cut-out in line with the balljoint location (Fig. 9.5).

21 Lightly lubricate the driveshaft splines with grease.

22 Refitting is the reverse of this procedure, noting the following points:

    a) Use the service replacement bolts - if required (paragraph 8).

    b) Use new split pins and new hub nuts.

    c) When tightening the hub nut, have an assistant apply the foot brake. The necessary torque (200 lbf ft) can be achieved with a force of 200 lbf on a 1 ft lever, 50 lbf on a 4ft lever and so on.

    d) Once the hub nut is correctly tightened, it must be 'staked' into the cut-out in the driveshaft with a pin punch.

    e) Refer to paragraph 8, and check the front wheel alignment if necessary.

4 Front suspension strut - removal and refitting

1 It is difficult to work on the front suspension without one or two special tools, the most important of which is a set of adjustable spring clips which is Ford tool No. P.5045 (USA tool number T70P-5045). This tool or similar clips or compressors are vital and any attempt to dismantle the units without them may result in personal injury.

2 Get someone to sit on the wing of the car and with the spring partially compressed in this way, securely fit the spring clips.

3 Jack-up the car and remove the roadwheels.

4 Remove the two bolts retaining the hub bearing carrier to the suspension strut (photo 3,8). If these bolts are the type fitted in production (photo 3.7), they will have to be renewed with the bolts with a splined shank (Fig. 9.4).

5 From inside the engine compartment, remove the two top suspension mount bolts (photo 3.10), and carefully lift out the suspension strut.

6 Refitting is the reverse of this procedure, noting the following points:

    a) Use only the correct service replacement bolts (paragraph 4).

    b) After refitting, the front wheel alignment must be checked (Section 19).

5 Front suspension strut - dismantling and reassembly

1 When dismantling the suspension strut, suitable spring restrainers must be used. The non-adjustable type should have been fitted before removal of the suspension unit, Section 5. If an adjustable type, such as the Ford tool No. P.5045 (USA Tool No. T70P.5045) is being used, they should be fitted at opposite sides of the spring (Fig. 9.6), and tightened a little at a time until the spring tension is relieved.

2 Using a 6 mm Allen key to hold the piston rod, unscrew the top mount retaining nut and remove the nut and top mount components.

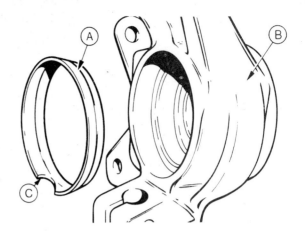

Fig. 9.5. Fit the dust shield (A) to bearing carrier (B) with cut-out (C) aligned with balljoint location (Sec. 4)

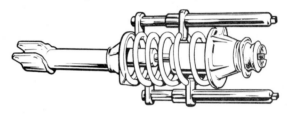

Fig. 9.6. Compressing the front coil spring (Sec. 5)

Lift off the spring.

3 Reassembly is the reverse of this procedure, noting the following points:

    a) Ensure that the top mount components are correctly assembled (Fig. 9.7).

    b) When releasing the spring compressors, make sure that the ends of the spring coils locate correctly in their seats.

6 Tie bar and bush - removal and refitting

1 Jack-up the front of the car and fit axle stands.

2 Unscrew and remove the nut from the front end of the tie-bar. Remove the washer.

3 Unscrew and remove the two nuts retaining the track control arm to the tie-bar (Fig. 9.8).

4 Slacken the track control arm balljoint pinch bolt, and pull down the balljoint and arm.

5 Remove the tie-bar bolts and remove the tie-bar from its front mounting bracket.

6 The tie-bar bush may be renewed without disconnecting the tie-bar from the track control arm. Unscrew and remove the three bolts holding the front tie-bar bracket, and remove the bracket.

7 Using a suitable sized mandrel, and a suitable piece of tubing, position the bracket between the jaws of a vice (Fig. 9.9). Tighten the vice to push out the bush.

8 Refitting is the reverse of this procedure, but note the following points:

    a) When pressing in the new bush, use a lubricant such as washing up liquid.

    b) When fitting the tie-bar to the track control arm, note that the bar should be fitted with the Ford stamp uppermost.

7 Track control arm, bush and balljoint - removal and refitting

1 Jack-up the front of the car and fit stands.

2 Unscrew and remove the track control arm inner pivot bolt and slacken the balljoint pinch bolt (Fig. 9.8).

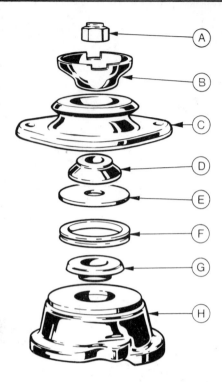

Fig. 9.7. Top mount components (Sec. 5)

A   Nut   E   Thrust washer
B   Retainer   F   Rubber seal
C   Top mount   G   Resin bearing
D   Spacer   H   Upper spring seat

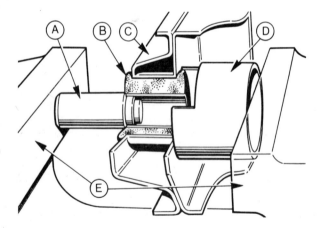

Fig. 9.9. Typical bush removal

A   Mandrel to fit inside bush   D   Pipe to fit outside bush
B   Bush   E   Vice jaws
C   Bush housing

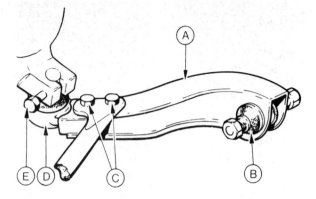

Fig. 9.8. Track control arm (Sec. 6 and 7)

A   Track control arm   D   Balljoint
B   Inner bush   E   Pinch bolt
C   Balljoint and tie bar bolts

Fig. 9.10. Levering out the shorter driveshaft (Sec. 8)

Fig. 9.11. Tapping out the longer driveshaft (Sec. 8)

3   Remove the two nuts retaining the track control arm to the tie-bar, and remove the arm and balljoint.
4   To renew the inner bush, position the arm together with a suitable size mandrel and a piece of pipe between the jaws of a vice (Fig. 9.9). Tighten the vice to push out the bush.
5   When refitting the bush, use a suitable lubricant such as washing up liquid.
6   Refitting is the reverse of the above procedure.

___

8   Driveshaft assembly - removal and refitting

___

1   Refer to Section 3 and carry out the work described in paragraphs 1 to 6 inclusive.
2   Where applicable, remove the three bolts retaining the centre bearing carrier to the side of the engine block at the right-hand driveshaft.
3   Position a drain tray under the transmission casing, and use a screwdriver to lever out the left-hand driveshaft (Fig. 9.10). or tap out the right-hand driveshaft (Fig. 9.11).
4   Insert a suitable plug (an old driveshaft stub is ideal) into the transmission casing to prevent the differential gears being dislodged if both driveshafts are being removed.
5   Withdraw the outer end of the driveshaft from the hub.
6   When refitting the driveshaft to the transmission, first fit a **new** circlip to the driveshaft end (photo).
7   Refitting is the reverse of this procedure. Refer to Section 3,

8.6 Fit a new driveshaft retaining circlip

Fig. 9.12. Expand the circlip and pull out the intermediate shaft (Sec. 9)

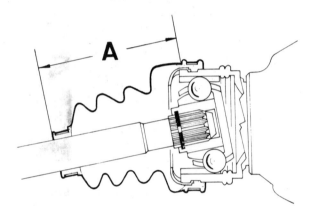

Fig. 9.13. Positioning the driveshaft bellows (Sec. 9)

paragraph 22 b), c) and d). Finally, top up the transmission oil as described in Chapter 6.

9 Driveshaft assembly - dismantling and reassembly

1   Gently tap the raised portion of each bellows clamp to loosen the clamp. Unhook and remove the clamp and slide the bellows along the intermediate shaft.

2   To disengage the constant velocity joints at the inner and outer ends of the driveshaft, first wipe off any surplus grease.

3   Using a pair of circlip pliers, expand the retaining circlip and pull out the intermediate shaft (Fig. 9.12). Remove the circlip.

4   To dismantle the centre joint on the right-hand driveshaft (where applicable) unscrew and remove the Allen screws retaining the joint halves.

5   Expand the retaining circlip, and pull the right-hand shaft from the constant velocity joint.

6   Firmly tap the universal joint from the end of the driveshaft. The dust cap and bearing race can then be removed from the shaft, followed by the bracket and bearing.

7   Examine the bearing race and cone for damage or wear, and if necessary, renew the bearing race, bracket and cone as a complete unit.

8   Check the constant velocity joints for damage or wear and renew them if necessary. Examine all circlips and bellows for wear, and renew as necessary.

9   Where applicable, refit the bearing bracket and bearing race onto the left-hand intermediate shaft. Refit the dust cap and tap on the universal joint.

10 Repack the centre joint with approximately 1½ ounces (40 grammes) of molybdenum based lithium grease such as Castrol MS3.

Fig. 9.14. Crimping the bellows clamp (Sec. 9)

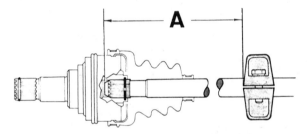

Fig. 9.15. Positioning the torsion damper (where fitted) (Sec. 9)

A —   300 mm (11.8 in) ± 2.0 mm (0.08 in)

11 Fit the right-hand intermediate shaft into the joint, and retain it with the circlip. Connect the bellows and then retain the centre joint halves with the Allen screws.

12 Repack each inner and outer joint with approximately 1½ ounces (40 grammes) of molybdenum based lithium grease such as Castrol MS3.

13 Slide the bellows onto the intermediate shaft then push the shaft into the constant velocity joint until the circlip snaps into its groove.

14 Refit the bellows to the joint. The bellows on the transmission joint should be fitted so that with the shaft at a 10° to 20° angle, dimension 'A' in Fig. 9.13 is 2.75 in (70 mm). The hub joint bellows dimension 'A' should be 3.7 in (95 mm) when the joint is straight.

15 Tighten the **new** clamps until the bellows are just held, then engage the clamp hook in the next hole. Crimp the clamp to fully tighten it (Fig. 9.14).

16 If a torsion damper has been removed (where applicable) it should have been refitted to give the dimension shown in Fig. 9.15.

10 Rear axle tube - removal and refitting

1   Slacken the rear wheel bolts, chock the front wheels, jack up the rear of the car and fit axle stands.

2   Open the bonnet and slacken, but do not remove, the two bolts securing the exhaust pipe to the manifold.

3   Unhook the exhaust system from its hangers, and gently lower it.
4   Unscrew the through bolt securing the Panhard rod to the axle casing (Fig. 9.3), and lower the rod.
5   Slacken the handbrake cable adjuster locknut, and unscrew the adjuster (refer to Chapter 7 if required).
6   Disconnect the brake fluid hoses from the axle brackets, and plug or tape the ends to prevent excess loss of fluid or entry of dirt.
7   Position a suitable block, such as a trolley jack, under the centre of the axle tube to take the weight.

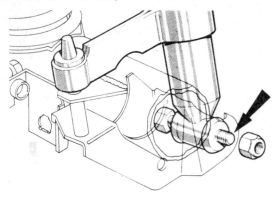

Fig. 9.16. Removing the lower shock absorber bolt (Sec. 10)

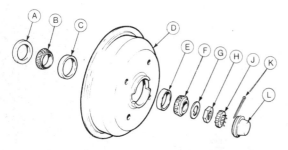

Fig. 9.17. Rear hub and drum components (Sec. 11)

A   Grease retainer   G   Tab washer
B   Inner bearing   H   Retaining nut
C   Bearing cup   J   Nut retainer
D   Brake drum and hub   K   Split pin
E   Bearing cup   L   Grease cap
F   Outer bearing

12.4 Shock absorber upper mount

8   Remove the two through bolts securing the shock absorbers and, where applicable, the stabiliser bar to the axle tube (Fig. 9.16).
9   Using a suitable lever, prise the shock absorber off its locating peg.
10 Remove the through bolts securing the trailing arms to the axle and remove the axle tube from the car.
11 Refer to Chapter 7 and remove the brake assembly from the axle tube.
12 Refitting is the reverse of the removal procedure, noting the following points:

> a) It is recommended that none of the through bolts are fully tightened until they have all been fitted.
> b) Refer to Chapter 7, Section 17 and adjust the handbrake cable.
> c) Refer to Chapter 7, Section 12 and bleed the braking system.

11 Rear hub bearings - removal, refitting and adjustment

1   Slacken the rear wheel bolts, chock the front wheels and jack up the rear of the car. Remove the rear wheels and release the handbrake.
2   Using a screwdriver, prise the grease cap from the centre of the wheel hub.
3   Pull out the split pin and remove the nut retainer. Unscrew the hub nut and lift out the tab washer and outer bearing race (Fig. 9.17).
4   Pull off the hub and drum assembly.
5   Using a suitable screwdriver, lever out the grease retainer and lift out the inner bearing race.
6   Examine the bearing races and cones for signs of wear or damage, and any looseness of the rollers in the cage. In addition, place the races in their cones, and turn them by hand, feeling for any roughness.
7   If necessary, remove the bearing cones from the hub by tapping them progressively with a suitable drift. Take care not to raise any burrs on the hub surfaces.
8   Bearing cones and races should always be renewed as matched pairs. When fitting the cups, they should be tapped gently into place with a copper or brass drift.
9   Pack the bearings with a lithium based grease, and fit the inner bearing to its cup.
10 Apply a smear of grease to the lips of the grease retainer, and fit the retainer with the lips towards the bearing. Gently tap the retainer fully home.
11 Refit the hub and drum assembly, then the outer bearing race, tab washer and retaining nut.

Adjustment
12 Whenever refitting the rear wheel hub, and also at the recommended service intervals, the bearing should be adjusted as follows.
13 Tighten the hub nut to a torque of 27 lbf ft (3.7 kgf m) while rotating the hub. Slacken the nut 90°, then fit the nut retainer and a new split pin.
14 Refit the grease cap, and tap it into position.
15 Refit the wheels and lower the car to the ground.

12 Rear spring - removal and refitting

1   Slacken the wheel bolts, chock the front wheels and jack up the rear of the car. Fit axle stands, and remove the roadwheel.
2   Position an extended jack beneath the rear axle tube to take the weight.
3   From inside the rear of the car, remove the plastic cap from the shock absorber.
4   Remove the retaining nut, washer and rubber insulator from the top of the shock absorber (photo).
5   Unscrew and remove the trailing arm through bolt from the axle tube.
6   Unscrew the two stabiliser bar to body nuts and washers, where fitted.
7   Lower the jack far enough to remove the spring and insulator (Fig. 9.18).
8   If required, prise the bump rubber from its location in the axle tube.
9   Refitting is the reverse of this procedure.

Fig. 9.18. Rear spring insulator pad (Sec. 12)

13 Rear shock absorber - removal and refitting

1   Carry out the work described in Section 12, paragraphs 1 to 4 inclusive.
2   Unscrew and remove the nut and through bolt retaining the lower end of the shock absorber (photo) and the stabiliser bar, where fitted.
3   Lever the shock absorber off its loading peg, and remove it.
4   Apply a suitable lubricant such as washing up liquid to the locating peg bush, and lever the bush onto the peg. Apply a steady force, and allow the bush to 'creep' onto the peg (photo).
5   Position the shock absorber through bolt, refit the stabiliser bar where applicable, and fit the nut.
6   Refit the insulators at the top of the shock absorber, refit to the body and secure with the washer and nut (Fig. 9.19). Fit the plastic cap.
7   Refit the roadwheels, and lower the car to the ground.

14 Rear suspension bushes - removal and refitting

1   There are a number of rubber bushes incorporated in the rear suspension to help minimise the transmission of road vibrations through the bodywork. Many of these bushes can be renewed, normally when the associated component is removed.
2   *Trailing arm* bushes cannot be renewed and must be considered an integral part of the arm.
3   The *Panhard rod* is removed from the vehicle by unscrewing and removing the two through bolts. Push out the bushes by using suitable sized mandrels and tubing (such as a socket) between the jaws of a vice in a similar manner to that illustrated in Fig. 9.9.
4   The *stabiliser bar* to floor pan bushes can be removed after removing the two clamp nuts and washers, and the clamps. New bushes must be fitted with the splits facing the rear.
5   The *stabiliser bar connecting link* upper bush can be pressed out of the link after removing the spring clip from the pin (Fig. 9.20). The lower bush is only serviced complete with the link.
6   The *shock absorber* lower bush can be removed by locating suitable mandrels and tubing in a heavy vice (Fig. 9.9) and first pressing out the metal spacer sleeves. The rubber bushes can then be removed by hand. The shock absorber arm bush can be removed with a suitable lever.
7   *Bush refitting* is generally made easier by the use of a suitable lubricant such as washing up liquid or paraffin. If paraffin is used, do not soak the bush, as this will cause it to swell. Always ensure that the new bush is correctly located, with the flanges protruding equally.

15 Steering gear - removal and refitting

1   Before starting this job, set the front wheels in the straight-ahead position. Then jack-up the front of the car and place blocks under the wheels; lower the car slightly on the jack so that the trackrods are in a near horizontal position.
2   Remove the nut and bolt from the clamp at the steering gear. This clamp holds the coupling to the pinion splines (photo).

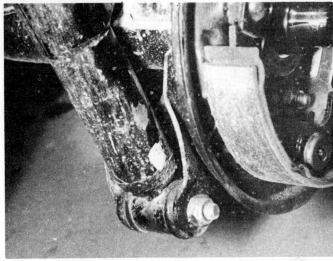

13.2 Shock absorber lower mount

13.4 Shock absorber locating peg

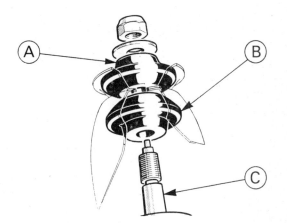

Fig. 9.19. Refit the shock absorber (C), lower (B) and upper (A) insulators (Sec. 13)

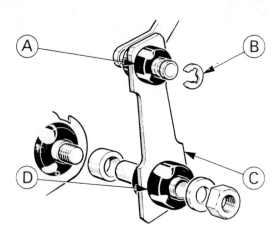

Fig. 9.20. Remove the spring clip (B) and press the upper bush (A) out of the link and lower bush assembly (C and D) (Sec. 14)

15.2 Steering shaft clamp bolt

3   Remove the split pins and castellated nuts from the ends of each trackrod where they join the steering arms. Separate the trackrods from the steering arms using a balljoint separator or wedges.
4   Knock back the locking tabs on the two bolts retaining each steering gear 'U' clamp, remove the bolts and lift out the steering gear.
5   Before refitting the steering gear make sure that the wheels have remained in the straight-ahead position. Also check the condition of the mounting rubbers round the housing and if they appear worn or damaged renew them.
6   Check that the steering gear is also in the straight-ahead position. This can be done by ensuring that the distances between the ends of both trackrods and the steering gear housing on both sides are the same.
7   Place the steering gear in its location on the bulkhead and at the same time mate up the splines on the pinion with the splines in the clamp on the steering column coupling.
8   Refit the two 'U' clamps using new locking tabs under the bolts, tighten down the bolts to the specified torque.
9   Refit the trackrod ends into the steering arms, refit the castellated nuts and tighten them to the specified torque. Use new split pins to retain the nuts.
10 Tighten the clamp bolt on the steering column flexible coupling to the specified torque, having first made sure that the pinion is correctly located in the splines.
11 Jack up the car, remove the blocks from under the wheels and lower the car to the ground. It is advisable at this stage to take the car to your local dealer and have the toe-in checked (see Section 19).

16 Steering gear - adjustment

1   For the steering gear to function correctly, the rack slipper adjustment must be correct. Ideally this will require the use of a dial gauge and mounting block, a surface table, a torque gauge and a splined adaptor. It is felt that most people will be able to suitably improvise using other equipment, but if this cannot be done and the equipment listed is not available, the job should be entrusted to your local vehicle main dealer.
2   To carry out the adjustments, remove the steering gear from the car as described in the previous Section. Mount the assembly in a soft jawed vice then remove the rack slipper cover plate, shim pack gasket and spring.
3   Using a dial gauge, measure the height of the slipper above the main body of the rack as the rack is transversed from lock-to-lock by turning the pinion. Note the height reading obtained.
4   Prepare a shim pack which, including the thickness of the rack slipper bearing gasket, is 0.002 to 0.006 in (0.05 to 0.15 mm) thicker than the dimension noted in paragraph 3.
5   Fit the spring gasket, shim pack and cover plate to the rack housing (gasket nearest cover). Apply a sealer such as Loctite to the cover

bolt threads, fit them and torque tighten to 5 to 6 lb f ft (0.6 to 0.9 kgf m).
6   Measure the torque required to turn the pinion throughout its range of travel. This should be 5 to 18 lbf in (6 to 21 kgf cm); if outside this range, faulty components, lack of lubricant etc., should be suspected.

17 Steering gear - dismantling, overhaul and reassembly

Note: The procedure given may be beyond the capabilities of many d-i-y motorists. Read through the Section before commencing any work and if not considered to be feasible, entrust the job to your local vehicle main dealer.
1   Remove and discard the wire retaining clips, remove the bellows and drain the lubricant.
2   Mount the steering gear in a soft-jawed vice and drill out the pins securing the trackrod housings to the locknuts. Centre-punch the pins before drilling then use a 5/32 in (4 mm or No. 22) drill but do not drill too deeply.
3   It is now necessary to unscrew the housings from the balljoints so that the trackrods, housings, locknuts and ball seats, can be removed. Ideally this requires the use of special tools which should be available from a vehicle main dealer but if improvised grips or wrenches are used take care that no parts are damaged (if parts are damaged, new items must be obtained).
4   Remove the rack slipper cover plate, shim pack, gasket, spring and slipper.
5   Remove the pinion bearing cover plate, gasket and seal.
6   Withdraw the pinion and bearing assembly. Note that the bearing is only supplied as a unit with the pinion.
7   Clean and inspect all the parts for damage and wear. Examine the bush in the end of the rack tube furthest from the pinion; if worn it can be pressed out and a new one fitted.
8   Commence reassembly by fitting the pinion upper bearing and washer into the housing.
9   Position the rack into the housing, and leave it in the central position.
10 Install the pinion, ensuring that after fitting the flat is towards the right-hand side of the vehicle (irrespective of right- or left-hand drive vehicles).
11 Fit the pinion bearing gasket, cover plate and seal, apply sealer to the bolt threads and tighten the bolt to 13 to 17 lbf ft (1.7 to 2.4 kgf m).
12 Assemble the rack slipper, spring, gasket, shim pack and cover plate, adjusting as described in the previous Section.
13 Lubricate the ball seats, balls and housings with SAE 90EP gear oil. Screw the locknuts onto the ends of the steering rack.
14 Assemble the ball seats, trackrod ends and housing. Tighten the housings to obtain a rotational torque of 5 lbf ft (0.7 kgf m) then lock

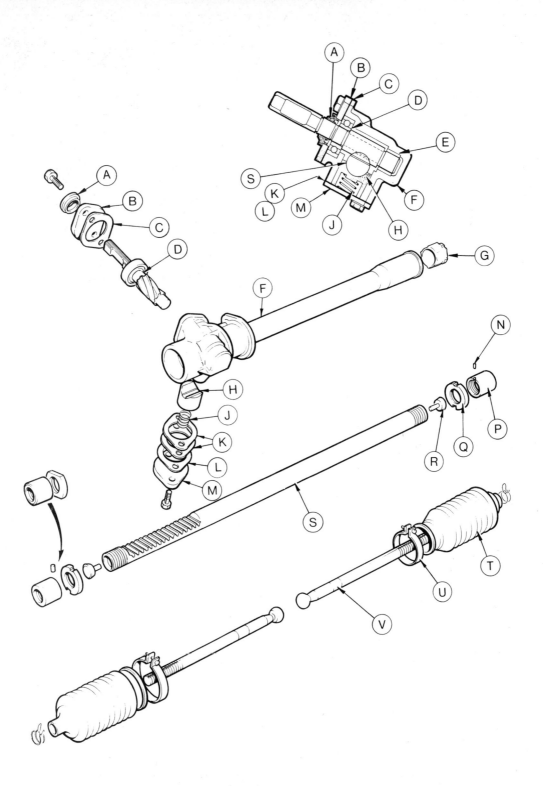

Fig. 9.21. Steering gear components (Sec. 17)

A Seal
B Cover plate
C Gasket
D Pinion and bearing assembly
E Lower bush

F Rack housing
G Rack support bush
H Rack slipper
J Spring
K Selective shims

L Gasket
M Cover plate
N Locking pin
P Ball housing
Q Locking ring

R Ball seat
S Rack
T Bellows
U Bellows clamp
V Track rod

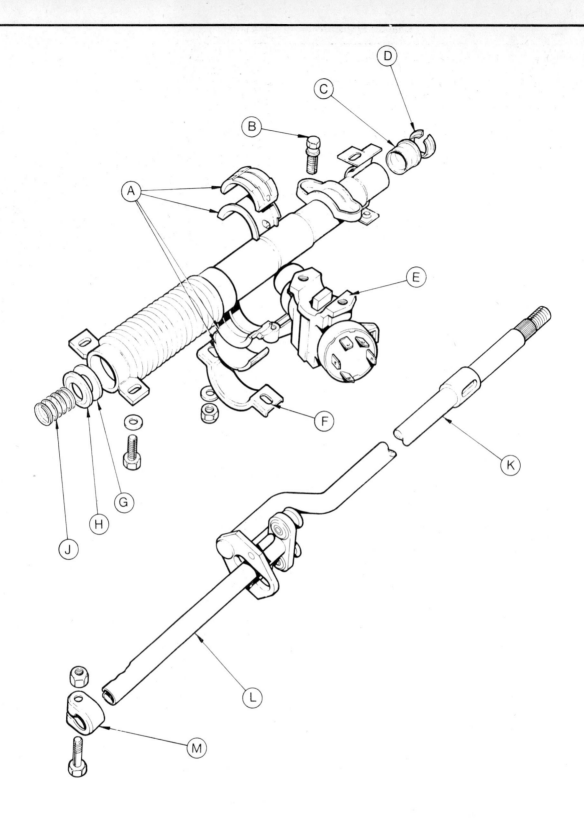

Fig. 9.22. Steering column components (Sec. 18)

A Steering column clamp inserts
B Shear-off bolts
C Upper bearing
D Tolerance ring

E Lock assembly
F Clamp
G Steel washer
H Nylon washer

J Spring
K Steering shaft
L Steering coupling
M Steering coupling clamp

them with the locknuts. Recheck the torque after tightening the locknuts.

15 Drill new holes (even if the old holes are in alignment), 5/32 in (4 mm or No. 22 drill) diameter, 0.38 in (9 mm) deep along the break lines between the housing and the locknut, approximately opposite the spanner locating hole in the housing.

16 Fit new retaining pins and peen over the surrounding metal to retain them.

17 Lightly grease the inside of the bellows where they will contact the trackrods, install one bellows ensuring that it locates in the trackrod groove; then fit a new retaining clip. Do not tighten the clip until the lock-in has been checked.

18 Add the specified quantity of steering gear oil, operating the rack over its range of travel to assist the lubricant in flowing. Do not overfill.

19 Fit the other bellows, but do not tighten the (new) clip yet.

20 Check the pinion turning torque, as described in paragraph 6 of the previous Section.

18 Steering column - removal, dismantling, reassembly and refitting

1 Disconnect the battery earth lead.

2 Carefully prise out the motif from the centre of the steering wheel and then unscrew the wheel retaining nut, but do not remove it.

3 Ensure that the roadwheels are in the straight-ahead position then pull the steering wheel free, and remove the nut and wheel.

4 Remove the direction indicator actuator cam.

5 Unscrew the upper shroud retaining screw and remove the upper shroud.

6 Unscrew the three lower column shroud retaining screws and remove the lower shroud.

7 Unscrew the two screws and lower the dash panel trim. Slacken the choke cable clamp and allow the cable to hang down.

8 Remove the light switch, wiper switch and multi-function switch from the column (two pairs of screws, one multi-plug each).

9 Disconnect the multi-plug from the ignition switch.

10 Insert the ignition key and turn it to disengage the steering column lock. Leave the key in the 'I' (accessories) position.

11 Remove the two steering column retaining bolts and two nuts. Lift the column assembly from the vehicle.

12 Drill off the steering column lockbolt heads, or tap them round with a pin punch, then use suitable grips to pull out the bolt shanks. Remove the steering lock (refer to Chapter 8 if necessary).

13 Lift out the tolerance ring and tap out the upper column bearing sleeve.

14 To remove the steering shaft, slacken the pinion shaft pinch bolt at the steering gear (photo 15.2). Pull the steering shaft from inside the car.

15 Remove the steel and nylon spacers and the anti-rattle spring from the shaft. Disconnect the steering coupling.

16 Inspect all parts for wear or damage, and renew if necessary.

17 Reconnect the steering coupling. Apply smears of grease to the nylon and steel spacers and refit them to the steering shaft.

18 Refit the steering shaft into the car and engage it with the steering gear.

19 Position the steering column lock around the column, with the lock bolt engaging in the hole in the tube. Fit new shear-off bolts, and tighten them progressively until the heads break off. Turn the ignition key to retract the lockbolt, and leave it in position 'I' (accessories).

20 Tap the upper bearing into the steering column, refit the column over the steering shaft and lightly retain the column with the two nuts and two bolts.

21 Temporarily fit the upper shroud and move the column to give a shroud to instrument panel clearance of 0.28 in (7.0 mm). Tighten the retaining nuts and bolts and remove the upper shroud.

22 Check that the steering coupling is still fully engaged (photo) then tighten the steering shaft pinch bolt at the steering gear.

23 The remainder of the refitting procedure is the reverse of removal, taking care to centralise the steering wheel.

19 Steering angles and front wheel alignment

1 Accurate front wheel alignment is essential for good steering and

18.22 Check the steering coupling engagement

tyre wear. Before considering the steering angle, check that the tyres are correctly inflated, that the front wheels are not buckled, the hub bearings are not worn or incorrectly adjusted and that the steering linkage is in good order, without slackness or wear at the joints.

2 Wheel alignment consists of four factors:

Camber which is the angle at which the front wheels are set from the vertical when viewed from the front of the car. Positive camber is the amount (in degrees) that the wheels are tilted outwards at the top from the vertical.

Castor is the angle between the steering axis and a vertical line when viewed from each side of the vehicle. Positive castor is when the steering axis is inclined rearwards.

Steering axis inclination is the angle when viewed from the front of the car, between the vertical and an imaginary line drawn between the upper and lower suspension strut pivots.

Toe-in is the amount by which the distance between the **front** inside edges of the roadwheels (measured at hub height) is less than the distance measured between the **rear** inside edges.

3 The angles of camber, castor and steering axis are set in production and are not adjustable.

4 Front wheel alignment (toe-in) checks are best carried out with modern setting equipment but a reasonably accurate alternative is by means of the following procedure.

5 Place the car on level ground with the wheels in the 'straight-ahead' position.

6 Obtain or make a toe-in gauge. One may easily be made from a length of rod or tubing, cranked to clear the sump or bellhousing and having a setscrew and locknut at one end.

7 With the gauge, measure the distance between the two inner wheel rims at hub height at the front of the wheel.

8 Rotate the roadwheel through 180^0 (half a turn) by pushing or pulling the car and then measure the distance again at hub height between the inner wheel rims at the rear of the roadwheel. This measurement should be within the limits of 0.04 in (1.0 mm) greater and 0.24 in (6.0 mm) less than the one just taken.

9 Where the toe-in is found to be incorrect slacken the locknuts on each trackrod, also the flexible bellows clips and rotate each trackrod by an equal amount until the second reading is 0.10 in (2.5 mm) less than the first. Tighten the trackrod-end locknuts while the balljoints are held in the centre of their arcs of travel. It is imperative that the lengths of the trackrods are always equal otherwise the wheel angles on turns will be incorrect.

10 If new components have been fitted, set the roadwheels in the 'straight-ahead' position and also centralise the steering wheel. Now adjust the lengths of the trackrods by turning them so that the trackrod-end balljoint studs will drop easily into the eyes of the steering arms. Measure the distances between the centres of the balljoints and the grooves on the inner ends of the trackrods and adjust, if necessary, so that they are equal. This is an initial setting only and precise adjustment must be carried out as described in paragraph 9.

20 Wheels and tyres

1 Check the tyre pressures weekly (when they are cold).
2 Frequently inspect the tyre walls and treads for damage and pick out any large stones which have become trapped in the tread pattern.
3 If the wheels and tyres have been balanced on the car then they should not be moved to a different axle position. If they have been balanced off the car then, in the interests of extending tread life, they can be moved between front and rear on the same side of the car and the spare incorporated in the rotational pattern.
4 Never mix tyres of different construction or very dissimilar tread patterns.
5 Always keep the roadwheels tightened to the specified torque and if the bolt holes become elongated or flattened, renew the wheel.
6 Occasionally, clean the inner faces of the roadwheels and if there is any sign of rust or corrosion, paint them with metal preservative paint.
Note: Corrosion on aluminium alloy wheels may be evidence of a more serious problem which could lead to wheel failure. If **corrosion** is evident, consult your Ford dealer for advice.
7 Before removing a roadwheel which has been balanced on the car, always mark one wheel and hub bolt hole so that the roadwheel may be refitted in the same relative position to maintain the balance.

21 Fault diagnosis

Before diagnosing faults from the following chart, check that any irregularities are not caused by:

1 *Binding brakes.*
2 *Incorrect 'mix' of radial and crossply tyres.*
3 *Incorrect tyre pressures.*
4 *Misalignment of the bodyframe.*

Symptom	Reason(s)
Steering wheel can be moved considerably before any sign of movement of the roadwheels is apparent	Wear in the steering linkage, gear and column coupling.
Vehicle difficult to steer in a consistent straight line - wandering	As above. Wheel alignment incorrect (indicated by excessive or uneven tyre wear). Front wheel hub bearing loose or worn. Worn balljoints.
Steering stiff and heavy	Incorrect wheel alignment (indicated by excessive or uneven tyre wear). Excessive wear or seizure in one or more of the joints in the steering linkage or suspension. Excessive wear in the steering gear.
Wheel wobble and vibration	Roadwheels out of balance. Roadwheels buckled. Wheel alignment incorrect. Wear in the steering linkage, suspension balljoints or track control arm pivot. Broken front spring. Worn driveshaft joints.
Excessive pitching and rolling on corners and during braking	Defective shock absorbers and/or broken spring.

Chapter 10 Bodywork and fittings

Contents

1 General description

The body is of a monocoque all-steel, welded construction with impact absorbing front and rear sections.

The vehicle has two side doors and a full-length lifting tailgate for easy access to the rear compartment. The side doors are fitted with antiburst locks and incorporate a key operated lock; window frames are adjustable for position. The tailgate hinges are bolted to the underside of the roof panel and welded to the tailgate. Gas-filled dampers support the tailgate in the open position; when closed it is fastened by a key-operated lock.

An automatic bonnet (hood) locking mechanism operates when the bonnet is closed, a release lever being fitted at the edge of the instrument panel on the driver's side. The bonnet (hood) is hinged at the front and is held in the open position by a support stay.

A tilting sunroof is available as an option, being available in body colour or tinted glass. The rear edge of this panel is tilted up by an interior handle, or the complete panel can be removed during fine weather.

Toughened safety glass is fitted to all windows, the windscreen having an addition 'zone' toughened band in front of the driver. In the event of the windscreen shattering this zone crazes into large sections to give a greater degree of visibility as a safety feature. An optional glass/plastic/glass laminated windscreen is available on all models at extra cost. This has the advantage of cracking only, to give an even greater degree of visibility in the event of accidental damage. The front door windows have a conventional winding mechanism. On certain, variants, the front quarter window may be opened after rotating the catch. A heated rear window is available as an optional extra throughout the range.

All vehicles have individual reclining front bucket seats, which tip forward for rear seat access after operating a safety catch. The rear seat back on all models tips forward for increased luggage carrying capacity. Certain models are equipped with a load space cover panel, which lifts with the tailgate. The standard seat and panel upholstery is a vinyl material, but a cloth fabric trim is available for all models.

A padded facia crash panel is standard equipment. Deep pile wall-to-wall carpeting and inertia reel seat belts are available as optional extras on all models.

All models are fitted with a heating and ventilating system which operates by ram air when the car is moving, or by a blower when stationary or for increased airflow. The heater is operated from a central control panel and airflow is directed to the windscreen or car interior according to the control lever settings. A heavy duty heater is available for some markets, and USA models can be supplied with an optional air conditioning system.

2 Maintenance - bodywork and underframe

1 The condition of your car's bodywork is of considerable importance as it is upon this that the secondhand value of the car will mainly depend. It is very much more difficult to repair neglected bodywork than to renew mechanical assemblies. The hidden portions of the body, such as the wheel arches and the underframe and the engine compartment are equally important though obviously not requiring such frequent attention as the immediately visible paintwork.

2 Once a year or every 12,000 miles (19,000 km), it is a sound scheme to visit your local main agent and have the underside of the body steam cleaned. This will take about 1½ hours. All traces of dirt and oil will be removed and the underside can then be inspected carefully for rust, damaged hydraulic pipes, frayed electrical wiring and similar maladies.

3 At the same time the engine compartment should be cleaned in the same manner. If steam cleaning facilities are not available, then brush a water soluble cleaner over the whole engine and engine compartment with a stiff paintbrush, working it well in where there is an accumulation of oil and dirt. Do not paint the ignition system but protect it with oily rags when the cleanser is washed off. As the cleanser is washed away it will take with it all traces of oil and dirt, leaving the engine looking clean and bright.

4 The wheel arches should be given particular attention as undersealing can easily come away here and stones and dirt thrown up from the road wheels can soon cause the paint to chip and flake, and so allow rust to set in. If rust is found, clean down to the bare metal with wet and dry paper, paint on an anti-corrosive coating and renew the paintwork and undercoating.

5 The bodywork should be washed once a week or when dirty. Thoroughly wet the car to soften the dirt and then wash the car down with a soft sponge and plenty of clean water. If the surplus dirt is not washed off very gently, in time it will wear the paint down as surely as wet and dry paper. It is best to use a hose if this is available. Give the car a final wash down and then dry with a soft chamois leather to prevent the formation of spots.

6 Spots of tar and grease thrown up from the road can be removed with a rag dampened with petrol, which should then be washed off.

7 Once every six months, or every three months, if wished, give the

bodywork and chromium trim a thoroughly good wax polish, If a chromium cleaner is used to remove rust or any of the car's plated parts remember that the cleaner also removes part of the chromium so use sparingly.

3 Maintenance - upholstery and carpets

1 Remove loose mats and thoroughly vacuum clean the interior of the car every three months or more frequently if necessary.
2 Beat out the carpets and vacuum clean them if they are very dirty. If the headlining or upholstery is soiled apply an upholstery cleaner with a damp sponge and wipe off with a clean dry cloth.

4 Maintenance - vinyl roof covering

Under no circumstances try to clean any external vinyl roof covering with detergents, caustic soaps or spirit cleaners. Plain soap and water is all that is required with a soft brush to clean dirt that may be ingrained. Wash the covering as frequently as the rest of the car.

5 Minor body damage - repair

The photo sequence on pages 198 and 199 illustrates the operations detailed in the following sub-sections.

Repair of minor scratches in the car's bodywork

If the scratch is very superficial and does not penetrate to the metal of the bodywork, repair is very simple. Lightly rub the area of the scratch with a paintwork renovator (eg, T-Cut), or a very fine cutting paste, to remove loose paint from the scratch and to clear the surrounding bodywork of wax polish. Rinse the area with clean water.

Apply touch-up paint to the scratch using a thin paintbrush, continue to apply thin layers of paint until the surface of the paint in the scratch is level with the surrounding paintwork. Allow the new paint at least two weeks to harden; then blend it into the surrounding paintwork by rubbing the paintwork, in the scratch area with a paintwork renovator (eg, T-Cut), or a very fine cutting paste. Finally apply wax polish.

An alternative to painting over the scratch is to use Holts 'Scratch-Patch'. Use the same preparation for the affected area; then simply pick a patch of suitable size to cover the scratch completely. Hold the patch against the scratch and burnish its backing paper; the patch will adhere to the paintwork, freeing itself from the backing paper at the same time. Polish the affected area to blend the patch into the surrounding paintwork. Where the scratch has penetrated right through to the metal of the bodywork, causing the metal to rust, a different repair technique is required. Remove any loose rust from the bottom of the scratch with a penknife, then apply rust inhibiting paint (eg, Kurust) to prevent the formation of rust in the future. Using a rubber nylon applicator, fill the scratch with bodystopper paste. If required, this paste can be mixed with cellulose thinners to provide a very thin paste which is ideal for filling narrow scratches. Before the stopper-paste in the scratch hardens, wrap a piece of smooth cotton rag around the top of a finger. Dip the finger in cellulose thinners and then quickly sweep it across the surface of the stopper-paste in the scratch; this will ensure that the surface of the stopper-paste is slightly hollowed. The scratch can now be painted over as described earlier in this Section.

Repair of dents in the car's bodywork

When deep denting of the car's bodywork has taken place, the first task is to pull the dent out, until the affected bodywork almost attains its original shape. There is little point in trying to restore the original shape completely, as the metal in the damaged area will have stretched on impact and cannot be reshaped fully to its original contour. It is better to bring the level of the dent up to the point which is about 1/8 in (3 mm) below the level of the surrounding bodywork. In cases where the dent is very shallow anyway, it is not worth trying to pull it out at all.

If the underside of the dent is accessible, it can be hammered out gently from behind, using a mallet with a wooden or plastic head. Whilst doing this, hold a suitable block of wood firmly against the impact from the hammer blows and thus prevent a large area of bodywork from being 'belled-out.'

Should the dent be in a section of the bodywork which has a double skin or some other factor making it inaccessible from behind, a different technique is called for. Drill several small holes through the metal inside the dent area - particularly in the deeper sections. Then screw long self-tapping screws into the holes just sufficiently for them to gain a good purchase in the metal. Now the dent can be pulled out by pulling on the protruding heads of the screws with a pair of pliers.

The next stage of the repair is the removal of the paint from the damaged area, and from an inch or so of the surrounding 'sound' bodywork. This is accomplished most easily by using a wire brush or abrasive pad on a power drill, although it can be done just as effectively by hand using sheets of abrasive paper. To complete the preparations for filling, score the surface of the bare metal with a screwdriver or the tang of a file, or alternatively, drill small holes in the affected area. This will provide a really good 'key' for filler paste.

To complete the repair see the Section on filling and respraying.

Repair of rust holes or gashes in the car's bodywork

Remove all paint from the affected area and from an inch or so of the surrounding 'sound' bodywork, using an abrasive pad or a wire brush on a power drill. If these are not available a few sheets of abrasive paper will do the job just as effectively. With the paint removed you will be able to gauge the severity of the corrosion and therefore decide whether to replace the whole panel (if this is possible) or to repair the affected area. New body panels are not as expensive as most people think and it is often quicker and more satisfactory to fit a new panel than to attempt to repair large areas of corrosion.

Remove all fittings from the affected area except those which will act as a guide to the original shape of the damaged bodywork (eg, headlamp shells etc). Then, using tin snips or a hacksaw blade, remove all loose metal and any other metal badly affected by corrosion. Hammer the edges of the hole inwards in order to create a slight depression for the filler paste.

Wire brush the affected area to remove the powdery rust from the surface of the remaining metal. Paint the affected area with rust inhibiting paint (eg, Kurust); if the back of the rusted area is accessible treat this also.

Before filling can take place it will be necessary to block the hole in some way. This can be achieved by the use of one of the following materials: Zinc gauze, Aluminium tape or Polyurethane foam.

Zinc gauze is probably the best material to use for a large hole. Cut a piece to the approximate size and shape of the hole to be filled, then position it in the hole so that its edges are below the level of the surrounding bodywork. It can be retained in position by several blobs of filler paste around its periphery.

Aluminium tape should be used for small or very narrow holes. Pull a piece off the roll and trim it to the approximate size and shape required, then pull off the backing paper (if used) and stick the tape over the hole; it can be overlapped if the thickness of one piece is insufficient. Burnish down the edges of the tape with the handle of a screwdriver or similar, to ensure that the tape is securely attached to the metal underneath.

Polyurethane foam is best used where the hole is situated in a section of bodywork of complex shape, backed by a small box section (eg, where the sill panel meets the rear wheel arch - most cars). The usual mixing procedure for this foam is as follows: Put equal amounts of fluid from each of the two cans provided in the kit, into one container. Stir until the mixture begins to thicken, then quickly pour this mixture into the hole, and hold a piece of cardboard over the larger apertures. Almost immediately the polyurethane will begin to expand, gushing frantically out of any small holes left unblocked. When the foam hardens it can be cut back to just below the level of the surrounding bodywork with a hacksaw blade.

Bodywork repairs - filling and re-spraying

Before using this Section, see the Sections on dent, deep scratch, rust hole, and gash repairs.

Many types of bodyfiller are available, but generally speaking those proprietary kits which contain a tin of filler paste and a tube of resin hardener (eg, Holts Cataloy) are best for this type of repair. A wide flexible plastic or nylon applicator will be found available for imparting a smooth and well contoured finish to the surface of the filler.

Mix up a little filler on a clean piece of card or board - use the hardener sparingly (follow the maker's instructions on the packet) otherwise the filler will set very rapidly.

Using the applicator, apply the filler paste to the prepared area; draw the applicator across the surface of the filler to achieve the correct contour and to level the filler surface. As soon as a contour that approximates to the correct one is achieved, stop working the paste - if you carry on too long the paste will become sticky and begin to 'pick-up' on the applicator. Continue to add thin layers of filler paste at twenty-minute intervals until the level of the filler is just 'proud' of the surrounding bodywork.

Once the filler has hardened, excess can be removed using a Surform plane or Dreadnought file. From then on, progressively finer grades of abrasive paper should be used, starting with a 40 grade production paper and finishing with 400 grade 'wet-and-dry' paper. Always wrap the abrasive paper around a flat rubber, cork, or wooden block - otherwise the surface of the filler will not be completely flat. During the smoothing of the filler surface the 'wet-and-dry' paper should be periodically rinsed in water. This will ensure that a very smooth finish is imparted to the filler at the final stage.

At this stage the 'dent' should be surrounded by a ring of bare metal, which in turn should be encircled by the finely 'feathered' edge of the good paintwork. Rinse the repair area with clean water, until all of the dust produced by the rubbing-down operation is gone.

Spray the whole repair area with a light coat of grey primer, this will show up any imperfections in the surface of the filler. Repair these imperfections with fresh filler paste or bodystopper, and once more smooth the surface with abrasive paper. If bodystopper is used, it can be mixed with cellulose thinners to form a really thin paste which is ideal for filling small holes. Repeat this spray and repair procedure until you are satisfied that the surface of the filler, and the feathered edge of the paintwork are perfect. Clean the repair area with clean water and allow to dry fully.

The repair area is now ready for spraying. Paint spraying must be carried out in a warm, dry, windless and dust free atmosphere. This condition can be created artificially if you have access to a large indoor working area, but if you are forced to work in the open, you will have to pick your day very carefully. If you are working indoors, dousing the floor in the work area with water will 'lay' the dust which would otherwise be in the atmosphere. If the repair area is confined to one body panel, mask off the surrounding panels: this will help to minimise the effects of a slight mis-match in paint colours. Bodywork fittings (eg. chrome strips, door handles etc.), will also need to be masked off. Use genuine masking tape and several thicknesses of newspaper for the masking operation.

Before commencing to spray, agitate the aerosol can thoroughly, then spray a test area (an old tin, or similar) until the technique is mastered. Cover the repair area with a thick coat of primer; the thickness should be built up using several thin layers of paint rather than one thick one. Using 400 grade 'wet-and-dry' paper, rub down the surface of the primer until it is really smooth. While doing this, the work area should be thoroughly doused with water, and the 'wet-and-dry' paper periodically rinsed in water. Allow to dry before spraying on more paint.

Spray on the top coat, again building up the thickness by using several thin layers of paint. Start spraying in the centre of the repair area and then, using a circular motion, work outwards until the whole repair area and about 2 inches of the surrounding original paintwork is covered. Remove all masking material 10 to 15 minutes after spraying on the final coat of paint.

Allow the new paint at least 2 weeks to harden fully; then, using a paintwork renovator (eg, T-Cut) or a very fine cutting paste, blend the edges of the new paint into the existing paintwork. Finally, apply wax polish.

6 Major body damage - repair

Because the body is built on the monocoque principle and is integral with the underframe, major damage must be repaired by competent mechanics with the necessary welding and hydraulic straightening equipment.

If the damage has been serious it is vital that the body is checked for correct alignment as otherwise the handling of the car will suffer and many other faults such as excessive tyre wear and wear in the transmission and steering may occur.

There is a special body jig which most large body repair shops have

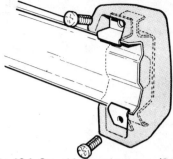

Fig. 10.1. Over-rider securing screws (Sec. 8)

and to ensure that all is correct it is important that this jig be used for all major repair work.

7 Maintenance - locks and hinges

Once every 6 months or 6,000 miles (10,000 km) the door, bonnet and tailgate hinges should be lubricated with a few drops of engine oil. Door striker plates can be given a thin smear of grease to reduce wear and ensure free movement.

8 Bumpers and over-riders - removal and refitting

Over-riders
1 All over-riders are secured to the bumper by two screwed clamps (Fig. 10.1).
2 Removal is a simple matter of unscrewing and removing the two screws and lifting off the over-rider. On vehicles equipped with a headlamp washer system, simply pull the hose from the over-rider.
3 When refitting over-riders with a headlamp washer nozzle, they should be positioned centrally to the headlamps, and the nozzles adjusted accordingly (Chapter 8, Section 33).

Front bumper
4 Pull off the hose from the headlamp washer nozzle, where fitted.
5 From inside the wheelarch, remove the nut, spring washer and flat washer from the front fixing stud, and the screw and washers from the side fixing location, from each side of the car.
6 Refitting is the reverse of this procedure, but do not fully tighten the nuts and screws until the front bumper has been aligned.

Rear bumper
7 Remove the license plate (number plate) lamps from the bumper (Chapter 8, Section 28).
8 Open the tailgate and remove the spare wheel cover.
9 Remove the nut and washer from each rear retaining stud.
10 Pull back sufficient sealing material from the inner quarter panel cut-outs to expose the bumper side retaining screws. Remove the screws.
11 Refitting is the reverse of this procedure.

9 Radiator grille - removal and refitting

1 Unscrew and remove the three screws and washers securing the grille and lift away the grille.
2 When refitting the grille, ensure that the special nuts are correctly located in their apertures in the front body panel, and that the spire clip is in position on the mounting tab on the upper edge of the grille aperture.
3 Refit the grille, and tighten the retaining screws after checking correct alignment.

10 Windscreen - removal and refitting

1 If you are unfortunate enough to have a windscreen shatter, or should you wish to renew your present windscreen, fitting a new one is one of the few jobs which the average owner is advised to leave to a

This sequence of photographs deals with the repair of the dent and scratch (above rear lamp) shown in this photo. The procedure will be similar for the repair of a hole. It should be noted that the procedures given here are simplified - more explicit instructions will be found in the text

In the case of a dent the first job - after removing surrounding trim - is to hammer out the dent where access is possible. This will minimise filling. Here, the large dent having been hammered out, the damaged area is being made slightly concave

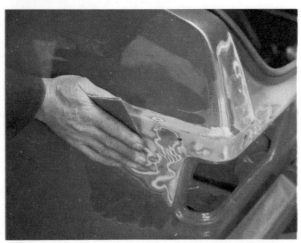

Now all paint must be removed from the damaged area, by rubbing with coarse abrasive paper. Alternatively, a wire brush or abrasive pad can be used in a power drill. Where the repair area meets good paintwork, the edge pf the paintwork should be 'feathered', using a finer grade of abrasive paper

In the case of a hole caused by rusting, all damaged sheet-metal should be cut away before proceeding to this stage. Here, the damaged area is being treated with rust remover and inhibitor before being filled

Mix the body filler according to its manufacturer's instructions. In the case of corrosion damage, it will be necessary to block off any large holes before filling - this can be done with zinc gauze or aluminium tape. Make sure the area is absolutely clean before ...

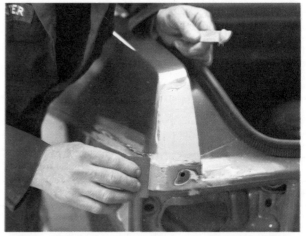

... applying the filler. Filler should be applied with a flexible applicator, as shown, for best results: the wooden spatula being used for confined areas. Apply thin layers of filler at 20-minute intervals, until the surface of the filler is slightly proud of the surrounding bodywork

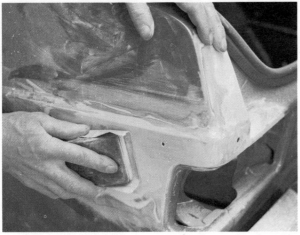

Initial shaping can be done with a Surform plane or Dreadnought file. Then, using progressively finer grades of wet-and-dry paper, wrapped around a sanding block, and copious amounts of clean water, rub-down the filler until really smooth and flat. Again, feather the edges of adjoining paintwork

The whole repair area can now be sprayed or brush-painted with primer. If spraying, ensure adjoining areas are protected from over-spray. Note that at least one-inch of the surrounding sound paintwork should be coated with primer. Primer has a 'thick' consistency, so will fill small imperfections

Again, using plenty of water, rub down the primer with a fine grade of wet-and-dry paper (400 grade is probably best) until it is really smooth and well blended into the surrounding paint-work. Any remaining imperfections can now be filled by carefully applied knifing stopper paste

When the stopper has hardened, rub-down the repair area again before applying the final coat of primer. Before rubbing-down this last coat of primer, ensure the repair area is blemish-free - use more stopper if necessary. To ensure that the surface of the primer is really smooth use some finishing compound

The top coat can now be applied. When working out of doors, pick a dry, warm and wind-free day. Ensure surrounding areas are protected from over-spray. Agitate the aerosol thoroughly, then spray the centre of the repair area, working outwards with a circular motion. Apply the paint as several thin coats.

After a period of about two-weeks, which the paint needs to harden fully, the surface of the repaired area can be 'cut' with a mild cutting compound prior to wax polishing. When carrying out bodywork repairs, remember that the quality of the finished job is proportional to the time and effort expended

professional but for the owner who wishes to attempt the job himself the following instructions are given.

2   Cover the bonnet with a blanket or cloth to prevent accidental damage and remove the windscreen wiper blades and arms as detailed in Chapter 8.

3   There are two methods of removing the windscreen. The first method can be used with any type of windscreen, and **must** be used with a laminated screen. The second method should only be attempted with a toughened screen.

4   First determine which type of screen is fitted. If in doubt, examine the trademark etched into the glass. This will contain the word 'TOUGHENED' or 'LAMINATED', or 'T' or 'L'. Then refer to the method applicable.

5   Remove the interior mirror, (Section 28).

First method

6   From inside the car, use a small screwdriver to ease the weatherstrip over the metal flange. Work progressively along the top and down the sides of the screen until the glass, complete with weatherstrip can be pushed out.

Second method

7   Put on a pair of lightweight shoes and get into one of the front seats. With a piece of soft cloth between the soles of your shoes and the windscreen glass, place both feet in one top corner of the windscreen and push firmly (see Fig. 10.2).

8   When the weatherstrip has freed itself from the body flange in that area, repeat the process at frequent intervals along the top edge of the windscreen until, from outside the car, the glass and weatherstrip can be removed together.

9   If you are having to renew your windscreen due to a shattered screen, remove all traces of sealing compound and broken glass from the weatherstrip and body flange.

10   Gently prise out the clip which covers the joint of the chromium finisher strip and pull the finisher strip out of the weatherstrip. Then remove the weatherstrip from the glass or, if it is still on the car (as in the case of a shattered screen) remove it from the body flange.

11   To fit a new windscreen start by fitting the weatherstrip around the new windscreen glass.

12   Apply a suitable sealer to the weatherstrip to body groove. In this groove then fit a fine but strong piece of cord right the way round the groove allowing an overlap of about 6 in (15 cm) at the joint.

13   From outside the car place the windscreen in its correct position making sure that the loose end of the cord is inside the car.

14   With an assistant pressing firmly on the outside of the windscreen get into the car and slowly pull out the cord thus drawing the weatherstrip over the body flange (see. Fig. 10.3).

15   Apply a further layer of sealer to the underside of the rubber to glass groove from outside the car.

16   Refit the finisher strip into its groove in the weatherstrip and refit the clip which covers its joint.

17   Carefully clean off any surplus sealer from the windscreen glass before it has a chance to harden and then refit the windscreen wiper arms and blades, Chapter 8.

11 Tailgate window glass - removal and refitting

1   Where applicable, remove the window glass wiper arm and blade, and carefully disconnect the heater element connections.

2   Carefully prise out the mylar insert from the rubber moulding.

3   If possible, obtain help from an assistant and carefully use a blunt bladed screwdriver to push the weatherstrip lip along the upper transverse section under the tailgate aperture flange. When approximately two thirds of the weatherstrip lip has been treated in this manner, pressure should be applied to the glass from inside the car. The glass and weatherstrip can then be removed from the outside.

4   Clean the lip of the window aperture, and the glass and weatherstrip if they are to be used again. Do not use solvents such as petrol or white spirit on the weatherstrip as this may cause deterioration of the rubber.

5   When refitting, initially fit the weatherstrip to the glass then insert a drawcord in the rubber-to-body groove so that the cord ends emerge at the bottom centre with approximately 6 in (15 cm) of overlap. During this operation it may help to retain the weatherstrip to the glass by using short lengths of masking tape.

6   On British built vehicles only, apply a suitable sealer to the body flange. Position the glass and weatherstrip assembly to the body aperture and push up until the weatherstrip groove engages the top transverse flange of the body aperture. Ensure that the ends of the draw cord are inside the car, then get the assistant to push the window firmly at the base whilst one end of the draw cord is pulled from the weatherstrip groove. Ensure that the cord is pulled at right-angles to the flange (ie, towards the centre of the glass) and that pressure is always being applied on the outside of the glass in the vicinity of the point where the draw cord is being pulled.

7   When the glass is in position, remove any masking tape which may have been used then seal the weatherstrip to the glass.

8   Lubricate the mylar insert with a rubber lubricant and refit it.

9   Refit the wiper arm and blade (where applicable), and reconnect the heater element connections.

12 Door rattles - tracing and rectification

1   The most common cause of door rattles is a misaligned, loose or worn striker plate. However, other causes may be:

   a) Loose door or window winder handles.
   b) Loose or misaligned door lock components.
   c) Loose or worn remote control mechanism.

2   It is quite possible for rattles to be the result of a combination of the above faults so a careful examination should be made to determine the exact cause.

3   If striker wear or misalignment is the cause, it should be renewed

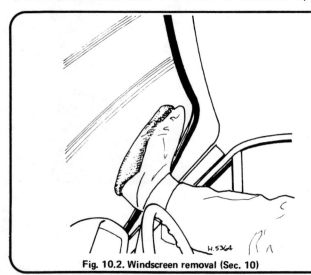

Fig. 10.2. Windscreen removal (Sec. 10)

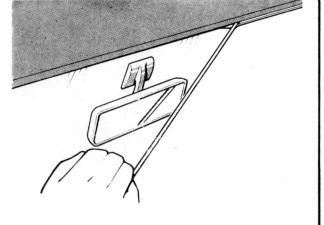

Fig. 10.3. Refitting the windscreen (Sec. 10)

or adjusted as necessary. The procedure is detailed in Section 14.

4   Should the window wiper handle rattle, this can be easily rectified by inserting a rubber washer between the escutcheon and the door trim panel.

5   If the rattle is found to be coming from the door lock it will probably mean that the lock is worn and therefore should be renewed as described in Section 16.

6   Lastly, if it is worn hinge pins causing rattles, they should be renewed.

13 Door - removal and refitting

1   Although the doors are bolted to the hinge pillar, access to the retaining nuts is only possible after the removal of a large number of items of interior trim. For this reason, a more practicable method is to remove the hinge pins.

2   Open the door and remove the plastic plugs from the top of the upper and lower hinge pins.

3   With an assistant supporting the weight of the door, use a suitable diameter drift and knock the upper pin downwards out of the hinge.

4   Remove the lower hinge pin in a similar manner.

5   Refitting is the reverse of this procedure.

14 Door striker - removal, refitting and adjustment

1   Slacken the striker locknut, then unscrew and remove the striker and dished washer (Fig. 10.4).

2   With the locknut screwed fully onto the striker, and the smaller diameter of the washer facing the locknut, screw the striker into the lock pillar, but do not tighten the locknut.

3   Open and close the door, adjusting the position of the striker until the door closes fully and easily. Tighten the locknut.

4   As a final check, the dimension shown in Fig. 10.5 should be 0.6 in (14.5 mm).

15 Door trim panel - removal and refitting

1   Carefully prise out the window winder handle cover.

2   Remove the winder handle retaining screw and pull off the handle and escutcheon (photo).

3   Remove the two armrest retaining screws, turn the armrest through 90° and pull out the top fixing.

4   Carefully prise out the remote control bezel and unscrew the private lock button (photo).

5   Where applicable, carefully prise the seven trim panel capping retaining clips from the door and remove the capping.

6   Using a broad screwdriver blade or spatula, carefully prise the trim panel clips from their locations, and remove the panel (photo).

7   Where fitted, remove the six retaining screws, and lift off the map pocket.

8   Whenever the trim panel is removed, take the opportunity to remove any loose material from within the door, and ensure that the drain holes are clear.

9   Refitting is the reverse of this procedure, noting that with the window closed the winder is in its lowest position.

16 Door lock assembly - removal and refitting

1   Remove the door trim panel as described in Section 15, and remove the plastic sheeting.

2   Unscrew the interior private lock knob.

3   Using a small screwdriver prise the clips from the exterior handle and lock cylinder rods (photo), and the remote control rod, and detach the rods from the lock.

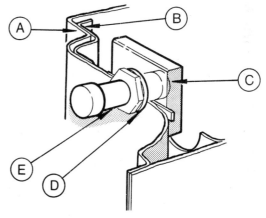

Fig. 10.4. Door striker assembly (Sec. 14)

A   Lock pillar   D   Washer
B   Reinforcement   E   Striker pin
C   Door striker anchor plate

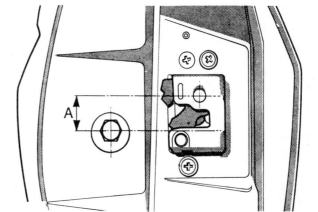

Fig. 10.5. Door striker checking dimension (Sec. 14)

15.2 Removing the window winder handle

15.4 Removing the interior door handle bezel

15.6 Removing the door trim panel

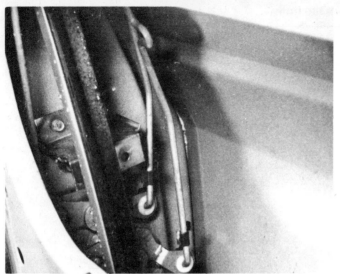

16.3 Exterior handle and lock cylinder control rods

16.4 Door lock retaining screws

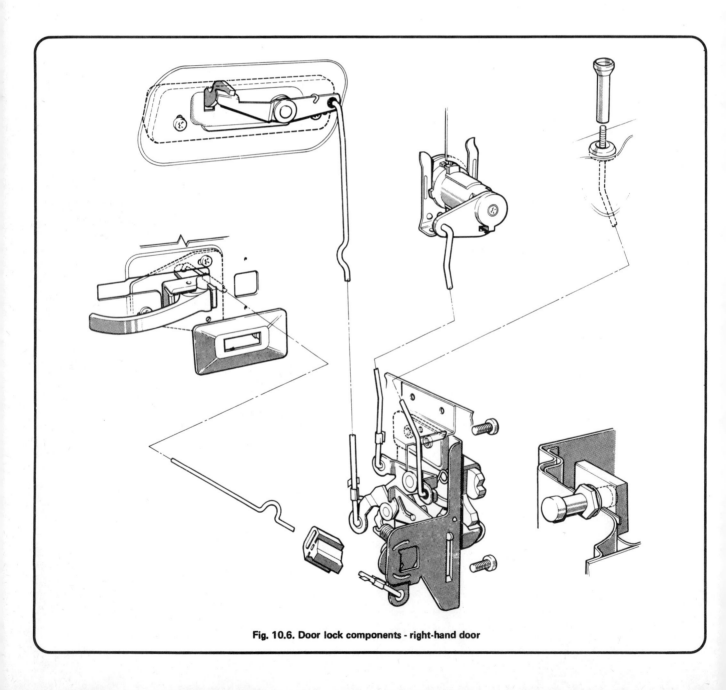

Fig. 10.6. Door lock components - right-hand door

4   Remove the three lock retaining screws (photo) and remove the lock from inside the door, manoeuvring the private lock rod as necessary.

5   Remove the private lock rod, retaining clips and three white and one black bush from the lock (Fig. 10.7).

6   Refitting is the reverse of this procedure, using petroleum jelly to assist when inserting the rods into the bushes.

17 Door handles - removal and refitting

1   Remove the door trim panel, Section 15. Also refer to Fig. 10.6.

Exterior handle

2   Using a small screwdriver, prise off the clip retaining the exterior handle rod to the door lock. Detach the rod from the lock.

3   Remove the two handle retaining screws, and remove the handle, guiding the rod from the door.

4   Disengage the rod from the handle bush.

5   When refitting the bush, warm it first in hot water.

6   When refitting the rod to each bush, lubricate the end with petroleum jelly.

7   When refitting the rod to the exterior handle, the hooked end should point to the rear.

Interior handle

8   Using a small screwdriver, prise off the clip retaining the interior handle rod to the door lock. Detach the rod from the lock.

9   Push the rod retainer from the panel (Fig. 10.7).

10 Remove the two retaining screws (photo), remove the handle from the door and guide the rod clear.

11 When refitting, slide the retainer onto the free end of the operating rod and guide the handle and rod into the door shell.

12 Refit the handle, and loosely secure with the two screws.

13 Refit the operating rod to its bush in the door lock, and refit the retaining clip.

14 Slide the retainer along the rod and push it into the cut-out in the inner panel.

15 Push the handle to its rearmost position (photo 17.10) and tighten the two screws.

18 Door lock cylinder - removal, overhaul and refitting

1   Remove the door trim panel, Section 15.

2   Prise off the securing clip, and disengage the lock cylinder rod from the door lock bush.

3   Pull down and remove the retaining clip (photo). Remove the lock cylinder assembly and rod from the door.

4   Disengage the operating rod from the lever, and carefully note the position of the end cap, lever and cylinder spring.

5   Remove the crosshead screw and lift off the end cap, lever and spring (Fig. 10.8). Insert the key into the lock and pull out the lock barrel.

6   Remove the sealing pad from outside the lock cylinder, and the 'O' ring from inside.

7   Refit the 'O' ring and sealing pad to the lock cylinder.

8   With the key in the lock barrel, insert the barrel into the cylinder with the tab on the barrel located in the cylinder groove.

9   Refit the spring with the legs crossing around the small lug on the cylinder.

10 Refit the lever on the cylinder, then fit the end cap with the tag located between the spring legs.

11 Refit the crosshead screw, then check that the key can rotate 90° on either side of the central position.

12 Refit the operating rod to the lever, with the free end pointing to the rear (Fig. 10.9).

13 Refit the rod and cylinder assembly into the door, and retain the cylinder by tapping the retaining clip upwards.

14 Refit the operating rod to its bush in the door lock, and secure it with the clip. Refit the door trim panel.

19 Door window regulator assembly - removal and refitting

1   Remove the door trim panel (Section 15).

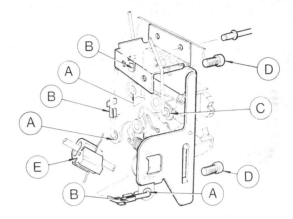

Fig. 10.7. Door lock components (Sec. 17)

A   White bushes
B   Connecting rod clip
C   Black bush
D   Retaining screws
E   Connecting rod retainer

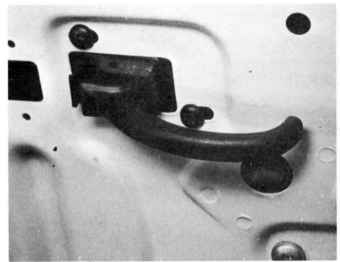

17.10 Interior door handle retaining screws

18.3 Pull down the lock cylinder retaining clip

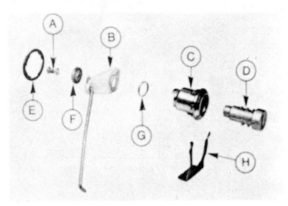

Fig. 10.8. Lock cylinder components (Sec. 18)

A Screw   E Sealing pad
B Lever and rod   F End cap
C Key housing   G Spring
D Lock barrel   H Retaining clip

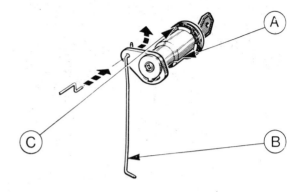

Fig. 10.9. Refitting the lock operating rod (B) and sealing pad (C) to the lock housing (A) (Sec. 18)

19.3 Remove the window regulator retaining screws

19.4 Unhook the regulator from the window glass

2 Peel off the plastic sheet.
3 Temporarily refit the winder handle and lower the window. Remove the four gear plate fixing screws (photo).
4 Draw the regulator assembly towards the rear of the door to disengage it from the runner at the base of the window (photo).
5 Push the window glass up and use adhesive tape on each side of the glass and over the window frame to retain it. If it is to be left for any length of time, additionally use a wooden support.
6 Withdraw the regulator from the door.
7 Refitting is the reverse of the removal procedure, alignment being obtained by adjusting the pivot plate as necessary.

20 Door window glass - removal and refitting

1 Remove the door trim panel (Section 15) and peel off the plastic sheeting.
2 Using a small screwdriver and a pad of protective material, prise off the inner and outer door weatherstrip (Fig. 10.10).
3 Wind down the window, and remove the upper and lower quarter window frame screws (Fig. 10.11).
4 Pull the quarter window assembly upwards and rearwards at 45° to remove it.
5 Slide the window glass sideways to disengage the glass bracket from the regulator arm. Hold the regulator arm clear of the glass and remove the glass from the door.

Fig. 10.10. Removing the inner door weatherstrip (Sec. 20)

6 Note the position of the bracket on the lower edge of the glass, then remove it by tapping with a hide mallet.
7 Refitting is the reverse of this procedure.

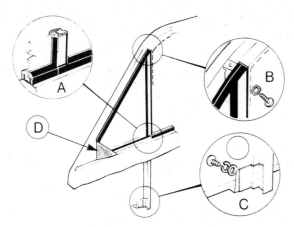

Fig. 10.11. Remove the upper (B) and lower (C) screws from the quarter window frame (A) (Sec. 20) (D) is the adhesive pad

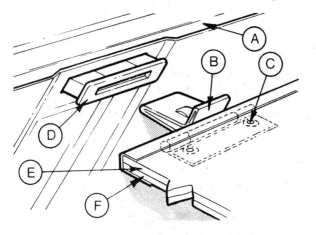

Fig. 10.12. Parcel shelf hinge retention (Sec. 21)

A	Rear seat back	D	Hinge retainer
B	Hinge bracket	E	Parcel shelf
C	Bracket retainer	F	Parcel shelf

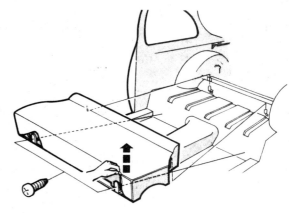

Fig. 10.13. Removing the rear seat cushion (Sec. 21)

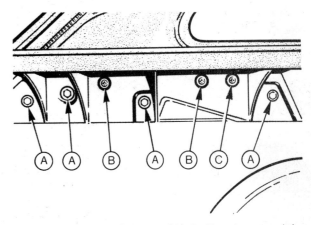

Fig. 10.14. Parcel shelf bracket screws (A), C pillar trim screws (B) and Quarter trim panel screw (C) (Sec. 21)

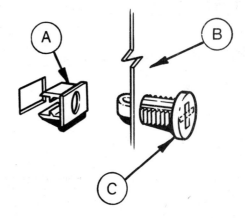

Fig. 10.15. Prise the special rivet (C) from the trim panel (B) and its retainer (A) (Sec. 22)

21 Rear quarter trim panel - removal and refitting

1   Remove the rear parcel shelf, where fitted, by first unhooking the lifting strap from the tailgate. Depress the top edge of the two shelf hinge brackets (Fig. 10.12) and pull the shelf from the seat back. Remove the shelf.
2   Unlatch the rear seat back, then pull the spring pins from each seat back pivot. Carefully prise the pivot bushes from each body side panel, and slide them along the pivots. Remove the rear seat back from the car.
3   Carefully lift the trim at the front of the rear seat cushion and remove the two securing screws (Fig. 10.13). Unhook the rear edge and remove the cushion from the car.
4   Remove the rearmost screw securing the scuff plate to the body.
5   Remove the load space trim panel, Section 22.
6   Remove the parcel shelf bracket front screw (Fig. 10.14).
7   Using a braod screwdriver blade, carefully prise the upper trim panel clips from their locations and pull the panel forward to disengage the parcel shelf support.
8   Prise out the remaining trim clips and lift the panel from the car
9   Refitting is the reverse of the above procedure.

22 Load space trim panel - removal and refitting

1   Carefully prise out the special rivet from the rear lower corner of the trim panel (Fig. 10.15).
2   Pull the panel to the rear to disengage it from the rear quarter trim panel, then inwards and downwards to unclip it from the body side rail.
3   Refitting is the reverse of this procedure.

23 Bonnet (hood) release cable - removal and refitting

1   From inside the car, unscrew and remove the two screws securing the bonnet release lever to the cowlside panel.
2   From inside the engine compartment, unhook the grommet from the hood lock (photo) and disengage the cable end from the lock lever.
3   Pull the cable through the engine bulkhead and into the car.
4   When refitting the cable, ensure that the sealing grommet is correctly located in the engine bulkhead.

23.2 Unhooking the bonnet lock cable

24.2 Remove the bonnet hinge bolts

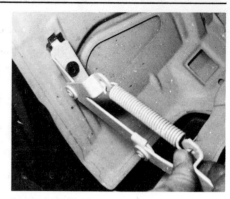

24.3 Remove the bonnet stay securing screw

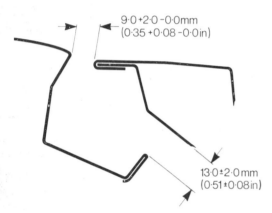

Fig. 10.16. Align the tailgate to 0.35 in (9.0 mm) from roof and 0.51 in (13.0 mm) from weatherstrip flange (Sec. 25)

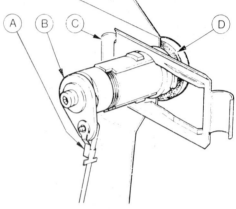

Fig. 10.17. Tailgate lock (B), operating rod clip (A), spring retainer (C) sealing pad (D) (Sec. 26)

24 Bonnet (hood) - removal, refitting and adjustment

1   Remove the radiator grille (Section 9).
2   Using a soft pencil, mark the outline of the bonnet hinges on the front panel (photo).
3   Open the bonnet and remove the crosshead screw securing the bonnet stay to the bonnet, and disengage the stay (photo).
4   With an assistant supporting the bonnet, unscrew and remove the four hinge securing bolts, two each side.
5   For storage it is best to stand the bonnet on an old blanket and allow the underside to lean against a wall, suitably padded at the top to avoid scratching the paint.
6   Refitting is a reversal of the removal procedure. However, before fully tightening the securing bolts, ensure that the hinges are aligned with the scribed marks. This will ensure correct alignment.
7   If it is found that the bonnet requires adjustment, this can be achieved by slackening the four hinge to body bolts, and the two bonnet lock to body bolts. Move the bonnet as necessary to give a gap at the rear edge of 0.25 in (6.0 mm), and a gap at the sides of 0.16 in (4.0 mm), equal on both sides. Tighten the four hinge bolts. Move the bonnet lock to ensure the rear edge of the bonnet is flush with the body panel, then tighten the lock bolts.

25 Tailgate assembly - removal and refitting

1   Open the tailgate and detach the heated rear window connectors. Unhook the rear parcel shelf supports, where fitted.
2   Pull down the tailgate weatherstrip from the roof, and carefully prise off the headlining clips in the area of the tailgate hinges.
3   Using a soft pencil, mark around the tailgate hinges.
4   Unscrew the two screws (one each side) retaining the dampers to the tailgate, and remove the screws and spacers.

5   With an assistant to support the weight, unscrew and remove the four nuts and washers from each hinge and lift off the tailgate.
6   For storage, stand the tailgate on an old blanket and allow it to lean against a wall, suitably padded at the top to avoid scratching the paint.
7   When refitting the tailgate, do not finally tighten the hinge nuts until the hinges are aligned with the previously made marks.
8   Check that the gap between the tailgate and roof edge is to specification (Fig. 10.16) and that gaps down each side of the tailgate are equal. Adjust the lock striker plate, Section 27.

26 Tailgate lock and latch - removal and refitting

Lock

1   Using a broad screwdriver blade, carefully prise out the tailgate trim panel clips, and remove the panel.
2   Prise off the clip and disconnect the operating rod from the lock cam.
3   Slide the retaining clip to one side (Fig. 10.17) and lift it over the lock. Remove the lock and sealing pad from the tailgate.
4   Refitting is the reverse of this procedure.

Latch

5   Carry out the work described in paragraphs 1 and 2.
6   Unscrew the three bolts and remove the latch complete with operating rod.
7   Refitting is the reverse of this procedure.

27 Tailgate striker plate - removal and refitting

1   Open the tailgate then carefully scribe a mark around the striker to

facilitate refitting.

2   Remove the two bolts and washers and take off the striker plate (photo).

3   Refitting is the reverse of the removal procedure, following which adjustment can be made if found necessary to obtain satisfactory opening and closing of the tailgate.

28 Interior mirror - removal and refitting

1   The Fiesta interior rear view mirror is glued to the windscreen, and will not need to be removed unless either the mirror or windscreen is broken or to be changed.

2   To remove the mirror, grasp it firmly with both hands, and push forward to break the adhesive bond (Fig. 10.18).

3   Fiesta windscreens obtained from a Ford dealer have a square of shaded glass with a piece of protective paper over them. Similarly, mirrors have an adhesive pad supplied with them, or the adhesive pad can be obtained separately.

4   Clean all traces of glass, old adhesive or grease from an existing mirror using methylated spirit.

5   Allow the windscreen to warm for at least one hour at room temperature (68°F, 20°C).

6   Warm the mirror base against a radiator for 10 - 15 seconds, firmly press a new adhesive pad onto the existing mirror base (if applicable) then peel off the protective backing.

7   Peel the backing paper from the windscreen patch (if applicable) then press the mirror firmly into place on the windscreen patch. Hold the mirror firmly in position for at least one minute.

29 Instrumental panel crash padding - removal and refitting

1   Refer to Chapter 9, Section 18 and carry out the work described in paragraphs 1 to 9 inclusive. Slacken the choke cable clamp and move the choke cable to one side.

2   Refer to Chapter 8, Section 38 and remove the instrument cluster.

3   Carefully prise out the centre air vent to expose the upper crash pad retaining screw. Remove the screw.

4   Remove the retaining screw below the ashtray. Remove the ashtray.

5   Remove the single screw each side retaining the crash pad to the door hinge pillar (Fig. 10.19).

6   On Ghia variants, remove the three screws retaining the driver's glove pocket, and push the pocket with fuse box and light switch forward, clear of the crash pad.

7   Pull off the heater control knobs, remove the two screws and lift off the heater trim panel.

8   Unscrew and remove the four nuts from the steering column support bracket.

9   Ease the crash pad forward to gain access to the rear of the switch panel, and pull off all leads and multiplugs.

10 Remove the two screws retaining the heater controls, then pull the hoses from the facia vents.

11 Fully remove the crash pad from the car (Fig. 10.20).

12 Refitting is the reverse of this procedure, ensuring that the crash pad cut-out (Fig. 10.22) is located over the peg on the steering column bracket.

30 Centre console - removal and refitting

1   Unscrew and remove the gear lever knob, and pull the gaiter free of the console.

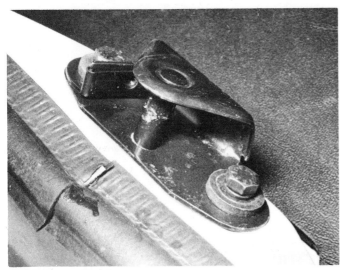

27.2 Tailgate striker plate

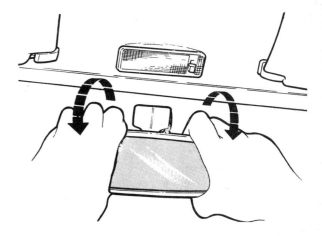

Fig. 10.18. Grasp firmly and push to remove the mirror (Sec. 28)

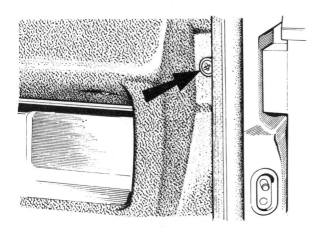

Fig. 10.19. Crash pad to hinge pillar screw (Sec. 29)

Fig. 10.20. Lifting out the crash pad (Sec. 29)

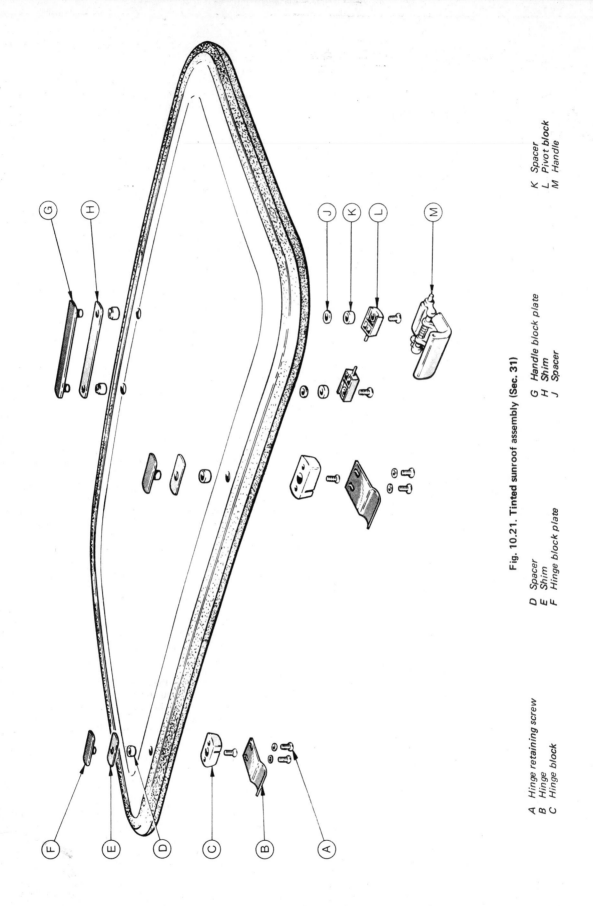

Fig. 10.21. Tinted sunroof assembly (Sec. 31)

A Hinge retaining screw
B Hinge
C Hinge block

D Spacer
E Shim
F Hinge block plate

G Handle block plate
H Shim
J Spacer

K Spacer
L Pivot block
M Handle

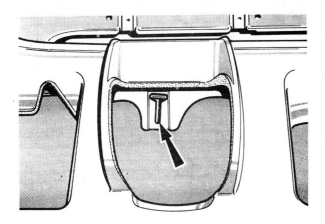

Fig. 10.22. Crash pad cut out (Sec. 29)

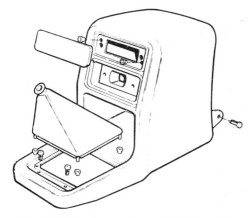

Fig. 10.23. Centre console assembly (Sec. 30)

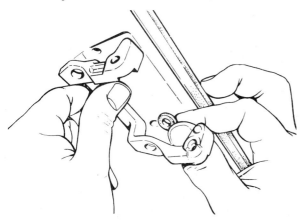

Fig. 10.24. Inserting a washer to adjust sunroof height (Sec. 31)

2   Remove the two screws, exposed by the removal of the gaiter, from the rear of the console, and two from the front (Fig. 10.23).
3   Pull out the console sufficiently to gain access to the rear, and disconnect the leads from the rear of the clock and/or radio.
4   Check that the mounting bracket securing screws are fully

tightened.
5   Refitting is the reverse of this procedure, not forgetting to reset the clock where applicable.

31 Sunroof components - removal, refitting and adjustment

Hinges
1   Unscrew and remove the two screws retaining each hinge to either the sunroof or hinge block, as appropriate.
2   When refitting, lightly tighten the hinge screws at the centre of the hinge slots. Fit the roof to the car and adjust the hinge position as necessary before fully tightening the screws.

Handle
3   To remove the handle, unscrew and remove the single screw from each handle pivot, and lift off the pivots and handle.
4   Refitting is a reversal of this procedure.

Hinge retainers
5   With the sun roof removed, pull off the weatherstrip from the front edge of the aperture.
6   Remove the headlining clips, and pull down the headlining as necessary.
7   Remove the two screws and push the retainer forward out of its location. Carefully withdraw the retainer.
8   When refitting the retainer, first fit a new seal.

Handle bracket
9   With the sunroof removed, unscrew the single screw retaining the bracket cover and remove the cover.
10 Unscrew and remove the two bolts and lift away the bracket.

Adjustment
11 To adjust the sunroof horizontally, slacken the two screws retaining each hinge to the roof panel or hinge block as appropriate. Move the roof to its correct position, and tighten the screws.
12 The height of the front edge of the roof should not need adjusting.
13 To adjust the height of the rear edge of the roof in its closed position, add or remove washers between the handle bracket and the roof as required (Fig. 10.24).

32 Air conditioning system - general

Where the car is equipped with an air-conditioning system, the checks and maintenance operations must be limited to the following items. No part of the system must be disconnected due to the danger from the refrigerant which will be released. Your Ford dealer or a refrigeration engineer must be employed if the system has to be evacuated or recharged.
1   Regularly check the condition of the system hoses and connections.
2   Inspect the fins of the condenser (located ahead of the radiator) and brush away accumulations of flies and dirt.
3   Check the compression drivebelt adjustment. There should be a total deflection of ½ in (13 mm) at the centre of the longest run of the belt. Where adjustment is required, move the position of the idler pulley.
4   Keep the air-conditioner drain tube clear. This expels condensation produced within the unit to a point under the car.
5   When the system is not in use, move the control to the 'OFF' position. During the winter period operate the unit for a few minutes every three or four weeks to keep the compressor in good order.
6   Every six months, have your Ford dealer check the refrigerant level in the system and the compressor oil level.

Metric conversion tables

Inches	Decimals	Millimetres	Millimetres to Inches		Inches to Millimetres	
			mm	Inches	Inches	mm
1/64	0.015625	0.3969	0.01	0.00039	0.001	0.0254
1/32	0.03125	0.7937	0.02	0.00079	0.002	0.0508
3/64	0.046875	1.1906	0.03	0.00118	0.003	0.0762
1/16	0.0625	1.5875	0.04	0.00157	0.004	0.1016
5/64	0.078125	1.9844	0.05	0.00197	0.005	0.1270
3/32	0.09375	2.3812	0.06	0.00236	0.006	0.1524
7/64	0.109375	2.7781	0.07	0.00276	0.007	0.1778
1/8	0.125	3.1750	0.08	0.00315	0.008	0.2032
9/64	0.140625	3.5719	0.09	0.00354	0.009	0.2286
5/32	0.15625	3.9687	0.1	0.00394	0.01	0.254
11/64	0.171875	4.3656	0.2	0.00787	0.02	0.508
3/16	0.1875	4.7625	0.3	0.1181	0.03	0.762
13/64	0.203125	5.1594	0.4	0.01575	0.04	1.016
7/32	0.21875	5.5562	0.5	0.01969	0.05	1.270
15/64	0.234275	5.9531	0.6	0.02362	0.06	1.524
1/4	0.25	6.3500	0.7	0.02756	0.07	1.778
17/64	0.265625	6.7469	0.8	0.3150	0.08	2.032
9/32	0.28125	7.1437	0.9	0.03543	0.09	2.286
19/64	0.296875	7.5406	1	0.03937	0.1	2.54
5/16	0.3125	7.9375	2	0.07874	0.2	5.08
21/64	0.328125	8.3344	3	0.11811	0.3	7.62
11/32	0.34375	8.7312	4	0.15748	0.4	10.16
23/64	0.359375	9.1281	5	0.19685	0.5	12.70
3/8	0.375	9.5250	6	0.23622	0.6	15.24
25/64	0.390625	9.9219	7	0.27559	0.7	17.78
13/32	0.40625	10.3187	8	0.31496	0.8	20.32
27/64	0.421875	10.7156	9	0.35433	0.9	22.86
7/16	0.4375	11.1125	10	0.39270	1	25.4
29/64	0.453125	11.5094	11	0.43307	2	50.8
15/32	0.46875	11.9062	12	0.47244	3	76.2
31/64	0.484375	12.3031	13	0.51181	4	101.6
1/2	0.5	12.7000	14	0.55118	5	127.0
33/64	0.515625	13.0969	15	0.59055	6	152.4
17/32	0.53125	13.4937	16	0.62992	7	177.8
35/64	0.546875	13.8906	17	0.66929	8	203.2
9/16	0.5625	14.2875	18	0.70866	9	228.6
37/64	0.578125	14.6844	19	0.74803	10	254.0
19/32	0.59375	15.0812	20	0.78740	11	279.4
39/64	0.609375	15.4781	21	0.82677	12	304.8
5/8	0.625	15.8750	22	0.86614	13	330.2
41/64	0.640625	16.2719	23	0.90551	14	355.6
21/32	0.65625	16.6687	24	0.94488	15	381.0
43/64	0.671875	17.0656	25	0.98425	16	406.4
11/16	0.6875	17.4625	26	1.02362	17	431.8
45/64	0.703125	17.8594	27	1.06299	18	457.2
23/32	0.71875	18.2562	28	1.10236	19	482.6
47/64	0.734375	18.6531	29	1.14173	20	508.0
3/4	0.75	19.0500	30	1.18110	21	533.4
49/64	0.765625	19.4469	31	1.22047	22	558.8
25/32	0.78125	19.8437	32	1.25984	23	584.2
51/64	0.796875	20.2406	33	1.29921	24	609.6
13/16	0.8125	20.6375	34	1.33858	25	635.0
53/64	0.828125	21.0344	35	1.37795	26	660.4
27/32	0.84375	21.4312	36	1.41732	27	685.8
55/64	0.859375	21.8281	37	1.4567	28	711.2
7/8	0.875	22.2250	38	1,4961	29	736.6
57/64	0.890625	22.6219	39	1.5354	30	762.0
29/32	0.90625	23.0187	40	1.5748	31	787.4
59/64	0.921875	23.4156	41	1.6142	32	812.8
15/16	0.9375	23.8125	42	1.6535	33	838.2
61/64	0.953125	24.2094	43	1.6929	34	863.6
31/32	0.96875	24.6062	44	1.7323	35	889.0
63/64	0.984375	25.0031	45	1.7717	36	914.4

1 Imperial gallon = 8 Imp pints = 1.16 US gallons = 277.42 cu in = 4.5459 litres

1 US gallon = 4 US quarts = 0.862 Imp gallon = 231 cu in = 3.785 litres

1 Litre = 0.2199 Imp gallon = 0.2642 US gallon = 61.0253 cu in = 1000 cc

Miles to Kilometres		Kilometres to Miles	
1	1.61	1	0.62
2	3.22	2	1.24
3	4.83	3	1.86
4	6.44	4	2.49
5	8.05	5	3.11
6	9.66	6	3.73
7	11.27	7	4.35
8	12.88	8	4.97
9	14.48	9	5.59
10	16.09	10	6.21
20	32.19	20	12.43
30	48.28	30	18.64
40	64.37	40	24.85
50	80.47	50	31.07
60	96.56	60	37.28
70	112.65	70	43.50
80	128.75	80	49.71
90	144.84	90	55.92
100	160.93	100	62.14

lb f ft to Kg f m		Kg f m to lb f ft		lb f/in^2 : Kg f/cm^2		Kg f/cm^2 : lb f/in^2	
1	0.138	1	7.233	1	0.07	1	14.22
2	0.276	2	14.466	2	0.14	2	28.50
3	0.414	3	21.699	3	0.21	3	42.67
4	0.553	4	28.932	4	0.28	4	56.89
5	0.691	5	36.165	5	0.35	5	71.12
6	0.829	6	43.398	6	0.42	6	85.34
7	0.967	7	50.631	7	0.49	7	99.56
8	1.106	8	57.864	8	0.56	8	113.79
9	1.244	9	65.097	9	0.63	9	128.00
10	1.382	10	62.330	10	0.70	10	142.23
20	2.765	20	144.660	20	1.41	20	284.47
30	4.147	30	216.990	30	2.11	30	426.70

Index

Printed by
Haynes Publishing Group
Sparkford Yeovil Somerset
England